Style Standards: Voice, Tone, Sentence Quality, Word Choice (Diction)	Style Standards: Grammar, Usage, Punctuation, Spelling, Format	Other Standard (Instructor's Choice)
☒ Voice/tone are always distinctive, appropriate, engaging. ☒ Sentence quality is almost always high, appropriate, fluent, varied. ☒ Diction is consistently appropriate, fresh, clear.	☒ Demonstrates strong understanding of sentence boundaries. ☒ Grammar, usage, punctuation help promote essay's ideas. ☒ Demonstrates highly proficient use of Standard Written English. ☒ All format standards are skillfully used.	
☒ Voice/tone are usually distinctive, appropriate, engaging. ☒ Sentence quality is usually high, appropriate, fluent, varied. ☒ Diction is usually appropriate, fresh, clear.	☒ Demonstrates strong understanding of sentence boundaries. ☒ Grammar, usage, punctuation almost always help promote essay's ideas. ☒ Demonstrates proficient use of Standard Written English. ☒ All format standards are skillfully used.	
☒ Voice/tone are inconsistent. ☒ Sentence quality is adequate, not as fluent and varied. ☒ Diction is usually appropriate and clear.	☒ Essay contains a few sentence boundary problems. ☒ Grammar, usage, and punctuation are adequate, with some errors. ☒ Demonstrates adequate use of Standard Written English. ☒ Most format standards are used.	
☒ Voice/tone need some development. ☒ Sentence quality is low, sometimes not fluent or varied, and idiomatic. ☒ Diction is sometimes inappropriate, unclear, and limited.	☒ Essay contains more sentence boundary problems. ☒ Errors in grammar, usage, and punctuation begin to hinder communication. ☒ Shows limited experience with Standard Written English. ☒ Some format standards are not used.	
☒ Voice/tone need much development. ☒ Sentence quality is low, not fluent, not varied, unidiomatic. ☒ Diction is often inappropriate, unclear, and limited.	☒ Shows little understanding of sentence boundaries. ☒ Numerous errors in grammar, usage, and punctuation hinder communication. ☒ Shows lack of experience with Standard Written English. ☒ Many format standards are not used.	

Insightful
Writing

A PROCESS RHETORIC WITH READINGS

zebroski@stcc.edu

Insightful Writing

A Process Rhetoric with Readings

FIRST EDITION

David Sabrio

Texas A&M University-Kingsville

Mitchel Burchfield

Southwest Texas Junior College

WADSWORTH
CENGAGE Learning™

Australia • Brazil • Japan • Korea • Mexico • Singapore • Spain • United Kingdom • United States

WADSWORTH
CENGAGE Learning

**Insightful Reading, A Process Rhetoric
with Readings, First Edition**

David Sabrio, Mitchel Burchfield

Executive Publisher: Patricia Coryell

Editor-in-Chief: Carrie Brandon

Sponsoring Editor: Joann Kozyrev

Senior Marketing Manager: Tom
Ziolkowski

Senior Development Editor: Meg
Botteon

Associate Project Editor: Carrie Parker

Art and Design Manager: Jill Haber

Cover Design Director: Tony Saizon

Senior Photo Editor: Jennifer Meyer Dare

Senior Composition Buyer: Chuck
Dutton

New Title Project Manager: James
Lonergan

Editorial Assistant: Daisuke Yasutake

Marketing Assistant: Bettina Chiu

Editorial Assistant: Jill Clark

Cover image: © Dimension Image/Alamy

Photo credits: p. 78: © Redlink/CORBIS;
p. 96: © Jeff Greenberg/Photoedit; p. 121:
© Mark Richards/Photoedit; p. 141:
© Lucas Jackson/Reuters/CORBIS;
p. 155: © Brian Bahr/Getty; p. 214: Photo
by Kate Turning, model Atong Arjo/LA
Models; p. 215: Used with permission;
p. 249: © Carlos Barria/Reuters/CORBIS;
p. 263: © Robert Brenner/PhotoEdit;
p. 282: © Jeff Zelevansky/Reuters/
CORBIS; p. 293: © Reuters/CORBIS.

Text credits are on page C-1, which is
hereby considered an extension of the
copyright page.

For product information and technology assistance, contact us at
Cengage Learning Academic Resource Center, 1-800-423-0563

For permission to use material from this text or product,
submit all requests online at **www.cengage.com/permissions**
Further permissions questions can be e-mailed to
permissionrequest@cengage.com

Library of Congress Control Number: 2007926607

ISBN-13: 978-0-618-87026-4

ISBN-10: 0-618-87026-1

Wadsworth
20 Channel Center Street
Boston, MA 02210
USA

Cengage Learning products are represented in Canada by Nelson
Education, Ltd.

For your course and learning solutions, visit **www.cengage.com.**

Purchase any of our products at your local college store or at our preferred
online store **www.ichapters.com.**

Printed in China by China Translation & Printing Services Limited
4 5 6 7 12 11 10 09

*We dedicate this book to
all of our family members
—our first and abiding teachers—
and to all of our other teachers,
past and present.*

Brief Contents

Preface **xv**

Introduction: Learning to Learn **1**

Part I

Looking Inside the Writing Process **17**

Chapter 1:   Writing and Learning   **19**

Chapter 2:   Discovering Ideas   **41**

Chapter 3:   Revision and Style   **62**

Part II

Looking Outside for Insights **71**

Chapter 4:   Family   **73**

Chapter 5:   Relationships Beyond the Family   **95**

Chapter 6:   Language   **114**

Chapter 7:   The Nation   **136**

Chapter 8:   The World   **151**

Part III

Writing for a Purpose **167**

Chapter 9:   Specialized Writing Tasks   **169**

Chapter 10:   Argument and Persuasion: Influencing an Audience   **181**

Chapter 11:   Research and Writing with Sources   **219**

Part IV

A Portfolio of Readings **243**

Chapter 12:   Cultural Identities   **245**

Chapter 13:   Work   **259**

Chapter 14:   Consumerism   **275**

Chapter 15:   The Environment   **290**

Glossary   **G1**

Credits   **C1**

Index   **I1**

Contents

PREFACE   xv

Introduction: Learning to Learn   1
READING: David Sabrio, "Learning Styles"   2
What's Your Learning Style?   5
READING: David Sabrio and Mitchel Burchfield, "Multiple Intelligences"   9
STUDENT ESSAY: Richie Saavedra, "Not a Perfect Person"   14
     Insightful Writing: Writing to Learn   15

PART I

LOOKING INSIDE THE WRITING PROCESS   17

1 Writing and Learning   19

The Writing Process   20
     Differences Between Speaking and Writing   23
     Keeping a Journal   23
Reading Effectively   25
     Getting Started: Strategies for Generating Ideas   25
     Thesis Statement   29
Organizing, Drafting, and Shaping   29
     Paragraphs   29
     Body Paragraphs   30
     Opening Paragraphs   32
     Closing or Concluding Paragraphs   34
STUDENT ESSAY: Melissa Anne Scott, "Tips for a New Preschool Teacher"   35
STUDENT ESSAY: Ricky Varela, "My Hobby"   38
     Insightful Writing   39

2 Discovering Ideas   41

Revision   42
     Global Revision   43
     Sentence-Level Revision   43
READING: Dianne Hales, "Getting Yourself Back on Track"   44
READING: Ben Fong-Torres, "He Wails for the World"   47

Getting Started: Preparing and Generating   51
Organizing, Drafting, and Shaping   52
Revision: Getting Feedback   53
Evaluation of Your Writing Process and Peer Responding   57
STUDENT ESSAY: Michael Verderber, "An Alienated Asian"   60
Insightful Writing   61

3 Revision and Style   62

Revising for Some Common Sentence-level Problems   63
Sentence Fragment   63
Comma Splice   64
Run-on or Fused Sentence   65
Achieving Clarity and Eliminating Awkwardness   65
Sentence Combining for Variety   66
Dividing or Shortening Long Sentences for Clarity   67
Insightful Writing   68

PART II

LOOKING OUTSIDE FOR INSIGHTS   71

4 Family   73

READING: Virginia Satir, "Peoplemaking"   74
READING: Cris Beam, "The Changing American Family"   80
Getting Started: Preparing and Generating   85
STUDENT ESSAY: David Lee Canales, "Family Values"   88
Organizing and Developing Your Essays   90
Developing Body Paragraphs   90
STUDENT ESSAY: Marissa Mullen, "My Family Traditions"   92
Insightful Writing   93

5 Relationships Beyond the Family   95

READING: Ricardo Sandoval, "Food" from "Fabric of a Nation"   97
READING: Linda Rosenkrantz, "Fashion" from "Fabric of a Nation"   98
READING: David Oliver Relin, "We Just Forge Ahead—and Believe"   101

Getting Started: More Strategies for Organizing Ideas   **105**

STUDENT ESSAY: Ricky Varela, "Fashion of the Times"   **110**

Insightful Writing   **112**

Language   114

READING: Penni Wild, "The Shameful Secret
of Illiteracy in America"   **116**

READING: Janice Castro, "Spanglish Spoken Here"   **118**

READING: Dennis Baron, "Language and Society"   **122**

Getting Started: Interviews and Conversations   **130**

STUDENT ESSAY: Brittney A. Dimas, "Reading and Writing"   **133**

Insightful Writing   **134**

The Nation   136

READING: Bill Moyers, "America's Religious Mosaic"   **137**

READING: Elie Wiesel, "We Choose Honor"   **143**

Getting Started: Broadening Your Perspectives   **147**

STUDENT ESSAY: Orry Arthur, "Tragedy of September 11, 2001"   **148**

Insightful Writing   **150**

The World   151

READING: Elie Wiesel, "When Passion Is Dangerous"   **152**

READING: Robert Moss, "We Are All Related"   **157**

Getting Started: Venturing Beyond Your Comfort Zone   **161**

STUDENT ESSAY: Sue Williams, "Some Aspects of Indian Culture"   **163**

Insightful Writing   **165**

PART III

WRITING FOR A PURPOSE   167

Specialized Writing Tasks   169

Essay Exams   **170**

Preparing for the Essay Exam   **170**

Writing the Essay Exam   **172**

SAMPLE STUDENT ANSWERS   175
In-Class Essays   176
Standardized Essay Exams   178
    Insightful Writing   179

10 Argument and Persuasion: Influencing an Audience   181

READING: Robert E. Litan, "The Obligations of September 11, 2001"   182
READING: Bruce Chapman, "A Bad Idea Whose Time Has Passed"   183
Some Basics of Argument and Persuasion   185
    Four Common Strategies to Strengthen Arguments   186
    Looking at Different Perspectives on an Issue   188
Organizing an Argument Essay   189
    Putting It All Together   191
SAMPLE STUDENT ESSAY: "It's Time for a New Animal Shelter"   191
STUDENT ARGUMENT ESSAY: Jessica Ryan, "Class Segregation"   194
Some Common Fallacies   195
READING: Max Schulman, "Love Is a Fallacy"   199
Rogerian Argument   206
SAMPLE ROGERIAN ESSAY: "How Can We Best Help the Animals?"   207
Evaluation: A Common Form of Argument   208
STUDENT EVALUATION ESSAY: Elizabeth J. Cook,
    "Lost Maples State Natural Area"   210
    Getting Started: Constructing Effective Arguments   212
Evaluation of Visual Media   213
STUDENT ESSAY COMPARING TWO ADS: Holly Remmers, "Secret vs. Soft & Dri"   216
    Insightful Writing   218

11 Research and Writing with Sources   219

Planning Your Research   221
Selecting a Topic, Research Question, and Thesis   222
    Topics   222
    Research Questions   223
    Thesis Statement   223
Finding and Evaluating Sources   224
    Evaluating the Credibility of Online Sources   225
    Finding Online Sources   225
    Evaluating a Website   225
    Evaluating the Credibility of Print Sources   226
    Interviews   227

Developing a Working Bibliography   **229**

Avoiding Plagiarism   **230**

How to Take Notes from Sources and Document Them   **230**

    Summarizing the Main Ideas   **231**

    Paraphrase   **233**

    Quotation   **234**

    Other Strategies for Avoiding Plagiarism   **235**

STUDENT ESSAY: Amy Wolter, "On This Day in 1986"   **237**

    Insightful Writing   **241**

PART IV

A PORTFOLIO OF READINGS   243

12 Cultural Identities   245

READING: Vanessa Colon, "Learning to Let Go: Tradition Binds College Hopefuls to Families"   **246**

READING: Roy H. Saigo, "Lessons from Executive Order 9066"   **250**

READING: Laila Al-Marayati, "It Could Happen Here"   **252**

READING: Michael Quintanilla, "The Great Divide"   **254**

13 Work   259

READING: Bridget Kulla, "Ten Majors That Didn't Exist 10 Years Ago"   **260**

READING: Barbara Moses, "Find Work That You Love"   **264**

READING: Ana Veciana-Suarez, "Working Just to Live Is Perverted into Living Just to Work"   **269**

READING: Winston Fletcher, "It's Time to Make Up Your Mind"   **272**

14 Consumerism   275

READING: Donna Freedman, "Living 'Poor' and Loving It"   **276**

READING: Brian Swimme, "How Do Our Kids Get So Caught Up in Consumerism?"   **279**

READING: Llewellyn H. Rockwell, Jr., "In Defense of Consumerism"   **283**

READING: Hillary Mayell, "As Consumerism Spreads, Earth Suffers, Study Says"   **286**

15 The Environment   290

READING: Mitchell E. Golden, "Debate, What Debate?"   **291**

READING: Chuck Blake, "Rumors of Our Climatic Demise Have Been Greatly Exaggerated"   **294**

READING: Kyeann Sayer, "A New Student Generation Accepts the Global Warming Challenge"   **297**

READING: Rachel Carson: "A Fable for Tomorrow"   **300**

GLOSSARY   **G1**

CREDITS   **C1**

INDEX   **I1**

Preface

Insightful Writing: A Process Rhetoric with Readings, is a "bridge" text. From its inception in 2002, we have developed the book to be used in writing courses at two levels: the highest developmental writing level and the first-semester college writing level.

From 2002 through 2007 *Insightful Writing* has been used and classroom-tested by approximately twenty teachers and more than one thousand students at two post-secondary institutions: a community college and a regional state university.

Insightful Writing takes an "aims-based" approach to writing, emphasizing the various purposes for which one writes. At the same time we include sufficient material about the traditional methods of organization (and reading selections that use these methods) to give students practice in writing essays based on the more common organizational methods.

This text is based on research on what works in the writing classroom, along with more than fifty years' cumulative teaching experience between the two authors. *Insightful Writing* combines the best of both innovative and time-tested classroom teaching strategies. Between the two of us, we have taught all levels of post-secondary writing courses, from basic writing through graduate seminars. We have made conference presentations and published articles in rhetoric/composition.

We know of no other first-year writing text that combines all of the following features:

▶ Cooperative learning
▶ Stasis theory
▶ Integration of writing, reading, speaking, and listening
▶ Reading selections and writing activities that help students learn about themselves, how to be successful academically, and the importance of lifelong learning
▶ Sequenced writing activities that begin by asking students to write about themselves and then move outward to subjects beyond the self
▶ Critical thinking and self-assessment activities

Insightful Writing can be paired with any handbook. We recommend *The Open Handbook* by Ann Raimes and Maria Jerskey (Wadsworth, 2007).

While developing *Insightful Writing,* we have worked under the assumption that college enrollments will become more diverse in the years to come. Therefore we have tried to represent the widest range of voices in our reading selections.

Resources for teachers and students

▶ **Annotated Instructor's Edition.** This desk copy of the complete student text, provided free to teachers, includes helpful teaching tips, classroom support suggestions, answers or possible responses to all questions, and ideas for additional activities.

▶ **NEW! Cengage Learning WriteSPACE™** encompasses the interactive online products and services integrated with Cengage Learning (Developmental Writing and Composition) textbook programs. Students and instructors can access Cengage Learning WriteSPACE content through text-specific Student and Instructor Websites, via Eduspace, Cengage Learning's online Course Management System, and through additional course management systems including BlackBoard/WebCT.

  ▶ **Cengage Learning WriteSPACE™ Instructor Website** for *Insightful Writing.* Instructors can access Cengage Learning WriteSPACE content at any time via the Internet. Resources include an Instructor's Guide, sample syllabi, diagnostic tests, and quizzes.

  ▶ **Cengage Learning WriteSPACE™ Student Website** for *Insightful Writing.* Students can access Cengage Learning WriteSPACE content at any time via the Internet. Resources include a library of e-Exercises; Plagiarism Prevention Zone; and glossary flashcards. Some content may be passkey protected.

Cengage Learning WriteSPACE™ with Eduspace® Online Writing Program

Eduspace, Cengage Learning's Course Management System, offers instructors a flexible, interactive online platform to communicate with students, organize material, evaluate student work, and track results in a powerful grade book. In addition to Cengage Learning WriteSPACE resources, students and instructors using Eduspace benefit from Course Management, Tools Practice Exercises, Online Homework, Cengage Learning Assess, Safe Assignment, and an Online Handbook.

Acknowledgments

At Cengage Learning we would like to thank Lisa Patterson, who first brought a very early version of *Insightful Writing* to the attention of editors at Cengage Learning; Joann Kozyrev, who saw even before we did what the early version of the book could become; Meg Botteon, with whom we worked the closest and the longest, whose probing questions and suggestions made every chapter better; Daisuke Yasutake, who made sure we had the resources we needed and helped with permissions issues; Tom Ziolkowski , who has done a splendid job publicizing and marketing the book; Sara Planck of Matrix Productions; Janet Tilden, who is a superb copy editor; and Carrie Parker, for her careful attention to every detail of the book's design and production.

Many teachers, who reviewed the manuscript at various stages of development, made valuable suggestions for improving the book:

Sue Anne Braley, North Harris College
Deborah Core, Eastern Kentucky University
Tyler Farrell, University of Dubuque
Susan S. Ford, Thomas University
Ann Foster, Santa Rosa Junior College
Billie J. Jones, Shippensburg University
Julie M. Kissel, Washtenaw Community College
Marisa A. Klages, LaGuardia Community College-CUNY
Robert A. Mayer, College of Southern Idaho
Marcia A. Rogers, Orange Coast College
Christine M. Tutlewski, University of Wisconsin–Parkside
Bradley A. Waltman, Community College of Southern Nevada
William W. Ziegler, J. Sargeant Reynolds Community College

We would like to thank Stephen Williams for help with legal issues. We also thank Beatrice Newman of the University of Texas–Pan American, who allowed us to use a checklist that she developed to help students revise their own drafts.

At Texas A&M University–Kingsville, David would like to thank the graduate teaching assistants, instructors (especially Jaya Goswami) and students who used earlier versions of *Insightful Writing* from 2002 to 2007; and the students who gave us permission to use their essays as sample and model essays. Many teachers and students helped us improve the book. David also thanks his colleagues in the Department of Language and Literature who taught his courses when he took a sabbatical leave in the spring 2007 semester to do major revision and expansion of the book. For supporting his sabbatical leave request David thanks his chair, Susan Roberson; his Arts & Sciences dean, Ronn Hy; the provost, Kay Clayton; and the president, Rumaldo Juarez. Finally, and most importantly, David thanks Sue, Rob, Cristin, Stephen, and Elizabeth Sabrio.

At Southwest Texas Junior College, Mitchel would like to thank his colleagues (especially Albert Hernandez) and students who used earlier versions of *Insightful Writing* from 2002 to 2007. Without the encouragement and support from his many friends at Southwest Texas Junior College, he would have been unable to pursue the creation of this book. The conversations and substantive feedback he received from Albert Hernandez, Michel Stocks, Helen Strait, and other members of the English faculty have contributed to the quality and depth of the book. Mitchel also thanks his favorite teacher and friend, David Sabrio, for being an excellent example of a professor who follows and continues to support his students long after they leave the classroom. Finally, Mitchel thanks Jan, Ann, and David Burchfield, as well as Fredrick and Erin Hostetler.

Introduction: Learning to Learn

I don't divide the world into the weak and the strong, or the successes and the failures, thoset who make it or those who don't. I divide the world into learners and nonlearners.

> *There are people who learn, who are open to what happens around them, who listen, who hear the lessons. When they do something stupid, they don't do it again. And when they do something that works a little bit, they do it even better and harder the next time. The question to ask is not whether you are a success or a failure, but whether you are a learner or a nonlearner.*
>
> Benjamin Barber, quoted in When Smart People Fail,
> by Carole Hyatt and Linda Gottlieb

From birth to death, we are all learners. Especially as infants and children, we learn an incredible amount of information and an enormous number of behaviors. Unfortunately, many people believe that learning stops when they leave the classroom. Nothing could be further from the truth! One reason why the graduation ceremony from high school or college is called "commencement" (beginning) is that many graduates are just beginning the next stage of their "education" in the real world.

JOURNAL WRITING

Respond to the above quotation by Benjamin Barber with some personal accounts of when you were a learner and when you were a nonlearner, both in school and out of school. What kinds of people do you know who are good examples of either learners or nonlearners? What sorts of traits do learners have in common? What do nonlearners have in common?

Different people learn in different ways. The different ways in which people learn are sometimes called *learning styles*. There is no one "right" way to learn. If you are aware of the way in which you learn most effectively, you can use that awareness to your own advantage when studying new material. The idea is not to learn everything in exactly the same way, but to use your learning strengths to help diversify or "flex" your learning styles. Knowing your learning styles will help you become more flexible and better able to learn a wide variety of material.

Before You Read

1. Before reading the following essay, "Learning Styles," from beginning to end, take a moment to read just the opening and just the closing paragraph. Put into your own words, either by telling a classmate or by writing in your notebook, what you believe to be the main point or thesis of the essay.

2. What do you think the body paragraphs will be about?

While You Read

1. As you read, underline or highlight key sentences. Remember key sentences are often at the beginnings and ends of paragraphs.

2. What questions occur to you while you read the essay? Write those questions down. What do you agree with or disagree with most strongly?

3. Underline the words you don't know and look up the definitions in a good college-level dictionary.

4. Meet with one or more classmates outside of class and take turns reading aloud sections of the essay.

Reading

Learning Styles

BY DAVID SABRIO

1 Although we are learning new things every day, probably few of us have actually sat down and reflected on exactly how and under what conditions we learn most effectively. Psychologists, however, have quite extensively studied the various ways in which people learn. The

ways that people acquire knowledge are called learning styles. Most people learn in a variety of ways; however, many people, when they have a choice, often favor one method of acquiring knowledge over another. Most learners tend to favor one or two out of four predominant learning styles. These four learning styles are based on the physical senses used by the learner when acquiring new information. Knowing your particular strengths in the area of learning styles will enable you to become a more effective learner.

2   The first type of learner is the tactile-kinesthetic learner. This person likes a "hands-on" approach to learning. Learners favoring this style like to touch and manipulate the objects they are learning about. They are "doers"; they prefer to participate physically in whatever they are learning, rather than listen to someone talk about it. Practical applications are more important to them than a lot of abstract talk and thought. These learners tend to enjoy labs, field trips, and cooperative education combining applied work experience with instructional classes. Athletes, craftspeople, artists, mechanics—people who enjoy physical activity or making or building things—often are tactile-kinesthetic learners.

3   The next type of learner favors hearing and speaking as ways of learning. Learners in this group would probably rather have someone explain something to them instead of reading about it. These types of learners often tend to be social, enjoying learning by participating in a group rather than by learning alone. They also may like to repeat in their own words what they were just told, as a way of checking their understanding of new concepts. These learners would probably enjoy any profession that requires them to use speech to interact with many different people every day. Sales representatives, social workers, and most people in "service" jobs (helping people) probably learn well by listening and speaking.

Other learners enjoy reading and writing   4 as ways of learning. These people often do well in traditional, structured school settings. They may also like to read a lot both in and out of school, and they often perform well on standardized, multiple-choice exams. In addition, they may enjoy independent study courses. Although they may not particularly enjoy writing, they typically do well in writing tasks. Given a choice of reading to learn about something or listening to someone talk about it, they frequently choose to read. These types of learners are found in a number of professions that require much reading and analysis of written material. Journalists, teachers (especially language teachers), librarians, lawyers, some researchers, and technical writers/editors usually learn well through reading and writing.

Finally, many people learn most effectively   5 by looking at pictures, diagrams, and other visual materials. If you would rather watch the television news than read the newspaper, or if you would rather look at illustrations or pictorial representations than read about a topic, or if you would rather "see the movie" than "read the book," then you may be a predominantly visual learner. Visual learners often use symbols, pictures, and color schemes to enhance their memory. Because visual learning is one of the first ways that people learn when young, many learners continue throughout their lives to have a visual component to their ways of learning. Visual learning is reinforced in today's culture by the widespread use of advertising logos, television, and movies. This group of learners is composed of a wide variety of people in many different professions, among them art, advertising, the television/motion picture industry, and some technical/scientific fields.

In addition to exhibiting these four major   6 ways of learning, people also have another tendency when learning. Some people like to learn alone, while others like to learn in groups. Although people who like to learn and work alone can be found in many different professions, they are often found in professions that involve scientific, mathematical, and technical knowledge. In addition, traditional school and work settings have often emphasized studying and working alone. Recently, however, more and more people are discovering the benefits of learning and working in groups and teams. Both in schools and in the workplace, we are seeing more and more emphasis on teamwork and collaborative efforts.

7   Another tendency in learning is whether one is a "splitter" or a "lumper." A "splitter" is said to be field independent, one who can focus on a narrow learning task without needing to know how this narrow task fits into the "big picture." A field independent learner is often good at analyzing, that is, breaking complex things down into smaller parts. A "lumper," on the other hand, is said to be field sensitive, one who likes to know how the narrow task fits into the larger scheme of whatever is being studied. A field sensitive learner may want a specific context in which to situate newly learned material.

This type of learner may also be good at synthesizing, that is, making connections among several related ideas.

8   One key point to remember about these learning styles is that almost everyone has, at one time or another, used all of these styles. However, you may also recognize that you tend to feel more comfortable with one or two of these styles in much of your high school and college learning. Think about the strengths and limitations of each style. One reason for knowing more about your learning styles is not to pigeonhole or simplistically categorize yourself, but rather to recognize your learning strengths and to attempt to broaden or "flex" the ways in which you learn. You will also probably notice that your college instructors or your employers may favor one or two learning styles over others. Your knowledge of their learning preferences may help you learn from them more effectively. One key to academic and career success is to adapt to the requirements of each situation and to choose the learning style needed for the specific task that you have to perform.

Thinking Critically About the Reading

1. What is the main idea or thesis of this essay?

2. What is the main topic of each body paragraph?

3. How do the ideas here relate to your own experience? Rank the learning styles and tendencies from most influential to least influential in your own life.

4. How can you use the information in the essay to become a more successful student?

5. Discuss the essay with one or more classmates. How do your classmates' responses to the essay influence your own response to the essay?

6. Think of a family member or friend who has a learning style very different from yours. What is the person like? How is this person different from you? What can you learn from him or her? What can he or she learn from you?

7. Using a dictionary when necessary, define the following words in their appropriate context: predominant (paragraph 1), manipulate (2), cooperative education (2), tactile (2), kinesthetic (2), pictorial (5), logos (5), collaborative (6), splitter (7), lumper (7), synthesizing (7), pigeonhole (8), and simplistically (8).

JOURNAL WRITING

In this and future journal writing activities throughout the book, practice your paragraph writing skills by developing separate paragraphs for each topic you respond to. Remember, you may be able to develop a single journal writing prompt into several related but distinct paragraphs.

1. What is your first reaction to the "Learning Styles" essay? What is your predominant learning style? What has been your most recent experience using this learning style?

2. What is your reaction to the results of your learning styles questionnaire on pages 6–8? What surprised you the most? How are the results of your classmates similar to or different from your results? What learning experiences can you recall that either confirm or contradict your discoveries about your predominant learning styles?

3. Recall an academic situation in which you learned something well and relatively easily. What was the subject? What predominant learning style did you use? Now recall an academic situation in which you had difficulty learning something. What was the subject? What predominant learning style did you use?

What's Your Learning Style?

The following brief questionnaire will give you some idea about your preferred learning styles. Remember that this is a nonscientific questionnaire, and that there are no right or wrong answers. Just be honest when answering the questions. If you want more specific information about your learning styles, the counseling and testing office on your campus may be able to give you a more detailed questionnaire about the ways in which you learn best.

The first ten questions help you determine whether you learn best in one of the following ways: by doing ("hands-on" experience), by hearing and speaking, by reading and writing, by seeing pictures and diagrams, or by a combination of these four learning styles. For each number, choose the answer that best describes your way of learning.

1. If you were taking a history class and studying a battle in the U. S. Civil War, would you rather learn about the battle by

    A. going to the battlefield and walking over the ground where the battle took place?

    B. listening to a Civil War historian talk about the battle?

    C. reading a book or article about the battle?

    D. watching a movie or TV documentary about the battle?

2. If you were studying a play by Shakespeare, would you rather learn about it by

    A. participating in a production of the play, that is, taking an acting role?

    B. listening to a record or audiotape, or listening to classmates read the play in class?

    C. reading the play alone and keeping a journal of your reactions to and questions about the play?

    D. attending a live performance or watching a movie or videotape of the play?

3. If you were studying about how your state government works, would you rather learn about it by

    A. participating in a "pretend" legislative session for a period of time?

    B. hearing an expert on state government talk about how government works?

    C. reading about how your state government works?

    D. watching a TV documentary about how your state government works?

4. In the past, the kinds of teachers you generally liked the best were those who

    A. got students involved by using hands-on classroom activities.

    B. included lots of class discussions among students and teacher.

    C. required lots of reading, note-taking, and report writing.

    D. used lots of visual aids, such as TV, movies, video clips, charts, and diagrams.

5. When studying for a test in history, or English, or government, do you like to

    A. participate in activities that require you to make something or to physically act out some aspect of your studies?

    B. listen to someone talk about the material, or listen to audio tapes of the teacher's lecture?

    C. read books or chapters and take notes?

    D. draw diagrams, look at pictures, or watch videotapes, lectures, or TV programs that cover the material?

6. In your spare time, do you often like to

    A. make, build, or repair things, or do physical activities?

    B. talk to friends and relatives?

    C. read books or magazines, write letters, or keep a diary?

    D. watch TV or movies, or play video games?

7. When you graduate from college, would you like a job that

    A. involves using your hands and moving your body?

B. involves lots of talking and listening to people?

C. involves lots of reading, analyzing what you read, and writing reports?

D. involves using lots of diagrams, charts, pictorial images, and video?

8. When doing a term project for a history or English class, would you prefer

A. making something, such as a model log cabin or model whaling ship?

B. speaking in front of the class?

C. reading some extra material and doing a written report?

D. making a poster, collage, video or audiotape on some aspect of the subject?

9. When learning new material in your English or government class, would you rather

A. participate in a role-playing game?

B. listen to an informative talk on the subject?

C. read the chapter and outline or summarize it?

D. watch a videotape of the material, or see a slide presentation?

10. To learn about some current news event or story, would you rather

A. experience or take part in the event?

B. talk about it with one or more people?

C. read about it in a newspaper or magazine?

D. watch the news or a news special on TV?

Now go back and look at your answers to the first ten questions. If you marked mostly "A" answers, then you tend to learn best by "hands-on" experience, by doing. If you marked mostly "B" answers, then you tend to learn best by speaking and listening to teachers and classmates. If you marked mostly "C" answers, then you tend to learn best by reading and writing. If you marked mostly "D" answers, then you tend to learn best by looking at pictures, movies, videos, and diagrams. If your answers were spread out over several choices, then you probably have no one dominant learning style.

The next set of questions, numbers 11–17, will help you determine whether you learn best alone or in a group.

11. When you are studying for a history, government, or English test, would you rather

A. study alone?

B. study with one or more classmates?

12. Suppose you are assigned a class project in English or history. The project is due three weeks from now. Would you rather

A. work on the project alone?

B. work on the project with one or more classmates?

13. Suppose your history or English instructor divided up the class into groups of four or five students to discuss and report on a reading assignment.

A. Would you often feel uncomfortable in this study group?

B. Would you often feel at ease in this study group?

14. What is your overall attitude toward studying with a group of classmates?

A. Studying with a group of classmates is usually not very profitable for me.

continued

I can learn the material better on my own.

B. Studying with a group of classmates is usually profitable for me. I usually benefit from group study.

15. Suppose your history or English teacher assigned some library research. Would you rather

A. do the research on your own?

B. do the research with one or two classmates?

16. In your academic activities, would you describe yourself as mainly

A. competitive?

B. cooperative?

17. In general, the kind of study activity I like best is

A. studying alone.

B. studying with a small group

On questions 11–17, if you marked mostly choice "A," then you prefer to learn alone. If you mostly marked choice "B," then you prefer to learn in groups or teams.

The final set of questions, numbers 18–21, will help you determine whether you tend to be a "splitter" or a "lumper." That is, are you better at breaking down your lessons into many small parts and remembering those parts (splitting), or are you better at getting the "big picture" and seeing how various parts of the lesson fit together (lumping)?

18. In your experience, how have you performed on multiple-choice exams and standardized tests in general?

A. I have usually done well on these tests.

B. I have usually not done very well on these tests.

19. How good are you at memorizing large numbers of facts, such as definitions for a vocabulary test?

A. Usually good.

B. Usually not so good.

20. Which of the following sentences best describes the way you learn more effectively?

A. I learn better in a highly structured environment in which my teacher has planned out every part of the lesson.

B. I learn better in an unstructured environment in which I have some say-so about how to learn the material.

21. When beginning the study of a new chapter or new material in school, do you usually

A. plunge right into the material, giving attention to all the specific details?

B. try to get a general overview of the subject by first reading introductions and conclusions, or by making connections between the new material and material that you have already studied?

On questions 18–21, if you marked mostly choice "A," then you are probably more of a "splitter" in your approach to learning. That is, you are good at learning many small bits of information, even though you may not see clearly how all the bits of information fit together. If you marked mostly choice "B," then you are probably more of a "lumper" in your approach to learning. That is, you learn better by first getting the overall "big" picture before plunging into the specific details of a learning task.

Writing About Your Learning Style

Write an essay in which you discuss some major failures and major successes when you attempted to learn something. Reflect back on your life and think of one or two instances in which you were very unsuccessful in learning something in school. Also, think of one or two instances in which you were very unsuccessful in learning something not associated with school. What do these instances have in common? Now think of some instances—both in school and out of school—in which you were very successful in learning something. What do these instances have in common? What is your purpose for writing? Who will your readers or audience be?

For this assignment, you may want to relate an experience that you had, an experience that illustrates either successful or unsuccessful learning. An experience is often related to an event or events in your life. Therefore, you may want to tell about a particular sequence of experiences you had related to learning.

Relating a sequence of events or a series of experiences is a form of narration, or telling a story. Narration has long been one of the most common methods of developing ideas for an essay or story.

Narratives are often told chronologically, that is, in sequence of time. It is easy to develop a draft of a paragraph using narration. You simply begin writing about what happened, from beginning to end. At this drafting stage, do not discard any ideas. You can do that later in the writing process. If you find that your narrative paragraph is getting too long, you may have to divide a series of events into more than one paragraph, with each paragraph focusing on one part of the series of events.

Reading

The following essay, written by David Sabrio and Mitchel Burchfield, draws extensively on developmental psychologist Howard Gardner's book *Multiple Intelligences: The Theory in Practice* (1993)*. A recipient of many awards, Howard Gardner is a professor in the Harvard Graduate School of Education. He is best known for his theory of multiple intelligences—the idea that there is no one simple kind of human intelligence, but an array of different kinds of intelligences.

Apply the "Before You Read" and "While You Read" questions on page 2.

———

*From *Multiple Intelligences* by Howard Gardner. Reprinted by permission of Basic Books, a member of Perseus Books Group.

Multiple Intelligences

BY DAVID SABRIO AND MITCHEL BURCHFIELD

1 Over the years many people in traditional academic settings have tended to define intelligence in certain ways, ways that some educators consider to be too narrow. Howard Gardner is one of these educators. He believes intelligence, or intelligences, should be defined much more broadly:

2 [T]here is an alternative vision that I would like to present—one based on a radically different view of the mind, and one that yields a very different view of school. It is a pluralistic view of mind . . . acknowledging that people have different cognitive strengths and contrasting cognitive styles. . . . One such approach I have called my "theory of multiple intelligences." (6–7)

3 Gardner has defined eight different intelligences among humans. Although we usually feel stronger and more comfortable in two or three of these areas, most of us have a combination of all eight intelligences. Knowing more about all eight may help us enhance our already-strong intelligences and build up those that may need some development.

Linguistic Intelligence

4 Linguistic intelligence is associated with those who enjoy and do well in tasks that involve reading and writing. These people may also be able to learn other languages with less difficulty than many people. Those with linguistic intelligence may keep diaries or write journals; they may be voracious readers, often reading for entertainment; they may have written stories when young. People with linguistic intelligence can be found in professions such as the teaching of language, literature, and writing. They may be creative writers (poets and novelists, for example), journalists, technical writers or editors, even attorneys and physicians. They may be good at analyzing written data for business, industry, and government. They often write advertising copy for companies. They are more likely to subscribe to newspapers and magazines.

Logical-Mathematical Intelligence

5 Next is logical-mathematical intelligence, which also includes scientific ability. "One form of logical-mathematical intelligence is the scientific practice of deduction and observation" (19). Two components of this kind of intelligence are the following: "the process of problem solving is often remarkably rapid" (20), and the nature of this intelligence is "nonverbal" (20). People with this kind of intelligence usually perform well in math and science courses in school and on the math and science parts of standardized tests such as the SAT and ACT. People with logical-mathematical intelligence are often math or science teachers; physicians and pharmacists; research scientists in business, industry, the government, and universities; biologists and chemists; and engineers. For reasons which are both complex and not yet fully understood, this kind of intelligence is more often associated with males than with females.

6 In our society, these first two intelligences have been given a high degree of value. As Gardner points out,

7 [W]e have put linguistic and logical-mathematical intelligences, figuratively speaking, on a pedestal. Much of our testing is based on this high valuation of verbal and mathematical skills. If you do well in language and logic, you should do well in IQ tests and SATs, and you may well get into a prestigious college, but whether you do well once you leave is probably going to depend as much on the extent to which you possess and use the other intelligences. (8–9)

8   Think for a moment about why and how our culture puts a high value on these two kinds of intelligences. Gardner adds, "Although I name the linguistic and logical-mathematical intelligences first, it is not because I think they are the most important—in fact, I am convinced that all [eight] of the intelligences have equal claim to priority" (8). We now turn to the remaining six intelligences.

Spatial Intelligence

9   "Spatial intelligence is the ability to form a mental model of a spatial world and to be able to maneuver and operate using that model" (9). This "spatial world" may be very large or very small. Are you the kind of person who hardly ever gets lost, who has a good sense of direction, who can find your way from point A to point B by looking at a map? Then you probably have good spatial intelligence. Gardner continues, "Sailors, engineers, surgeons, sculptors, and painters, to name just a few examples, all have highly developed spatial intelligences" (9). To this list we can add airplane pilots; mechanics; architects and landscapers; dentists; interior designers; drafting technicians; and many craftspeople, such as carpenters, plumbers, and others involved in building and renovating structures. If you like to do arts and crafts projects or build any kind of model or structure or machine, you probably have good spatial intelligence.

Musical Intelligence

10   The fourth category is musical intelligence (17–18). People manifest this intelligence by playing musical instruments, composing music, singing, having perfect pitch, and listening to and enjoying many different forms of music. Those with musical intelligence are often music teachers, composers, conductors, professional singers and instrument players. To a lesser degree, those who are in school band programs, take music lessons, sing in choirs, and just enjoy singing or listening to different kinds of music all have some musical intelligence. If you enjoy Broadway musicals and concerts, you probably have some degree of musical intelligence. People with this ability often find it easy to sing the harmony (as opposed to the main melody) of a song. Because of the major role that popular music plays in our culture, many different kinds of people—though they may not be professional musicians—have some level of musical intelligence.

Bodily-Kinesthetic Intelligence

11   Next is bodily-kinesthetic intelligence, which is "the ability to solve problems or to fashion products using one's whole body, or parts of the body. Dancers, athletes, surgeons, and craftspeople all exhibit highly developed bodily-kinesthetic intelligence" (9). To generalize, anyone who engages in physical activity while working or playing has a degree of this intelligence. This large category would include farmers, ranchers, police officers, firefighters; people who assemble things or work in warehouses; trainers, physical education teachers, and coaches. As you may have noticed, there is some overlap between this category and the "spatial intelligence" category. Anyone who likes to make or build products has some bodily-kinesthetic intelligence. This intelligence has a high profile in our culture because of the prominence of high school, college, and professional sports such as football, baseball, basketball, and golf. Think of how fascinated many people are with someone's ability to throw, catch, kick, or hit a ball.

Interpersonal Intelligence

12   The sixth intelligence is interpersonal intelligence, which Gardner defines as "the ability to understand other people: what motivates them, how they work, how to work cooperatively with them" (9). Gardner continues:

13   Interpersonal intelligence builds on a core capacity to notice distinctions among others; in particular, contrasts in their moods,

temperaments, motivations, and intentions. In more advanced forms, this intelligence permits a skilled adult to read the intentions and desires of others, even when these have been hidden. (23)

14   According to Gardner, this intelligence can be found in successful "salespeople . . . clinicians . . . religious or political leaders, teachers, therapists, and parents" (9, 23). Also included in this group are school counselors and those who are good listeners and who are effective at giving advice and counsel to others. We have all known people who are considerate of others and who make us feel comfortable when we are around them. In addition, we usually enjoy being with people who give positive affirmations of our character or efforts. Those who work effectively in cooperative and team efforts tend to have interpersonal intelligence.

Intrapersonal Intelligence

15   The seventh category is intrapersonal intelligence, which Gardner defines as "a capacity to form an accurate, veridical [truthful, genuine] model of oneself and to be able to use that model to operate effectively in life" (9). Expanding on this basic definition, Gardner states that this kind of intelligence is

16   knowledge of the internal aspects of a person: access to one's own feeling life, one's range of emotions, the capacity to effect discriminations among those emotions and eventually to label them and to draw upon them as a means of understanding and guiding one's own behavior. A person with good intrapersonal intelligence has a viable and effective model of himself or herself. (24–25)

17   As Gardner points out, "[T]his intelligence is the most private" (25), so it manifests itself in one or more of the other seven intelligences. People with this kind of intelligence cannot be easily classified into a few professions. Rather, these people can be found in a wide variety of careers; they tend to know their strengths and weaknesses. This knowledge is usually accumu-

lated over a period of years. As you may have guessed, people who are emotionally and intellectually mature are more likely to have intrapersonal intelligence. We have all met people who are comfortable with who they are, who do not have to put on airs or pretend to be something or someone they are not. We might say that all those who are living fulfilling lives and who have spent some time (formally or informally) doing some honest self-assessment (or self-evaluation or self-reflection) have a degree of intrapersonal intelligence.

Naturalist Intelligence

In his book *Intelligence Reframed: Multiple Intelligences for the Twenty-First Century,* published in 1999, Gardner added "Naturalist Intelligence" to his original list of seven. According to Gardner, one who possesses naturalist intelligence "demonstrates expertise in the recognition and classification of the numerous species—the flora and fauna—of his or her environment" (*Intelligence Reframed* 48). Other signs of naturalist intelligence are "extensive knowledge of the living world" (48) and "fascination with plants and animals and a drive to identify, classify, and interact with them" (50). This intelligence "represents the ability to understand, identify, and work with plants, animals and other natural objects. This is the intelligence of the farmer or horticulturist, the veterinarian, the botanist, the environmentalist and the marine biologist" (www.education.com/teachspace/intelligences). Naturalist intelligence is displayed by people who "best understand the world through their own environment. . . . They believe that nature, ecological issues and animals are important" (www.education.com/teachspace/intelligences). Other kinds of people who have naturalist intelligence are those who work with animals in zoos, in research, and in the wild. Even people who keep and enjoy pets have some naturalist intelligence. Also sharing this intelligence are gardeners, bird-watchers, and those who work to make the environment a cleaner, safer place.

19   Knowledge of these eight intelligences can help us to expand our notions of what it means to have intelligence, to recognize and acknowledge the different kinds of intelligences in ourselves and others, and even to strengthen or develop one or more of our own intelligences. As Gardner states,

20   I think of the intelligences as raw, biological potentials . . . work[ing] together to solve problems, to yield various kinds of cultural endstates—vocations, avocations, and the like. . . . In my view, the purpose of school should be to develop intelligences and to help people reach vocational and avocational goals that are appropriate to their particular spectrum of intelligences. People who are helped to do so, I believe, feel more engaged and competent, and therefore more inclined to serve the society in a constructive way. (9)

Thinking Critically About the Reading

1. Where is the essay's thesis statement? If the author does not provide a thesis statement, develop one that fits the article.

2. Why do you think that logical-mathematical intelligence is more often associated with men than with women? What aspects of our culture or society may contribute to this view? In what ways has this view been changing?

3. From your own experience, what evidence can you think of that supports the view that our society puts a high value on linguistic intelligence and logical-mathematical intelligence?

4. Give examples of how the schools that you have attended recognize or do not recognize, develop or do not develop, all eight intelligences.

5. What are some practical steps that educational institutions can take to recognize or to help students develop a wider range of intelligences?

6. As the article mentions, standardized tests such as the ACT and SAT evaluate mainly linguistic and logical-mathematical intelligences. What are some arguments for and against the use of standardized tests in the process of admitting students to colleges?

7. Using a dictionary when necessary, define the following words in their appropriate context: pluralistic (paragraph 1); cognitive (1); figuratively (5); pedestal (5); kinesthetic (8); motivations (9); therapists (9); intrapersonal (10); veridical (10); viable (10); flora (11); fauna (11); botanist (11); vocations (12); avocations (12); spectrum (12).

Essay Assignment

Writing About Multiple Intelligences

Do a "multiple intelligences" assessment of yourself. Which two or three of the intelligences are you strongest in? Give examples of how you have shown these strengths, both in school and out of school. In which two or three intelligences do you believe you need the most development? Give examples.

Remember, the main purpose for getting to know more about your learning preferences is not to pigeonhole yourself, but rather to build on your strengths. As you progress through college, try to become more flexible in the ways in which you learn. Flexibility in your learning styles will help you become more successful in whatever career you choose and in developing lifelong learning skills. We close this Introduction with an essay written by one of our students in response to a prompt about learning experiences.

Student Essay

Not a Perfect Person

Richie Saavedra
Dr. Sabrio
English 1301-015
12 September 2006

Thesis statement
Plan of organization— two sentences

1   Learning is the foundation of life, in which one will either succeed or fail. Everything a person learns during one's lifetime is important and allows one to grow as a whole. Personally, I have experienced both failures and successes. Two areas in which I experienced failure were learning mathematics and learning how to weld. On the other hand, I also experienced success in Air Conditioning Technology and playing football.

Topic sentence
Development of first topic of paragraph

2   Two areas in which I have experienced failure include learning about mathematics and welding as a job. Since junior high school, numbers would confuse me, and the thought of fractions and percentages would make me want to give up. Even when I would make an effort to study and do homework, my grades would never reward me. When I entered high school, my algebra teacher would not spare the time to explain the information in detail. My geometry teacher was very patient and taught me as much as I needed to know about this subject. By showing his patience, he would stay after school three days a week to tutor me. Another area in which I experienced failure was learning how to weld for a job. Since my father was a technician, I would go with him to different welding jobs as an assistant in the summer. I began helping my father with welding when I was fourteen. Every time I would try to weld copper tubing, it would break apart. Now, at age twenty-two, it

Transition and development of second topic

is still very hard for me to weld. Coincidentally, the two areas I was unsuccessful in have some similar characteristics. Both mathematics and welding require measurements and calculations, so I could not calculate as a result of my poor mathematical skills.

3   On the other had, I have also experienced successes in life, such as learning about air conditioning and refrigeration during school. After I graduated from high school, I attended Texas State Technical College, in which I majored in Air Conditioning and Refrigeration Technology. An advantage in going into this field was that I gained experience while working with air conditioners and refrigerators at a young age. These classes were very interesting and caught my attention during the hands-on learning. Several of my professors encouraged me to help with lab classes because of the experience I had with this field.

4   Moreover, another experience in my life in which I experienced success was playing football. This sport had an interesting effect on my personal life away from school. One of my good childhood memories I always remember was playing football with my father. I remember him complimenting me on my natural ability to play, which increased my love for the game. As I grew older, I noticed when I was not working or in school I was always playing football. Every time I would play, it would somehow relieve my stress and I would forget about my worries. All of the passion I had for the game of football stayed with me when I moved to Harlingen, where I played semi-professional football for the Harlingen Wolverines.

5   Being an air conditioning tech and a football player were not only successes, but they also shared some traits. These traits include performing hands-on procedures, having coordination, and working out in the sun. When I was in school, I always preferred learning by hands-on experiences. I felt that I learned more information out of lab classes rather than lectures.

6   In conclusion, every person has attempted to learn something, whether it was school related or not. Of all of these lessons learned, everyone has experienced both failures and successes. When I would not succeed, I would learn from my mistakes and try harder the next time around. In my opinion, when one experiences failure, it only makes one stronger.

Insightful Writing: Writing to Learn

One of the major themes of this book is that writing is a powerful tool of learning. Writing is a very complex activity, one that is influenced by many different parts of one's brain, personality, culture, background, and previous experiences. When we write, we develop our mental capacities far beyond the confines of the particular assignment we are working on at the moment.

When we write in different college courses or situations, for different audiences, for different purposes, we are helping to develop a mental web or matrix that strengthens our cognitive abilities in many areas.

One of the reasons we began this book with learning styles and multiple ways of learning is to suggest that, whatever your predominant learning style or whatever intelligences you are strongest in, writing will help you develop virtually all your learning styles and intelligences.

PART I

Looking Inside the Writing Process

Chapter 1: *Writing and Learning*

Chapter 2: *Discovering Ideas*

Chapter 3: *Revision and Style*

1 Writing and Learning

"Why do I need to learn to write? In my job, I won't have to do much writing."

"I'm just getting a two-year degree. People in my line of work don't write very much."

"I'll just use the telephone, computer, or have face-to-face meetings in my business. I know people in the same profession, and they say that they don't have to write very often."

Do these comments sound familiar? These are some reactions that students have when told that they must take a writing course in college. You may have these or similar ideas about the uses of writing in your own life and job.

And there is absolutely nothing wrong with having these kinds of doubts. In fact, such thoughts indicate that you are interested in relating your educational experiences to your "larger" world, the world beyond the four walls of the college classroom, beyond an academic world that may seem overly narrow to you.

We ask, however, that you consider writing in three broader ways. First, instead of thinking of writing as an isolated skill, think of it as an extension of what we have been doing since we were infants. Writing is merely one of several important kinds of communication; just like listening, speaking, and reading. Therefore, we will try throughout this book to indicate the many interconnections among all of these important communication skills. Second, although one of the major purposes of writing is communicating information and points of view to others, this is not the only purpose. We hope that you will discover what many writers have found over the years: Writing can be a very powerful form of learning about both the self and the world. Finally, research has indicated that writing helps develop critical thinking and analytical skills, which are useful skills to have both inside and outside the classroom. Writing, therefore, can be used to communicate, to learn, and to develop higher-order thinking skills.

And please consider this final note about jobs and careers. It's very difficult for many students to predict exactly what they will be doing five, ten, or fifteen years from now. According to a U.S. Bureau of Labor Statistics survey conducted in April 2000, the average person holds more than nine jobs between the ages of 18 and 34—often completely changing his or her basic occupation. Given the fact that many people change careers and that the requirements of many careers are changing constantly, it may be better not to close off any of your options so early in your educational development. And remember, even if you don't use your writing skills very much on the job, writing is still one of the most useful forms of learning, self-discovery, and sharpening the mind. If there is any single lesson to be gained from your college experience, it is that learning is a lifelong activity. It is not an isolated chore that you endure passively for several years.

The Writing Process

All successful writers have some kind of procedure for producing a finished piece of writing. However, this procedure varies so widely from writer to writer that it is difficult to talk about *the* writing process, or *one* writing process. So we will present a brief composite: a procedure that highlights the main steps that many successful writers go through when they write. Incidentally, because the writing process is often difficult to explain in words (sounds ironic, doesn't it?), we will sometimes use analogies or comparisons between writing and more familiar activities or objects to help us get our ideas across.

To begin, the term *writing process* may be a bit misleading, because the process often begins even before we actually start writing. We often begin thinking—consciously or unconsciously—about a writing project before any words are actually typed or written on the page. Because the process includes this very important thinking component, some writing instructors prefer to use the term *composing process,* because this term includes both the thinking and writing aspects of the process.

Two questions of utmost importance should arise whenever you begin a writing project. The first one is "What is my purpose?" That is, what do I want to achieve or accomplish in this piece of writing? What main point do I want to get across? The second question is "Who are my readers, or who is my audience?" (We will use the terms *reader(s)* and *audience* interchangeably throughout this text.) We will examine these two crucial questions more carefully later in the book.

The following four-step procedure, then, summarizes some of the main steps that successful writers follow. Remember, however, that we are being somewhat arbitrary and artificial in the way we divide or partition this complex thinking/writing activity. Remember, too, that people have always divided or partitioned complex activities or organisms or objects in order to understand them better.

The first step is preparing or generating. This is a thinking/quick writing activity in which you get down on paper any thoughts or ideas as quickly as possible. We call this step "thinking on paper." This step, sometimes called "prewriting," is often most difficult for inexperienced writers because they think they must have their thoughts perfectly formed in their heads before they write those thoughts down. Not true. In fact, the very act of writing our thoughts down often helps us to clarify them in our own minds. In addition, because we use previous thoughts, ideas, and experiences in our writing, we have—in a sense—always already begun our essays before we actually sit down to "begin" a specific writing task! Remember always to keep in mind your purpose and your audience. Later we will point out some specific strategies for generating ideas for your essays.

The next step is organizing/drafting/shaping. In this step you take the rough ideas from step one and group them according to similarities. After you put all the like ideas together, you may have two, three, four, or more separate groups of ideas. These groups of ideas will form the basis of your body paragraphs. After you have a sense of what the body of your essay contains, you will have an easier time drafting out two specialized paragraphs—the opening paragraph and the closing paragraph. At this point you should have a pretty good idea of what the overall organization of the essay looks like.

There is no single essay structure that fits every situation. However, most essays that you write in college and most writing tasks on the job and in everyday life will share some common traits. One of these is a three-part structure: a beginning, a middle, and an end, or to put it another way, an opening or introductory paragraph, some body paragraphs, and a closing or concluding paragraph. Therefore, the overall "look" of your essay on the page will be something like Figure 1.1.

Please don't misunderstand us. Writing essays involves much more than pouring content into prefabricated molds. And the number of body paragraphs will vary depending on several factors, such as the assignment, your instructor's directions, and the amount of time you have to write. But the above structural pattern can help you organize your ideas

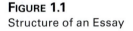

FIGURE 1.1
Structure of an Essay

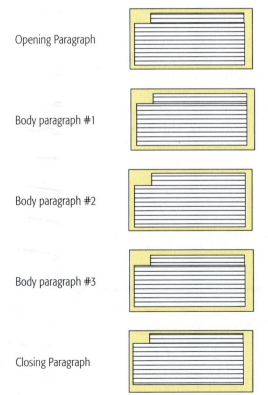

Opening Paragraph

Body paragraph #1

Body paragraph #2

Body paragraph #3

Closing Paragraph

more effectively as your writing matures. We will discuss more detailed ways to organize essays in succeeding chapters.

The third step is revising, that is, "looking again" at all aspects of the draft. "Revising" here does not mean checking for punctuation and spelling, but rather looking at the larger concerns of the draft: What ideas have I left out that I should have included? How can I change the order of the body paragraphs for greater effectiveness? What is in the draft that does not belong? How can I improve sentence quality and word choice? Ideas for revisions come from three main sources: your instructor, yourself, and your classmates. Later in the book we will provide you with systematic ways to revise your essays.

The final step is editing and proofreading. Here you give your essay one or two (or more) careful re-readings, looking especially for oversights in grammar, usage, punctuation, spelling, and format. In Chapter 3 we will include strategies for becoming a more effective editor and proofreader.

So there it is—a commonly used composing process. But don't let the step-by-step clarity of the above procedure fool you. In actual practice, the process is much messier, with one or more steps blending into and out of other steps. A rough drawing that represents this process might look something like the diagram in Figure 1.2). Notice all the loops, false starts, and dead ends. But also notice that you have a general map for getting you from a tentative beginning to a satisfying end.

All we can say is that throughout this term you will, with the assistance of your instructor and classmates, continue developing the composing procedure that is most effective for you. We do ask that you have no preconceived, rigid notions right now about how you write best. A procedure that at first feels uncomfortable to you may actually help you become a more effective writer if you work with it for a while.

FIGURE 1.2
The Writing Process

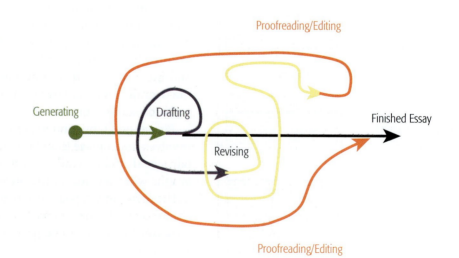

Differences Between Speaking and Writing

You may have heard conflicting advice in this area: "You should write the way you speak." "For heaven's sake, don't write the way you speak!" As with much conflicting advice, each side of the conflict has something useful to say.

Writing the way you speak is in one sense essential for you to communicate in your authentic voice. So a good way to begin getting your ideas down on paper is precisely to imagine you are having a conversation with someone. We have frequently read hard-to-follow sentences in student essays; but when we have conferences with these students and ask them to talk to us, to tell us what they were trying to say, they are usually able to tell us much more clearly what they were trying to communicate. We simply ask students to write down what they say and substitute that spoken sentence for the original, muddled sentence.

When advising students not to write the way they speak, teachers usually mean that writing—especially the kind done in college and on the job—is more formal, conforming more closely to the conventions of "standard written English" or "edited American English." The kinds of speaking and writing we do with family, friends, and acquaintances (everyday conversations and personal letters or e-mails, for example) are usually much less formal, more colloquial.

Does this mean that such speaking and writing are inferior to the kinds we do at college and on the job? Not at all! We simply have different conventions, standards, and levels of usage for different situations. Just as we wear different styles of clothing for different occasions, so do we also use different "styles" of language for different occasions. We will go into much more detail on these topics in Chapter 6, which focuses on language. One mark of educated people is not that they always use formal language, but that they use the language appropriate to the situation.

Keeping a Journal

One of the best ways we know of to learn how to write more effectively is—you guessed it—to write! Moreover, we suspect that if your writing were risk-free, that is, if you knew that your instructor would not rip your writing to shreds with red ink, you would be more likely to develop a very important skill that many inexperienced writers lack: fluency. Fluency is the ability to write ideas down readily, to generate large chunks of discourse in a relatively short period of time. Keeping a journal, or writer's log, will help you build that ever-important capability, fluency.

Recognizing the importance of fluency and self-confidence in the early part of a writing course, instructors allow students to develop ideas, make connections and discoveries, and take chances without worrying too much about concerns such as organization, sentence quality, grammar, usage, punctuation, and spelling.

Throughout this book we will give you the opportunity to develop your fluency by doing some journal writing. Sometimes the journal topics will be related to the essays you are writing, and sometimes they will not. In any case, use these journal writing activities to develop your fluency while at the same time developing your ideas.

Some instructors may want you to write your journals in a thin spiral notebook devoted solely to your journal writing. Others may want you to keep an electronic journal, or blog, and submit entries electronically. In order to get into the habit of developing your ideas fully and increasing your writing fluency, try making each journal entry at least 250 words long. There is, of course, nothing magical about this 250-word length. Your instructor may choose to adjust this length up or down. Also, don't confuse journal writing with keeping a diary. A diary often tells simply what you did each day. Journal writing is often more reflective, or comments on what you are reading, or is preparation for an upcoming essay.

JOURNAL WRITING

Here are some suggestions for early-in-the-term journal writing:

1. Write a brief autobiography (a history of your life told by yourself) as a way of introducing yourself to your classmates and your instructor. Concentrate on those past events in your life that helped to make you who you are.

2. What kinds of writing activities did you do in all previous college or high school writing classes? How much did you write? What kinds of paragraphs or essays did you write? What do you feel are your strengths and shortcomings as a writer?

3. How do you feel about being in this particular writing class? What have you heard from students and teachers about this course? How do you think this course will or will not help you in your other courses?

4. What are your short-term and long-term goals for yourself? How do you see your college work fitting into these goals? What major obstacles stand in the way of reaching your goals?

5. When you are not working or attending classes, what kinds of activities do you enjoy doing as hobbies or pastimes? Why do you enjoy these activities? How did you become interested in these activities?

6. What questions or concerns do you have about this particular college campus?

7. Besides this course, what other courses are you taking this term?

8. What job(s) have you had in the past, and what job(s) do you hold while attending college? Which job(s) have you enjoyed most? Why? Which have you enjoyed least? Why?

Reading Effectively

As part of this textbook's "whole language" approach to writing, we include a number of reading selections throughout the book. Some of these selections will be used as sources of ideas for discussion and writing, others will be used as models to help you organize your own essays more effectively, and all have been carefully chosen to help promote your development as a person with reflective insight and a positive attitude toward life. In particular, we want you to become a lifelong learner who is able to adapt to a changing world. You will also encounter reading, some of it very heavy, in your other college courses. It would be a good idea, then, to know how to read effectively, so that you can get as much as possible out of each course you take.

One important point to remember is that people read differently for different purposes. When reading the daily newspaper or a news magazine, or when reading for entertainment, we may not need to concentrate on every detail, nor would we have to devote our undivided attention to our reading.

When reading academic or work-related material, however, we use different strategies. The most important strategy is to be an active reader. Become involved. Use as many senses as you can. When many students read for their college courses, they may lie down on a couch or bed and read silently. This is probably the least effective reading method.

Getting Started: Strategies for Generating Ideas

Beginnings are often the most difficult part of a writing assignment. Who would have thought that a piece of blank paper or a blank computer screen would be so intimidating? But there it is. What do you do? Perhaps we should first tell you what *not* to do. Do not wait for the perfect first sentence of the opening paragraph of your essay to become magically formed in your head. Chances are it won't. But that is perfectly all right and normal.

One often overlooked way in which writers generate material for their essays is hard to talk about because it goes on quietly, often without writers being consciously aware of it. This is the subconscious turning over of

Using some or all of the following strategies will make you a more active, hence a more effective, reader:

- Read with a pen, pencil, or highlighter in hand and a notebook or piece of paper at your side. As you read, write down any questions that occur to you. Try to summarize each section or paragraph of the reading. Remember that beginnings and endings are usually places of emphasis in writings. Authors often place their most important ideas here. So pay careful attention to beginnings and endings of book chapters, essays, and individual paragraphs.

- Use a pen, pencil, or highlighter to underline key passages in the reading. Also, underline and look up in a dictionary any words that are unfamiliar to you. This may seem like a chore now, but this activity will help build your vocabulary and will assist you in your other courses as well as in your career.

- Talk about the reading with one or more classmates. Trying to explain an essay to someone will really test your own understanding of the essay.

- If you don't understand something about a reading, ask your instructor at the appropriate time in class. Carefully thought out questions, which can be very valuable to class discussions, indicate to your instructor that you have read the material.

- The greater the number of language activities (listening, speaking, reading, writing) you use while reading, the more effective reader you will be.

ideas in our heads when we are not consciously working on our writing project. Some writing teachers call this process the "cooking" or "incubating" stage. At random times during any part of the day or night—while you are driving to class, daydreaming, taking a shower, lying in bed just before dozing off or just after waking up—an idea will strike you. We recommend that you get into the habit of listening to this voice from the back of your mind and jotting down a note to yourself. Otherwise, the idea will slip away as quickly and mysteriously as it came.

Here are several strategies for generating material when you are stuck, or even if you are not. The main point to remember about all of these strategies for generating ideas is that you are not writing a draft of your essay yet, but you are accumulating ideas and materials to use in your essay.

Focused Freewriting   One of the most effective and widely used methods for generating material is called focused freewriting. It goes by this name because you are focusing on an actual essay subject, and you are free to write anything that comes to mind about this subject. In this activity you simply write down on paper (or type) as fast as you can anything that comes to mind related to the subject you are writing your essay about. We sometimes call this activity "thinking on paper." You may write words, phrases, sentences, or perhaps even short paragraphs if you want to develop a topic at that particular moment.

Whatever you do, do not worry at this time about concerns such as organization, sentence quality, word choice, punctuation, or spelling. Worrying about these aspects of writing now will hinder your free flow of ideas. Also, don't decide now which ideas to keep and which ideas to discard. At this point, keep everything. You will probably wind up with some unusable ideas, but you'll have plenty of time to throw those away later.

In some ways, getting started on an essay is like turning on an old water faucet that has not been used in six months. When you turn on the faucet, what comes out at first? Dirty, rusty water, small corroded bits of the interior of the pipe, perhaps some air that makes the pipe sputter and spurt. But what happens after you keep the faucet open for a while and let the water run? The water begins to run clear. Something similar happens during focused freewriting. You may get some gunky, corroded ideas at first, but you will also eventually get much usable material. So turn on your "idea-generating faucet" and let the ideas run onto the page or screen.

Brainstorming Another method of generating ideas is brainstorming. This strategy may work better for you if you tend to learn better by talking and listening with a small group of classmates. Brainstorming is similar to focused freewriting in the sense that you are trying to generate many ideas in a short period of time. However, a writer using focused freewriting immediately begins putting ideas onto the page, usually working alone.

Brainstorming, on the other hand, emphasizes talking and listening with a small group of writers first (try three students per group) and then slowly getting ideas onto paper as the brainstorming session progresses. One principle behind brainstorming is that two or three minds are better than one when you are generating ideas. An important point to remember is this: Each person in the brainstorming group must feel a sense of responsibility to participate fully by both talking and listening carefully, and also to remain focused on the subject under discussion. You should also jot down brief notes and ideas as the session progresses, so that you have a summary of what was discussed. You can then expand these notes more fully on your own time after the brainstorming session. At the end of an effective brainstorming session, each person in the group should feel that he or she has contributed ideas to the others as well as benefited from the comments and questions of the others. Remember also that a brainstorming session is not the time to be critical of other people's ideas. You'll have time to discard ideas later.

Also, don't be afraid to speak up, even if your mind has not fully formed the point you want to make. Sometimes the act of speaking or writing actually helps us form our ideas and make connections as we speak. And sometimes sharing our ideas helps us clarify them in our own minds.

Clustering or Mapping   Yet another method of generating ideas early in the composing process is clustering or mapping. This technique may be better suited to people who are more visually oriented, who learn better by visualizing diagrams or actually drawing on paper visual representations of ideas.

You begin this method by writing the key term of your subject in the middle of a sheet of paper and drawing a circle or box around the term. Then you begin thinking of various ways in which your subject can be divided into various subtopics that you want to discuss. These terms you also write down and circle or box, drawing a line from these secondary terms to the main subject in the middle of the page. Continue to add and connect terms until you have a page full of relationships between various aspects of the subject. Perhaps the best way to demonstrate clustering is to—you guessed it—draw you a picture! The clustering illustration in Figure 1.3 was done for the essay "Tips for a New Preschool Teacher" that is included later in this chapter.

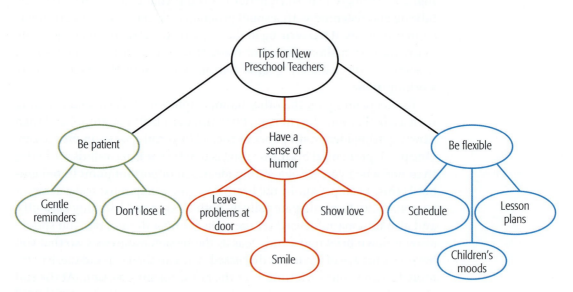

Figure 1.3
Example of Clustering

The preceding three strategies for generating ideas will help you get going early in your writing. Your instructor may also add other methods of getting ideas down on paper quickly. You need not use all three of these methods for every writing task. Why not experiment and see which technique works best for you? You may discover that different techniques work better for different writing tasks.

Thesis Statement

During your preparing/generating activity, you are always aware that you have to focus on some specific subject for your essay. You constantly remind yourself of your purpose for writing and the audience for whom you are writing. Out of all of these considerations will grow your thesis statement. This is the most important part of the entire essay, the sentence or sentences that tell your readers what you plan to do in your essay. Sometimes you will be able to formulate your thesis statement very early in your preparing/generating activity. At other times you may have to formulate your thesis statement slowly during the course of your preparing/generating activity. At any rate, by the end of this activity, you should have at least a rough or working version of your thesis statement written down both as a guide for you and as a promise or commitment of what you intend to do or show for your readers.

Some instructors may require you to include a plan of organization after your thesis statement. The plan of organization lists the major topics in the order in which you will discuss them in your essay.

Organizing, Drafting, and Shaping

Once you have spent some time generating ideas and material for your essay, you are ready to organize or shape that material into a working draft. Although you will eventually rework and revise your material, this early draft will give you some sense of what the final draft may look like.

Paragraphs

Because this second step in the composing process involves writing paragraphs, we will present a quick review of paragraph basics.

Most essays consist of an organized sequence of paragraphs. Paragraphs are the essential building blocks of essays. Imagine how difficult an essay would be to understand if it consisted of one enormously long paragraph.

A paragraph can be defined as a block of prose, usually a minimum of several sentences long, whose first line is indented one tab or five spaces from the left margin. A paragraph usually develops a single topic. Think of a paragraph as a subdivision of an essay. Paragraphs help both the writer and the reader.

Paragraphs help the writer organize ideas into separate blocks of prose, based on similarity of ideas. Paragraphs also help the writer present several different topics to the reader in a structured way.

In addition, paragraphs help the reader navigate through an essay. They help the reader digest or assimilate related bits of information one piece at a time. Paragraphs help the reader know where the essay begins, where each new topic begins, and where the essay ends.

Paragraphs, then, are organizational tools that help both writers and readers navigate more easily through an essay. The more effectively paragraphs are written, the more effective the essay will be.

There is no hard and fast rule about how many sentences and words a paragraph should contain. Many factors come into play to guide writers on paragraph length. Even something as seemingly insignificant as the width of columns helps determine paragraph length. In general, the narrower the column, the fewer sentences a paragraph contains. Look at newspapers and newsmagazines, which usually have very narrow columns. You will find many paragraphs that consist of only one or two sentences. In the kinds of writing that students do in college, with the much greater page width of standard-sized typing paper, paragraphs tend to contain more sentences.

We can classify paragraphs into three basic kinds, based on where in the essay they appear. The three most common kinds of paragraphs are the following:

- Body paragraphs
- Opening or introductory paragraphs
- Closing or concluding paragraphs

In general, opening and closing paragraphs tend to be shorter than body paragraphs. Since opening and closing paragraphs are often difficult to write without first knowing what the body paragraphs of an essay will contain, we will discuss these specialized paragraphs after we discuss body paragraphs.

Body Paragraphs

One way to begin shaping your rough ideas from the generating activity is to try to group your ideas into two to four main topics, based on similarity of ideas. These groups of similar ideas will become the material for your body paragraphs, with each paragraph discussing one topic.

Readers often expect body paragraphs—especially in college and career-related writing—to have certain general qualities. If your body paragraphs exhibit these qualities, you will have begun fulfilling the expectations of your reader, thus taking an important step in gaining his or her interest.

May we digress briefly to make a point? One way to remember important facts is to associate them with an acronym, a word formed from the first letters of the words in a particular phrase. For example, "scuba" is an acronym for "self-contained underwater breathing apparatus," and "laser" is an acronym for "lightwave amplification by stimulated emission of radiation." To give you an idea of how well acronyms work, we still recall the names of the Great Lakes because of an acronym given by a fifth-grade teacher more years ago than we care to remember! That acronym is "HOMES": Huron, Ontario, Michigan, Erie, and Superior.

Here is an acronym for remembering some key traits of an effective body paragraph: **DUCTT**. (We added the extra "t" for a reason which you will see soon.) A duct is any tube or enclosure that conveys a substance such as air or liquid. You are probably in a room right now that uses a duct to bring in cool or warm air. So a duct helps to focus substances such as air or water, putting them where they are needed. And using the DUCTT acronym will remind you to put features into your body paragraphs to make them more effective. Here are five traits of an effective body paragraph, each trait beginning with a letter of the acronym:

D evelopment

U nity

C oherence

T ransitions

T opic Sentence

Let's look more closely at each of these traits.

Development   Body paragraphs are usually fully developed with details, specific examples, and explanations. One mark of inexperienced writers is that they tend not to develop their ideas fully. Typical body paragraphs in college writing range in length from about 80 to 160 words.

Unity   A body paragraph is unified when it develops only one topic and when every sentence in that paragraph is somehow tied back to the main topic of the paragraph. Therefore, a short essay that discusses four main topics will usually contain four body paragraphs.

Coherence   Coherence means that the paragraph flows smoothly from one sentence to the next, that each sentence is clearly and logically connected to the one before it and the one after it. A coherent paragraph is one that lets readers understand the connections between the sentences.

Transitions   Transitions are words, phrases, or even sentences that help tie a paragraph together, that help link the sentences together. Using transitions helps give coherence to a paragraph. Some obvious transitions are "first," "next," "and," "for instance," and "another." Less obvious transitions include words that show logical relationships ("as a result") and repetitions of key words.

Topic Sentence   The topic sentence is the key sentence of a body paragraph. It tells the reader what the paragraph contains. After reading this one sentence, the reader should have a reasonably good idea of what the paragraph is about. While you are developing your skills and confidence as a writer, it may be a good idea to place your topic sentence first in each body paragraph. Remember, the first sentence of a paragraph is a point of emphasis. It is important to understand, though, that in your reading, you will see body paragraphs that use topic sentences in positions other than the first, and other paragraphs may only imply—without clearly stating—their topic sentences.

Opening Paragraphs

Once you have drafted your body paragraphs, you are now in a better position to know more clearly what should go into the opening and closing, or introduction and conclusion, of your essay.

You may be wondering, "Wait a minute! I thought that I was supposed to write my opening paragraph first, before I write the body paragraphs." Of course you can do that, if you have a good idea for writing an effective opening paragraph. But many writers find that beginnings are hardest and that they often get stuck trying to write the perfect opening paragraph. This "stuck" feeling is sometimes called "writer's block." Writing your body paragraphs first, then, has two big advantages. First, you avoid getting stuck and frustrated at the very beginning of your essay, and second, knowing what your body paragraphs contain will allow you to write an opening paragraph that "fits" your essay perfectly.

What makes a good opening paragraph? One key is to grab your reader's interest, to cause the reader to think, "Hey, this looks interesting. I want to continue reading this!" Another key is to let the reader know the main idea, or thesis, of the whole essay. Let's take a closer look at these two factors.

The second key for writing an effective opening paragraph is to include a clear thesis statement. Remember, too, that readers are more likely to recognize your thesis sentence if you place it in a position of emphasis: either the beginning or the end of a paragraph. One advantage of placing your thesis statement in the first sentence of the opening paragraph is that your reader knows immediately the main idea of the essay. One advantage of placing your thesis statement in the last sentence of the

Here are some suggestions for grabbing your reader's interest in the opening paragraph:

1. Begin with a question, especially one directed to your readers. Questions such as these help pull your readers into your essay. "Have you ever wondered how compact discs are made?" "What would you do if your car broke down on an expressway of an unfamiliar city?"

2. Begin with a short narrative or story related to the topic of your essay.

3. Begin with a general statement that orients your readers toward the more specific thesis of your essay.

4. Begin with some unusual or little-known fact regarding your subject.

Experiment with these and other methods for capturing your reader's interest at the beginning of your essay.

opening paragraph is that you can orient the reader to the general subject before focusing on your specific thesis. Another advantage of placing the thesis statement at the end of the opening paragraph is that you can use one or more key words or phrases contained in the thesis statement as tools of organization and coherence for the opening paragraph. For example, look at the following introductory paragraph.

```
Working with children can be one of the most reward-
ing experiences in any person's life. The old adage,
"It takes a village to raise a child," proves to be
true when working at a nursery school. Every teacher
works together to provide the best possible learn-
ing environment for young children. The prospect of
dealing with small children every day is daunting.
There are a few points that new teachers can remem-
ber to get through the day. First, be flexible. Sec-
ond, have a sense of humor. Last of all, remember to
be patient.
```

Notice that the thesis statement comes towards the end of this opening paragraph. This statement tells readers what the writer will discuss in the body of the essay. Also, notice that the writer gives a plan of organization in the last few sentences of the introduction.

Here, then, is one structuring tool for writing well-organized opening paragraphs. This idea was developed a number of years ago by college

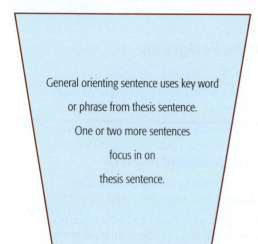

FIGURE 1.4
Funnel Structure of an Opening Paragraph

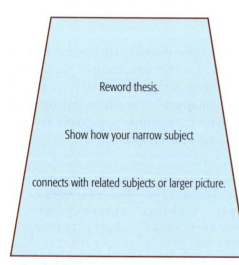

FIGURE 1.5
Inverted Funnel Structure of Closing
Paragraph

writing teacher Sheridan Baker. Remember that this is not the only way to organize your opening paragraph. Many writers, however, when they are developing their skills and confidence, find this structure useful.

The funnel-like shape of the diagram in Figure 1.4 suggests the broad-to-narrow or general-to-specific movement of the opening paragraph. One final word about the length of the opening paragraph: Your opening paragraph need not be very long to get its job done. In academic essays of the kind that you will be writing, an opening paragraph of about sixty to eighty words is usually sufficient.

Closing or Concluding Paragraphs

Your closing paragraph does not need to be elaborate, nor does it need to be as long as your body paragraphs. What it should do is let the readers know that you are finished, that you have accomplished what you set out to do. The first way of presenting your conclusion is to reword your thesis statement at the beginning (position of emphasis) of the closing paragraph. Rewording your thesis statement will signal to the reader that you are wrapping up your essay. We say "rewording" because if you use in this paragraph exactly the same thesis statement, word for word, from your opening paragraph, then readers might be put off by the repetition and monotony.

The second way of letting your readers know that you have finished is not introducing any new topics in the closing paragraph. If you did introduce a new topic here, your readers might feel cheated if you did not discuss it fully.

Third, you probably do not need to summarize the main topics you covered in your essay. Shorter essays usually do not need summaries in the closing paragraph. You will, however, sometimes see summaries in the closing paragraphs of longer essays.

One strategy for crafting a closing paragraph is to reword your thesis and then show how the specific subject in your essay connects with related subjects. That is, you show how your narrow subject fits into a larger picture. One way to think of this structure is to picture an inverted funnel, like the diagram in Figure 1.5.

Here is a sample closing paragraph. It is the closing paragraph of the same essay from which we took the opening paragraph above.

If a new preschool teacher remembers these tips,
she will be showered with adoration. Being flexible allows children to understand the teacher is
there on their terms. A sense of humor shows children that the teacher came to work to have a good
time with them as well as teach them. Last of all,
if a teacher is patient above all else, children will
learn patience and respect. If this career path is
one you end up walking down, be prepared for the
best walk of your life.

Notice that the student did not merely repeat the three main responsibilities of preschool teachers. Instead, she reworded her thesis to emphasize the overall responsibility of teachers to make learning fun.

Here is the entire essay from which we have shown the opening and
closing paragraphs. This essay illustrates the points we have been discussing in this chapter. It's not perfect; few essays are. But reading it will
give you a concrete idea about how an essay comes together.

Student Essay

Tips for a New Preschool Teacher

Melissa Anne Scott

Thesis statement

Topic sentence

1   Working with children can be one of the most rewarding experiences in
any person's life. The old adage, "It takes a village to raise a child," proves
to be true when working at a nursery school. Every teacher works together
to provide the best possible learning environment for young children. The
prospect of dealing with small children every day is daunting. There are a
few points that new teachers can remember to get through the day. First, be
flexible. Second, have a sense of humor. Last of all, remember to be patient.

2   Working with preschoolers can be a challenging experience. Just by
walking into a classroom, a parent, the director, or even another child can
sense the mood of the room. Teachers must be flexible in order for a classroom to run smoothly. A daily schedule helps to keep children organized
and alert to what comes next in the classroom. Lesson plans made a week or
so in advance help to keep the teacher on top of her class. Lesson plans also
need to be flexible, in case another teachable opportunity occurs during the
day. Also, if children become tired, the teacher may have to change the day
around them.

Topic sentence

3 A sense of humor is a main ingredient for getting through the day. Children come up with the best stories, songs, and actions that can keep a teacher smiling. It is always best when teachers leave their problems at the door. A teacher can go to work having had the worst morning, but the minute a child runs to her and gives her a hug, her problems melt away. Children just want to be loved. Sometimes children do things that are not correct, but a teacher has to look at preschoolers and smile because they are just learning, and need the guiding hand of a teacher with a good attitude.

Topic sentence

4 Last but not least, patience is the key. A preschool teacher may have to tell a child numerous times what is right and wrong. Teachers will have to constantly remind them of manners, schedules, and rules. Just remember, they are children. They haven't lived in the world as long as adults have, and it will take time to remember what is expected of them. The minute a teacher loses her patience, it is best to take a step back, breathe, and rethink what it will take to help the child. This will make it easier for the teacher to revisit the situation and use a clear head when redirecting the child.

Reworded thesis

5 If a new preschool teacher remembers these tips, she will be showered with adoration. Being flexible allows children to understand the teacher is there on their terms. A sense of humor shows children that the teacher came to work to have a good time with them as well as teach them. Last of all, if a teacher is patient above all else, children will learn patience and respect. If this career path is one you end up walking down, be prepared for the best walk of your life.

▶ Essay Assignments

Writing About Learning

In order to give you practice in using the composing process, your instructor may assign one of the following essay subjects or other choices for writing an essay. These subjects are for essays based on personal experience and observation:

1. Who are the three best teachers you have had so far in your education? How or why were they the best? How have they influenced you? What event or incident can you relate about each teacher that illustrates his or her effectiveness as a teacher? What positive traits do all three have in common?

2. What are some important lessons that you have learned while working in jobs that you have had? Concentrate especially on lessons that are difficult to learn from books. Use examples or brief narratives to illustrate your main points.

3. Think of some activity that you and your family have done over the years, something that has turned into a family tradition, such as celebrating a holiday, having a family reunion, or going to the same place for vacation. Write about this activity in such a way that your reader gets a sense of what the activity is like.

4. What are your main goals for this semester, and how do you plan to accomplish these goals? You may have personal goals, academic goals, family goals, and goals related to any work that you do.

5. Think of a hobby or pastime that you are really interested in and know about, perhaps something that you have been doing for a number of years. Write an essay about the rewards of taking up _____ as a hobby or pastime.

6. Tell a story or give a narrative about the most embarrassing, or the proudest, or the most difficult, or the most memorable event that you have experienced or witnessed so far.

PRACTICAL TIPS   Format for Academic Essays

In academic writing students are expected to follow a certain standard format so that the essay is presentable and professional. Your instructor may add to or modify these guidelines.

1. Word process and double space your essays. Use black ink, standard font (such as Times New Roman), and font size 12. Leave one-inch margins at top, bottom, and right and left sides of each page. Number each page with your last name and page number at the upper right corner of the page. You do not need a cover sheet. Any standard college-level writing handbook contains information on the proper formatting of essays.

2. Give your essay an appropriate title, centered, and not underlined.

3. Hand in ALL work. This includes prewriting, drafts, peer responses, and final draft.

4. After word processing your essay, save your work on a disk, and print two copies: one for yourself and one to hand in. Make these copies before you turn off the computer.

The following essay responds to "Essay Assignments," topic #5, on a hobby or pastime, written in the appropriate academic format.

Student Essay

My Hobby

Ricky Varela
Dr. Saenz
English 1301-006
21 September 2006

Ricky Varela
Dr. Saenz
English 1301-006
21 September 2006

Thesis statement

1   Hobbies and pastimes are activities that portray how one feels on the inside, where no one else can see. Hobbies bring out good feelings and incorporate those feelings into the best of the activity. People may not know what hobby they actually like until they put in the time and effort to look for it. The search is the real thrill of finding a hobby because, when it is found, the rewards are great and the feelings are comforting. For me, the hobby is playing the drums. Though I did not know it at the time, I found my hobby when I was four years old, banging on pots and pans.

Topic sentence
Development of topic

2   Playing the drums takes a lot of self-discipline and respect for what needs to be done. The mind of the performer must be set on the task at hand. A drummer has to be focused on what his part is and be aware of everyone else's parts that are important. In order to be aware of this, the drummer must take apart a song and know each part in great detail. He must have the willpower to sit down and figure out how his part mixes with everyone else's. The patience that goes into this is the most important part. It is said that practice makes perfect, but for a drummer, it is perfect practice makes perfect. The time put into practice should be more than the time spent studying, eating, and sleeping all combined. I learned how to discipline myself by locking myself in my room for hours at a time. I could practice whatever parts I needed to practice. I would find recordings of all musical pieces that I was to practice. I would study the techniques of the drummers on the recordings and incorporate what they played into what I played. If I didn't like the technique, then I would find another recording. This type of practice took a lot out of me. However, all the work paid off for me in the end. I became a better player and am now able to practice for a long time with ease.

Topic sentence
Development of topic

3   Many people can listen to music and say they like it, but can they say that they really appreciate it? Through the studies of percussion and music that I have done, those who are involved in some type of musical organization seem to love and appreciate music more. If one can understand all the

details that go into the making and playing of music, then the love for music would come as a tool to understanding it. Music can be interpreted in many ways. One person might say a song is about love because of its slow tempo. Another person might say that the song is a dramatic song that involves a lot of emotion and feelings. No matter what the interpretation, the appreciation is there.

Topic sentence
Development of topic 4   Playing the drums has another type of emotional background to it. It might be of a different style than the musical way. If one listens to a drum solo and says that he likes it because it is fast and flashy, then he is looking at it from one perspective, the non-musical way. If another person who is trained in the art hears the solo, he might be more specific about it and say he liked it because it used a great deal of dynamics as well as many intricate rhythms to add color and texture to the solo piece. This is just a really fancy way to say that it was fast and loud. This type of appreciation only comes to those who are actually serious about learning the art of making music through the percussion instruments.

Topic sentence
Development of topic 5   Music is a great way to meet new friends and make lifelong connections with people who have the same interests. I have personal experience with this. I have been in many jazz bands throughout my career and have met many people in the process. If I ever need help with a playing gig or just need some advice from friends, then I know I can count on these guys to help me in any way possible. I would do the same for these people also. We all have a mutual relationship through music. The ages of these friends vary from as young as twelve to older than forty. Sometimes I might meet an older musician who would give me good advice, but those are few and far between. Each of these friends can help with a different aspect of music as well as life. These relationships are the core of what making music is. Music starts with friends. It may begin with one person showing another how to play or just giving advice. These people might be coworkers or bosses or audience members. Last night after I played a performance, someone from the audience asked me to play in his band on weekends for pay.

Restatement of thesis 6   Playing the drums puts me in a place where I am the star and no one can touch me. It can fulfill the need for competition as well as self-worth. I hope everyone has at least one hobby that takes them to a place where they are invincible.

Insightful Writing

Some people believe that great writers are born, not made. While there may be a grain of truth to that belief, most college writing teachers believe, as we do, that virtually every college student is capable of learning how to be a competent writer, to advance beyond the writing level at which he or she entered the course.

This chapter gave you a blueprint for building your essay-writing skills. There is nothing mysterious about learning how to write more effectively. It takes time, work, and practice. We also want to point out a connection that many new college writers have not considered. There is a definite, significant link between how well one reads and how well one writes. That is, strong readers usually have the potential to develop into strong writers. Those who have difficulty reading have a much harder time developing their writing skills. For this reason, we include in this book strategies to improve your reading skills.

You will find out very quickly that many college courses require a great deal of reading. One challenge is to develop your reading skills to meet the reading demands. One opportunity is to use your increased reading abilities to strengthen your writing skills.

2 Discovering Ideas

There is an Indian belief that everyone is a house of four rooms: a physical, a mental, an emotional and a spiritual room. Most of us tend to live in one room most of the time, but unless we go into every room every day, even if only to keep it aired, we are not complete.

Rumer Godden, House of Four Rooms

There is one person you have to live with every day of your life: yourself. So the better you know and like yourself, the better you'll get along with yourself. It is very important for you to have a positive concept of who you are, to have high self-esteem. It is much better to live with someone you like than with someone you despise.

As we have seen, one excellent way to learn and discover more about yourself is to write about yourself. Remember, writing is not just a tool for communicating; it is also a very powerful tool for self-discovery, learning, and developing higher-order thinking skills.

JOURNAL WRITING

In the quotation at the beginning of this chapter, Godden mentions four "rooms" that make up the "house" of one's personality. Write a few sentences describing the four rooms of your personality: the physical, the mental, the emotional, and the spiritual. In which "room" do you spend most time? Why? What people and experiences have influenced you in each of these four rooms? How have you changed over the years in terms of spending time in each room? In other words, do you spend less or more time in one or more rooms now than you used to? Why?

This prompt is tailor-made for a response of four separate paragraphs, each one focusing on one of the four "rooms" of one's personality. One of the most common ways to develop a paragraph is through the use of examples or illustrations. These examples or illustrations support your general statements about a topic. For example, if you state that you spend a lot of time in your "physical" room, the reader would like to see examples and illustrations of this assertion.

In the previous chapter, we introduced the writing process and began to explore the first stages of that process: generating ideas, and organizing, drafting, and shaping those ideas. The next stages of the writing process are revising and editing/proofreading.

Revision

One of the most important activities in the composing process—and unfortunately one of the most neglected—is revision. *Revision* means re-seeing—that is, looking again at what we have written. Successful writers tell us over and over that careful revision is what makes their writing stand out.

Before we go any further, we want to clear up a misconception about revision. Many inexperienced writers believe that successful writers need to do little or no revision because they get everything right the first time. Not true! They are successful precisely because they spend so much time on revision. Unfortunately, many students associate revision with punishment: "You didn't get it right the first time; write it over again."

We would like you to associate revision with achievement. The more you revise, the greater the likelihood your writing will be successful. In fact, one trait that distinguishes successful writers from unsuccessful writers is that successful writers spend much more time revising and take their writing through more drafts than unsuccessful writers.

PRACTICAL TIPS	Questions for Global Revision

1. What topics have I left out that could have been included?

2. What topics have I included that could have been left out?

3. What ideas need fuller development or elaboration?

4. How can I put my body paragraphs into a more effective order?

5. How can I make the opening paragraph more attention-grabbing?

6. How can I make the closing paragraph more effective?

Notice that these questions center on larger concerns such as ideas, development, organization, and paragraphing.

Questions to ask at this level of revision include the following:

1. Does my draft indicate that I understand the concept of sentence boundaries? That is, have I eliminated all sentence fragments, comma splices, and run-on sentences?

2. What sentences may be difficult for my readers to follow? How can I revise them for clarity?

3. Do I have too many short sentences? (Having too many short sentences makes your writing sound choppy and immature.)

4. How many sentences begin with the same word or phrase? (If too many sentences begin in the same way, your writing will sound monotonous and repetitious.)

Global Revision

What exactly is revision? We will begin by telling you what it is not. It is not fixing the punctuation and spelling, getting commas in the right places, and getting the format to look good. These activities are important, but they usually come after revision, in the proofreading/editing step. (We will discuss that step next.) Revision means looking again at the larger or "global" concerns of your draft.

Sentence-Level Revision

After attending to these "global" revisions, you can go to the next level of revision, sentence quality.

Before You Read

1. Before reading the following essay, "Getting Yourself Back on Track," take a moment to read just the opening and closing paragraphs. Put into your own words, either by telling a classmate or by writing in your notebook, what you believe to be the main point or thesis of the essay.

2. Look at the titles of each subsection of the article. What do these titles tell you about the contents of the body paragraphs?

While You Read

1. As you read, underline or highlight key sentences. Remember, key sentences are often at the beginnings and ends of paragraphs.

2. What questions occur to you while you read this essay? Write these questions down. What do you agree or disagree with most strongly?

3. As you read, keep a written record of your summary of and comments on or responses to each paragraph. How do the ideas in this essay speak to you personally?

4. Meet with one or more of your classmates during this class or outside of class and discuss the different reactions and responses that you and your classmates have to the article. How are your interpretations similar to or different from those of your classmates?

Readings

The following article was first published in *PARADE* magazine in September 2004. It offers some practical strategies for reaching your potential.

Getting Yourself Back on Track

BY DIANNE HALES

Are you stuck in a job you hate? Afraid to make decisions? Unable to climb the corporate ladder? Here's expert advice on how to live up to your potential.

1   Five years after graduation, an economics major still temps as a bookkeeper. A legal secretary has dropped so many evening courses over 20 years that she still doesn't have her bachelor's degree. An audiovisual technician finds himself in one dead-end job after another.

2   These men and women share a common enemy: themselves. By procrastinating, missing deadlines and engaging in other self-defeating behaviors, they routinely undermine their chances for success.

3   "Everybody ducks out of one challenge or another," says psychologist Kenneth W. Christian, author of *Your Own Worst Enemy: Breaking the Habit of Adult Underachievement*. "But if you're a chronic underachiever, whenever you run into difficulty, you want to curl up and suck your thumb. You seek comfort rather than hard work.

You make excuses to avoid facing your fears. And you end up with a life that's unfulfilling, because you miss out on the satisfaction that only comes from tackling something hard."

4   Underachievement—failure to live up to potential—exists in every age group, at every job level and in every field, from sales to sports. Christian estimates that one in four adults has the problem. But sufferers should take heart, notes psychologist Pamela Brill, author of *The Winner's Way*. "Underachievement isn't a permanent condition," she says, "but a mind-set—a behavior pattern that you can change."

The Roots of Self-Sabotage

5   The key, psychological research reveals, is how much control you think you have over your life. "High achievers tend to assume responsibility,

attributing positive results to their own actions," says psychologist Susan Battley of Stony Brook, N.Y. "Underachievers may feel very little control over their lives, so they may not have the same motivation to work to make things happen. They like to believe things will turn out the same, whatever they do."

6 Although underachievement can start in grade school, adults usually don't sense a problem until their late 20s. "The Bart Simpson, underachieving-and-proud-of-it thing isn't cute after a certain age," says Christian. "Often, young adults who don't want to leave behind the world of adolescence, where anything is possible, won't commit to any one job or career. They just drift along." Other underachievers hit a plateau in their 30s and see younger colleagues advancing faster. As their self-defeating behavior continues, they sink deeper into disappointment.

7 "It doesn't take long before underachievers lose confidence that they could perform well even if they tried their best," Christian adds. "Instead of pursuing a path leading to a sense of meaning and delight, they lower their expectations and settle for less. Before they know it, they're 40 and at the edge of depression, or 50 and having a midlife crisis."

8 At any age, self-sabotage stems from fear— both of failure and of success. "If you're afraid of what success will bring, you'll find a way to fail," says Noah St. John, author of *Permission To Succeed*. "Success may bring higher standards, more work, more responsibilities. And the best way to stay in your comfort zone and not succeed is not to finish things. You can always find an excuse so it's not your fault, and people will expect less of you in the future."

How To Stop Shooting Yourself in The Foot

9 If you want to break the habit of underachievement, here are some ways to start:

10 **Say goodbye to the way things were.** "Ask yourself what you would leave behind if you got a promotion," says Kenneth Sole, a consulting social psychologist in Lee, N.H. "Would you miss the people you work with? Would you have to move? Only when people come to terms with the losses that any change brings can they see its benefits and move into the future."

11 **Take a personal audit.** "Identify what you really want to achieve," says Kenneth Christian. "Get rid of everything that stands in the way. And keep working regardless of how frustrated or inadequate you may feel."

12 **Put your goals in writing.** "High achievers have goals and plans," Susan Battley observes. "Underachievers live in wish mode." Start with "stretch goals" that are both a reach and reachable, so you can accumulate a confidence-building series of small wins. "And remember: Nothing becomes a goal until you write it down."

Are You Sabotaging Yourself?

❏ Do you procrastinate and constantly put things off?

❏ Do you miss deadlines?

❏ Do you hold back rather than engage fully and passionately in your life?

❏ Do you fail to complete projects or tasks?

❏ Do you try to get by with the least possible amount of effort?

❏ Do you quit things just as you begin to succeed at them?

❏ Are you stuck in what you thought would be a temporary situation?

❏ Do you blame others or bad luck when you don't succeed?

❏ Do you get an "itchy" or uncomfortable feeling inside when you think about what you're making of your life?

The more times you answer "yes," the more likely it is that you are getting in the way of your own success.

---

13 **Use the language of change.** Tune in to the messages you send yourself. Eliminate "weasel words," such as "I'll try" or "I hope to," and declare what you will do positively. Switch from saying "I have to" and "I should"; instead, say "I will." Challenge automatic negative assumptions ("I couldn't do that") by asking yourself, "Why not?" "Try to neutralize irrational fear," says Battley.

14 **Take baby steps.** "Think of *one* small thing you can do today that will make you feel better tomorrow," says Christian. "One daily change, especially if it helps you finish something you started, can change the trajectory of your life."

15 **Tackle self-defeating habits.** Identify three behaviors that have resulted in the most lost opportunities. For example, if you always procrastinate, open the mail as soon as it arrives and return e-mails the same day.

16 **Get support.** Recruit a friend or colleague to encourage you to reach your goals. Surround yourself with positive people who don't make you feel inferior or defensive, and train yourself to tune out the negative words of others.

17 **Be your own Monday-morning quarterback.** Top competitors analyze and learn from each performance. Like them, focus on what you did well and what you can correct—and aim to do better the next time.

18 For more information, visit: www.maxpotential.com and www.susanbattley.com.

Thinking Critically About the Reading

Working with one or two classmates, discuss your answers to the following questions.

1. What is the author's main purpose in writing this essay? Who is her audience?

2. Where is the article's thesis statement? If the author does not provide a thesis statement, develop one that fits the article.

3. The author mentions three books that help people develop strategies to be successful in life. List the titles and authors of these books. Choose one of these books and use an Internet search engine or website, such as amazon.com, to find and print a brief summary and review of the book you chose. Bring the printed summary and review to class and be ready to report your findings to your classmates.

4. Get two different colored highlighters or pens. Go through the article and, using one of the highlighters or pens, mark all the actions or traits of high achievers. Using the other highlighter or pen, mark all the actions or traits of underachievers. Compare your list with those of your classmates. Help each other to develop more complete lists.

5. Discuss the essay with one or more classmates. How do your responses to the essay differ from those of your classmates? How do your classmates' responses influence the way that you interpret the essay?

6. Although this article was written mainly for those who are already working full time, show how many of the suggestions may be applied to those attending college. From your own experiences or the experiences of those you know, give some specific examples of actions or traits of high academic achievers and of academic underachievers.

7. Using a dictionary when necessary, define the following words in their appropriate context: temps (1); procrastinating (2); psychologist (3); chronic (3); adolescence (6); commit (6); plateau (6); sabotage (8); audit (11); neutralize (13); irrational (13); trajectory (14).

This article, about musician Carlos Santana, appeared in *PARADE* magazine, March 30, 2003. Work through the same "Before You Read" and "While You Read" questions applied to the previous reading, "Getting Yourself Back on Track."

He Wails for the World

BY BEN FONG-TORRES

Carlos Santana might have gone bad in Tijuana. But destiny brought him to America, where he created the evocative sound and healing vision that appeals across generations and ethnicities.

1 Carlos Santana makes no bones about it. "If I hadn't come to America," he says, "I probably would've been dead by now."

2 I'm visiting Santana, one of the world's most admired and enduring musicians, at his offices in the industrial section of San Rafael, Calif. Santana has had several musical lives. He first became known as the Latin-rock pioneer who scored such hits as "Evil Ways" and "Black Magic Woman," both in 1970. Then, after several musical, spiritual and personal transformations, he came back in 1999 with the superhit CD *Supernatural*. His latest, *Shaman*, was No. 1 its first week out, last October.

3 I wanted to learn the secret of Santana's longevity in music and why he feels he owes his life to America.

4 He was born in 1947 in Mexico, the second son of José Santana, a popular violin player who supported his wife and seven children with his traveling mariachi band. Carlos spent his boyhood in the rural village of Autlán and later in Tijuana. He studied violin and guitar and dutifully learned traditional Mexican music, earning money by playing for tourists on the streets.

5 Then, he says, he discovered American rock and blues music, which he heard on the radio.

He became entranced with the electric guitar of B.B. King and the gritty blues of Muddy Waters. By age 13, he was playing in a rock band in Tijuana dance halls, alternating with strip acts.

6   Despite his attraction to the American sound, Carlos hid and stayed behind when his family moved to San Francisco in 1960. He played guitar in Tijuana's bars and strip clubs until, a year later, his parents sent his older brother Antonio to fetch him.

7   "They brought me here kicking and biting," he says. "I wanted to stay in an environment in Tijuana where I was around grown-up musicians and prostitutes." And he didn't want to go to school in San Francisco. "I said, 'This is my university right here. This is where you learn the real music, man!'"

8   The teen, in fact, was learning more than music in Tijuana. Life on the streets was fast, he recalls. "Fast everything. I was going toward the path of becoming an alcoholic. It was part of 'the fuel,' as we call it."

9   In San Francisco, a flower-powered rock music scene was blossoming at the Fillmore Auditorium and the Avalon Ballroom. Newly arrived, Carlos was the outsider trying to look and listen in. Though he had formed a band, he made his living toiling at a fast-food restaurant, giving most of his earnings to his family. Hungry for music, Carlos says, he would try to sneak into the Fillmore, only to be tossed out by the owner, the late rock promoter Bill Graham.

10 One night, Santana paid his way in and got a chance to join in a jam session. He impressed not only the audience and other musicians but Graham as well. Santana recalls their exchange: "Graham said, 'Hey, you have a band?' I said, 'Yeah!' He said, 'Would you like to open for The Loading Zone and The Who?' I said, 'Yeah!' It was 1967, and America had welcomed him.

11 Graham became a champion of Santana— and more. He got the band a slot at the Woodstock festival in 1969 and introduced them to the song "Evil Ways," which became their first big hit.

12 Santana's band, a melting pot of black, white and Latino musicians, brought a new sound to rock music. It was, simply put, a blend of all their musical influences: Top 40, R&B, Afro-Cuban, Mexican, Latin, jazz and blues. The exotic mix—Santana's crying guitar, Gregg Rolie's rollicking Hammond B-3 organ and a battalion of drums, congas and timbales—tore its way onto the radio and millions of turntables. Other bands followed suit. "Next thing you know," Santana says, "the Rolling Stones, Jimi Hendrix, Chicago—everybody's got congas."

13 Rock music made Santana wealthy. He bought a house for his parents in San Francisco. Remembering their difficult beginnings in Autlán—the town had no running water, and his mother washed their clothes in a river—he made sure there was a washing machine. "I feel really grateful," he says, "that most of my dreams are manifested."

14 Success also brought him nightmares: stress, physical ailments, ego trips among musicians, financial problems—and drugs. Santana admits to taking some but adds, "I didn't like being fogged. I like clarity."

15 He focused more and more on his abiding passion: to grow musically. "I wanted to become more intoxicated," he says, "with how [Brazilian composer] Antonio Carlos Jobim made this song or how [jazz sax legend] John Coltrane arrived at that scale."

16 In the years following the band's first success, Santana explored spirituality and fused jazz into his music, with sporadic hits and usually respectable sales. Then came *Supernatural*. He'd been turned away by several record companies when he was signed to Arista by Clive Davis, former president of Columbia Records, Santana's original label. The other companies had told him, "You're too old. It's over."

17   In fact, he'd only just begun. *Supernatural,* which included younger stars such as Lauryn Hill and Rob Thomas, sold 25 million copies and won nine Grammys. "The main word that I heard," Santana says, "was 'phenomenon'—the phenomenon of connecting with grandparents, parents, teenagers and Little children." He credits his daughters Stella, 17, and Angelica, 12, and son Salvador, 19, for making him aware of the younger artists. *Shaman*—with singers ranging from pop star Michelle Branch and funky hip-hopper Citizen Cope to opera star Placido Domingo—followed in 2002. It was an instant hit.

18   At 55, Santana looks fit and trim. He maintains a regimen of frequent walks and tennis. He does it, he says, for Deborah, his wife of 30 years, and their family. He adds that he doesn't want to wind up on shows like VH1's *Behind the Music,* which chronicles rock stars' ups and, mainly, downs. "I want my life to be a testament of triumph, not of tragedy," he says. "There's so much tragedy and fear on TV. I want to do something different."

19   The key to his success, Santana says, is discipline. "Teens don't want to hear that. They think they can just snap their fingers, and *voila!* But with discipline comes knowledge, coordination, balance, muscle memory, confidence—things that make it possible to hit the bull's-eye three times in a row. But you must practice."

20   For all his success in this country, Santana is concerned about a jittery mood in America. He called his new CD *Shaman,* he explains, "because a shaman is a spiritual healer, and we all need a serious healing right now, from a vibration of anger and fear and over-the-top patriotism. I think humanity should have a higher priority than any nation."

21   Since he told me he'd be dead if it weren't for America, I ask Santana what he feels he owes this nation. "What I owe the U.S.," he says, "is for me to behave with compassion and respect and dignity."

22   Santana wishes for a world where, as he puts it, "we have passion for compassion, and children are taught spiritual values." Music can help, he says: "I'm a firm believer that if you play a certain kind of music, you can dismantle the violence on this planet. That's what *Shaman* and *Supernatural* are about—healing, sharing spiritual information, inviting individuals to look at the bigger picture, to feel the sacredness of the family. Then, hopefully, we can behave with a lot more dignity toward each other."

Thinking Critically About the Reading

Working with one or two classmates, discuss your answers to the following questions.

1. Where is the article's thesis statement? If the author does not provide a thesis statement, develop one that fits the article.

2. What were some of the musical influences on Santana as he grew up in Mexico and the U.S.?

3. Describe the "new sound" that Santana and his band brought to rock music.

4. What were some positive and negative results of Santana's success?

5. How did Santana grow musically and spiritually in his later years?

6. What do you think Santana means when he says, "[W]e all need a serious healing right now, from a vibration of anger and fear and over-the-top patriotism"? This article was published in March 2003. What do you know about this time period in the U.S. that might help you answer this question?

7. What kind of world does Santana wish for, and how can music help transform the world?

8. Using a dictionary when necessary, define the following words in their appropriate context: longevity (3); mariachi (4); blues (5); entranced (5); gritty (5); toiling (9); exotic (12); congas (12); timbales (12); manifested (13); abiding (15); scale (15); sporadic (16); phenomenon (17); regimen (18); voila (19); jittery (20); shaman (20); compassion (21); dignity (21); dismantle (22).

Explorations

1. Visit one of the two websites listed at the end of the article "Getting Yourself Back on Track." Summarize and respond to the information that seems useful to you. Bring your journal to class and be prepared to make a brief report to your classmates.

2. Reflect on your own life, in school or at work or both, and, using the list you generated from the article "Getting Yourself Back on Track," write about some of the times when you exhibited actions or traits of high achievers. Again, using the list you generated from the article, write about some of the times when you exhibited actions or traits of underachievers. (*Note:* In this and all writing and discussion activities for this class, you should never feel pressured to reveal anything about yourself that you would prefer to keep private.)

3. Carlos Santana went through a process of self-discovery for many years, learning about who he was and what his profession was going to be. Up to this point in your life, what activities have you participated in that might help you choose a profession or career, or might help you eliminate a profession or career that you do not like?

4. In your experience or the experiences of those around you, what positive influences has music had on your life or in the lives of those around you?

5. In addition to being praised for its positive influences, music has been criticized for its negative influences or for sending harmful messages to listeners. What examples can you give of music with negative influences or harmful messages? For example, some rap music has been criticized for being anti-woman and homophobic.

6. What kinds of music do you listen to? What is it about this music that makes you want to listen to it? Who or what influenced you to listen to the kinds of music that you listen to?

7. Think of a song that you really like. Type out the lyrics or print them out from the Internet. Then analyze the song, discussing what it means to you. What is a possible theme (central meaning or unifying idea) of this song? Why does this song appeal to you?

8. Choose one of the preceding seven topics that you did not write about. Do some focused freewriting for ten minutes, generating as many ideas as you can. Share your freewriting with classmates.

Essay Assignments

Writing About Achievement

1. Write an essay in which you discuss two or three times in your life when you exhibited actions or traits of underachievers. What were they? When did they happen? What were the results of these actions? In what positive or negative ways were you affected? In the same essay, write about two or three times in your life when you exhibited actions or traits of high achievers. What were they? When did they happen? What were the results of these actions? In what positive or negative ways were you affected? Your audience or readers are your classmates and instructor, who would like to know more about you as a person. Your purpose is to give your readers some idea of the kinds of experiences that have helped to shape you into who you are. A secondary purpose may also be to help you understand yourself better.

2. Choose one of the "Explorations" related to the Carlos Santana article and develop it into an essay.

Getting Started: Preparing and Generating

You have already begun working on this subject by reading and responding to the above essay and by doing some journal writing on this subject. In addition to these two ways of generating ideas (reading and journal writing), we have already discussed in Chapter 1 three other ways of getting ideas on paper:

- Focused freewriting
- Brainstorming
- Clustering or mapping

Use one or more of these "prewriting" or "generating" strategies for getting ideas down on paper quickly. ("Prewriting" is a term used to refer to all the thinking, idea gathering, and other preparation one does prior to writing the first draft of an essay. Prewriting is usually a messy process.

The term *prewriting* is somewhat misleading, because one actually does quite a bit of writing during this stage of the writing process.)

Remember, your goal at this point is not to write the perfect opening paragraph, but to let the ideas flow from your head to the paper or screen. You may feel more comfortable talking with classmates in order to generate ideas, or talking into a tape recorder, or jotting your ideas down on paper. Whatever method you use, one important point to remember at this stage is to keep the ideas flowing and to include all ideas. Don't toss out any ideas at this point. You will have time to toss out ideas later in the composing process.

At the end of a successful generating or prewriting stage, you should have several pages of ideas, notes, possibilities, sentences, and perhaps even a few ideas that you were able to develop into rough paragraphs. This is the material that you will shape into a first rough draft. You should also have by this time a pretty good idea of your thesis, the main point of your essay. With your working thesis and audience written down on your "scratch" paper, you are now ready to go on to the next step in the composing process.

Organizing, Drafting, and Shaping

Remember, you do not have to begin writing your first rough draft with the opening paragraph. If you feel more comfortable working on the body paragraphs first, by all means do that. The DUCTT (Development, Unity, Coherence, Transitions, Topic sentence) acronym from Chapter 1 will help you write effective body paragraphs.

When you are developing your body paragraphs, one element that makes them more effective is the use of specific examples and details. Notice how the authors of the article earlier in this chapter use specific examples, instances, events, and illustrations for each of the four main parts of the body of their essay. If we could strip away the content of a typical body paragraph and look at its underlying structure or framework, we would often see something like this:

Transition _____ Topic Sentence _____

_____. Example _____

_____. Explanation of example

_____

_____. Transition _____. Example _____

_____. Explanation of

example _____

_____

Please understand that the preceding diagram is just a way to give you some sense of the order of a body paragraph. As you gain confidence and experience, you will find yourself modifying and manipulating basic guidelines such as the ones just given.

Revision: Getting Feedback

"OK, great," you say. "But how do I know what to revise?" We will discuss three ways of getting feedback about your drafts. These three ways come from three different sources: your instructor, your classmates, and yourself.

Your Instructor   Probably the most common source of ideas for revision is your instructor. You hand in an essay or draft to your instructor, and it comes back to you with written suggestions for improving it. Be sure to read all the comments carefully and to revise based on those comments. If you are not sure about a particular comment, ask your instructor about it. A variation on this method of response is that some instructors may ask you to hand in with your essay a blank audiotape. As the instructor reads your essay, he or she will talk into a tape recorder, giving you a running commentary about what went well and what could be improved in your essay. When your instructor returns the essay and tape to you, you listen to the recorded comments and make the revisions.

Sometimes, instead of writing comments on your essay or draft, some instructors may arrange a face-to-face conference, either in the classroom or in their office. An advantage of face-to-face conferences, besides the fact that you and your instructor get to know each other better, is that you can immediately clear up any confusion about exactly how to revise the draft. Another advantage is that, by being given an opportunity to talk aloud about your draft, you can often hit upon some good ideas for improving it.

Even if your instructor does not require a formal conference with you in his or her office, it is always a good idea to visit your instructor during his or her office hours to talk about a draft of an essay that you are working on. We recommend that you visit your instructor concerning the first essay that is assigned. Taking the initiative to visit your instructor will show that you are interested in doing the best possible work in the course. You should of course take with you a draft, or at least a partial draft, so that you and your instructor have something specific to talk about. It may be a bit intimidating to go to your instructor's office for a conference. Studies show, however, that students who periodically meet with their instructors outside of class on academic matters tend to be more successful in college.

Your Classmates   Another good source of ideas for revising your drafts is your classmates. Getting feedback from your classmates is often called "peer response." Your "peer" is your equal, or in this case, someone enrolled in the same course as you. Students are sometimes reluctant to participate in peer response activities. You or your classmates might think, "I don't feel qualified to give advice on revising essays," or "I don't want to take advice from my classmates! If they were good writers, they wouldn't be here in the first place." We understand your concerns, but we ask you to consider the following ideas. First, you know more about good writing than you give yourself credit for. Second, you don't have to be an excellent writer to give suggestions or ask questions in order to help classmates improve their writing. Finally, writers, even good ones, sometimes work so closely with their material for so long that an "outside" perspective, a more "distant" response, a "fresh" set of eyes, is just what they need. In the event that you and your classmate disagree on a suggested revision, you can always consult your instructor.

When peer response is done well, both the writer and the responder benefit because each one learns something about the elements of effective writing. Like any other activity, practice helps. The more peer responding you do, the better you'll get at peer responding. There are two keys to benefiting from peer responding: (1) practicing cooperative learning, and (2) having a checklist to follow for giving systematic feedback.

Practicing Cooperative Learning   Cooperative learning means learning together for mutual benefit so that you and your classmates come away from the activity with the feeling that everyone has both given and received useful ideas about effective writing.

The first activity to do before exchanging drafts with a classmate is to write down at the end of your draft two or three questions that you want your classmate to answer. Try to phrase your questions in such a way that they require more than just a "yes" or "no" answer. For example, instead of writing, "Are my transitions between paragraphs effective?" write, "How can I improve my transitions between paragraphs?"

Even with the best of intentions about cooperative learning, you may still feel lost when asked to respond to a classmate's draft. When you receive your classmate's draft, you may ask, "Where do I begin?" To help you respond to a draft in a systematic way, we provide a Peer Response Checklist.

You can use this checklist throughout the term for all of the drafts that you will be responding to. Your instructor may add questions to the checklist for specific kinds of essays that you will write during the course of the term.

- Cooperative learning is active learning; it is not a "spectator sport." You must get involved with your classmates' drafts and really try to give useful feedback.

- Cooperative learning is mainly positive learning. Point out what works in your classmate's draft, what you liked the most. Does this mean that you cannot make suggestions for improving your classmate's draft? Not at all. But avoid put-downs and harsh criticisms. Instead of saying or writing, "Your introduction is terrible," why not say or write, "When I read your introduction, I did not get a clear idea of what the essay was going to be about." In general, giving your reactions and thoughts or asking questions as you read your classmates' drafts is better than making simple criticisms with no suggestions for improvement.

- The tendency of students who have not participated in cooperative learning activities is often to think "If I don't say anything bad about my classmate's draft, then she won't say anything bad about mine. Then we'll both be happy." This approach is something like the eleventh commandment among students: "Thou shalt not criticize another student's work." This type of attitude leads to cooperative mediocrity—nobody benefits. You do not have to be critical or offensive in order to make suggestions for improving a classmate's draft.

- Unless you plan to be a hermit and live in a cave for the rest of your life, knowing how to participate in cooperative learning activities will be a great benefit in your career or profession. More and more U.S. businesses are moving to environments that emphasize team cooperation rather than individual competition. In recent national surveys, employers rank "the ability to work effectively in teams" very high in evaluating employees.

What if your classmate suggests a change or makes a comment that you believe will not improve your draft? Discuss the issue with your instructor.

If there is time, your instructor may allow two rounds of peer responding, during which you will respond to the drafts of two different classmates. At the end of these two rounds, you will receive two sets of responses from two different classmates. These responses will almost certainly help you to improve your draft before you hand in the final version of your essay to your instructor.

Yourself   The third source of feedback for a draft of your essay is yourself. When you need to revise a draft of your essay, you may not always have your classmates or instructor around to help. Because you will often

PEER RESPONSE CHECKLIST | Guide for Essay Drafts

Read through your classmate's entire draft once. Then go back and respond to the following questions. Some questions require you to write answers or suggestions on a sheet of paper. You will give this sheet to your classmate at the end of the peer responding activity. Other questions can be answered by writing on your classmate's draft. To help your classmate and instructor see your comments, put your comments in a different color to make them stand out from the surrounding text.

1. What do you like best about the draft? Why?

2. Underline or highlight the thesis sentence. If you cannot find a thesis sentence, say so.

3. Underline or highlight the topic sentence of each body paragraph. If you cannot find a topic sentence, say so.

4. What one or two topics do you think the author could have included in order to make the essay more effective?

5. Suggest a more attention-grabbing opening for the essay, if you believe the essay needs one.

6. Place brackets [ ] around the two or three sentences that are hardest to understand and need revision.

7. What surprised you the most as you read the draft?

8. Circle—but do not correct—any problems and errors you see in grammar, usage, punctuation, spelling, or format.

9. Answer the questions that your classmate wrote at the end of the draft.

10. Do this last activity if there is time. To see if the draft has a sense of proportion, count the number of words in each paragraph and write those numbers down. Most college-level essays should contain several well developed body paragraphs along with an opening and closing paragraph that are shorter than the body paragraphs.

have to revise your own drafts, it is a good idea to have a systematic strategy for revision.

One good self-revision strategy is to leave time between completing a rough draft and doing the final draft. If you try to revise your essay immediately after drafting it, you will be so tired of it and so close to it that you will not be able to see many of the draft's shortcomings. Ideally, you should allow several days between writing the first draft and writing the final draft. But we do not live in an ideal world. Even a half day or overnight may be time enough to give yourself some distance from your draft so that you can look at it more objectively.

The following worksheet (pages 58–59) is useful for giving your draft a thorough going-over. This worksheet is adapted from one developed by Professor Beatrice Newman of the University of Texas-Pan American. It has been used successfully for years. Once again, a key to making this self-responding activity work is to become actively involved in your revision process.

So there you have it: three strategies for receiving or generating responses to your drafts so that you can revise them thoroughly. We recommend that you experiment with all three of these strategies to see which ones work best for you.

One final point about revision: Revision usually works better when you have large units of time (weeks, days, hours) to work with rather than small units of time (minutes). Therefore, revision works much better on essays written outside of class than on those written in class or under similar time constraints. In a later chapter we will discuss strategies for revising timed essays such as those written in class or in a testing situation.

Evaluation of Your Writing Process and Peer Responding

The self-evaluation writing activity on page 60 is a good tool for assessing how well you use the writing process and how helpful your classmate is in responding to a draft of your essay.

Please respond to the self-evaluation questions as fully and honestly as possible.

Essay number _____

Paragraph	Number of Sentences in This Paragraph	Number of Words in This Paragraph
Opening para.	_____	_____
1st body para.	_____	_____
2nd body para.	_____	_____
3rd body para.	_____	_____
4th body para.	_____	_____
Closing para.	_____	_____
Total Sentences _____	Total Words _____	

Total number of words divided by total number of sentences = _____. This is your average sentence length. In general, if your average sentence length is about 10 to 12 words or fewer, your writing may sound choppy and immature. You should probably work on combining some shorter sentences. If your average sentence length is 25 words or higher, your writing may be difficult and confusing to read. You should probably divide long sentences into two shorter sentences. Aim for an average sentence length of about 16 to 22 words. Of course, this is only an average. Not every sentence has to be exactly this long. In fact, sentence length should vary in your final draft. Strive for a balance between long and short sentences. A short sentence may be more effective for making a strong point at the end of a paragraph, while a longer sentence may be appropriate when you are explaining a complex idea or describing a situation.

Working title of essay (Make sure the title reflects the subject of the essay. If you have several alternative titles, write them all down here.):

_____

First sentence of essay: _____

_____

Last sentence of opening paragraph: _____

_____

First sentence of first body paragraph: _____

_____

First sentence of second body paragraph: _____

_____

First sentence of third body paragraph: _____

_____

First sentence of fourth body paragraph: _____

_____

First sentence of closing paragraph: _____

_____

The above key sentences are the "guideposts" of your draft. They should give you and your readers a pretty clear summary of the main idea (thesis) and major topics to be discussed. If they do, then your essay is probably effectively organized. If they do not, then you probably need to work on improving the overall organization of your draft.

1. Circle all transition words and phrases in your draft. (Transitions help link earlier sentences and paragraphs to later sentences and paragraphs. They may be obvious, such as "first," "next," "then," or "finally." They may emphasize a point made earlier: "this," "that," "these," "those." Or they may be repetitions of key terms.)

2. Write a more attention-grabbing opening paragraph for your draft. How can you pull your readers in and motivate them to continue reading?

3. Which part of your essay do you like best? Why? How can you expand or capitalize on this "best" part?

4. Which part of your essay still needs more work to make it better? What can you do right now to improve it?

5. If you had to develop one topic in your draft more fully, which would it be? What kinds of new ideas would you add?

6. If you had to take out one topic in your draft, which would it be? Why?

7. If you had to add a new topic to your essay, what would it be? Why?

This self-responding worksheet should help you generate many ideas and ways to improve your draft. The more often you use it, the better you will get at revising your own writing.

1. Describe in as much detail as possible the exact procedure you went through in preparing the essay that you handed in today. Recount each step you took from the time the essay was assigned to the time you handed it in. What did you do first, next, and so on? How much time did you spend on each step in your writing process? When during the day or night did you do each step in your process?

2. What is your opinion of the effectiveness of the peer responding activities that you did recently? How helpful were your classmate's comments and questions about your draft? In what areas were the comments most helpful, least helpful? To what extent did you follow your classmate's suggestions? How helpful do you think you were in responding to your classmate's draft? What suggestions do you have for improving the effectiveness of peer responding sessions?

3. What aspects of preparing this essay were easiest for you? What aspects were most difficult? What strategies do you plan to use next time in order to overcome these difficulties? If you were able to give your essay one more complete revision, what would you do to improve the essay? What would you do differently if you could do this assignment over again?

4. How was your procedure in writing this essay similar to or different from your procedure in writing past essays, either in high school or college?

You may add anything else that you believe is relevant.

Student Essay

The following essay is the end result of a successful use of the composing process. It was written by a student who discovered something about himself and his ancestry.

An Alienated Asian

Michael Verderber

Thesis statement

1   Growing up, I always had the sneaking suspicion I was a bit different from the rest of my community. On the surface, it was nothing that I thought too deeply of. After all, I was merely a child. But throughout my secondary education and especially during a trip to Vietnam, I began to become more aware of my ethnicity and took pride in my Vietnamese ancestry.

Topic sentence

2   I grew up in a small town in the Rio Grande Valley of South Texas, an area that is predominantly represented by the Hispanic culture. As a child, I noticed no differences between me and the other kids around me, but when it came down to "duking" it out on the playground, racial insults were

inevitable. From my racially different opponents, I would frequently hear insults like "Chinese boy" and "rice," which were stereotypical interpretations of the Vietnamese culture. This was the first catalyst in the cultural gears that were now set in motion. By the third grade, and thanks in part to frequent skirmishes on the playground, I began to grow more aware of my own culture as a contrast to others around me. To add perspective, my brother and I were the only two Asian kids in a town of 10,000.

Topic sentence

3   Throughout junior high, this view subsided a bit, but returned with a vengeance come the ninth grade. My school would frequently have "Hispanic Awareness" rallies and celebrations, and I could not help but feel alienated. I was having another culture's "awareness" nearly crammed down my throat without any consideration of my own. Sure, I appreciate any and all cultures, but what of my own? Why was no one celebrating mine? I was the minority among minorities.

Topic sentence

4   To add to this confusion, I come from two different cultures. My father is a Caucasian from New England, my mother is Vietnamese, and I was living in Texas. I did not feel torn within my own paradox; my Caucasian and Asian sides were perfectly balanced, I felt. However, it was in my own school where difference presided. People always said things like, "I thought you looked different. I couldn't figure out what you are." Well, I'm half-Caucasian, half-Vietnamese, and all pride.

Topic sentence

5   I went to Vietnam between my ninth- and tenth-grade years and I was rocked. For the first time, I saw true poverty; my family in Vietnam had nearly nothing and would constantly barrage me with gifts. These were gifts that they could not afford, but felt obligated to give me because I was family. It broke my heart, and at that moment I truly understood my culture.

Reworded thesis

6   When I was younger, I felt a sense of alienation within a culture different from my own. However, over the years and through life's experiences I have grown more and more aware of, and proud of, my own Vietnamese culture.

Insightful Writing

One common image of a "typical" writer is that of someone working alone late into the night, cranking out page after page of polished writing. While this image may have some validity, the much more common path to polished prose—and probably much more successful—is the path of collaboration, getting feedback from different sources, and working through multiple drafts. Inexperienced writers may see revision as punishment for not getting the writing right the first time. Experienced writers know that the best writing is almost always the result of revision, with input from peers and instructors or editors.

Writers are sometimes too close to their material to get insights, but a fresh pair of eyes or a different perspective can often help writers see and develop insights that they would have missed if they had not taken advantage of opportunities for feedback and revision.

3 Revision and Style

So far we have discussed generating ideas, drafting the essay, and revising it. We now come to the final step in the composing process: editing and proofreading. This is the step in which we deal with concerns that you probably associate with "English": sentence quality, word choice or diction, grammar, usage, punctuation, mechanics, spelling, and formatting.

We have purposely left these concerns to the end of the composing process. Why? We have seen many students who were so afraid of making proofreading and editing mistakes early in their writing tasks that they were not able to generate adequate ideas or organize their ideas effectively. Students often feel paralyzed early in the composing process because they have been made so aware of error, of all the things that can go wrong, that they try to do too much at the same time. They try to generate ideas, organize them, and edit and proofread all at once.

Imagine what would happen at a home building site if all the tradespeople and craftspeople arrived and started working at the same time: The foundation pourers, the framers, the plumbers, the electricians, the drywall hangers, the painters, the insulation crew, the roofers, the air conditioning/heating technicians. You get the picture. It would be utter chaos! That's what happens when writers, especially inexperienced writers, try to do everything at once.

We believe that you can edit and proofread more effectively if you wait until you have something more substantial to work with, something like a reasonably complete and revised draft. We focus first on improving sentence quality.

Revising for Some Common Sentence-level Problems

When we talk we are rarely aware of problems with punctuation or incompleteness of sentences. We "punctuate" our talking with pauses, changes in emphasis, using a rising or falling voice, and so on. If we are talking and our listener feels we are being unclear and incomplete, we can clarify or complete our ideas right then and there.

When we write, however, especially in academic and business settings, we must be sure that our sentences are clear and complete and that they don't run into one another. In other words, we have to be sure that we write in complete sentences and that our sentences are properly separated according to the conventions of standard written English. The good news is that you probably are already using these conventions in the vast majority of your writing. The challenge is to be able to recognize your mistakes and to fix them. We will concentrate here on three common sentence-level problems: the sentence fragment, the comma splice, and the run-on or fused sentence. These three errors tend to hinder communication with readers and cause confusion, and are therefore often considered major errors.

Sentence Fragment

The sentence fragment is a piece or part of a sentence. It is punctuated like a complete sentence. That is, it usually begins with a capital letter and ends with a period, but for some grammatical reason it is not considered a complete sentence. Here are some examples of sentence fragments:

- Even though I wrote about how new wave music talked my kind of language.
- So by teaching and learning more about it myself and wanting others to learn about it too.
- Especially my dad because he would always advise me not to do drugs.

Many of our students tell us that after reading a sentence fragment, they feel as if the writer has left them "hanging" there, either wanting more information or thinking that the writer should have joined the fragment with the sentence before or after it.

> **PRACTICE: Recognize and Avoid Sentence Fragments**
>
> To show that you understand what a sentence fragment is, try writing a short paragraph (no more than 60 words) that includes one sentence fragment. Then exchange paragraphs with a classmate and see if he or she can locate and correct the fragment.

A very good way to recognize and avoid sentence fragments is to study them in the context of your and your classmates' essays. Your instructor may collect passages from student essays that contain typical sentence fragments and distribute them to you so that you have a better sense of what sentence fragments look like and how to correct them. And remember, our purpose in pointing out errors in students' essays is never to belittle or make fun of anyone, but rather to help them learn to become more successful writers.

Comma Splice

To "splice" means to join or unite. An electrician often splices two wires together, and sailors sometimes have to splice two ropes together. A comma splice is joining two complete sentences with just a comma. In standard written English, a comma is not strong enough, by itself, to join two complete sentences. Here are some examples of comma splices:

- You don't want to have your head too high, if the teacher can see your eyes she knows when you are going to fall asleep.
- You have been playing around too much, you need to do your work.
- Don't worry about turning everything off, just make sure that everything is stacked up and clean.

Notice that the usual pattern for a comma splice looks like this:

Complete sentence, complete sentence.

> **PRACTICE: Recognize and Avoid Comma Splices**
>
> Again, one way to show that you understand what a comma splice looks like is to include one on purpose in a passage. Write a short paragraph that contains a deliberate comma splice. Then exchange paragraphs with a classmate and see if you can locate and correct the comma splice.

Just as with sentence fragments, the best way to recognize and avoid comma splices is to analyze them in your own writing and that of your classmates. If your instructor notices that your writing tends to contain many comma splices, then you may want to look at every comma that your finished essay contains so that you can be sure that your final draft contains no comma splices.

There is one common sentence pattern that does use a comma along with a coordinating conjunction to join two sentences. You can see this pattern in Figure 3.1.

Notice that the comma must be used along with the coordinating conjunction in order for it to join two complete sentences.

	, for	
	, and	
	, nor	
Complete sentence	, but	complete sentence
	, or	
	, yet	
	, so	

FIGURE 3.1
Coordinating Conjunctions

Since acronyms help people remember important ideas, here's one to help you remember the seven coordinating conjunctions: FANBOYS. No, this is not a new rap group or band; it is a word formed by taking the first letter of each of the seven coordinating conjunctions (For, And, Nor, But, Or, Yet, So).

Run-on or Fused Sentence

A run-on or fused sentence is created by running two complete sentences together with no punctuation between the two sentences. Here are some examples:

- You should learn on your own if you can't learn on your own, then get help from a tutor. But don't cheat.

- That is all right we will try harder next time.

- My band and choir teachers had a great impact on me they helped me decide to go into the field of music education.

> **PRACTICE: Recognizing and Avoiding Run-on/Fused Sentences**
>
> Write a short paragraph that contains a run-on or fused sentence and see if a classmate can pick out and correct the error. As with the previous two errors, this one is also best studied in the context of your and your classmates' essays.

These three sentence-level errors—fragments, comma splices, and run-on or fused sentences—are usually considered major oversights. They greatly hinder your readers' attempts to follow your ideas and to make meaning of your words. However, don't be overly concerned about these errors during the early stages of the writing process. Many of these errors will probably disappear as you attempt to make your draft clearer. The time to take a really close look at your essay for these errors is the proofreading and editing stage.

Achieving Clarity and Eliminating Awkwardness

When we speak or write, especially in business or educational settings, we want to be clearly understood by our audience. If we do not make ourselves clear when we speak, our listeners can ask us immediately to clarify our point. When we write, however, we may not be available to our readers when they are reading our words. So we must be extra careful to be clear and precise in our writing.

We have purposely put off discussing clarity until now because we believe it is very important for you to first develop your fluency—your ability to get words on paper easily, to let the words flow. Once you have the words on paper (or on the computer screen) through your use of the preparing and drafting strategies that we discussed earlier, then you are ready to go back and clarify your writing.

One way to achieve clarity is to have a classmate read a paragraph of your essay to see if he or she can understand the points you are trying to get across. If your classmate has trouble understanding a sentence, try explaining that sentence using different words. That is, talk through what you were trying to say. Frequently you will find that explaining an unclear passage to someone will help to clear it up.

A similar way to achieve clarity is to read your essay aloud to a classmate. Often, as you read, you or your classmate will notice a sentence that needs clarifying. The sentence may be too long, or it may not flow from the previous sentence, or it may be too wordy.

All of what we have said about achieving clarity applies just as well to eliminating awkward sentence constructions. "Awkwardness" in sentence structure is a catch-all term to indicate that you can probably find a more effective way of saying whatever you want to say. A good way to eliminate awkward constructions is to "talk out" the sentence in several different forms. That is, try saying the same thing in several different ways, writing each version down on scratch paper. Then you or your peer responder can choose the version that best communicates your idea.

Sentence Combining for Variety

Inexperienced writers often tend to write short sentences, one after another, in their essays. There is really nothing wrong with short sentences, especially if they are clear. But too many short sentences in a row tend to make your writing sound choppy, monotonous, and immature.

How can you tell if you are writing too many short sentences in a row? There are no hard and fast rules about judging how many short sentences are too many, but try figuring out the average sentence length of each of the paragraphs in your draft. To find the average sentence length, just count every word in a paragraph, and then count the number of sentences in that paragraph. (What qualifies as a sentence? For now we will say that a sentence is a word group that begins with a capital letter and ends with a period or other end punctuation, such as a question mark.) Next, divide the number of words by the number of sentences. The resulting number is your average sentence length. If this number is 12 or lower, then your paragraph can probably benefit from combining some short sentences.

For example, look at the preceding paragraph. The number of words is 136, and the number of sentences is 8. One hundred thirty-six divided by 8 equals 17. So our average sentence length for the paragraph is 17 words. A rough guideline to follow for your own writing in college and business is an average of about 15 to 22 words per sentence. Remember, this is just an average. You will have sentences that are longer and shorter than this average. In our paragraph, for instance, only three of the eight sentences fall within the "average" length of 16 to 22 words. The shortest sentence contains only 5 words, and the longest contains 32.

PRACTICE: Lengthening Sentences

Take a look at the following paragraph and suggest ways in which the writer could have combined or even added words to some of the short sentences.

A firefighter's career includes a lot of work. He has to make sure the floors of the firehouse are spotless. He never knows when an unexpected visitor will arrive. Another chore he has to do is to cook for the firefighters who are on duty. Have you ever eaten chili for seven days straight? Think of all the heartburn! His last task is not that easy. He has to wash and wax the fire truck. This is a pretty big job if you ask me.

This paragraph is 85 words long and contains 9 sentences. So the average sentence length (85 divided by 9) is 9.4 words. You can probably think of several ways to combine some of these shorter sentences.

Once again, the best place to go to practice sentence combining is your own drafts.

Dividing or Shortening Long Sentences for Clarity

In addition to sometimes writing many short sentences in a row, you may occasionally write a "monster" sentence that is so long that your readers find it difficult to understand. Again, we cannot give a hard and fast rule, but if you write a sentence that is about 34 words or longer, chances are that readers may have trouble understanding the sentence.

Don't be too concerned about sentence-level problems early in your writing process. Some of these problems will take care of themselves as you sharpen your ideas in the drafting and revision steps of the composing process. Remember, you want to work on your fluency first, then your clarity.

After you have addressed issues of fluency and clarity, then comes the time to look carefully at correctness. Editing and proofreading skills may take some time to master, but they are important aspects of the overall

Practice: Clarifying Long Sentences

Take a look at the following examples of long sentences. How would you improve them?

1. First, the reason I came about choosing this major is that my talent is based on music and that's what makes me happy so by teaching and learning more about it myself and wanting others to learn about it too, I will do well in this major.

2. That way whenever you go out there in the world and that you would have to write a paper for an interview in a job or anything else that you are going to do in life you can say that the teacher you had for English was a really good teacher.

3. The reason that I would like to pursue this as a career would be for the reason that I've always wanted to be a nurse but I've learned that there is a greater demand for medical assistants and it takes less time and pays very well.

composing process. Essays may exhibit thoughtful insights and display solid organization; but if the essays contain numerous errors overlooked in editing and proofreading, readers often become distracted and frustrated trying to navigate through the errors. As writers, we want readers to focus on the content of our essays, not to wonder why we did not put forth the time and effort to write an effective essay. The "Practical Tips" box on page 69 contains five specific strategies to help you become a better editor/proofreader. If you follow these strategies, we guarantee that your final product will be better than if you had not used these strategies.

Insightful Writing

The chapters in Part I have taken you through the composing process. We have divided the process into four steps, moving from fluency of ideas, to clarity of ideas, to correctness of style:

1. **Preparing or Generating (Fluency)**

2. **Drafting or Shaping (Clarity)**

3. **Revising (Clarity)**

4. **Editing and Proofreading (Correctness)**

To discuss each of these steps clearly and fully, we have had to separate them from each other and focus on one step at a time. However, as you have probably discovered, and as any successful writer will tell

Five Strategies for Effective Editing and Proofreading

1. **Read your essay out loud**. We guarantee that you will not catch all of your errors if you proofread silently. It is amazing how often our mind "sees" words as correct when they really are not. But reading out loud doubles the the number of senses—from one (seeing) to two (seeing and hearing)—that you use to catch errors. Did you catch the error two lines above?

2. **Read slowly**. One way to force yourself to read slowly, besides reading out loud, is to point to each word of your essay while you read. You can point to each word with either a pen or your finger. In a sense, you are using the additional sense of touch in this proofreading technique.

3. **Read for one type of error at a time**. If, for example, you know that you tend to write comma splices, then proofread once looking for just that one error. If you have trouble with pronoun-antecedent agreement, then go through your essay focusing on that one problem.

4. **Begin proofreading with the last sentence of the essay**. Then proofread the next to last sentence, and continue reading each sentence in this order until you finally read the first sentence of the essay. Reading this way forces you to focus on each sentence more in isolation from the surrounding sentences. Instead of being distracted by concerns such as ideas, logic, coherence, and transitions (all of which you attended to in earlier steps of the composing process), you are forced to look more carefully at the individual grammar, usage, punctuation, and spelling of isolated sentences. This strategy may also help students who say, "I can usually do well on grammar drills isolated from my essays, but I can't seem to apply my knowledge to my own writing." This strategy helps you treat your essay more like a grammar drill, but in the context of your own writing.

5. **Leave time between the last revision and the editing/proofreading step**. At this stage, as during earlier stages of the writing process, allowing an adequate amount of time can make your essays more effective. If you try to edit and proofread your essay immediately after revising it, you will be so tired and so familiar with the words that you will miss many oversights in your essay. Ideally, you should try to leave at least one day between the time you revise and the time you edit and proofread. The next time you get an essay assignment, try this: Divide into three equal parts the time from when the essay is assigned to the time it is due. Generate a draft during the first third of the time allotted. Revise the draft during the second third. Proofread/edit the draft during the final third. For example, if you are assigned an essay that is due in six days, work on generating ideas and drafting during the first two days. Then work on revising during the next two days. Finally, work on proofreading/editing during the last two days. And please leave time for printing off the final version of your essay. We are almost convinced that computers, printers, and disks know when student essays are due, and too often they tend to break down when we need them the most!

you, the actual practice of writing is usually much more jumbled, much messier, and more intertwined than we have suggested in our "linear" presentation. Attempting to describe any complex activity in a logical, coherent way is always difficult. But the fact that we cannot describe it accurately in all its infinite complexity does not mean that we should not attempt to describe it at all. We believe that a detailed overview of a generalized writing process can help you use your time more productively to become a more effective writer.

PART II

Looking Outside for Insights

Chapter 4: *Family*

Chapter 5: *Relationships Beyond the Family*

Chapter 6: *Language*

Chapter 7: *The Nation*

Chapter 8: *The World*

4 Family

Family life is too intimate to be preserved by the spirit of justice.

It can be sustained by a spirit of love which goes beyond justice.

Reinhold Niebuhr

The oldest social institution of human civilization is the family. It has outlasted the tribe, Greek city-state, Roman Empire, British Empire, and Soviet Union. Families probably existed before the first tribe was formed and will still exist after various forms of government that currently hold power cease to exist. Aside from the obvious function of perpetuating the human race, there must be something about the "family" as a form of organization that is extremely effective.

JOURNAL WRITING

Do you agree or disagree with the basic message contained in the quotation by Reinhold Niebuhr? Is it possible for a parent to give every child equal time and attention? Should all children be treated exactly the same? Should the mother and father share all the duties of parenting on an equal basis? Recall a few incidents from your own life that would serve as an example to illustrate your viewpoint or opinion about the practicality of "justice" as opposed to "unconditional love" in a family.

Before You Read

1. Before reading the introduction to *Peoplemaking* take a moment to read just the second and final paragraphs. Put into your own words, either by telling a classmate or by writing in your notebook, what you believe to be the main point or thesis of the reading selection.

2. Look at the structure of the reading selection. Notice that the author has several "lists" or "sets of questions" in which she provides an outline of the main topics in her book. How effective is this technique for introducing a book?

While You Read

1. As you read, underline or highlight key sentences. Remember, key sentences are often at the beginnings and ends of paragraphs.

2. What questions occur to you while you read this selection? Write these questions down. What do you agree or disagree with most strongly?

3. Underline the words whose meanings you do not know and look up the definitions in a good college-level dictionary.

4. As you read, keep a written record of your summary of and comments on or responses to each paragraph. How do the ideas in this essay speak to you personally?

5. Meet with one or more of your classmates during this class or outside of class and discuss the different reactions and responses that you and your classmates have to the article. How are your interpretations similar to or different from those of your classmates?

Reading

Today we hear psychologists and counselors talk about "functional" and "dysfunctional" families. These words are becoming part of the current vocabulary. What makes a family successful or unsuccessful? The answers to these questions and others were pioneered by people like Virginia Satir, who wrote the book *Peoplemaking* in 1972. The following reading is from the introduction to her book about her experiences as a family therapist.

Peoplemaking

BY VIRGINIA SATIR

1 When I was five, I decided that when I grew up I'd be a "children's detective on parents." I didn't quite know what it was I would look for, but even then I realized that there was a lot going on in families that didn't meet the eye. There were a lot of puzzles.

2 Now, forty-five years later—after working with some three thousand families, ten thousand people—I am finding that there are indeed a lot of puzzles. Family life is something like an iceberg. Most people are aware of only about one-tenth of what is actually going on—the tenth that they can see and hear—and often they think that is all there is. Some suspect that there may be more, but they don't know what it is and have no idea how to find out. Not knowing can set the family on a dangerous course. Just as a sailor's fate depends on knowing about the iceberg *under* the water, so a family's fate depends on understanding the feelings and needs and patterns that lie beneath everyday family events.

3 Fortunately, through the years I have also found solutions to many of the puzzles, and I would like to share them with you in this book. In the chapters that follow we will be looking at the underside of the iceberg.

4 In this age of expanding knowledge about the atom, outer space, human genetics, and other wonders of our universe, we are also learning some new things about people's relationships with people. I believe that historians a thousand years from now will point to our time as the beginning of a new era in the development of man, the time when man began to live more comfortably with his humanity.

5 Over the years I have developed a picture of what the human being living humanly is like. He is a person who understands, values, and develops his body, finding it beautiful and useful; a person who is real and honest to and about himself and others; a person who is willing to take risks, to be creative, to manifest competence, to change when the situation calls for it, and to find ways to accommodate to what is new and different, keeping that part of the old that is still useful and discarding what is not.

6 When you add all this up, you have a physically healthy, mentally alert, feeling, loving, playful, authentic, creative, productive human being; one who can stand on his own two feet, who can love deeply and fight fairly and effectively, who can be on equally good terms with both his tenderness and his toughness, know the difference between them, and therefore struggle effectively to achieve his goals.

7 The family is the "factory" where this kind of person is made. You, the adults, are the *people-makers*.

8 In my years as a family therapist, I have found that four aspects of family life keep popping up in the troubled families who come to me for help. They are—

> the feelings and ideas one has about himself, which I call *self-worth;*

> the ways people work out to make meaning with one another, which I call *communication;*

> the *rules* people use for how they should feel and act, which eventually develop into what I call the family system; and

> the way people relate to other people and institutions outside the family, which I call the *link to society.*

9 No matter what kind of problem first led a family into my office—whether a nagging wife

Virginia Satir, *Peoplemaking* (Palo Alto, CA: Science and Behavior Books, 1972).

or an unfaithful husband, a delinquent son or a schizophrenic daughter—I soon found that the prescription was the same. To relieve their family pain, some way had to be found to change those four key factors. In all of these troubled families I noticed that—

self-worth was low;

communication was indirect, vague, and not really honest;

rules were rigid, inhuman, nonnegotiable, and everlasting; and

the linking to society was fearful, placating, and blaming.

10 Fortunately, I have also had the joy of knowing some untroubled and nurturing families—especially in my more recent workshops to help families develop more fully their potential as human beings. In these vital and nurturing families, I consistently see a different pattern—

self-worth is high;

communication is direct, clear, specific, and honest;

rules are flexible, human, appropriate, and subject to change; and

the linking to society is open and hopeful.

11 No matter where a surgeon studies medicine, he is prepared to operate on human beings anywhere in the world, because the internal organs and the limbs will be the same. Through my work with families, troubled and nurturing, in the United States, Mexico, and Europe, I have learned that families everywhere have certain working parts in common, too. In all families—

every person has a feeling of worth, positive or negative; the question is,

Which is it?

every person communicates; the question is,

How, and what happens as a result?

every person follows rules; the question is,

What kind, and how well do they work for him?

every person is linked to society; the question is,

How, and what are the results?

These things are true whether the family is 12 a *natural* one, where the man and woman who sired and conceived the child continue to care for him until he is grown; a *one-parent* one, where one parent leaves the family by death, divorce, or desertion, and all of the parenting is done by the remaining parent; a *blended* one, where the children are parented by step-, adoptive, or foster parents, not by the persons who brought them into the world; or an *institutional* one, where groups of adults rear groups of children, as in institutions or the modern-day commune.

Each of these forms of family has its own 13 special problems in living, and we will return to them later. But basically, the same forces will be at work in all of them; *self-worth, communication, rules,* and *linking to society.*

In this book I will talk more about each of 14 these crucial factors, to help you discover how they are operating in your own family and how they can be changed to reduce problems and increase the vitality and joy you can find with one another. Think of my words not as the voice of a so-called expert, but as the accumulated experience of someone who has shared the happiness and sorrow, the hurt and anger and love, of many families.

I am not going to scold anyone in this book. 15 As a matter of fact, I should probably pin medals on many of you for doing the best you know how with a difficult situation; the very fact that you are reading a book like this tells me that you really care about the well-being of your family. It is my hope, however, that I can give you something more valuable than medals: namely, some new ways to find a better life together as a family.

16   The relationships in a family are extremely complex. To make them a little easier to understand, I will use many *as ifs*. These won't add up to the kind of sophisticated model the scholar constructs, but rather they will offer you a variety of ways of looking at your family system, in the hope that you'll find some that have real meaning for you.

17   As you read, you will come upon suggested experiments or exercises. I hope you will do each one as you come to it, even if at first it seems simple or foolish. Knowing *about* the family system won't change anything. You must learn *how* to make that system work vitally yourself. These experiments are positive, concrete steps your family can take to become less troubled and more nurturing. The more members of your family who take part in them, the more effective they will be. You will begin to *feel* your system working and sense whether it is leading to trouble or growth.

18   Perhaps you might wonder how to get the rest of your family members to participate in these exercises with you. This might be especially true if ruptures are already occurring in your family.

19   My suggestion is that you become thoroughly familiar with what you are asking so you will be able to more clearly present your request. If you feel enthusiastic and hopeful about what you think might happen, you will probably communicate a sense of excitement, which will make the invitation attractive and make your family members want to try along with you. By setting your request in a simple straightforward question—Will you participate with me in an experiment that I think might be useful to us?—you maximize the opportunity for a positive response.

20   The problem most people encounter is that they try to badger or demand or nag their family members to go along with them. This turns the transaction into a power struggle, which usually works in the opposite direction. It is possible that at this point in time, things are so ruptured nothing can be done. The chances are pretty good that if your family members live under the same roof, they will be willing to at least try.

21   I have seen much pain in families. Each one has moved me deeply. Through this book I hope to ease that pain in families whom I may never have a chance to meet personally. In doing so, I hope also to prevent the pain from continuing into the families their children will form. Some human pain is unavoidable, of course. But as a people, we don't always put our efforts in the right place, to change what we can and to work out creative ways to live with what we can't change.

22   There is some possibility that just reading this book may evoke a little pain for you. After all, facing ourselves has its painful moments. But if you think there may be a better way of living together as a family than the way you are living now, I think you'll find this book rewarding.

Thinking Critically About the Reading

Working with one or two classmates, discuss your answers to the following questions:

1. What is the author's main purpose in writing this introduction? Who is her audience?

2. What are the four important "aspects of family life" mentioned by Satir? What techniques does she use to emphasize these aspects?

3. What does the author mean when she says that the following chapters will be the underside of an "iceberg"? What other comparisons does the author make? What does the author compare family life to?

4. What specific examples or evidence does the author use to establish her "authority" or "credibility" as an expert on families?

5. Discuss the reading selection with one or more classmates. How do your responses to the essay differ from those of your classmates? How do your classmates' responses influence the way that you interpret the reading selection?

6. Using a dictionary when necessary, define the following words in their appropriate context: humanly (5); manifest (5); authentic (6); therapist (8); schizophrenic (9); prescription (9); nonnegotiable (9); placating (9); nurturing (10); commune (12).

What do you think the family relationships are of the family in the photograph celebrating the Chinese New Year? What do you think is in the red packets?

1. Using the classifications in the reading, describe the type (natural, one-parent, blended, or institutional) of family you had as a child, young adult, and adult.

2. How would you evaluate some of the individuals in your family in terms of the four forces described by Virginia Satir?

   a. Self-worth (high or low)
   b. Communication (honest or not honest)
   c. Family system of rules (open to change or rigid)
   d. Linking to society (hopeful or fearful)

3. How do you think the family environment you were raised in affected your individual learning style? Did it help or hurt? Explain.

Explorations

1. Interview an elderly member of your family and record (with a tape recorder or video camera) some aspect of your family's history.

2. Conduct a genealogical search on the Internet about your ancestors. Share your results with family members and friends.

Before You Read

1. Before reading the entire article, take a moment to read just the opening and closing paragraphs. Put into your own words, either by telling someone or by writing in your notebook, what you believe to be the main point or thesis of this article.

2. Look at the titles of each subsection of the article. What do these titles tell you about the contents of the subsections?

While You Read

1. As you read, underline or highlight key sentences. Remember, key sentences are often at the beginnings and ends of paragraphs.

2. What questions occur to you as you read this article? Write these questions down. What do you agree or disagree with most strongly?

3. As you read, keep a written record of your summary of and comments on or responses to the subsections of the article. How do the ideas of this article relate to your own experiences?

4. Meet with one or two of your classmates during this class or outside of class and discuss the different reactions and responses that you and your classmates have to this article. How are your interpretations similar to or different from those of your classmates?

Reading

This reading about family first appeared in *American Baby* magazine in May 2005.

The Changing American Family

BY CRIS BEAM

Shifting Demographics

1 If all you did was watch television commercials for minivans, you might think that the traditional All-American family was still intact—Mom, Dad, dog, and the 2.5 kids buckle up and drive off every day on TV. But ads (depending on your perspective) are either selling aspirations or guilt: This is the family you're supposed to have, supposed to want.

2 In real life, in big cities and in smaller towns, families are single moms, they're stepfamilies, they're boyfriends and girlfriends not getting married at the moment, they're foster parents, they're two dads or two moms, they're a village. In real life, in 2005, families are richly diverse.

3 And only getting more so.

4 In fact, the very definition of "family" is changing dramatically. The year 2000 marked the first time that less than a quarter (23.5 percent) of American households were made up of a married man and woman and one or more of their children—a drop from 45 percent in 1960. This number is expected to fall to 20 percent by 2010.

5 **Why the Changes?** The change in the makeup of the American family is the result of two primary factors, says Martin O'Connell, chief of fertility and family statistics at the U.S. Census Bureau, which collects such figures every 10 years. First, more babies (about a third) are now born out of wedlock, and second, divorce rates continue to climb so that nearly half of all marriage contracts are broken.

What's Normal Now?

6 The overall attitude toward relationships and commitment has shifted. More than half of female high school seniors say that having a child outside of marriage is acceptable, according to a recent poll from the University of Michigan Survey Research Center. And census data shows that 26 percent of all households are made up of a single person, living alone (as opposed to 13 percent back in 1960)

7 While a good portion of these singles are likely senior citizens, others are younger career folks who don't feel yesteryear's societal pressure to rush into partnerships.

8 "In 2002, the median age for a woman's first marriage was 27," says O'Connell. That's five years older than it was even in 1980. Sometimes young singles establish their individual identities so solidly that they never marry, even if they have children. These couples may partner up—but without the papers.

9 **Adoption, no marriage:** Such was the case with Steve Wilson and Erin Mayes, a couple in their mid-30s living in Austin, Texas. They've been together for 10 years, own a home together, and though they've talked about it, have decided it isn't necessary to get married. Still, they wanted a family and, last June, adopted a baby boy.

10 **Wedding after baby:** Another example is Jared and Lori Goldman, of San Mateo, California. Their relationship was relatively new when Lori got pregnant in 2000. They agreed to raise the child together but didn't get engaged. But not long after their daughter was born, Jared proposed. "Reverse order worked better for us," he says. Lori agrees: "Our wedding felt more meaningful happening on its own time instead of on the traditional schedule. What girl wants a shotgun wedding?"

11 **Single moms on the rise:** Of course, because currently one-third of all babies are born out of wedlock, it's no surprise that many mothers remain single. When she got pregnant, Pam Hansell says her boyfriend initially seemed supportive. Then he began dodging her phone calls and e-mails, and eventually cut contact. Deeply hurt but determined to give her child a good life, Hansell moved in with her parents, outside of Philadelphia, and gave birth to a daughter in March. "When I realized I couldn't count on the father, it was devastating. I'm so thankful that family and friends have stepped in," Hansell says.

12 **Two dads:** Finally, Dean Larkin and Paul Park are living out another common-in-today's-world scenario. They live together in Los Angeles, and Larkin has a 21-year-old daughter from a previous marriage. Now he and Park are planning a second child, via a surrogate mother. They'd like to marry, but gay marriage is not legal nationally.

13 **Reactions from the Trenches** Perhaps no one has a better ringside seat to all these untraditional family setups than those involved in the childbirth industry. "I've seen unmarried couples come in, lesbian couples, mothers who have been here with one father and then come in with a new father—the family dynamics and structures have changed a lot over the past 25 years," says Barbara Hotelling, president of Lamaze International and a long-time childbirth instructor.

14 Based in Rochester Hills, Michigan, Hotelling probably sees a good cross section of American families and, while she doesn't ask the marital status of her students, estimates that around 20 percent are unmarried, compared with maybe 5 percent when she first began her career.

15 Hotelling has shifted her language with the times. She says she used to call her students moms and dads, but now, "I say 'moms and partners' and hope nobody screams."

The Marriage Advantage

16 According to 1999 figures from the Population Resource Center, families in which the mother is the head of the household are, by and large, living on less. Because of the wage gap, female-headed households earn, on average, $26,164 a year; male-headed households earn $41,138 per year; and married households earn $56,827 per year.

17 Then, there are the more than 1,100 federal benefits that married households can take advantage of during a lifetime. Under the Family and Medical Leave Act, married partners can take leave from work when their spouse gets sick; unmarried partners cannot. Federal Medicaid laws permit only married couples to keep their homes when one partner needs nursing home care; an unmarried partner can lose the house. When a married person dies, the spouse inherits Social Security benefits; an unmarried partner gets nothing.

18 All told, according to the Los Angeles-based American Association for Single People and cited in an October 2003 *Business Week* article, with health benefits, retirement, and so on, married families can "earn" 25 percent more than unmarried ones.

19 **Marriage Penalties** How does this stack up with the so-called "marriage penalty" that

people complain about at tax time? Two of the major tax penalties were eliminated in 2003, says Fred Grant, a senior tax analyst at Turbo Tax, a corporation that produces electronic tax preparation programs.

20   Used to be, married couples filing jointly had a lower standard deduction than two singles living together, and married couples (in the lowest two income brackets) got bumped into a higher tax bracket on a combined income, thus paying more taxes overall. Now, only the richest three tiers pay more as marrieds than as cohabiters.

21   There are a few other penalties married couples face (for example, they need a lower combined income to qualify for a $1,000 per-child tax credit), but, Grant warns, taxes are such a complex soup incorporating home ownership, itemizations, and more, it's almost impossible to state assertively which type of family comes out ahead tax-wise.

22   **Money, Marriage—and Children** What is safe to say is that the kids of untraditional families can wind up penalized. Of course, there are many possible scenarios. In the best cases, kids living with, for instance, only their mother also receive financial support from a father. But as many single moms will tell you, not all fathers pay their full share of childcare costs.

23   Statistics also show that there are many kids lacking basic health insurance—at last count, about 8.4 million, according to the U.S. Census. All told, there are 11 million children (16 percent) living at or below the poverty line, and while that's not broken down into the number of kids with married or unmarried parents, it's a sure bet that many impoverished kids are in untraditional families.

Single and Satisfied

24   Though a growing number of couples are fine with never getting married, the vast majority of cohabiting relationships change into either marriage or separation after an average of 18 months, says Susan Brown, PhD, associate professor of sociology at Bowling Green State University's Center for Family and Demographic Research and a contributor to the 2002 collection of essays and studies *Just Living Together*. She says that according to some research, there may be a psychological cost to raising a family without the mental safety net of marriage.

25   "I've found that cohabiters are more depressed than married people, and it seems to be because of relationship instability," Brown says. That means most unmarried parents who live together get married eventually—or break up and seek other potential spouses.

26   **The Growth of Gay Families** According to the Urban Institute, 2 in 5 gay or lesbian couples live in a house with children under age 18. But because the U.S. Census Bureau doesn't figure same-sex relationships into their data, it's hard to pinpoint exactly how many children are living with gay or lesbian parents.

27   The American Academy of Pediatrics (AAP) places its bet between one and nine million children, which means somewhere between 1.4 percent and 12.5 percent of all kids. While the AAP issued a statement saying that children of same-sex couples deserve two legally recognized parents, no state can grant federal marriage benefits to these couples, and only one state—Massachusetts—allows state rights, such as the guarantee that unmarried parents can visit a child in the hospital.

28   **Two moms, one donor:** One couple, Sue Hamilton and Christy Sumner, used a sperm bank when they decided to have a baby. While the couple isn't able to marry in their home state of California, Hamilton recently adopted their daughter, which is legal there. Negotiating state laws puts extra stress on gay and lesbian families, but Hamilton and Sumner have encountered a few sympathizers. "One of the hospital workers fell in love with our family," Hamilton says.

29　"She thought it was nutty that birth certificates have to read 'mother' and 'father,' and typed up a mock certificate that just has our names on it."

30　**Can Your Employer Help You?** Some large employers are scrambling to catch up to how families are changing. Traditionally, companies required workers to be married if they wanted benefits for household members. But now, "in order to attract and retain quality employees, the benefits need to be more flexible," says Kevin Marrs of the American Society of Employers, an organization that tracks information for firms in the Detroit area. He concedes, however, that because domestic partner benefits can cost a company more money, many small independent businesses don't yet offer them.

Families, Privileges, and the Law

31　Few laws protect untraditional families. In fact, at this point federal laws don't prohibit discrimination based on marital status, so unmarried families can and do face discrimination in these key areas:

- housing
- employment
- adoption
- insurance
- child custody
- hospital visitation
- the ability to make a decision for a partner or child in an emergency

32　Wilson and Mayes are lucky—their decision to not get married is made easier by the fact that their state, Texas, permits common-law marriage status. Declaring that lets them enjoy joint health coverage through Mayes's employer, and it smoothed the adoption process. If all states had such laws, a great many people would benefit. But only 16 states recognize common-law marriage—and three of those require couples to prove they've been living together since the '90s, according to Nolo Press, which publishes plain-English legal information.

33　**Why Aren't Laws Catching Up to How We're Living?** To many politicians, pushing for marriage is easier than changing laws. President Bush proposed spending $1.5 billion over five years on a Healthy Marriage Initiative to encourage couples (especially in poor communities) to marry. The money hasn't been approved, but the Department of Health and Human Services is running the program.

34　"Bush [advocates] marriage among low-income populations as a way to ameliorate poverty. But I'm not sure that's the answer," Brown says.

35　Daniel Lichter, a sociology professor at Ohio State University, goes even further. In his 2003 study, "Is Marriage a Panacea?" he shows that poverty rates for disadvantaged women who marry and then divorce are actually higher than for women who never marry in the first place. (One thought is that the loss of financial stability as a direct result of divorce—which costs money in itself—may set women back.) So getting married doesn't always ease the financial burden of raising kids, and it certainly doesn't help open the rigid boundaries of what "counts" as a family.

36　The answer probably lies in making sure all families—whether Mom and Dad drive the minivan to soccer practice or Mom piles her stepkids onto the city bus—receive the same kinds of rights, benefits, and treatment. Access to affordable childcare and living wages are also more direct solutions.

37　Discrimination against unmarried families is still real. But those families also have the love and courage it takes to press for change. Says Hamilton, "It really doesn't matter what kind of relationship the parents are in—what matters is the love they have for their child. That is what makes a family."

Thinking Critically About the Reading

1. Where is the article's thesis statement? If the author does not provide a thesis statement, develop one that fits the article.

2. In paragraph 4, the author refers to the definition of "family," but does not define this key term. Look up the definition of "family" in two dictionaries, one published twenty or more years ago, and one published recently. How are these two definitions different? Now formulate a definition of "family" based on your experience and understanding of this article.

3. What two primary factors account for the change in the makeup of the American family?

4. How have attitudes toward relationships and commitment shifted over the years?

5. What current variations of "family" does the author discuss in paragraphs 9, 10, 11, and 12?

6. Give some specific examples of changes in families noticed by those working in the childbirth industry.

7. What are some financial advantages of living in a married household?

8. Give some examples of how families headed by gay or lesbian couples have grown in recent years.

9. Why are employers and lawmakers sometimes slow to respond to the realities of the changing family?

10. In general, do federal laws protect untraditional families? In what areas do untraditional families face discrimination?

11. Using a dictionary when necessary, define the following words in their appropriate context: demographics (1); intact (1); aspirations (1); fertility (5); statistics (5); shotgun wedding (10); surrogate (12); Lamaze (13); cohabiters (20); impoverished (23); sociology (24); concedes (30); common-law marriage (32); ameliorate (34); panacea (35).

JOURNAL WRITING

1. What aspects of the article did you have the strongest positive or negative reaction to? Explain.

Explorations

1. Think of two or three of your closest friends. How would you describe the family that each friend is a part of? Traditional? Nontraditional? What positive and negative effects do you see resulting from the type of family situation your friends are in?

Getting Started: Preparing and Generating

In Chapter 2 we discussed introductory and concluding paragraphs in some detail. This chapter will give you a strategy to tie together the concepts of purpose and audience with the structure of the overall essay. As you have probably noticed, we believe that it is very important for

---

PRACTICAL TIPS — Five Useful Questions

When you are writing an essay to be read by someone other than yourself, there are five basic questions you can use to help determine the overall purpose of your essay. These questions can be used in the preparing/generating (step 1) and the organizing, drafting, and shaping (step 2) steps of the writing process. Which of these questions does your essay's thesis statement and major conclusion answer?

1. Does IT exist?
2. What is IT?
3. How did IT get that way?
4. Is IT good or bad?
5. What should we do (or not do) about IT?

The answers to these questions are closely related to the thesis and major conclusion of your essay. You probably will not know what your major conclusion or thesis will be when you start to write an essay.

---

you to determine your purpose and audience for every essay you write. One reason for stressing purpose and audience is to make sure you compose a clear and effective thesis statement and major conclusion for your essay.

The "preparing/generating" techniques discussed in Chapter 1 will help you focus your thoughts about a topic. Use listing, brainstorming, focused freewriting, and/or clustering/mapping to discover what you really know about a specific topic and discover what you really want to say about that specific topic.

You can also use the five questions mentioned to generate ideas and then organize your ideas for your essay. First, substitute the topic you are writing about for the word "IT" in each of the questions. Your topic may be one that requires you to use a short phrase in place of the word "IT." Second, respond to the questions by writing a tentative (temporary) thesis statement for each question. On five separate sheets of paper, write one of the tentative theses at the top of the page. Third, look at the material you have generated from the listing, brainstorming, etc., and decide what ideas would best support each tentative thesis. Fourth, group your ideas by listing them under the appropriate thesis sentence as you start to see ideas that are related to a tentative thesis. Finally, add any additional thoughts about the topic on the sheet that has a tentative thesis that seems to be associated with your idea. Remember to think of examples, short explanations, and reasons that would support a thesis.

After you have put on paper some of your ideas, make a decision to use one of the five questions as the controlling idea for the thesis of your essay. Some of the ideas listed on the paper with the tentative thesis will serve as subjects for the topic sentences of the body paragraphs. The other four sheets of paper may be very useful for possible subjects for the body paragraphs too. You probably will not be able to use all of your notes for one particular essay assignment. Your task is to make wise decisions about what is appropriate to use and what is not. If you feel a little confused at this point and don't think you know how to make wise decisions, don't worry—it's all part of the writing process. Every time you go through the process of writing an essay, you will gain experience.

MAKING CONNECTIONS | Determining Your Audience

Ask yourself the following questions about your audience:

- What type of background information do you think they have about your topic?

- How old are they?

- Do you have some specific examples in your notes that you think would have a special appeal to your audience?

You should also look for key words in your essay assignment that will help you determine your audience: Classmates, Instructor, Specialists, Non-Specialists, or General Audience.

The more experience you gain, the greater your knowledge will be. While you will not become a writing expert overnight, you will develop the wisdom and expertise to choose the right examples and ideas from your notes.

An important decision for you to make in addition to finding a purpose for your essay is to decide who the audience will be for your essay. Sometimes you will be given a specific audience as part of an essay assignment. If this is the case, you will not have to decide who your readers will be. Whether the audience is of your own choice or not, you should spend some time thinking about the characteristics of your audience.

The examples and supporting ideas you choose from your initial activities of listing, brainstorming, freewriting, or clustering/mapping should be related to the readers of the essay as well as the purpose of the essay. Some of the ideas you may have generated may be appropriate for your classmates to read, but definitely not suitable for a general audience of elderly people, middle-aged adults, young adults, teenagers, and children. You have to pick examples that fit your audience to ensure reaching your basic goal of communication.

With your purpose and audience (readers) clearly in mind, you can start supporting your thesis with examples, facts, and other reasons. The number of examples you choose to use, the amount of detail you include, and how you organize the ideas are three factors that influence the development of your essay.

▶ Essay Assignment

Writing About Family

Write an essay about a special tradition in your family or a family that you have known. Choose one of the following purposes:

1. Describe the tradition (which may be related to holidays, birthdays, yearly vacations, family reunions, or something else) and explain why it is special to you. Your major conclusion and thesis will answer the question, "What is IT?"

This prompt asks you to describe a family tradition. Body paragraphs are often developed by description. Description is the use of words to appeal to one or more of the reader's senses. The five senses are those of seeing, hearing, smelling, tasting, and touching. As you describe your family tradition, try to help your readers experience that tradition by giving descriptive detail. What did that special campground look like? What did all the young cousins sound like when they were playing? What did the holiday meal smell and taste like? What did the sand inside your swimsuit feel like?

2. How did this tradition get started? How old is the tradition? Do you think it will continue to happen in the future? How did the tradition become special to you? Your major conclusion and thesis will answer the question, "How did it get that way?" Decide who your readers will be for this essay.

The following student essay is an expansion of Journal Writing prompt #2 following the excerpt from Virginia Satir's *Peoplemaking*:

Student Essay

Family Values

David Lee Canales
Dr. Burchfield
English 1301
12 October 2006

1   All my life I've had a natural type of family. I am glad to say that I was lucky and very fortunate to be blessed with both a mother and father who have always cared for me throughout my tough experiences. We also share mutual respect for one another and create support whenever we feel down in the dumps. On the other hand, we all know things are not always perfect and that the Brady Bunch, fun-loving, highly spirited family doesn't exist. With that in mind, I was cursed with three other siblings and a dog that constantly fight and whine for space, including me. In terms of describing the four forces mentioned by Satir, which are self-worth, communication, the family system, and the link to society, I have both positive and negative experiences within the household that reflect my family values.

2   Satir explains in *Peoplemaking* that self-worth involves the feelings and ideas one has about himself or herself. In evaluating my self-worth, I had a very negative experience growing up in high school. I was always at the top of my class and kept up with my grades, but when I couldn't live up to my classmates' expectations as being the best, my flaws seemed over-exaggerated, which made me feel like I was dumb. Basically, my self-worth was constantly being shot down and extremely low. I believe that I was very

Thesis statement

Topic sentence—first two sentences of paragraph
Development of first topic

affected by my troubles in high school, but I never really showed any negative emotion in class. Everyone thought that I was always content, but inside the frustration was ripping me apart. Instead, this negativity was brought to the family along with my irritability and moodiness, which wasn't good. However, my comforts were my parents, who always tried to create a perfect environment that I could handle while trying to cope with my challenges at school. My siblings weren't a curse anymore, because they also brought up my self-esteem. All this in return brought the family closer together and cleared any previous negativity that was present.

Transition and topic sentence
Development of second topic

3   In addition, my positive self-worth could only be achieved with yet another strong aspect in any family relationship: communication. Communication has to be one of the most important aspects, because it is the only way that any problem can be resolved. For example, after I came back from school, I couldn't reach out to anyone else that I felt was trustworthy other than my parents. We actually had to sit and talk about my problems. While I wasn't the only one who felt insecure about life, my family began to talk about many topics including school and some positive issues that were happening around us. Communication within our family has always been kept honest and valued with great importance. Our open communication, along with good humor, has made us even stronger and will continue to grow as we get older.

Transition and topic sentence
Development of third topic

4   I also learned that a family system must be established within a household to keep it structured and organized. This family system, according to Virginia Satir, is the rules that people use for how they feel and act. The rules that my parents made were very understandable and essentially crucial in my upbringing. Rules must be made in order to maintain structure within a family or any other formal organization. On the other hand, rules must be appropriate and flexible so that issues in the family become resolved and negotiable. As far as I'm concerned, my brothers and I never had rigid rules that were harsh or strict in any manner. We were disciplined at times when we were younger, but we never behaved poorly or deserved maltreatment either. As I got older, I even started creating rules for my parents to work with concerning my views. Our mutual agreement helped us get a better understanding of each other and continues to strengthen us as a unit.

Transition

Topic sentence
Development of fourth topic

5   Along with strong self-worth, open communication, and a flexible family system, Satir also mentions the last factor while discovering different families as a therapist. The last aspect is the link to society: the way people relate to other institutions outside the family. For example, my mother is an elementary school teacher, and among her many duties, her job must be to get involved with all her students as well as the parents. I believe that without that connection she wouldn't be doing her job, which in turn would affect other people's views about her. The same goes for our family and the people around us. We must keep that positive connection around us open.

Furthermore, our outlook definitely reflects how we perceive our loved ones and ourselves, with respect and care. I never saw any negatives in my family when confronting other people outside of my family. I, on the other hand, am not always welcoming when it comes to meeting new people. I am not blaming anyone, but it takes a lot for me to develop trust even among my friends. I have had plenty of people in my life who have hurt me, and that is where the challenge began for me.

Restatement of thesis 6   Thus, my family is really average and basic but not without its flaws. We still argue and disagree many times. I still hold my weekly grudge match against my brothers, but we forgive and forget. They are *mi familia,* my family, as well as my comfort zone, and I will try my best never to take them for granted.

As mentioned earlier in the book, the length of your essays will vary, depending on factors such as the subject, your instructor's directions, the amount of time allotted, and other factors. The opening paragraph will usually be the introduction, and the closing paragraph will be the conclusion. That leaves a flexible number of body paragraphs in which you can support your thesis with facts, details, examples, and believable reasons. Each paragraph will have a topic sentence that is related to your thesis and major conclusion.

Organizing and Developing Your Essays

Developing Body Paragraphs

We discussed the key traits of an effective body paragraph in Chapter 1. Do you remember the acronym we mentioned to help you remember the five traits? Take a moment and write down (on a separate sheet of paper) as much as you can of the acronym and the traits the letters stand for. How many of the five traits of an effective body paragraph did you remember?

In this section we will give you some more ideas about how to write body paragraphs. Remember that often you will write the body paragraphs before you write the introductory and concluding paragraphs. Let's concentrate on the technique of giving examples in your body paragraphs to support your thesis.

Effective Examples in Body Paragraphs

Here is another acronym to help you learn the ART of writing effective examples in body paragraphs:

The acronym "**A R T**" stands for:

Accurate details

Related to the thesis

Typical examples

Accurate details This means you should use specific details or facts that describe the example. The details can provide the reader with important information that answers the questions *Who? What? When? Where? Why?* and *How?* These six questions are sometimes called the "Reporter's Formula" or "Reporter's Questions." These questions are especially useful when generating ideas about an event.

Related to the thesis Use examples that are clearly related to your thesis or are connected to your thesis in a logical way. Sometimes it

is easy to get so involved writing about an example that a shift in the focus of an essay occurs. You can prevent this from happening by asking yourself, "Does this example really have something to do with the thesis?"

Typical examples Choose examples that your readers are probably familiar with. If your readers know something about the example from their own experience, they will more easily accept the example as support for your thesis. This characteristic is particularly important when you are writing an essay that is attempting to persuade your reader that your opinion or viewpoint is correct.

Use these characteristics as a guide to choose examples from your notes. Remember, the ART of using effective examples is an ability that is learned. No one is born knowing how to choose the right examples for an essay.

Consider the second choice in the essay assignment in this chapter:

Write an essay about a special tradition in your family or a family that you have known. How did this tradition get started? How old is the tradition? Do you think it will continue to happen in the future? How did the tradition become special to you? Your major conclusion and thesis will answer the question, "How did IT get that way?"

The examples that you will use in the body paragraphs of an essay in response to this question will be specific traditions that you choose from your preparing/generating activities. How do you go about making sure that each example is fully developed?

Student Essay

The following student essay is based on the assignment that asks students to discuss family traditions.

My Family Traditions

Marissa Mullen
Dr. Sabrio
English 1301
October 6, 2006

Thesis statement

1   For the first eleven of my seventeen years my family shared organized traditions. We spent every birthday and Christmas at my paternal grandmother's house. These were times when my father's entire family gathered to celebrate together. We celebrated together until the death of the family matriarch fragmented the family. Though the traditions no longer go on, I remember what we used to do.

Topic sentence

Development of topic sentence

2   I remember every birthday we had at my grandmother's. We always went to visit my grandmother, Momo, for birthdays. She would bake me my favorite cake, a chocolate cake smothered in coffee-flavored chocolate icing. Everyone would gather around the table, light all the candles and sing "Happy Birthday" to me. I loved to pick the candles out of the cake to get as much of the icing as I could. My mother and I always fought over who got the candles. Needless to say, I always won. I don't remember any single birthday more than any other, but I do remember loving all the attention and the good feeling that everyone had come to see me. A few years ago I won first place in a cooking contest using Momo's icing recipe.

Topic sentence

Development of topic sentence

3   My favorite traditions revolved around Christmas. Every Christmas Eve we would gather to eat dinner and open presents. It was probably fairly hectic for the adults trying to make the food and keep an eye on all five children. We weren't terribly rambunctious; however, with two sets of siblings, there were quite a few arguments. The night would always start with everyone hurriedly preparing the food. My cousin and I, who were very close in age, jumped at the chance to set the table. There were two tables, the adult table and the children's table. I don't remember there ever being a certain age when we got promoted, but both tables were always full as adults shifted around. Every year Momo would make a peach cobbler that was my favorite part of the meal.

Topic sentence (sub-topic of Christmas topic)

Development of topic

4   After we ate dinner, everyone would gather in the living room to open presents. We didn't open our gifts from Santa, but we opened the presents

from the rest of the family. There was a certain way we would do this. The youngest would open her presents first. It was the same order every year. First my cousin Tiffany would open hers, then it was my turn, then my cousin Michelle, followed by my brother Lindsey, and finally my cousin Mark. Now that I look back on it, that order was probably the only way that the adults thought the kids would stay preoccupied while the rest of the family opened their gifts. Momo would always put all the children's presents in little Christmas stockings on the small tree that was in the center of the living room. Once the kids started to get cranky, we would call it a night and head home. It was a thirty-minute drive that I intentionally slept through, so when I got home I could play with my new toys.

Topic sentence
Development of topic

5   After Momo's death in 1996, our family seemed to grow apart. We of course tried to revive the tradition for a year or two afterwards, but for some reason it never worked out. There didn't seem to be the driving force bringing us all together anymore. My extended family still communicates on occasion and manages to gather when there is some sort of crisis. Eventually I fear that a crisis will be the only reason for communication.

Restatement of thesis

6   My immediate family still attempts to continue some sort of holiday tradition, although as the years go by, I see that dissolving as well. It doesn't mean that we don't care. It means that we no longer feel it necessary. We continue to exchange gifts for birthdays and Christmas. It just isn't the same as when I was a child.

Insightful Writing

As you proceed through the four steps of the composing process with your current essay assignment (Step 1: Preparing/Generating; Step 2: Organizing/Drafting/Shaping; Step 3: Revising; Step 4: Editing and Proofreading) it is entirely possible that you will gain some new insights about your own education and the ways in which you and your family value language and literacy. The word "insight" can be defined as *the ability to perceive the true nature of a situation or understand the hidden nature of something*. Be aware of these moments of discovery and take note of them. Write them down in the form of a note and be sure to include these insights in your essay if you consider them appropriate for your audience. We can assure you that college instructors like to read essays and journal entries with their students' insights into various issues and topics. Reading essays and journals that contain insights is more interesting for instructors, and we get a certain satisfaction in knowing that our students are growing in their awareness of themselves and the world. We feel so strongly about the insightful nature of writing that we include it in the title of this textbook.

The ability to gain an insight into a topic is not just a matter of luck. It can be developed by knowing what questions to ask about a topic. We have tried to provide a foundation for you to develop the "active" reading strategies you need to write meaningful essays containing your insights. Review the section on Reading Effectively in Chapter 1 (pages 25–29). Also, look at the "Before You Read," "While You Read," and "Thinking Critically About the Reading" questions in Chapters 1 and 2. Refer to these sections as you read the rest of the reading selections in this book, and also remember the "five useful questions" and the "reporter's formula" contained in this chapter. We want you to develop the habit of using them as you read, but we realize that you will need to modify the activities to fit your own learning style and the particular article or reading selection that you are studying.

5 Relationships Beyond the Family

God gives us our relatives—thank God we can choose our friends.

Ethel Watts Mumford (1878–1940),
U.S. novelist, humor writer. The Cynic's Calendar, p. 1
(written with Addison Mizner and Oliver Herford, 1903)

 As you move from childhood to adulthood, the amount of time you spend with your family starts to diminish, and the time you spend with your peers and various groups increases. More than likely, you are spending considerable time in a group called a "college class" as you read this chapter.

Typically, people like to spend time with other people who have similar interests. They join clubs that meet on a regular basis, or they get together for sports like softball, bowling, or golf. People also belong to groups that are simply necessary for making a living. Yes, we are talking about groups of employees at a job. Unless you are independently wealthy, you will probably belong to a group that works together at a business or organization. If it is a large business, you may not have a lot in common with many of your coworkers. Over time, however, you will establish lasting friendships (or relationships) with quite a few of these "strangers."

Humans have common needs and desires that form a foundation for building healthy relationships. The key ingredient to forming relationships is communication—all types of communication. As you will read in the articles chosen for this chapter, the very clothes we wear communicate with others on a nonverbal level, and one of the most common needs we all share, food, can serve as a vehicle to learn about other cultural groups. It is interesting to note that the word *companion* originally meant "a person that you share bread or food with."

Before You Read

1. Before you read the following articles, take a moment to read just the opening and closing paragraphs of each article. Put into your own words, either by telling a classmate or writing in your notebook, what you believe to be the main point or thesis of each article.

2. What do you think the body paragraphs will be about?

While You Read

1. As you read, underline or highlight key sentences. Remember, key sentences are often at the beginnings and ends of paragraphs.

2. What questions occur to you as you read these two articles? Write them down. What do you agree or disagree with most strongly?

3. As you read, keep a written record of your summary of and comments on or responses to each paragraph. How do the ideas in these two articles speak to you personally?

4. Meet with one or more of your classmates during class or outside of class and discuss the different reactions and responses that you and your classmates have to these articles. How are your interpretations similar to or different from those of your classmates?

Examine the diversity of people in this urban farmers' market. Is the comparison "America is a melting pot" (metaphor) accurate, or do you feel "America is like a salad bowl" (simile) a better description?

Readings

The following excerpts from a magazine article, "Fabric of a Nation," focus on food and fashion in the United States. The amazing diversity of the food we eat and the clothes we wear results from a combination of the diverse cultural heritage of the population and the "globalization" of our daily life. As you read the selections, think about times when you met with friends at a restaurant for a meal or party and how the experience of sharing food provided a common basis for communication. The food and service were either great, or average, or bad. In each case you probably talked about your viewpoint on the matter and listened to the views of your friends.

Food

BY RICARDO SANDOVAL

1 They gave up their languages, their styles of dress—their very ways of life. But it was going to take more than moving to the United States to make immigrants give up their familiar foods. Their identities were tied to tables heaped with old-country favorites: German *Sauerkrauteintopf* (sauerkraut and pork stew); Italian *Gnocchi di patate* (potato dumplings); Jewish *Nockerl* (egg dumplings); Polish *Kielbasa w Sosie Pomidorowym* (sausage with tomato sauce); Greek *Dolmadakia Yialandji* (stuffed grape leaves).

2 The basic ingredients for these dishes, along with thousands of other international favorites, are now regular stock on American grocery shelves. Need more proof? Look no farther than your nearest fast-food eatery with its dizzying meld of such items as Mexican pizza, teriyaki hamburgers, Cajun-spiced French fries and Chinese-style chicken salad.

3 "There is no way to talk about a single American food tradition," says Nancy Harmon Jenkins, Maine-based ethnic food historian and writer for *The New York Times* and *Food and Wine* magazine. "Our food customs are derived from all other parts of the world. In time they all got mixed together."

4 Many of those traditions had variegated histories even before they came to the New World.

For instance, the humble Mexican taco, originally a corn tortilla dish, has been changed by Spanish and American influences. Its American version comprises a deep-fried tortilla stuffed with ground beef and various additions such as cheese, sour cream, mild salsa, lettuce and tomato.

5 Some of the most entrenched traditional American foods like pumpkin pie and "puffed" breakfast cereal are early products of European and Native American ingenuity. Pie was an English concept the Colonists adapted with the help of Native Americans, who introduced them to pumpkin and squash; the settlers finished off the cooked pulp by adding sweeteners and Asian spices like cinnamon and nutmeg. Colonial housewives served popcorn with sugar and cream for breakfast after American Indians showed them the versatility of the New World's predominant grain.

6 Food historians trace the origins of seemingly the most American of foods to other lands. Peanuts come from South America. Oranges were first picked in Asia, taken to Africa and the Middle East by Arab traders, then brought to the New World by travelers from the Mediterranean countries. Potatoes from the Andes went to Europe with homebound explorers, gained wide acceptance, then returned to the

New World as a major food crop with immigrants from Ireland and central Europe.

7   Of all the foods inherent in the American diet, corn ranks second only to wheat as the most universally grown and used today. It goes back thousands of years to Mexico. By the time European explorers took samples home, the grain was a staple throughout the Western Hemisphere.

8   The list of American favorites adopted from other cultures continues to increase. "The current health kick has exposed more Americans to Asian dishes," Jenkins points out. "People are going back to basic, unprocessed foods and minimalist dishes common to peasants and previously known as 'poverty food.'" For example, brown rice is the healthier, increasingly popular alternative to the processed white variety. And leaner meats (turkey, chicken and fish) are replacing well-marbled beef.

9   "Over countless generations people from different countries have been doing great things with a limited number of local ingredients," says Michael Batterberry, founding editor of *Food Arts* magazine. "Now there is a whole world of ingredients to choose from and cook with. The idea of Global Village cooking is finally becoming the norm."

Fashion

BY LINDA ROSENKRANTZ

10   Visit a shopping center or stand on a busy street corner anywhere in the U.S.A.: You'll see global influences in the clothes of virtually every passer-by. The man over there wears an Aran sweater and a dashiki. That one wears a Ukrainian embroidered vest over his tie-dyed shirt. A woman sports a brilliant blue beret to complement her American Indian turquoise jewelry. "The wearing of a single foreign garment, like the dropping of a foreign word or phrase in conversation," says Alison Lurie in *The Language of Clothes* (Random House, 1981), "is meant not to advertise foreign origin or allegiance but to indicate sophistication."

11   That wasn't the case, however, during the first half of the 20th century. Then immigrants to the United States couldn't wait to get rid of their foreign fashions and get into something more American. The impetus was to adopt the new land's styles. Authentic ethnic clothing ended up in trunks tucked out of sight (except for an occasional wedding or parade), and out of memory.

12   During the '30s, '40s and '50s, any lack of ethnic memory was made up for by the imagination of American designers. Thus the kimonos and Spanish shawls, Fair Isle sweaters and argyle socks, boleros, kilts and Tyrolean pinafores worn by Americans from Schenectady to Sacramento bore but little resemblance to their Old World inspirations. Add the impact of the Hollywood Dream Machine. When Edith Head designed Dorothy Lamour's first sarong for the 1936 film *The Jungle Princess,* she initiated a vogue for all things tropical that lasted until the end of World War II. The mandarin-collared dresses Jennifer Jones wore in 1955's *Love Is a Many-Splendored Thing* triggered a trend toward Asian-inspired styles.

13   In the turbulent '60s fashion became overtly political. With the onset of the Civil Rights and Women's Liberation movements, folk music and rock 'n' roll; with the proliferation of hippies and flower children, drugs, Zen and other Eastern religions, clothing (as well as hair length) became a social statement. You were what you wore. Concerts and crash pads were populated by people wearing embroidered caftans and djellabas from Morocco; Moorish

burnooses; Mexican wedding dresses, ponchos, serapes and embroidered shirts; Arabian harem and drawstring pants; sheepskin-lined Afghan jackets; Indonesian batiks; Indian block prints and mirror-decorated fabrics.

14 The great rage was tie-dyeing—a fabric-patterning method used in Indonesia and India to produce uniquely mottled, brightly hued sun-bursts of color that were perfectly suited to the free-spirited Age of Aquarius.

15 African-Americans began to express their racial identity and pride by wearing dashikis. "The adoption of [aboriginal] African costume signified the racial pride inculcated by the Civil Rights movement," according to Joel Lobenthal, author of *Radical Rags: Fashions of the Sixties* (Abbeville Press, 1990).

16 In the late '60s and '70s the hippie-ethnic look expanded to welcome Native-American influences. Feathers, fringed leather, turquoise beads, silver bracelets and soft suede boots were the rage. High-fashion designers—Giorgio di Sant' Angelo, Ralph Lauren, Oscar de la Renta, Halston and Anne Klein—incorporated all of these features into their lines.

17 Fashions have always been indicators of the political and social pulse—thus styles of the '80s and '90s became more conservative. Ralph Lauren and Laura Ashley established English country as a standard; very expensive European-designed clothes (labels conspicuously attached on the outside for all to see) were a short-lived fad. Now it's the style to "Buy American" and "Buy cheap." But even the red-white-and-bluest of fashions are so enmeshed with ethnic influences that we often forget where they end and the American standard begins.

Thinking Critically About The Readings

1. Find a thesis statement for the "Food" article and one for the "Fashion" article. If an article does not contain one, develop an appropriate thesis statement that fits the article.

2. List the authoritative sources (magazines, books, and experts) used by the authors.

3. Where do peanuts come from?

4. What is the history of the "humble" Mexican taco?

5. Consider the following statements by Nancy Jenkins: "There is no way to talk about a single American food tradition," and "Our food customs are derived from all other parts of the world. In time they all got mixed together." Do you agree with these statements? Why or why not?

6. Using a dictionary when necessary, define the following words in their appropriate context: meld (paragraph 2); variegated (4); ingenuity (5); versatility (5); predominant (5); minimalist (8); marbled (8); dashiki (10); embroidered (10); beret (10); complement (10); turquoise (10); sophistication (10); inculcated (15); hippie-ethnic (16); conspicuously (17); enmeshed (17).

What groups or organizations do you belong to or have you belonged to? Are the members of some of these groups or organizations similar in their backgrounds, or are the members from diverse backgrounds? Compare the types of groups you belong to and determine the shared values or beliefs that hold them together. (Think of groups related to family, school, church, social interests, athletics; and hobbies or pastimes.)

Explorations

1. Did you recognize the name of any of the exotic foods described in the first paragraph of the reading selection? Either alone or in a small group, try to add to this list as many unusual foreign names of food (without the common English name) in a three-minute time frame. Trade lists with another group in the class or another class member and provide the common English name for the foreign names. One way to organize your list of foods is to classify them into separate groups based on some similarity or principle of classification. For example, you might classify foods into groups based on the foods' country of origin, or the ethnic or cultural group often associated with the foods.

2. What foods would you never give up, even if you moved to a foreign country? Compare your list with the other students in the class and look for the most frequent response. Construct a chart to show the results and/or prepare a PowerPoint® presentation. Make a class presentation.

3. Obtain a copy of one of the magazines or books mentioned in the article and choose an article or book chapter to read. Present a short oral report to the class or write a brief review of the article or chapter.

4. Plan a dinner party for your group (4 to 5 class members) with an international sampler menu. (You do not have to actually buy and prepare the food.) Write the names and countries of the foods you plan to serve. Stage a "mock" dinner party, complete with dialogue, and make a class presentation with your group (about 5 minutes in duration).

Before You Read

1. Before reading the following article, take a moment to read just the opening and closing paragraphs. Put into your own words, either by telling a classmate or by writing in your notebook, what you believe to be the main point or thesis of the article.

2. Look at the titles of each subsection of the article. What do these titles tell you about the contents of the body paragraphs?

While You Read

1. As you read, underline or highlight key sentences. Remember, key sentences are often at the beginnings and ends of paragraphs.

2. What questions occur to you as you read this article? Write these questions down. What do you agree or disagree with most strongly?

3. As you read, keep a written record of your summary of and comments on or responses to each paragraph. How do the ideas in this article speak to you personally?

4. Meet with one or more of your classmates during class or outside of class and discuss the different reactions and responses that you and your classmates have to the article. How are your interpretations similar to or different from those of your classmates?

The following article, "We Just Forge Ahead And Believe," written by David Oliver Relin, appeared in *PARADE* magazine on November 2, 2003. As you read, compare your experiences in high school with the experiences of the students and teachers at the high school featured in the article.

We Just Forge Ahead—and Believe

BY DAVID OLIVER RELIN

Despite limited resources, Roy Sunada helped transform John Marshall Fundamental Secondary School into one of the country's most-improved high schools.

1 Einstein peers down encouragingly. Shakespeare oversees everything with a sly smile. And Joe DiMaggio balances a bat on his shoulder with the confidence of a champion. Everywhere you look in Room 106, you see something inspiring. From the portraits that gaze upon the rapt ninth-graders to the baseball caps from Harvard and Berkeley on the walls, every inch of this classroom at Pasadena's John Marshall Fundamental Secondary School urges students to aim high.

But the most inspiring presence in Room 106 2 is pacing in front of the class. Wearing a white button-down shirt and a rainbow-hued Scooby-Doo tie, Roy Sunada is at work doing that most difficult thing: convincing teenagers there's nothing they can't achieve. At this moment, he's pressing his students to recall an obscure fact about the reign of King Philip the Fair. "C'mon, people, reach for it," he urges. "I know you know this." After blurting out the correct answer,

Michael Jimenez, 15, throws his arms up in victory, like he's just hit a game-winning home run. Sunada rewards him with the merest nod of approval, a look that says, "Good, but don't get too excited. You have much more work ahead of you."

3   If this was a rich prep school, the scene in Sunada's classroom might not seem so remarkable. But Marshall Fundamental is a poor public school in greater Los Angeles. More than 70% of the 1700 students are Hispanic or African-American, and 60% of the students' families qualify for free or reduced-price lunches. That makes the success Sunada has spearheaded here all the more revolutionary.

4   In the six years since Sunada took over as Marshall's advanced placement coordinator, the number of students passing AP exams has exploded from 37 in 1997 to 187 last year. Now nearly 33% of Marshall students are enrolled in AP—rigorous college-level courses that bestow college credits if students pass the final exam. During the same period, the percentage of Marshall graduates attending colleges has surged from 57% to 88%. That's why, this year, Marshall was one of only three schools nationally to receive the prestigious College Board 2003 Inspiration Award for improving so dramatically and sending so many economically disadvantaged students on to college.

5   One on one, Roy Sunada seems an unlikely revolutionary leader. He speaks so softly that you have to strain to catch every word. And even after 34 years in education, he says, "Standing in front of a class still makes me nervous."

6   Sunada, 58, was born in a Japanese-American internment camp in Arkansas, where his family was confined during World War II. After the war, the Sunadas settled in Pasadena.

7   Sunada discovered his love for teaching as a student at UC Santa Barbara, where he taught a martial-arts class. He chose a career in education and quickly rose from classroom teacher to assistant principal to administrator. But eventually he had his fill of administrative work. Says Sunada, "I felt like I'd made enough money and gotten too far from what drew me to teaching: making a difference in the lives of young people."

8   In 1992, Sunada asked to return to the classroom. Marshall approached him about teaching AP European History. He agreed only if he could take over the school's entire AP program. Sunada says he returned to teaching with a single goal: to make college preparatory classes available to all students, not just the privileged few who typically take them. "People always ask me, 'What about classes for kids in the middle?'" Sunada says. "I tell them, 'They're called AP. What do you want? Kids to stay in the middle?'"

9   Surprisingly, in an era where schools are often measured by their students' performances on standardized tests, Sunada says he doesn't care how many Marshall students pass the AP exams. To him, just persuading teenagers to try college-level work is a success. "We demand that our students push themselves and improve, and in that way prepare for college," he says. "That's the only standard I care about."

10   So Sunada set out to expand the school's AP offerings, adding a dozen new courses, from economics to advanced calculus. The school even added AP chemistry and biology despite the fact that Marshall has no laboratories. "We don't worry about class size or lack of materials here," Sunada says. "We just forge ahead and believe, you know, that if we build the program, they will come."

11   Janice Campbell came to Sunada her freshman year. Living in foster and group homes with no role model for success, Janice had drifted through her academic life, earning average grades at best. "I asked Janice, like I ask every student, why she wanted to take my class," Sunada says. "She said, 'Because I'm tired of being stupid. I want to be smart, and your class has all the smart kids.'"

12   "My palms were all sweaty when I asked Mr. Sunada to be in his class," says Janice, now 18.

"I really didn't know if I could do it." After struggling her first semester, Janice improved her study habits, and she racked up AP course credits in English, history, economics, government, chemistry and biology during her time at Marshall, also excelling on the school's tennis team.

13   Janice entered Pasadena City College this fall. "If not for Mr. Sunada, I never even would have thought about college," she says. "After surviving his class, my self-esteem really increased, and I learned that I can do anything. More than that, being in AP felt like being a part of something—like I finally found the family I never had."

14   Many passionately committed teachers have been drawn to Marshall's experiment in inclusion. Patricia Kavanagh left a lucrative job in the television industry to teach AP English at Marshall. "I wanted to do something important with my life," she says. After seven years here, she takes pride in reeling off her students' accomplishments—how they routinely beat kids from LA's wealthiest prep schools in essay and oratory contests and have attended elite colleges from Stanford to Columbia. "The kids here might be a little tougher, and their language might be a little rough, but I see such greatness in them," she says. "With all they have to overcome in their lives, our kids are warriors."

15   Like almost everyone at Marshall, Kavanagh reserves her greatest praise for her soft-spoken AP coordinator. "A school can have all the money in the world and still not succeed," she says. "But having a Roy Sunada is priceless. He lives, breathes and eats his dream—success for teens who have never been near a college. Our students live to hear him praise them, and he makes other teachers want to impress him too."

16   For many Marshall students who come from cultures that steer them away from academic success, the dedication of their teachers is the anchor that keeps them on course. Growing up in a neighborhood with a pervasive gang presence, Michael Jimenez says he's aware that choices he makes now will determine the course of his life. Michael's brother-in-law, Esteban Martinez, had tried to distance himself from gang life once he decided he wanted a future. Then, one evening last year while hanging out at Michael's house, Esteban, 23, answered the door, and members of a local gang shot and killed him.

17   "I saw what happened to him," Michael says, "and that made me even more determined to choose the right path. I know I want to go to college. I know I want to be an example to my younger brothers and sisters. And I'm willing to work hard for it." That means enduring classes like Roy Sunada's, where Michael's notes will be collected and graded, and the exams are impossible to ace. "When you see how hard Mr. Sunada works to help you, how passionate he is, it should be no big deal to work hard right back."

18   Michael says he hopes to attend the Air Force Academy and to fly fighter jets. But today, his trajectory takes him once more to a desk in Room 106, to wrestle with the intricacies of European history in a class piloted by a stern workaholic in a Scooby-Doo tie—a man dedicated to catching and cultivating the potential in every student who passes through his door.

Thinking Critically About the Reading

1. Where is the article's thesis statement? If the author does not provide a thesis statement, develop one that fits the article.

2. Summarize Roy Sunada's family background and career path.

3. This article discusses the AP, or advanced placement, program. What is the AP program? What kind of AP program did your high school have? What experiences did you or your high school classmates have with AP courses and AP exams? To what extent was the AP program at your high school promoted by teachers, counselors, and principals?

4. The author uses two extended examples of students who have benefited from participation in the school's AP program. Briefly summarize the experiences of each student.

5. Using a dictionary when necessary, define the following words in their appropriate context: forge (title); peers (1); sly (1); rapt (1); hued (2); obscure (2); merest (2); rigorous (4); bestow (4); internment (6); confined (6); martial (7); lucrative (14); oratory (14); elite (14); pervasive (16); trajectory (18); intricacies (18); stern (18); cultivating (18).

JOURNAL WRITING

The preceding article highlights the importance of high school teachers who are committed to challenging students and helping them get the most out of their high school education. Develop a journal of about 200 words in which you discuss the two high school teachers who were most instrumental in helping you work up to your potential. Your instructor may ask you to expand this journal into a complete essay.

Explorations

1. Make arrangements with one of your teachers or counselors from the high school from which you graduated to give a talk to an eleventh- or twelfth-grade class about some of the challenges faced by new college students, and about some of the major differences between high school and college. Be sure to give the high school students time to ask you questions. Write a brief report on your talk to the high school students.

2. Meet with one or more of your high school teachers, counselors, or principals and discuss the activities and programs that your high school is providing to help prepare students for college. Also, discuss activities and programs in your high school that need improvement in order to better prepare its graduates for college.

Getting Started: More Strategies for Organizing Ideas

We introduced in Chapter 1 the acronym for remembering some key traits of an effective body paragraph—DUCTT:

D evelopment

U nity

C oherence

T ransitions

T opic Sentence

In Chapter 4, we introduced the **"ART"** of developing body paragraphs through examples (**A**ccurate details, **R**elated to thesis, **T**ypical examples). There are several additional strategies for the development of body paragraphs as well as full essays. Here is a brief list of techniques you can use:

Narration   This strategy involves telling a story or relating a series of events to support your topic sentence. If a narrative paragraph becomes too long, split it into two or more paragraphs, each with an appropriate topic sentence. The student who wrote "An Alienated Asian" (p. 60) used narration paragraphs skillfully to get across his main point.

Description   Effective description involves using words to appeal to one or more senses of your readers. Descriptive writing appeals to your readers' sense of sight, hearing, smell, taste, and touch. In descriptive writing, try to be as concrete and specific as possible so that readers get a clear sense of what you are describing. Elizabeth Cook's essay on Lost Maples State Park (p. 210) contains some effective descriptions of the park.

Examples   Using specific incidents and examples that are logically connected to the topic sentence is a solid strategy for developing paragraphs and supporting your argument. The examples should support your thesis or claim. Using examples is also sometimes called exposition, exemplification, or illustration. Earlier, we discussed developing paragraphs by including examples. Using examples is one of the most common methods of developing paragraphs and entire essays. Many articles in this book use examples as the major method of development; among them are the articles on learning styles (p. 2), food (p. 97), and fashion (p. 98).

Explanation   Consideration for your audience requires you to provide necessary information about the subject of the topic sentence. Information that answers the journalists' questions "Who, What, When, Where, Why, and How" is interesting to your readers. In fact, journalists make sure that these questions are answered in the first part of a newspaper story to satisfy their readers' curiosity. Taken as a group, the five Ws and one H are referred to as the "Reporter's Formula" or "Reporter's Questions." This method of development is especially useful when writing about an event (i.e., something that happens at a particular time in a particular place). Marissa Mullen, who wrote "My Family Traditions" (p. 92), uses some explanations in her paragraphs, along with narration and examples.

Process   Many writers whose audience wants to learn how something is made or how something is done use a process organization. The key element in any process is a series of steps, done in a prescribed order. This "how to" method of organization is one of the most commonly used structures today. You are familiar with the process method of development if you have ever read directions on how to prepare a meal, change the oil in your vehicle, install software on your computer, put together a toy for a child, or build something. The early chapters of this book took you through the process of writing an essay. Telling how to make something is one kind of process; another is explaining how something happens. For example, a political science book might tell how a bill becomes law, a chemical engineering student studies how oil is refined into gasoline, and someone studying for the medical field learns how heart disease develops into a life-threatening condition. Dianne Hales uses process in her article, "Getting Yourself Back on Track" (p. 44) to help readers become higher achievers.

Comparison/Contrast   In this development strategy, a writer discusses the similarities and differences between two like items, people, or ways of doing something. This method of organization is common because in everyday life we make choices about what goods or services to buy, what political candidates to support, and what approach will best solve a problem. A potential homeowner must decide whether a fixed-rate or adjustable-rate mortgage is best. A consumer must decide whether to buy this television or that one. County voters may be asked to decide whether to contract out garbage pickup services or have county workers provide the service.

Comparison/contrast is such a common method of organization that entire essays are structured around it. Two frequently used methods of organizing a comparison/contrast essay are described below.

The first method goes by several names: block method, subject-by-subject method, or whole-to-whole method. In this structure, the writer mentions everything about item A first and then mentions everything about item B next. To illustrate, suppose you are comparing and contrasting two restaurants. Using this first method of organization, you would structure your essay something like this:

❡ Introduction and thesis

❡ Atmosphere of restaurant A

❡ Service of restaurant A

❡ Prices of restaurant A

❡ Food of restaurant A

❡ Major transition, atmosphere of restaurant B

❡ Service of restaurant B

❡ Prices of restaurant B

❡ Food of restaurant B

❡ Restatement of thesis and conclusion

The second method is often called the part-to-part method or point-by-point method. In this structure, the writer chooses several appropriate topics and discusses both items being compared and contrasted under each topic. Let's take the same essay subject from the example above and structure it according to this second method:

❡ Introduction and thesis

❡ Atmosphere of restaurant A and restaurant B

❡ Service of restaurant A and restaurant B

❡ Prices of restaurant A and restaurant B

❡ Food of restaurant A and restaurant B

❡ Restatement of thesis and conclusion

Many readers may prefer this second method of comparison/contrast because the items are being compared and contrasted within each body paragraph. In the first method, the reader, while reading the second half of the essay, may have to refer back to the first half of the essay to see what was said about a particular topic.

Cause/Effect Often found in persuasive writing, this strategy analyzes the causes or effects (results, consequences) of a particular event or action. Students pursuing careers in law enforcement read about the causes of criminal activity in cities. Historians and politicians continue to debate the causes of the U.S. invasion and occupation of Iraq in March 2003. Various effects are also analyzed: Scientists study the effects of burning fossil fuels on the environment. Sociologists and government officials continue to analyze the effects of Hurricane Katrina on the people of the Louisiana and Mississippi Gulf Coast. In his article "America's Religious Mosaic" (p. 138), Bill Moyers discusses the causes of the renewed interest in religion in the U.S.

Division or Partition   This strategy involves taking one item and dividing or partitioning it into its component parts. Division or partition is one of the most common approaches we take in order to better understand whatever we are studying. Another term for division or partition is analysis, which involves taking a complex item, dividing it up, and studying each part carefully in order to understand the whole item better. Someone learning about auto mechanics studies the various components of a motor vehicle: the engine, the exhaust system, the electrical system, the suspension system, the chassis, the body, the interior. Someone hired by a large corporation as a manager trainee may have to rotate through all the company's departments: accounting, personnel, customer relations, manufacturing, and so on. Virginia Satir, in the excerpt from her book *Peoplemaking* (p. 75), uses division/partition when she analyzes the family in terms of the four elements that strengthen or weaken the family. In addition, the article on multiple intelligences (p. 10) takes the complex concept of "intelligence" and divides or partitions it into seven types, based on the writings of Howard Gardner.

Classification   This strategy involves categorizing or grouping people, places, things, or even examples in your paragraph according to common characteristics. Be sure your audience knows the principle of classification that you are using. Classification always applies to a large number of people, places, or things. Classification is used all the time to help make our lives easier. Classification is used in libraries, department stores, supermarkets, and newspaper "classified ads." Remember that the same group of items can be classified according to different principles, or in several different ways, depending on what your purpose is. For instance, students at your college can be classified according to major, or according to how many hours they have completed, or according to age, or according to ethnicity. Each of these classifications yields different information to be used for a different purpose. The student who wrote "Fashion of the Times" (p. 110) used classification to categorize the college students on his campus.

Definition   You will often use this strategy to clarify for your readers a specific context of an otherwise familiar word, or to narrow your particular understanding of an abstract concept such as *justice* or *friendship*. In an essay about family traditions you might define a word like *reunion* to make a point about what does or does not happen at your family reunion. A complex term or idea may require an expanded definition, including what it is not (negative definition), how the idea or term may develop over time, and what variations the definition may include. The essay on multiple intelligences (p. 10), in addition to being a division or partition of the term *intelligence,* can also be considered an expanded definition of "intelligence."

Facts and Statistics   Often used in tandem with such strategies as examples or definition, this pattern of development uses information from reliable sources that provides relevant information about your topic.

Analogy   This strategy makes use of comparisons between unlike objects or things that have similar characteristics to help communicate a concept or idea to your readers. In the previous chapter, Virginia Satir compares family life to an iceberg. Satir communicates the concept that a lot of activity in family life is hidden to most observers. She also compares a family to a "factory" that produces people instead of some consumable product. In an analogy, an item more familiar or more concrete to your readers is usually used to help them understand a less familiar or less concrete item: Planet earth is like a spaceship. An aircraft carrier is like a floating small town with a busy airport and a very powerful air force. Wetlands are like a giant sponge that helps soak up the storm surge of a hurricane. When making an analogy, be sure that you choose the comparison carefully and that the comparison helps illuminate your point. Otherwise, you may be accused of presenting a false or faulty analogy, which is a fallacy (a kind of error in reasoning). Analogies are used in several places in this book: Virginia Satir uses analogies in her article on families (p. 75). The chapter on language begins with a quotation by Robert MacNeil in which he makes an analogy between the language we speak and the clothes we wear.

All of the above methods of development can be used to develop body paragraphs or entire essays. Think of these methods of development as different strategies in your "organization toolbox." These strategies can help you expand your ideas in the most appropriate way, depending on your purpose and audience. In actual practice, writers tend to use more than one method of development in their essays and articles. Many of the articles in this book use mixed methods of organization.

Essay Assignments

Practicing Methods of Development

1. Write an essay describing two or three of your best friends. Use the body paragraphs to compare your friends to each other and to yourself. What are the similarities in backgrounds? What are the differences in backgrounds? What makes them your friends?

2. Write about your relationship with a non-family person who is very different from you. For instance, pick someone who grew up in a different part of the country or whose ethnic background is different from yours. It could be someone who is either older or younger than you. Describe the person. How would you define the relationship? Is it good or bad? What makes it that way? How have the two of you handled the differences?

3. Write an essay that discusses how today's fashions reflect membership in a group. Use your own personal experience to develop three examples of groups that tend to share a distinctive "look" or "fashion" that easily identifies them as members of a particular group. (Sorting people into groups based on the clothes they wear is a good example of the use of classification, one of the common methods of organizing an essay.)

The following essay was written in response to the preceding "Essay Assignment" # 3:

Student Essay

Fashion of the Times

Ricky Varela
Dr. Sabrio
English 1301
30 October 2002

Thesis statement and plan of development

1   If we look around the world and try to see how the world has changed, we would see too many changes to count. The one thing that has not changed is the fact that everyone can be classified in many ways; one of these ways is fashion. Fashion can describe the clothes that reflect how people feel, their cultural background, or what group they are associated with. Some of the fashion groups that I have noticed on this campus are the kickers, skaters, Goths, and the band geeks, just to name a few.

Topic sentence
Development of topic sentence

2   Here in this area, one of the most popular types of fashion is the country-western style. For instance, those who wear tight-fitting jeans with a belt buckle bigger than their head, cowboy boots, and a cowboy hat are

sometimes known as kickers. I believe the term "kicker" comes from the fact that these people enjoy walking through the fields and pastures kicking up cow patties, or shit. These people would come to be known as "shit-kickers," and I guess that it became too much to say the whole phrase, so it was shortened to "kickers." They usually reside on ranches or in rural areas and may have an accent befitting their country origins. These people may be gentle but sometimes lack the street-smart abilities of a big-city resident.

Topic sentence
Development of topic sentence

3   The group who wears their clothes five times the size of their bodies would sometimes be referred to as the skaters. Other parts of their wardrobe may be a baseball cap of some sort, a pair of tennis shoes, a skateboard, and a shirt with a picture or some catch phrase on it. The catch phrase may be of some skate company like Billabong or of a skateboard manufacturer. The clothing alone indicates that skaters have a different lifestyle from the kickers. These people tend to be more relaxed and not take life too seriously. The skater attitude is more happy-go-lucky than all others, and skaters feel positive about almost everything. The street-smart ability of this group would be the highest among all groups, but they might lack a great deal of book knowledge.

Topic sentence
Development of topic sentence

4   When looking through a crowd, one might observe that there are a growing number of people dressing in the style of the Goths. Before judging the appearance of someone in this group, one must understand some history. The Gothic people were a very religious group in the third century from Germany that migrated to Rome and soon threw the Romans out of power. The Goths themselves were soon overthrown and became outcasts. Today the Goths usually wear darker clothing, usually black; they may wear a cross of some sort. The dark clothing is usually a sign that they are trying to keep to themselves and not be very social. No, it does not mean that they are devil worshippers or involved in a cult that brainwashes all rules and knowledge of those they come in contact with. It simply means that they feel comfortable in clothing that is out of the norm. They do not want to be like anyone else but themselves.

Transition and topic sentence
Development of topic sentence

5   The final group, which I am a member of, is the band geeks. We are the entertainers of the world and enjoy doing what we do. We are always in the music building and hardly have any time away from school due to the constant practice and perfecting of skills. We usually have some type of clothing indicating that we have been a member of a certain band or organization dealing with music. A few examples would be the T-shirts that are given to all members of the marching band, the polo shirts given to the members of the jazz bands, and the shirts given to those who were members of a drum-and-bugle corps. One might also see us carrying a musical instrument along with us or a piece of music to practice on when we have a little free time. The thing about us is that many of us fit into more than one of these fashion categories.

People can be classified under more than one fashion group. These days people are so diverse that one day a person can be called a kicker and the next day be a skater. People are harder to stereotype nowadays. They go among others and are not criticized because of their fashion choices. We shouldn't judge people by what they look like, but by how they are on the inside. Jesse Jackson captures this thought with his statement, "Never look down on anybody unless you are helping him up."

Insightful Writing

At the end of the previous chapter we discussed ways to develop the ability to gain insights into a topic of study and share those insights with others. The great inventor Thomas Edison once said that genius is one percent inspiration and ninety-nine percent perspiration. That is, most of us are not geniuses and must rely on a lot of hard work and persistence. This is why you have probably heard many parents and teachers emphasize the importance of effort and "stick-to-it-tiveness" in whatever you do. In the long run, in almost every aspect of our lives, persistence and effort will carry the day more than genius will.

Another way to develop insights is to use some systematic method of inquiry into whatever topic you are studying. The long list of methods of organization that we just discussed can also be used as ways to jog your mind into developing more ideas and more connections on whatever you are writing about. Suppose you need to develop ideas about your high school. Why not quickly go through all the different methods of organization and do some focused freewriting? **Narrate** a story that captures your experience in high school. **Describe** some aspect of the school that you vividly remember. Give some **examples** of memorable experiences you had there. **Explain** some aspects of the school that your readers might find interesting. Recount the **process** by which something was done at your school. **Compare and contrast** your school with other schools that you may have attended or may know about from your friends. Discuss some of the **causes** of the successful programs of the school, and causes of some of the less successful programs of the school. What **effects** did the years at the school have on you and your classmates? Choose a particularly successful program and **partition** it into its component parts to discover why it is so successful. **Classify** the students of your graduating class into three or four groups based on some principle of classification that you or your audience may find useful. Give an extended **definition** of "high school" as you experienced it. What **facts and statistics** are most striking about your high school? What about graduation rates, dropout rates, the percentage of graduates who continue their education at a post-secondary institution? Where can you find this information? What **analogy** best helps outsiders understand your high school?

You could not possibly use all of the preceding information in one essay, but looking at, thinking about, and writing about something from multiple perspectives and different points of view can help you perceive and communicate flashes of insight that you may not have gotten if you had considered the topic from one angle only.

6 Language

It fascinates me how differently we all speak in different circumstances. There are very formal occasions, often requiring written English: the job application or the letter to the editor—the dark suit, serious-tie language, with everything pressed and the lint brushed off. There is our less formal out-in-the-world language—a more comfortable suit, but still respectable. There is language for close friends on weekends—blue-jeans and sweat-shirt language. There is family language, even more relaxed, full of grammatical shortcuts, family slang, echoes of old jokes that have become intimate shorthand—the language of pajamas and uncombed hair. Finally, there is the language with no clothes on; the talk of couples—murmurs, sighs—open and vulnerable language, at its least self-conscious.

Robert MacNeil, Wordstruck

Although Robert MacNeil writes about spoken language in the above quotation, his remarks apply equally to written language. To use MacNeil's analogy, all of us have had a great deal of experience with talking "blue jeans and sweatshirt" language, "pajamas and uncombed hair" language; and some of us have even used "language with no clothes on."

However, in educational and business settings, we are usually expected to talk and write "dark suit . . . with everything pressed" language. Because you are taking this writing course in a college setting, we have focused on "Standard Written English" or "Edited American English." This is the form of English that people are expected to use in most academic and business settings. Rightly or wrongly, fairly or unfairly, people are often judged by the language they use. If you use "blue-jean" language in a setting that requires "dress-up-suit" language, you may alienate your audience, making it much more difficult for you to achieve your purpose with that audience.

We also know that language is a very powerful tool that can be used for both positive and negative effects. You may have heard the following statement when you were a child: "Sticks and stones can break my bones, but words will never hurt me." Some believe that this statement is true, while others believe that words can hurt as much as—or perhaps even more than—sticks and stones. Unfortunately, words are too often used to put other people down or hurt their feelings. Fortunately, however, words can also be used to heal hurt feelings and build up positive relationships. We hope that, over the course of this term, you have become more sensitive to the power of language to heal and to hurt, to build up and to break down, to clarify and to confuse.

JOURNAL WRITING

Look carefully at the above quotation by Robert MacNeil. Give some examples in your own life of your different levels of speaking and writing in different circumstances. For example, how did your writing for a high school English course differ from your writing e-mail messages to friends? Or how does your speaking to a teacher differ from your speaking with a sibling or parent? Or tell about an incident in your life, or an incident that you witnessed, in which you or someone else used language that had either a positive or negative effect on the person(s) being addressed.

Before You Read

1. Before reading the following article, take a moment to read just the opening and closing paragraphs. Put into your own words, either by telling a classmate or by writing in your notebook, what you believe to be the main point or thesis of the article.

2. Look at the title of each subsection of the article. What do these titles tell you about the contents of the body paragraphs?

While You Read

1. As you read, underline or highlight key sentences. Remember, key sentences are often at the beginnings and ends of paragraphs.

2. What questions occur to you while you read this article? Write these questions down. What do you agree or disagree with most strongly?

3. As you read, write a summary of each paragraph and include your comments or responses to the material. How do the ideas in this article speak to you personally?

4. Meet with one or more of your classmates during class or outside of class and discuss the different reactions and responses that you and your classmates have to the article. How are your interpretations similar to or different from those of your classmates?

Readings

The following article, written by Penni Wild, discusses two of the most important uses of language—the ability to read and write. There are many degrees and levels of literacy, from the basic literacy of a child who is just learning how to read and write, to the advanced literacy of one who has developed reading and writing skills over several or many years. You may be surprised, even shocked, at the number of people in the United States (perhaps in your own community) and around the world who do not possess even the most basic literacy skills.

The Shameful Secret of Illiteracy in America

BY PENNI WILD

The word is not just a sound or a written symbol. The word is a force; it is the power you have to express and communicate, to think, and thereby to create the events in your life.

Don Miguel Ruiz

1 One New Jersey woman, "Maria," read at a third grade level. She held a job and fudged her way through everyday tasks without reading. When she would go to a restaurant, she would order what she knew was on the menu—a hamburger, salad or grilled chicken—or point to someone else's plate at the next table and ask "for what he's having." Maria even went so far as to keep her illiteracy a secret even from her husband of ten years. Because she could not read the mail, she would pretend that she forgot her glasses at work or say that she had been too busy to open the mail and ask her husband to do it. One day, they were walking past a shop window with a sign in it. As they looked at the display, the husband suddenly realized that his wife could not read. Maria was embarrassed and humiliated. But she sought help and now reads, works on a computer and teaches others to read.

2 In 2002, before the Subcommittee on Education Reform Committee on Education and the Workforce, United States House of Representatives, actor James Earl Jones testified:

"92 million Americans have low or very low literacy skills—they cannot read above the 6th grade level. To be illiterate in America—or anywhere for that matter—is to be unsafe, uncomfortable and unprotected. For the illiterate, despair and defeat serve as daily fare. Can any of us who do know how to read really understand the sadness that is associated with the inability to read? Can we truly relate to the silent humiliation, the quiet desperation that can't be expressed, the hundreds of ways that those who cannot read struggle in shame to keep their secret? The struggle out of illiteracy . . . is still a part of the story of America."

3 Today, our nation faces an epidemic that is destructive to our future. The disease is functional illiteracy. According to the most recent National Assessment of Educational Progress (NAEP), it has overtaken one-third of America's children by the fourth grade—including two-thirds of African-American students and almost half of all children in the inner cities.

4   The basic definition of literacy is the ability to read and write. So the basic definition of illiteracy is the inability to read and write.

5   Beyond the basic definitions, there is significance in the shocking statistics about the functionally illiterate. What illiteracy means is that millions may not be able to understand the directions on a medicine bottle, or be able to read their telephone bill, make correct change at a store, find and keep a job, or read to a child.

6   Illiteracy has long been viewed as a social and educational issue—someone else's problem. However, more recently we have come to understand the economic consequences of the lack of literacy skills for America and American business. Illiteracy has a significant impact on the economy. According to *Nation's Business* magazine, 15 million adults holding jobs today are functionally illiterate. The American Council of Life Insurance reports that three-quarters of the Fortune 500 companies provide some level of remedial training for their workers. And, a study done by the Northeast Midwest Institute and the Center for Regional Policy found that business losses attribute to basic skill deficiencies run into the hundreds of millions of dollars because of low productivity, errors and accidents.

7   In addition, as reported in the 1986 publication entitled *Making Literacy Programs Work: A Practical Guide for Correctional Educators* (for the U.S. Department of Justice, National Institute of Corrections), one-half of all adults in federal and state correctional institutions cannot read or write at all. Only about one-third of those in prison have completed high school.

8   Evidence indicates that the problem begins at home. A National Governors' Association Task Force on Adult Literacy reported that illiteracy is an inter-generational problem, following a parent-child pattern. Poor school achievement and dropping out before completing school are commonplace among children of illiterate parents. The reasons for illiteracy are as varied as the number of non-readers. The adult non-reader may have left school early, may have had a physical or emotional disability, may have had ineffectual teachers or simply may have been unready to learn at the time reading instruction began.

9   Because they are unable to help their children learn, parents who can't read often perpetuate the inter-generational cycle of illiteracy. Without books, newspapers or magazines in the home and a parent who reads to serve as a role model, many children grow up with severe literacy deficiencies. Clearly, there is no single cause of illiteracy. Adults have many reasons for requesting reading help. Many are prompted by the need for increased levels of literacy in their jobs. Others may wish to read to a child, read the Bible or write to a family member for the first time. All express a hope for a better quality of life through higher levels of literacy.

10   According to Barbara Bush, "It suddenly occurred to me that every single thing I worry about—the breakup of families, drugs, AIDS, the homeless—everything would be better if more people could read, write and understand."

11   Let us all do what we can to make illiteracy not a part of the story of American today but a part of America's past.

Thinking Critically About the Reading

1. The article begins with a quotation by Don Miguel Ruiz. Read and think carefully about this quotation. Give examples of how words can "create the events" in people's lives.

2. Where is the article's thesis statement? If the author does not provide a thesis statement, develop one that fits the article.

3. James Earl Jones said that to be illiterate is to be "unsafe, uncomfortable, and unprotected." Give examples of how illiteracy can have these consequences.

4. What are some of the economic consequences of illiteracy in America?

5. How do you explain the fact that U.S. prisons have some of the highest levels of illiteracy in the country?

6. The author mentions some causes of illiteracy in paragraphs 10 and 11. What are these causes? What additional causes of illiteracy can you add to this list?

7. What can you do in your own immediate and extended family to promote higher levels of literacy?

8. Using a dictionary when necessary, define the following words in their appropriate context: fudged (1); illiteracy (1); humiliated (1); despair (2); fare (2); desperation (2); epidemic (3); functional (3); deficiencies (7); inter-generational (9); ineffectual (10); perpetuate (11).

Spanglish Spoken Here

JANICE CASTRO

1 In Manhattan a first-grader greets her visiting grandparents, happily exclaiming, "Come here, sientate!" Her bemused grandfather, who does not speak Spanish, nevertheless knows she is asking him to sit down. A Miami personnel officer understands what a job applicant means when he says, "Quiero un part time." Nor do drivers miss a beat reading a billboard alongside a Los Angeles street advertising CERVEZA—SIX-PACK!

2 This free-form blend of Spanish and English, known as Spanglish, is common linguistic currency wherever concentrations of Hispanic Americans are found in the U.S. In Los Angeles, where 55% of the city's 3 million inhabitants speak Spanish, Spanglish is as much a part of daily life as sunglasses. Unlike the broken-English efforts of earlier immigrants from Europe, Asia and other regions, Spanglish has become a widely accepted conversational mode used casually—even playfully—by Spanish-speaking immigrants and native-born Americans alike.

3 Consisting of one part Hispanicized English, one part Americanized Spanish and more than a little fractured syntax, Spanglish is a bit like a Robin Williams comedy routine: a crackling line of cross-cultural patter straight from the melting pot. Often it enters Anglo homes and families through the children, who pick it up at school or at play with their young Hispanic contemporaries. In other cases, it comes from watching TV; many an Anglo child watching Sesame Street has learned uno dos tres almost as quickly as one two three.

4   Spanglish takes a variety of forms, from the Southern California Anglos who bid farewell with the utterly silly "hasta la bye-bye" to the Cuban-American drivers in Miami who parquean their carros. Some Spanglish sentences are mostly Spanish, with a quick detour for an English word or two. A Latino friend may cut short a conversation by glancing at his watch and excusing himself with the explanation that he must "ir al supermarket."

5   Many of the English words transplanted in this way are simply handier than their Spanish counterparts. No matter how distasteful the subject, for example, it is still easier to say "income tax" than impuesto sobre la renta. At the same time, many Spanish-speaking immigrants have adopted such terms as VCR, microwave and dishwasher for what they view as largely American phenomena. Still other English words convey a cultural context that is not implicit in the Spanish. A friend who invites you to lonche most likely has in mind the brisk American custom of "doing lunch" rather than the languorous afternoon break traditionally implied by almuerzo.

6   Mainstream Americans exposed to similar hybrids of German, Chinese or Hindi might be mystified. But even Anglos who speak little or no Spanish are somewhat familiar with Spanglish. Living among them, for one thing, are 19 million Hispanics. In addition, more American high school and university students sign up for Spanish than for any other foreign language.

7   Only in the past ten years, though, has Spanglish begun to turn into a national slang. Its popularity has grown with the explosive increases in U.S. immigration from Latin American countries. English has increasingly collided with Spanish in retail stores, offices and classrooms, in pop music and on street corners. Anglos whose ancestors picked up such Spanish words as rancho, bronco, tornado and incomunicado, for instance, now freely use such Spanish words as gracias, bueno, amigo and por favor. Among Latinos, Spanglish conversations often flow easily from Spanish into several sentences of English and back again. "It is done unconsciously," explains Carmen Silva-Corvalan, a Chilean-born associate professor of linguistics at the University of Southern California, who speaks Spanglish with relatives and neighbors. "I couldn't even tell you minutes later if I said something in Spanish or in English."

8   Spanglish is a sort of code for Latinos: the speakers know Spanish, but their hybrid language reflects the American culture in which they live. Many lean to shorter, clipped phrases in place of the longer, more graceful expressions their parents used. Says Leonel de la Cuesta, an assistant professor of modern languages at Florida International University in Miami: "In the U.S., time is money, and that is showing up in Spanglish as an economy of language." Conversational examples: taipiar (type) and winshiwiper (windshield wiper) replace escribir a maquina and limpiaparabrisas.

9   Major advertisers, eager to tap the estimated $134 billion in spending power wielded by Spanish-speaking Americans, have ventured into Spanglish to promote their products. In some cases, attempts to sprinkle Spanish through commercials have produced embarrassing gaffes. A Braniff airlines ad that sought to tell Spanish-speaking audiences they could settle back en (in) luxuriant cuero (leather) seats, for example, inadvertently said they could fly without clothes (encuero). A fractured translation of the Miller Lite slogan told readers the beer was "Filling, and less delicious." Similar blunders are often made by Anglos trying to impress Spanish-speaking pals. But if Latinos are amused by mangled Spanglish, they also recognize these goofs as a sort of friendly acceptance. As they might put it, no problema.

Thinking Critically About the Reading

1. This article was written in 1988. Do you believe that the positive attitude toward Spanglish expressed by the authors is shared by most people in the United States? Why do you believe this is so? Do you think the attitudes of people vary according to geographical location and cultural heritage?

2. Have you had any first-hand experience with hearing or using Spanglish? Divide into groups of three or four and list as many Spanglish examples as you can in a three-minute brainstorming session. Compare lists with other groups. What are the four most common examples?

3. What are the current population statistics for Hispanic Americans? Do a search on the Internet to find the latest estimates of the "spending power" of Spanish-speaking Americans.

4. Americans have borrowed many words from other languages over the course of history. For example, the word *pajamas* comes from Hindi (major language in India) and the word *rendezvous* comes from French. Many, many words related to food are commonly borrowed (for example, sushi, burritos, quiche, fettuccini). How is the popularity of Spanglish different from this kind of borrowing?

5. Previous waves of immigrants from European countries such as Germany, Italy, and Poland often discouraged the use of their native language in favor of English. They wanted their children to be successful in their new country and felt that it would be bad to have them speak their "old world" language. What were the advantages and disadvantages of this strategy? Do you agree or disagree with this strategy?

6. What does the author mean when she says that Spanglish "is common linguistic currency wherever concentrations of Hispanic Americans are found"?

7. Using a dictionary when necessary, define the following words in their appropriate context: fractured (3); syntax (3); patter (3); melting pot (3); phenomena (5); implicit (5); brisk (5); hybrids (6); incommunicado (7); linguistics (8); lean to (9); tap (10); gaffes (10).

JOURNAL WRITING

Give as complete an account as you can remember about your own introduction to literacy. What do you remember about being read to before you began school? What do you remember about learning to read and write? Who were the one or two people who encouraged you the most to develop your reading and writing skills? What experiences do you have, if any, with learning to read and write a second language? How has your life been affected—positively or negatively, in school or outside of school—by your knowledge and use of language?

The angle at which this photograph was taken lets us see the library like a "fly on the wall." Pretend you are listening to the conversations and thoughts of the people, and that you can see the computer screens. Write a short paragraph describing the dialog, actions and thoughts of these people.

Explorations

1. Locate a website that ranks countries of the world according to literacy rates. What are the ten countries with the highest literacy rates? What percentage of the population of each of these countries is literate? What traits or characteristics do these top ten countries have in common? Where is the United States ranked? How would you explain this ranking? What are the ten countries with the lowest literacy rates? What traits or characteristics do these bottom ten countries have in common?

2. Do some research on the literacy rate in your city, county, or state. What is the literacy rate? What programs does your city or county have to help increase the level of literacy?

3. Locate a literacy volunteer who teaches adults how to read, or a teacher who teaches reading to elementary school children. Develop some questions and interview one of them about teaching reading, the rewards, the frustrations, the success stories, and any other points of interest.

4. If you are a parent with young children, or someone who has younger siblings, what have you been doing or what can you do to encourage reading in your home? Take an inventory of your home. What books are visible? What kinds of reading activities go on in your home? How

often do your children or younger siblings see you reading, both for your college courses and for pleasure?

5. What are some reasons why certain words become offensive? What personal experience have you had with offensive language being used against you? Or what situations have you witnessed in which offensive language was used?

Before You Read

1. Before reading the following article, take a moment to read just the opening and closing paragraphs. Put into your own words, either by telling a classmate or by writing in your notebook, what you believe to be the main point or thesis of the article.

2. Look at the title of each subsection of the article. What do these titles tell you about the contents of the body paragraphs?

While You Read

1. As you read, underline or highlight key sentences. Remember, key sentences are often at the beginnings and ends of paragraphs.

2. What questions occur to you while you read this article? Write these questions down. What do you agree or disagree with most strongly?

3. As you read, keep a written record of your summary of and comments on or responses to each paragraph. How do the ideas in this article speak to you personally?

4. Meet with one or more of your classmates during class or outside of class and discuss the different reactions and responses that you and your classmates have to the article. How are your interpretations similar to or different from those of your classmates?

The following article, "Language and Society," was written by Dennis Baron, a professor of English and Linguistics at the University of Illinois at Urbana-Champaign. Baron has written and spoken widely about language; he has published books and articles about language and has spoken about language issues on radio and television. This article was written to accompany the PBS documentary "Do You Speak American?"

Language and Society

BY DENNIS BARON

Language is a social phenomenon. In America—as anywhere—it's shaped by contact, conflict and incredible cultural complexity. Dennis Baron explains how.

Is e-mail ruining the language?
Can I be fired for speaking Spanish on the job?
Are we less literate than we used to be?

1 These questions reflect how language is a social phenomenon. Although many linguists believe that humans are genetically programmed to learn language, it takes social contact to flip the switch that makes us talk. So, linguists study not simply the sounds, grammars and meanings of the world's languages, but also how they function in their social settings.

2 Language varies according to the social structure of a local speech community. For example, American English has varieties, dialects that are subsets of the larger linguistic whole called English. Some dialects vary by geography: In the North, you put the groceries in a bag; in the South, you put them in a sack.

3 Language also expresses solidarity or group identity. Language can separate insiders from outsiders, those in the know from those who didn't get the memo, the cool from the pathetically unhip, and, in the case of the Biblical shibboleth, friend from foe.

4 Members of small groups such as families, couples, friends, roommates and work groups all give their language a spin suited to the group's interests and experience. Members of a profession develop a jargon, an internally efficient job-related shorthand that permits them to impress, mystify or stonewall outsiders. In simple two-person conversation, language may reflect power differentials: One person may take charge while the other plays a subordinate role.

5 We sometimes label the language of larger social groups a social dialect, with differences in pronunciation and usage based on social class, ethnic factors, contact with other languages, gender or age. Let's take a look at some issues in social dialects.

Ebonics Emerges

6 African-American Vernacular English (AAVE)— sometimes known as Black English or Ebonics— is used by many African Americans, particularly those from working-class or inner-city areas. Black English clearly differs from other varieties of English in its vocabulary, grammar and pronunciation, but simply attaching it to one population group oversimplifies a complex situation.

7 Many African Americans do not speak Black English; many non-African Americans who live in inner cities do. Complicating matters further, African American influence—music, fashion, language—on American culture is very strong. As a result, some white American teenagers from the suburbs consciously imitate Black language features, to express their own group identity and shared opposition to mainstream culture.

8 Many people—African American or not— look down on Black English as an undesirable or ignorant form of the language. Others see it as a proud and positive symbol of the African-American experience. A few political activists or Afro-centrists insist that Ebonics isn't a dialect of English at all but rather a separate language with roots in Africa. And many people accept Black English as an important social dialect but argue that its speakers must also master

standard English in order to succeed in America today.

9   The debate illustrates a larger sociolinguistic point. We *all* master several different varieties of our language, standard and less so, that we deploy depending upon social contexts. In unfamiliar social situations, we feel linguistically inadequate and "don't know the right thing to say." Yet we can pick up the lingo of a new context if we are exposed to it long enough.

Word Wars Between the Sexes

10   Gender differences in the use of English are subtle. Nonetheless, notions of men's and women's language use abound: Men are said to swear a lot, to be more coarse and casual. Studies claim that American women know more color terms and men know tool names; that women use more qualifiers and diminutives; and that young women are more likely than men to end a declarative sentence with a rise in pitch, as if it were a question? In meetings or other professional contexts, men are said to speak more than women and interrupt them more often. On the other hand, women seem to carry the burden in mixed-gender conversations.

11   Clearly, these stereotypes aren't very trustworthy. It's probably not so much gender as gender *roles* that influence linguistic behavior. As gender roles change, gender differences in speech frequently disappear. Women who work as mechanics know the names of tools, and men who paint and decorate have to know their color terms.

12   Gender roles change, but they may not disappear. For example, although the taboo against women swearing has eased, both men and women students still report some degree of discomfort when women swear in mixed company.

Department of Ms. Information

13   In the 1970s, the U.S. Department of Labor rewrote its extensive list of job titles to eliminate gender bias, making language less patronizing,

more accurate and inclusive—by, for example, replacing "stewardess" with "flight attendant."

14   The case of the missing "Miss" illuminates more change. For some time people sought an alternative to Miss or Mrs. that did not indicate marital status, a title that would parallel the masculine title Mr. "Ms." took root (after decades of failed starts) in American usage in the 1970s, pronounced Miz to distinguish it from Miss. Since then, Ms. has undergone an interesting shift. Many young women use it either as a trendy alternative to Miss, or to indicate an unmarried woman (widowed or divorced) of their mother's generation. It's a good example of what can happen when planners decide a word should mean one thing, but users of the language adapt it to mean something else.

15   Another interesting development in gender-neutral vocabulary is the rise of *you guys* as a new kind of second person plural in American speech. Even though *guy* is usually masculine, the plural *guys* has become, for most people, gender neutral—and can even refer to an all-female group.

Minority Report

16   Human history can be viewed as what happens when groups of people speaking different languages encounter one another. The result isn't always pretty: language contact can lead to mutual understanding but also social conflict. Although it's the speakers who unite or clash, language often symbolizes what unites or divides people—and linguistic minorities often find their right to use their native language severely restricted by laws requiring the majority language in all sorts of situations.

17   The United States is founded on diversity and difference. In religion and ethnicity, we are a composite people. However, when it comes to language, diversity tends to give way to one common language: English. And although the very title *Do You Speak American?* suggests the broadness of American speech, there have always been

Americans who feel that if you don't speak the "American" language, you may not really be an American.

18 Americans initially accepted French in Louisiana and Spanish in California and the Southwest territories, but soon began requiring English-only in all public transactions. Government policy initially eradicated Native American languages, but has recently switched—in an effort that may come too late—to try to preserve them and encourage growth. Similarly, depriving African slaves of their linguistic roots was one way of controlling them.

19 Language loss is common for immigrants to the United States. During the pre-World War I waves of immigration from non-English-speaking countries, it was common for second-generation speakers to be bilingual in English and the language of the land they came from, and the third generation to be monolingual English speakers, unable to converse with their grandparents. There is some evidence that the switch to English has speeded up since the 1960s, skipping the bilingual middle generation altogether. Parents are monolingual in Spanish or Hmong or Ukrainian. Their children speak only English.

20 American schools have never dealt comfortably with their non-Anglophone students. In the nineteenth century, bilingual schooling was common, particularly in the heavily German areas of the Midwest. As immigration increased, public schools shifted overwhelmingly to English as the language of instruction. The Americanization movement of the early 1900s reinforced assimilation to English, often punitively. But there was no concerted effort to teach these students *how* to speak English. It should not be surprising that in this sink-or-swim environment, many students simply sank: More than half of students dropped out at the height of the great wave of Eastern European immigration.

21 Teddy Roosevelt once warned that the United States was in danger of becoming a polyglot boarding house. Instead we became a nation of monolingual English speakers. Language teachers tell a joke: What do you call a person who speaks two languages? Bilingual. What do you call a person who speaks one language? American.

22 Immigration reforms in the 1960s brought an influx of speakers of Spanish, as well as Russian and a variety of Asian languages—yet English continues to dominate the United States. In the 1970s, court-ordered bilingual education attempted to deal with the problems faced by minority-language speakers in the schools. Ideally, such programs use the students' native languages to instruct them in basic subjects (reading, writing, math, science and social studies) so that they don't fall behind while they get up to speed in English.

23 Highly effective when done well, bilingual education has been controversial because many people fear the programs are designed to preserve minority language, not to teach children English. California voters recently rejected bilingual education in favor of English immersion programs. Supporters of bilingual education fear that this reduction in language support services signals a step back to the isolationism of the early twentieth century.

24 Americans will continue to face issues of assimilation and minority language rights. Opponents of immigration see the English language as endangered and call for laws to make English the nation's official language. Still, the U.S. Census has reported for several decades that English is spoken by 95 percent or more of U.S. residents. Although bilingualism may be on the rise, the children of non-English-speaking immigrants are abandoning their heritage languages, becoming monolingual speakers of English with record speed.

Sociolinguistic Short-Takes

25 • *Do people swear more today than they used to?* We have no way to quantify how much

people used to swear, or even how much they swear today. It would be fair to say that people today swear more in public (and on radio and television and in film) than they did in the 1940s or 50s.

26 • *Is the language of blacks and whites diverging?* Some observers worry that the social distance between whites and African Americans may be increasing, which could in turn lead to greater linguistic differences.

27 • *Is e-mail ruining the language?* Critics object that it encourages misspelling and grammatical errors, makes people lazy, and is impersonal and overly informal. Even so, standards for e-mail started to emerge as soon as it became common. E-mail programs come with spelling- and grammar-checkers, advanced formatting capabilities, and graphics and sound. Many e-mail writers want their e-mails to read as if they have been written by someone who knows how to do things right.

28 • *Where do language standards come from?* Language standards—ideas about correct spelling, usage, grammar, and style—emerge by consensus within communities of language users. In some countries, government offices or language academies devise language policy, draw up standards and attempt to enforce them. There are no such mechanisms for English, though teachers, editors, writers, and self-appointed experts serve as language guardians, transmitting ideas of correctness and attempting to secure their adoption. Despite their efforts, there is no single standard of correctness in English. Instead, there are multiple standards that emerge from fluid communication contexts.

29 • *Can I be fired for speaking Spanish on the job?* That depends. Federal courts frequently side with the workers' right to use any language they want, particularly when on breaks or talking privately. The courts also allow employers to specify the language to be used when employees deal directly with the public, and more than half the states have adopted English as their official language—a designation more symbolic than enforceable. English doesn't need the protection of being an official language: the number of English speakers in America is rising and will not decline anytime soon. No other language, including Spanish, is positioned to become the majority national language. However, designation of English as official can put a chill on the use of other languages. In a period of increased globalization, a knowledge of the world's languages should help rather than hurt the U.S. position among the nations of the world.

30 • *Are literacy rates really too low?* We all agree that literacy—the ability to read and write—is one of the most important things that people need to succeed. Yet as experts disagree over how to define and measure literacy, the stakes have gone up. Is a high-school education enough? Can we say that a given score on a standardized test guarantees a comparable level of performance in real-world reading, writing, and calculating?

31 Every few years we have a literacy scare. Most recently, a report in the 1990s warned that almost half of American adults couldn't read, write, or calculate at adequate levels. At the same time, the vast majority of people interviewed considered their reading, writing and math perfectly adequate for their jobs and other everyday tasks. So, the assessment could simply mean Americans are too complacent about their literacy . . . or that testing doesn't really measure what we need to know.

32 After a report on literacy in crisis, politicians legislate more standardized testing. This forces schools to redirect their efforts to get

students past the standardized tests. Scores go up, things settle down for a while, then the next report comes out and the crisis cycle starts again.

33   Standardized tests have some ability to predict actual performance. But when schools devote too much time to test-taking skills and too little time to the actual literacy practices the tests are supposed to measure, actual progress is stymied. A more reliable measure of literacy might be the amount of time spent in and out of class on reading, writing, and numeracy. A 2003 report from the Brookings Institution indicates that two-thirds of American high school students spend less than an hour a day on homework. This suggests that students don't spend enough time on actual literacy tasks—and that is something that no test can address.

Suggested Reading/Additional Resources

- Chaika, Elaine. *Language: The Social Mirror.* 3rd ed. Boston: Heinle & Heinle, 1994.

- Wolfram, Walt, and Natalie Schilling-Estes. *American English.* Malden, MA: Blackwell, 1999.

Thinking Critically About the Reading

1. Where is the article's thesis statement? If the author does not provide a thesis statement, develop one that fits the article.

2. Paragraph 2 mentions dialects. What is a dialect? What dialect do you speak? As an example of a dialect difference between the northern U.S. and the southern U.S., Baron uses the words "bag" and "sack." What other examples can you think of in which people from different parts of the U.S. use different words to refer to the same item?

3. In paragraph 3 Baron states that language "expresses solidarity or group identity." Give some examples that support his statement.

4. In paragraph 3 Baron makes an allusion to the Biblical shibboleth. Look in the Old Testament, Book of Judges, Chapter 12, and explain the appropriateness of Baron's use of this reference.

5. In paragraph 4 Baron discusses jargon. What is jargon? Give some examples of the jargon of a particular profession, activity, craft, sport, or some other specialized activity that you know about.

6. In paragraphs 6 to 9 Baron discusses African American Vernacular English (AAVE). What is AAVE? Give some specific examples of AAVE.

7. In paragraph 7 Baron states that African American influence on U.S. culture is very strong in the areas of music, fashion, and language. Give some examples of this influence in each of these three areas.

8. In paragraph 9 Baron states that "we *all* master several different varieties of our language" that we use in different social contexts. What different varieties of language do you use, and what different situations? How does social context influence your choice of language variety?

9. In paragraphs 10 to 12 Baron discusses gender differences in the use of English. What differences between men's and women's language does Baron mention? What differences can you add that Baron does not discuss?

10. Since the 1970s there has been an attempt in the U.S. to eliminate gender bias in job titles. For example, "stewardess" was replaced with "flight attendant." Make a two-column list with gender-specific job titles in the left column and gender neutral job titles in the right column, as in "policeman" and "police officer." To what extent have attempts to use gender-neutral job titles been successful in the U.S.? What evidence can you use to support your position?

11. In paragraph 16 Baron states, "Human history can be viewed as what happens when groups of people speaking different languages encounter one another." Give some specific examples of these encounters. (Wars can be considered encounters.) Now think of some examples of encounters between people who speak the same language. Analyze all of your examples and those of your classmates. What conclusions can you draw?

12. In paragraph 19 Baron discusses language loss among immigrants to the U.S. According to Baron, what is a typical pattern of language loss among immigrants? Does this pattern reflect the experiences of your family?

13. In paragraphs 22 to 24 Baron discusses bilingual education. What is bilingual education? What experiences have you (or someone you know) had with bilingual education? What are some arguments in favor of bilingual education in the public schools? What are some arguments against bilingual education in public schools?

14. Paragraphs 25 to 30 contain six bulleted questions about language. Choose the three questions that you feel most strongly about and develop a response to each of these three questions.

15. The question in paragraph 27 asks whether e-mail is ruining the language. Make a list of ten nonstandard forms and usages that you have used or seen in e-mails. Focus on those forms and usages that would be inappropriate for use in a college essay.

16. Using a dictionary when necessary, define the following words in their appropriate context: literate (introductory questions); linguists (1); grammars (1); dialects (2); solidarity (3); pathetically (3); unhip (3); shibboleth (3); jargon (4); stonewall (4); subordinate (4); culture (7); Afrocentrists (8); sociolinguistic (9); deploy (9); contexts (9); lingo (9); subtle (10); qualifiers (10); diminutive (10); declarative (10); pitch (10); stereotypes (11); taboo (12); bias (13); patronizing (13); illuminates (14); second person (15); composite (17); eradicated (18); Hmong (19); Ukrainian (19); Anglophone (20); assimilation (20); punitively (20); Teddy Roosevelt (21); polyglot (21); immersion (23); heritage (24); quantify (25); consensus (28); globalization (29); legislate (32); stymied (33); numeracy (33).

1. What is jargon? Choose a profession, craft, activity, hobby, or sport. List and explain as many jargon terms as you can from the area you have chosen.

2. Look at question 12 in "Thinking Critically About the Reading." If the immigrant experience applies to you, your parents, or your grandparents, give an account of how you and your family met the challenges of learning English.

3. Question 13 above focuses on bilingual education in the schools. If you have had experiences with bilingual education in the schools, give an account of those experiences. Were they positive, negative, some of both? How would you evaluate the bilingual education program(s) that you experienced?

Explorations

For many of these explorations, the pbs.org website entitled "Do You Speak American?" (http://www.pbs.org/speak) contains some very useful resources.

1. Do some research on the dialect that you speak. What are some features of this dialect? Features include vocabulary words, pronunciation, accent, idioms.

2. One aspect of solidarity or group identity that Baron does not discuss is slang. Find a good definition of slang. Choose one group of speakers who use slang and discuss the slang of that group, using as many specific examples as possible. You might choose one of the following groups (there is some overlap of slang use between groups): college students, a particular ethnic minority, those in the military, skateboarders, surfers, valley girls.

3. Question 6 in "Thinking Critically About the Reading" focuses on African American Vernacular English (AAVE). Do some research on AAVE and develop a list of terms, sayings, accents, along with explanations, associated with AAVE.

4. Expand on question 9 above, about gender differences in language. Give at least three examples to support your statements.

5. Computers, the Internet, and various online activities have influenced the English language greatly since the 1980s. Focus on the jargon or the slang associated with computers and the Internet, and analyze your material. What conclusions can you draw?

Getting Started: Interviews and Conversations

Up to this point in the book, we have focused mainly on the reading and writing aspects of language. But in terms of the development of human language and our own language development from infancy, speaking and listening have always come before reading and writing. Some of the writing activities and explorations in this chapter require you to listen and speak, and to record what you hear and say. In learning more about language, dialects, jargon, slang, and literacy, you will have the opportunity to talk with people about their language experiences. One useful way to gather information is to conduct an interview in person, over the phone, or through e-mail.

One key to conducting a successful interview is careful planning. First, give yourself plenty of time to collect the information you need; do *not* wait two days before a draft is due before trying to set up an interview. Next, decide what information you need and who might best be able to help you gather that information. Then, contact the person or people whom you would like to interview and tell them about the overall purpose of the interview. That is, give them the "big picture." Knowing your overall purpose will help the potential interviewee determine if he or she can help you. Then set up a time for the interview that is convenient for both of you. Before the interview, develop and write down several questions that will help you get the information you need. It's usually better to ask open-ended questions that allow the interviewee to expand on answers. Try to avoid questions that require a simple yes or no answer.

After all the planning comes the actual interview. Be sure to thank the person for taking the time to answer your questions. Take your written questions to the interview and use them. During the interview, let the interviewee do most of the talking. Do not interrupt or argue; be tactful. Listen carefully and attentively, and take notes. If you would like to record the interview, get permission from the interviewee before you begin. Two advantages of an e-mail interview are that you have a written record of the interview and you are not limited to a face-to-face meeting. During the interview the discussion may go off in a direction that you did not anticipate but which may prove to be very useful. Be open to that possibility. If something is said that you do not understand, ask for clarification. At the end of the interview, thank the person again and ask for approval to contact him or her to clarify any information when you are drafting your writing assignment. You might even offer to give your interviewee a draft of the finished essay.

After the interview, expand your notes while the information is still fresh in your mind. Concerning the use of the interview information in your writing, use it as you would any other information, examples, and explanations. Most grammar handbooks cover information about the

Effective Interviews

Before the Interview

▶ Plan well in advance.

▶ Contact potential interviewee and give big picture.

▶ Set up interview.

▶ Develop open-ended questions.

During the Interview

▶ Use your written questions.

▶ Let interviewee do most of the talking.

▶ Be open to unanticipated direction of interview.

▶ Ask permission to record interview.

▶ Ask for clarification if necessary.

▶ Thank interviewee.

After the Interview

▶ Develop notes immediately.

▶ Use the interview information appropriately.

difference between direct quotations and indirect quotations, and how to document interviews in your list of sources at the end of your essay.

Gaining some experience as an interviewer has many practical advantages. You develop your organizational and interpersonal skills. You learn about conducting primary research and using it in an essay. You get experience in listening attentively and accurately. You get reinforcement that language is a complex web of speaking, listening, reading, and writing.

Essay Assignments

Writing About Language

1. In the quotation at the beginning of this chapter, Robert MacNeil mentions at least five levels of language usage and compares these levels with kinds of clothing: very formal (pressed dark suit), less formal (comfortable suit), language with friends (blue jeans and sweatshirt), language with family (pajamas), and language between couples (no clothes). Over the course of three or four days, keep a record of all the different kinds of language that you read (in college texts, newspapers, magazines), hear (on television and radio, and with employers, teachers, friends, family), and use (with employers, teachers, friends, family). Then write an essay in which you give examples of at least four of the five different levels of usage that you have used or have witnessed being used. Your essay should contain at least four body paragraphs,

each one focusing on a different level of usage that you have experienced or witnessed. Your purpose is to show that, whether we are aware or not, we all experience many different levels of language usage during the course of ordinary days. Your audience is your classmates and your instructor.

2. Think of a song that you have heard on the radio and that you like, one that contains a sentiment or message about life that you believe is important or worth knowing about. Write out the lyrics to this song. Also, look at the "op-ed" page of a newspaper. The op-ed page is "opposite the editorial page" and contains articles, commentaries, and essays by local or national columnists and sometimes guest essays written by local readers of the newspaper. If you do not subscribe to a newspaper, go to your college or public library. Most libraries subscribe to several newspapers. Read several op-ed essays to get a sense of the content of an op-ed column.

   Now take the song lyrics and rework or adapt them into an essay that might be suitable to appear on the op-ed page of a newspaper. You will probably have to add some examples from your own experience or the experiences of others to "flesh out" or develop more fully the ideas of the song. For example, suppose you choose a song that emphasizes the importance of making the most of every day that you are with your family members. Then your op-ed essay will use this major point as a thesis. Or perhaps you will choose a song that laments about being hurt in a love relationship. Your op-ed essay will focus on the same point.

3. Eliza Sporn, in *College Hill Independent,* has written:

   > Literacy is more than decoding words and stringing together sentences. It is even more than comprehending those sentences, forming them into meaningful narrative and reaching personal conclusions. Literacy is understanding the variety of forces that mold our lives. It is seeing these not as impersonal and unapproachable influences, but as factors we can understand and alter, if not fully control. We have power over our economic, political and social situations. We can change our lives and our communities. We can choose our goals and work toward achieving them. All of these forces are intricately tied to the power of the written word.

   Write an essay in which you discuss ways in which your own literacy has helped you understand "the variety of forces that mold" your life. How has literacy helped give you power over your "economic, political and social situations"? How has literacy helped you change your life and your community? If you feel that you do not have enough information to write about just yourself, you may include the experiences of one or more of your family members in your essay.

4. Choose one of the prompts from the Journal Writing or Explorations features and develop it into an essay.

5. All three articles in this chapter use literacy as a major focus. Compare/contrast the attitudes toward and treatment of literacy in any two of these articles. How are the attitudes and treatments similar? How are they different? What literacy challenges face your community (however you define it) over the next several years?

Student Essay

The following essay grew out of a journal entry written in response to the prompt about a student's introduction to literacy.

Reading and Writing

Brittney A. Dimas
Dr. Sabrio
English 1301-013
20 November 2007

Thesis statement 1   As a child, learning to read and write was one of my many goals. I remember waking up early on Sunday mornings and seeing my father reading a newspaper at the breakfast table. I also remember looking through the kitchen window and seeing my mother reading her favorite novel while relaxing on the porch swing. Sunday morning reading seemed to be a ritual in my family. I was constantly surrounded by books, and both my father and mother made it a point to read to me every night before tucking me in. During those nights, I remember wishing that I could read, as well. I knew school was just around the corner, and I looked forward to it greatly. For I knew that would be my time to learn to read and write.

Topic sentence 2   As I look back, I remember my first days of elementary school. I walked
Development of topic into a classroom filled with multicolored letters and words all over the walls.
sentence Of course, by that point I had seen letters and words many times before, but had no idea how to pronounce and read them myself. The first thing the teacher told me was "Do you see all those letters and words on the wall? You are going to learn what they stand for, and by the end of the year, you will have learned how to read." Immediately after hearing those words, I felt greatly intrigued by the idea of learning about letters and words. I soon found I would also be learning how to write, as well. This heightened my interest and suddenly I realized all the learning school had to offer. I felt as though I had found my place, even at my young age. I remember the first

lesson in class was to learn the alphabet and be able to sing it together with the class. Within a week, the entire class had learned the alphabet, and after only a few days more we were able to sing it as a class.

Topic sentence
Development of topic sentence

3   For weeks after that, we learned about each letter in the alphabet for three days at a time. Every time a new letter was introduced, each student received a letter book containing many different activities regarding the specific letter. For example, one book titled *The Letter G* contained an illustration consisting of both objects and animals beginning with the letter G. As a class, we were all required to label each object and animal correctly. This activity helped us learn more about the letter G and its different pronunciations, which I found evident in words such as grape and giraffe.

Topic sentence

4   After learning about each letter in the alphabet, we began to form small words, and after a short while we learned how to read them by pronouncing each letter, one at a time. Once we learned simple words, we were introduced to letters that came in pairs. When these letters were placed adjacent to one another, they made a specific sound such as ch–, ph–, and th–. After mastering adjacent letters, we moved on to learning about letters that remained silent under special circumstances. Silent letters in words were introduced by simple examples such as the silent B in comb or the silent K in knot. This lesson seemed to be the most challenging one of all, but after a few weeks of practice I began to improve. Soon, the class moved on to bigger words, and by the end of the year I had indeed learned to read.

Development of topic sentence

Restatement of thesis

5   For me, learning to read and write seemed to be a great challenge. I feel very privileged to have learned these skills at a young age. I believe it is from reading and writing that an individual can gain a great amount of knowledge. Even through this very assignment, I have realized the importance of learning to read and write. If I had not learned to read and write at a young age, I would have struggled greatly in my grade school years where both reading and writing are necessary in order to succeed. Through these skills, I have improved my speech. I hope to expand my knowledge of both reading and writing for years to come.

Insightful Writing

Whenever we apprehend or understand aspects of ourselves, others, or the world, we are gaining insights. Developing our abilities to gain insights is a lifelong process. We believe—and research has supported—that writing helps people develop critical and higher-order thinking skills, which in turn predispose people to get flashes of understanding, of insight, when interacting with others and with the wider world.

Insightful writing is the result of self-reflection, of interacting with peers and instructors, and of actively seeking different perspectives and points of view. Since our brains are rarely in the "off" position, we recommend that you keep a "writer's notebook" in which to write down ideas, perspectives, thoughts, connections, and flashes of insight about both academic and non-academic matters. And remember, your insights do not have to be brilliant flashes of genius along the lines of an Albert Einstein, a Marie Curie, or a Bill Gates. Your insights are what help you get a better sense of yourself, of others, and of the world.

7 The Nation

America is not like a blanket—one piece of unbroken cloth, the same color, the same texture, the same size. America is more like a quilt—many pieces, many colors, many sizes, all woven and held together by a common thread.

Jesse Jackson

The United States has too much "pluribus" and not enough "unum."

Unknown

Look at all the nations around the world. Look at a list of the most stable, the most economically solid, the most democratic nations, and you will almost certainly find that they all have something in common: a strong educational system from kindergarten through college. One of the main justifications for spending millions of dollars on a good public education system is that the payoffs for any nation are enormous: political and economic stability, an educated workforce, and people who are mindful of their responsibilities as citizens.

To be able to participate fully in local, state, and national conversations about what courses of action are best for our nation, we have to be able to understand, analyze, and evaluate all kinds of arguments, positions, situations, and political candidates. One of the best ways to prepare ourselves for the rigors of civic participation is to take advantage of the many opportunities to improve our abilities in reading, writing, speaking, and listening. Although you may not always see an immediate connection between your academic activities and your civic responsibilities, be assured that the critical thinking and creative abilities developed in this and other courses will prove to be very useful in your life as a citizen of this nation.

It has been said that there is strength in diversity. Do you agree or disagree with this statement? Write about how our country is either stronger because of the diversity present or weaker because of the diversity present. What evidence can you think of to support your opinion? Explain the second quotation above. Where have you seen the Latin words *E pluribus unum*? What do these words mean?

Before You Read

1. Before reading the following essay, take a moment to read just the first three paragraphs and the last three paragraphs. Put into your own words, either by telling a classmate or writing in your notebook, what you believe to be the main point or thesis of this article.

2. Go online and find an example of a mosaic. Print it and bring it to class. Reread the paragraph above that introduces this article and look carefully at the title of this article. Explain what the title "America's Religious Mosaic" might suggest. The title is an example of a metaphor, or comparison. What two things are being compared? How is this comparison appropriate?

While You Read

1. As you read, underline or highlight key sentences. Remember, key sentences often appear at the beginnings and ends of paragraphs.

2. What questions occur to you as you read the essay? Write those questions down. What do you agree or disagree with most strongly?

3. As you read, keep a written record of your summary of and comments on or responses to each paragraph. How do the ideas in this paragraph speak to you personally?

4. Meet with one or more of your classmates during class or outside of class and discuss the different reactions and responses that you and your classmates have to this article. How are your responses similar to or different from those of your classmates?

Readings

The following selection ("America's Religious Mosaic") appeared in *USA Weekend* on October 11–13, 1996. The author, Bill Moyers, is a noted commentator and journalist. Whereas Jesse Jackson, in the above quotation, compares the nation to a quilt, Moyers writes of a "mosaic." A mosaic is a

America's Religious Mosaic

BY BILL MOYERS

1 Something is happening in America that as a journalist I can't ignore. Religion is breaking out everywhere. Millions of Americans have taken public their search for a clearer understanding of the core principles of belief and how they can be applied to the daily experience of life.

2 The Gallup Organization reports that more Americans say religion plays a role in their lives today than did 10 years ago. Public confidence in both organized religion and the clergy has been renewed. Church attendance has held steady and in some instances—among teens, for instance—is up slightly. Another survey reports that "religion is a strong and growing force in the way Americans think about politics"—not only among the conservative activists of the Christian Coalition but also among Americans who describe themselves as politically moderate or liberal.

3 Religion is big news—a fact that was brought vividly home to me as I did research for *Genesis: A Living Conversation,* a new series that begins Wednesday on PBS stations. As the journal *Theology Today* notes: "People seem to want to talk about God. Recent novels, magazine stories and newspaper articles reflect a more serious attention to religious matters." One scholarly book, *A History of God,* remains on the popular bestseller list for more than a year. Another, *God: A Biography,* wins the Pulitzer Prize. The son of the Rev. Billy Graham appears on the cover of *Time* magazine as heir to his father's evangelical ministry. The media flock to cover tens of thousands of men—Promise Keepers—who gather in sports stadiums to renew their commitment to God, family and country. Buddhists and Roman Catholics launch dialogues to learn about each other's traditions.

Yearning for Certainty

4 We shouldn't be surprised by all this stirring. It's a confusing time, marked by social and moral ambivalence and, for many, economic insecurity. People yearn for spiritual certainty and collective self-confidence. In her classic study of ancient Greece, *The Greek Way,* historian Edith Hamilton writes that "when the world is storm-driven and the bad that happens and the worse that threatens are so urgent as to shut out everything else from view, then we need to know all the strong fortresses of the spirit which have been built through the ages."

5 For many people, this has meant turning—or returning—to the Bible as a guide through the chaos. I've lost count over the past year of people who have told me they have joined a Bible study group, sometimes one associated with a church or synagogue, often one improvised by laity. These Bible stories of struggle and redemption seem more than ever relevant to our storm-tossed time.

6 But there are new stories contributing to the religious ferment. They come from an amazing diversity of sources. Until this century, as *Encountering God* author Diana Eck reminds us, America's religious discourse was dominated by white male Protestant cultural conservatives

of European heritage. Their core values went largely unchallenged. Dissenting visions of America—of the role of women, of race, faith and language—rarely reached the mainstream. It is different now. The old "melting pot" is being supplanted by metaphors of "mosaic" or "tossed salad." America has become the meeting place for nearly all the living religions of the world.

7   When I first rode the New York City subway almost 30 years ago, I was impressed by the number of riders reading the Bible in Spanish. Now I am as likely to see someone reading the Koran. Islam is America's fastest-growing religion. Muslims now outnumber Episcopalians and Presbyterians, and soon may outnumber Jews. Along with Muslim minarets, Buddhist retreat centers and Hindu temples now dot our religious landscape.

8   Recently I interviewed Huston Smith, the renowned historian of religion. He told me that East and West are being "flung at one another, hurled with the force of atoms, the speed of jets, the restlessness of minds impatient to learn ways that differ from their own." When historians look back upon our years, Smith wrote in his classic study *The World's Religions*, "they may remember them not for the release of nuclear power but as the time in which all the peoples of the world had to take one another seriously, including our quest for meaning."

9   Because of this, some of the most interesting stories of our time are emerging in the intersection between the secular and the spiritual.

A New National Vision

10 One story is the attempt to find a new vision for America that has the authority and power of a religious vision but that is inclusive, not sectarian. We have seen what happens when a leader such as Nelson Mandela offers a vision so inclusive that an entire nation embraces a revolution that once seemed impossible. It happened in no small part because Mandela's old adversary, the white South African F.W. deKlerk, was moved

by his own religious faith to help fulfill that vision.

11 Watching their cooperation in the emergence of the new South Africa, I am reminded that at its best, religion's great accomplishment has been to create social bonds based on justice and mutual respect.

12 This doesn't mean we have to relinquish our distinctive traditions in what Diana Eck calls "an undifferentiating twilight where all cats are gray." Instead, in a democracy like ours, "we are all invited to be ourselves and yet to be engaged in critical and self-critical encounters with others as persons of faith."

13 Here is the dilemma: America strives to be a home to the world's religions in accordance with the dictates of democracy. Can a pluralistic America avoid the bitter fruits of religion—intolerance, ignorance and murderous fanaticism—that have occurred throughout history when faith is used as a wedge to drive people apart? How can I hold *my* truth to be *the* truth when so many others see truth so differently? When I put this question to Huston Smith, he answered: "We listen. We listen to what others say about their experience of reality. We listen as alertly as we hope they will listen to us."

The Lesson of Waco

14 As Smith talked, I remembered the Branch Davidian tragedy in Waco, Texas. Trying to assess in retrospect what went wrong, federal agents acknowledged that one factor contributing to the disaster was their failure to listen to the spiritual language issuing from the compound, garbled as it was.

15 Lawrence Sullivan, director of the Center for the Study of World Religions at Harvard University, was one of 10 experts asked by the Justice and Treasury departments to review the actions of federal agents. While the Branch Davidians obviously were not typical of American believers, government officials' handling of the crisis "may, in fact, reflect the marginal value

assigned to religion as a public matter," Sullivan wrote. He also worried about "the reduction of public religious convictions and actions to the realm of 'unconventional' behaviors."

16   He concluded: "What is disconcerting is the lack of knowledge about the historical role of religion in molding personal identities, shaping social identity, generating community and goals, transmitting values, sharpening critical moral sense, challenging the status quo and questioning authority."

17   Officials are not the only people who can be tone-deaf to religion. When it comes to understanding the role of faith in molding the lives, identity, values and moral sense of its adherents, most of us are religiously illiterate. The resurgence of religion in America, and the arrival on our shores of so many believers of different faiths, will test us. The scholar James Davison Hunter describes democracy as "the hard, tedious, perplexing, messy and seemingly endless task of working through what kind of people we are and what kind of communities we will live in." It requires good listeners.

18   The reward for listening can be great. I know. For much of the past year, in preparing the *Genesis* series, I have listened to people of different faiths talk about the great stories of the Bible's first book, stories that inspired three enduring world religions and the spiritual, ethical and literary imagination of Western civilization. We were filming the discussion for television, and I wanted a diversity of people from many stations of life and learning.

19   Our time together was notably enriched because we did not come from the same religion but from all three of the monotheistic faiths that trace their origins to Abraham: Judaism, Christianity and Islam. A Hindu took part, too, and a Zen Buddhist. Often we disagreed with each other, and sometimes the more we talked the more we disagreed. But a generosity of spirit prevailed in the circle.

20   While talking about these issues exposed our differences, it also brought us closer together—people who, for the most part, had been strangers. Sometimes we discovered that, in spite of our differences, we shared our deepest values with people who seemed most unlike us.

21   We hear a lot these days about "dialogue and democracy." Concerned about failing voter participation, nasty political campaigns and a declining sense of community, various organizations are convening thinkers and doers to address issues of civic renewal. Religion belongs in that conversation—religion as a wellspring of values reflecting different aspirations for our moral and political order; religion as the exercise of men and women to bring order out of the chaos of their lives; religion as the interpretation of experience itself.

22   At this moment between two centuries, as one millennium gives way to another, we Americans must debate what it means to be a nation. We must decide our identity as a people. How are we to write a new story for ourselves unless we learn to be open about our deepest religious beliefs with people not like us?

Thinking Critically About the Reading

1. Where is the article's thesis statement? If the author does not provide a thesis statement, develop one that fits the article.

2. What are some specific examples, or what evidence does Moyers present, that there is a renewed interest in religion in the U.S.?

3. What are some reasons for or causes of this renewed interest in religion?

4. What is one instance of one of "the most interesting stories of our time"?

5. What is a dilemma? What dilemma faces America?

6. What was the "Waco incident"? If you do not know, go online and find a brief recap of the incident. Print out the recap and bring it to class. According to Moyers, what were some lessons learned from the Waco incident?

7. What rewards did Moyers experience in preparing his *Genesis* series?

8. Toward the end of the article, Moyers mentions some indications that democracy is in decline. What three examples does he use?

9. How might religion help to alleviate some of these problems?

10. Using a dictionary when necessary, define the following words in their appropriate context: coalition (paragraph 2); ambivalence (4); chaos (5); synagogue (5); laity (5); ferment (6); discourse (6); metaphors (6); minarets (7); quest (8); secular (9); sectarian (10); adversary (10); pluralistic (13); retrospect (14); marginal (15); status quo (16); adherents (17); tedious (17); monotheistic (19); wellspring (21); aspirations (21); millennium (22).

Write a short fictional biography of the man in the photograph. Include details about his life such as occupation, age, marriage status, and birth place. Look at his clothes, jewelry, glasses, flag, etc. for clues. Why is he present at the demonstration?

Look back at your responses to the questions in the sections "Before You Read," "While You Read," and "Thinking Critically About the Reading." Choose one or two of your answers that you would like to explore in more depth and expand them into a journal entry of the length suggested by your instructor.

Explorations

1. Conduct a group discussion that considers the following quotation:

   "It is a well-known fact that we always recognize our homeland when we are about to lose it." Albert Camus (1913–1960), French-Algerian philosopher, author. "Summer in Algiers," in *Nuptials* (1939; reprinted in *Selected Essays and Notebooks,* ed. and tr. by Philip Thody, 1970).

2. Conduct a group discussion that considers the following quotation:

   "Nationalism is power hunger tempered by self-deception." George Orwell (1903–1950), British author. *Notes on Nationalism* (1945; reprinted in *Collected Essays,* 1961).

3. Conduct a group discussion that considers the following quotation:

   "A strong nation, like a strong person, can afford to be gentle, firm, thoughtful, and restrained. It can afford to extend a helping hand to others. It's a weak nation, like a weak person, that must behave with bluster and boasting and rashness and other signs of insecurity." Jimmy Carter (b. 1924), U.S. Democratic politician, President, 1976–1980. Speech, 14 Oct. 1976, New York City. Carter won the 2002 Nobel Peace Prize.

The following essay was written by Nobel Prize winning author Elie Wiesel and appeared in *PARADE* magazine on October 28, 2001, about six weeks after the September 11, 2001, terrorist attacks on the United States.

Before You Read

1. Before reading the following article, take a moment to read just the first two paragraphs and the last four paragraphs. Put into your own words, either by telling a classmate or by writing in your notebook, what you believe to be the main point or thesis of the article.

2. Recall where you were and what you were doing when you first heard about or saw on television the reports about the terrorist attacks of 9-11. What were your first reactions and the reactions of those around you?

While You Read

1. As you read, underline or highlight key sentences. Remember, key sentences are often at the beginnings and ends of paragraphs.

2. What questions occur to you while you read this article? Write these questions down. What do you agree or disagree with most strongly?

3. As you read, keep a written record of your summary of and comments on or responses to each paragraph. How do the ideas in this article speak to you personally?

4. Meet with one or more of your classmates during this class or outside of class and discuss the different reactions and responses that you and your classmates have to the article. How are your interpretations similar to or different from those of your classmates?

We Choose Honor

BY ELIE WIESEL

1 None of us will ever forget that sunny day in September when the United States was subjected to a man-made nightmare: a heinous terror attack unprecedented in contemporary history. It will remain shrouded in mourning in the violated memory of our country.

2 Would this terrible act drive us apart, I asked myself, or draw us together as a nation?

3 My wife and I were in a taxi in midtown Manhattan. We looked with disbelief at the gigantic clouds of smoke and ashes hanging over the lower part of the city. We listened to the radio and couldn't understand what we heard. Suddenly our hearts sank: Someone we love worked on Wall Street. Cell phones remained mute. At home, we found a message: He was all right.

4 Glued to television like so many others, we watched the first pictures. They were both surreal and biblical: the flames, the vertical collapse and disappearance of the world's two proudest towers. Many of us were stunned into silence. Rarely have I felt such failure of language.

5 I remember what I was thinking: "That's madness, madness." Two banal words, like an accursed mantra. Sheer madness. Terrorists wanted to die in order to spread death around them. They demanded neither ransom nor concessions. They proclaimed no belief and left no testament. But then what did they wish to affirm, negate or prove? Simply that life is not worth living? Some observers insisted that they were "courageous," since they wanted to die. I disagree: They wanted to kill and to do so anonymously. It would have taken more courage to live and explain why they had chosen murder. More questions, many of them,

came later: Faced with such immense suffering, how can one go on working, studying and simply living without sinking into despair? How is one to vanquish the fear that infiltrated our very existence? And how are we to console the families and friends of the more than 5,000 victims?

6   The pictures of missing victims, the sobbing of relatives, the farewell words on cell phones, the sight of hardened journalists weeping. . . Days and days elapsed, and the devastated site was still reminiscent of war-torn Europe in 1945.

7   I checked history books for a semblance of precedent for this terror. There may be one. In the 11th century, a certain Hasan-e Sabbah founded a secret small sect of assassins in Persia. Known as the Messengers of Death, they roamed around Islam clandestinely for years before fulfilling their mission. They killed people they did not know, for motives they themselves did not comprehend. Is Osama bin Laden a reincarnation of Hasan-e Sabbah? No. Those times and those violent "dreamers" are gone. The twenty-first century will not be theirs.

8   Why, then, the mass murder now? A human earthquake, it was caused by people whose faith had been perverted. There can be no justification for it. Can it be explained? Yes, by hatred. Hatred is at the root of evil everywhere. Racial hatred, ethnic hatred, political hatred, religious hatred. In its name, all seems permitted. For those who glorify hatred, as terrorists do, the end justifies all means, including the most despicable ones. If they could, fanatics of violence would slaughter all those who do not adhere to their ideological or religious principles. But this they cannot achieve and so they resort to simply arousing fear, the goal of terrorists since they emerged in history.

9   Only this time, they failed. The American people reacted not with fear and resignation but with anger and resolve. Here and there it was misguided and misdirected: Individual Muslims were assaulted and humiliated. That was and is

wrong. Collective blame is unwarranted and unjust. Islam is one of the world's great religions and most of its believers in our country are good and decent citizens. That had to be said and our leaders said it.

10   On the highest level of government, President Bush immediately charted the right path to follow by declaring war against terrorist leaders and all those who harbor and aid them. His address before the joint session of Congress made the American people experience a moment of greatness. The Senate and the House made us proud. Democrats and Republicans spoke with one voice. The White House, the State Department, the Pentagon lost no time in preparing for the battle to come. In a very short while, our entire nation and its allies were mobilized to wage a new world war whose aims are to identify, uproot, disarm and apprehend all those who were and are directly, or indirectly, linked to terrorist practitioners of mass murder.

11   One thing is clear: By their magnitude as well as by their senselessness, the terrorist atrocities constitute a watershed. Yes, life will go back to normal; it always does. But now there is a before and an after. Nothing will be the same. The political philosophy of governments, the national economy, the concern over security, the psychology of citizens, the weight of comradeship and hope: Everything has changed. One will not, as before, take a plane without considering the possibility of sabotage. Nor will one look at his or her neighbors without suspicion. We may never visit Lower Manhattan without pangs of sadness; we all know of someone who perished simply because he or she was there.

12   But the American people did not bend. Never have they been more motivated, more generous. Their behavior was praised the world over. Instead of trying to save themselves, men and women, young and old, ran to Ground Zero to offer assistance. Some stood in line for hours to donate blood. Hundreds of thousands

of sandwiches, sodas and mineral waters were distributed. Those who were evacuated from their buildings were offered food and shelter by neighbors and strangers alike. Rudy Giuliani, the most admired New Yorker of the day, appealed in vain over radio and television for volunteers to stay away; they kept coming. And then, one had to see the outpouring of affection and gratitude toward policemen and firefighters to believe it.

13 And so, the terrorists achieved the opposite of what they wanted. They moved people to transcend themselves and choose that which is noble in man. For in the end, it is always a matter of choice. Even when faced with the murderous madness of criminals, and in the presence of the silent agony of their victims, it is incumbent upon us to choose between escape and solidarity, shame and honor. The terrorists have chosen shame. We choose honor.

14 I belong to a generation that thinks it knows all that is possible to know about the thousand manners of dying but not about the best way of fighting death. And I know that every death is unjust, that the death of every innocent person turns me into a question mark. Human beings are defined by their solidarity with others, especially when the others are threatened and wounded. Alone, I am on the edge of despair. But God alone is alone. Man is not and must not be alone. If the terrorists believe they can isolate their living targets by condemning them to fear and sadness, they are mistaken. Americans have never been as united.

15 Nor has our hope been as profound and as irresistibly contagious.

Thinking Critically About the Reading

1. Where is the author's thesis statement? If the author does not provide a thesis statement, develop one that fits the essay.

2. Wiesel describes the television pictures of the September 11 attacks as "surreal and biblical" (paragraph 4). Explain as fully as possible what you think he means here.

3. What are some possible answers to the three questions posed by Wiesel in paragraph 5?

4. What historical precedent does Wiesel suggest for the September 11 terrorist attacks on the United States?

5. How does Wiesel briefly explain the terrorist attacks on the United States?

6. What were the "misguided and misdirected" (paragraph 9) reactions by some Americans to the September 11 terrorist attacks?

7. Wiesel writes that, after the attacks, "Everything has changed" (paragraph 11). In what way(s) have the attacks affected you, your family, and your community?

8. What kinds of American behavior were praiseworthy during and after the attacks?

9. Use the Internet or some other source to learn more about author Elie Wiesel. Print out the information and bring it to class. How does this knowledge affect your understanding of the essay, especially paragraphs 14 and 15?

10. Using a dictionary when necessary, define the following words in their appropriate context: heinous (paragraph 1); unprecedented (1); shroud (1); mute (3); surreal (4); banal (5); mantra (5); sheer (5); ransom (5); concessions (5); immense (5); despair (5); vanquish (5); infiltrated (5); elapsed (6); devastated (6); reminiscent (6); semblance (7); precedent (7); clandestinely (7); reincarnation (7); perverted (8); justification (8); despicable (8); ideological (8); resignation (9); resolve (9); humiliated (9); collective (9); unwarranted (9); apprehend (10); practitioners (10); atrocities (11); constitute (11); watershed (11); sabotage (11); pangs (11); vain (12); transcend (13); incumbent (13); solidarity (14); profound (15).

Journal Writing

Look back at your responses to the questions related to the Elie Wiesel article: "Before You Read," "While You Read," and "Thinking Critically About the Reading." Choose one or two of your answers that you would like to explore in more depth and expand them into a journal entry of the length suggested by your instructor.

Explorations

1. Both Bill Moyers and Elie Wiesel discuss religion in their essays. Look back at these two readings and give examples of both positive aspects and negative aspects of people's interpretation of religion.

2. Although Christianity and Islam share a common Old Testament ancestor (Abraham), people professing these two religions have had many conflicts over the years, beginning in the early middle ages. Using the Internet or other sources, learn more about one or more of the conflicts that divide people professing these two religions.

3. Using the Internet or other sources, learn more about the similarities and common beliefs between Christianity and Islam. What common ground do these two religions share?

4. Find someone who practices the Islamic faith and interview the person. Try to learn and understand more about Islam.

Getting Started: Broadening Your Perspectives

A college education serves many purposes, one of which is to broaden one's horizons beyond one's narrow experiences in a local community. Because this chapter focuses on our nation, we will suggest ways to learn and understand more about national issues. You have probably already noticed that most colleges require students to take at least one course in U.S. political science and one course in U.S. history. These courses are often excellent ways to help students get the "big picture" of U.S. politics and history. Other easily accessible sources are national newscasts on network and cable TV stations and various Web pages, such as msn.com. More traditional sources of national information are big-city daily newspapers (such as *The New York Times, Washington Post, Chicago Tribune,* and *Los Angeles Times*) and weekly newsmagazines such as *Newsweek* and *Time.* Your college library probably subscribes to several daily newspapers and weekly news magazines.

Essay Assignments

Writing About the Nation

1. Write an essay that explores the basic differences between three religions of your choice. Focus on the fundamental differences and make a judgment about whether they can coexist in a democratic society. (A prompt that asks you to discuss similarities and differences between two or more items is asking you to do a comparison/contrast. Comparison focuses on similarities; contrast focuses on differences. If the particular points of comparison or contrast are not specified in the prompt, then you get to choose the points of comparison and/or contrast. We recommend that you focus on major similarities and/or differences, and discuss no more than three or four major points or topics, unless instructed to do otherwise.)

2. Moyers stated in 1996 that there was a renewed interest in religion in the U.S., but does this interest still exist today? Write an essay stating your opinion and supporting it with specific examples and recent data.

3. Moyers refers to the "Waco" incident. Write an essay stating your opinion regarding the actions of the U. S. government in the incident. Do you think the country has learned "The Lesson of Waco" during the subsequent years?

4. Write an essay that explores the impact of the events of September 11, 2001, on religion in the United States. Has tolerance for differences in beliefs increased or decreased? As a result of September 11, what have you personally learned about being an American?

5. Choose one of the "Explorations" from this chapter and expand it into an essay.

Student Essay

The following student essay was written in response to question number 2 under "Before You Read," in relation to Elie Wiesel's article "We Choose Honor," about the terrorist attacks on the U.S. on September 11, 2001.

Tragedy of September 11, 2001

Orry Arthur
English 1301
Dr. Sabrio
November 30, 2006

Thesis statement

1 For many years America had been coasting along without a direct attack of any kind on us. Then, on September 11, 2001, we were attacked on this soil. The feeling of disbelief was in everyone's minds, but as we saw the authentic television shots of what had happened, actuality set in. I was frightened, as we all were, but I felt that our president and other high-ranking government leaders would lead this country back, and we would be the same nation as we have always been.

Topic sentence

Development of topic sentence

2 When I heard the announcement over the intercom describing the attack on the World Trade Center in New York City, I was sitting in my second-period history class at H. M. King High School here in Kingsville; and I will never forget the sinking feeling that completely overtook me. I believe that every American had the feeling of immediately wanting to do something to protect this country and our faith in the American way. Every day as I saw plans unfold to search and clean up, I felt proud and had a feeling of restored and renewed faith in my country. The president and his administration declared a war on terrorism, with a goal of bringing Osama bin Laden and Al Qaeda to justice. Other terrorist networks would be prevented in the future and blocked by pressure from our government. Economic and military sanctions against any and all states and organizations harboring terrorists would be in force. Increasing global surveillance and sharing intelligence would become world-wide among U.S. allies. The North Atlantic Treaty Organization (NATO) actually agreed to endorse a "hot" war against terrorism in the world. My history class in high school closely followed the aftermath actions daily, for the entire semester, after this attack. I recall that the death toll came to about three thousand people with many more missing and unaccounted for.

Topic sentence
Development of topic sentence

3 I felt extreme sadness for the families who lost their loved ones in these events. During one hijacking, some passengers and crew members were able

to make phone calls, and each time they reported that several hijackers were aboard each plane. In one instance, I recall hearing that the crew and passengers attempted to seize control of the plane. They were unsuccessful, and soon after that attempt, the plane crashed. The black box recording from the airplane revealed that these actions had taken place. These hijackings caused widespread fear and confusion in the United States. The rumors and reports that followed this day made everyone aware of how precious life is and how it can be changed in one second. I wondered, along with everyone I knew, how such a thing could happen in America and how so many innocent lives could be lost.

Topic sentence
Development of topic sentence

4   Late in the day of September 11, I began hearing that terrorists had been involved in the attacks. I couldn't believe that anyone could have so much hate in their heart that they would be a part of an attack in which they would sacrifice their own life to kill others. Immediately, I knew our country would be up against terrible times when confronting such twisted terrorists as these. Terrorists, who are fanatics and radicals, are not clear-thinking personalities, and there is no way of knowing what they will do in the future. We are smart to have in place the terror alert system in the country to keep the nation informed of possible attacks. These warnings constantly remind us that we need to be aware of the world's feelings of being unsettled. America should stay on the alert and realize that modern times are turbulent for every country.

Topic sentence
Development of topic sentence

5   Search and rescue operations for the victims and military operations against the perpetrators began immediately. The Twin Towers of the World Trade Center were totally destroyed, and many other buildings at the site were destroyed or badly damaged. Toxic conditions from the explosions and rubble made it extremely dangerous for rescue operations. Seeing the firefighters, policemen, and other public figures along with numerous unidentified volunteers coming to the aid of the victims of this tragedy gave me added faith in fellow Americans. The respect and homage paid to everyone involved made me more confident that America is the greatest place on earth. The sensible and stable response to this tragedy gave everyone a feeling that thorough investigating and planning were taking place before any retaliation would be made. I think everyone was ready to take action against the people who had caused these attacks, and the diligent search for the perpetrators was imminent.

6   The attacks had major global political ramifications. They were denounced worldwide. The damage, both physical and emotional, will remain in our memories forever. This nation will never forget the lives lost on nine-eleven, and America will always be stronger and better prepared because of this nightmare. Our military came to the front to protect America and for what it stands. These feelings caused by these events are ones of a great sense of security and patriotism in stressful times.

Restatement of thesis

Insightful Writing

We probably all feel inadequate when asked to provide insights into large, complex national issues. After all, you might ask, "What can my limited, local perspective add to this or that national debate?" First, an insight, even an insight into a national issue, is a personal flash of understanding or making a connection to help *you* understand the issue more clearly. Next, you may find that your voice, when joined together with the voices of thousands of others from small communities around the country, may find "traction" at the national level. Remember, too, that a number of solutions to national challenges began as local ideas and were implemented on a larger scale. Finally, the very activity of engaging in national debates, making connections among local, state, and national issues, makes more likely the possibility of an insight into a national issue from a local perspective.

8 The World

"I have enough to worry about in my own family and community. I can't be concerned with national affairs, much less world events. They don't affect me, and I can't influence them." This statement may have had some validity for many Americans before 1914 (the year World War I began). But in the twenty-first century—the age of instant electronic communication, of global economies, and of the United States' interactions with scores of countries around the world—global affairs affect us every day, whether we like it or not. The more we know about world affairs, the better informed we will be about making choices that affect us, our families, and our country.

The food we eat, the clothes we wear, the fuel we use to run our vehicles and the cost of that fuel, changes in the climate, immigration into the U.S., whether our family members or friends serving in the military will be deployed, the safety of travel, the jobs we have or seek: all these elements of our lives are affected to a greater or lesser degree by global affairs. Globalization—with all of its benefits, shortcomings, and challenges—is now a reality. How we react to globalization—beginning with reading, writing, speaking, and listening—may well influence our lives and the lives of those closest to us.

What do you think about America's role in the world? Should we try to help other nations with their internal problems, or should we concentrate our efforts on domestic issues? Or should we do some of both? How are you and other Americans affected by events that happen in other parts of the world?

Before You Read

1. Before reading the following article, take a moment to read just the first two paragraphs and the last five paragraphs. Put into your own words, either by telling a classmate or by writing in your notebook, what you believe to be the main point or thesis of the article.

While You Read

1. As you read, highlight or underline key sentences. Remember, key sentences often appear at the beginnings and ends of paragraphs.

2. What questions occur to you as you read this essay? Write these questions down. What do you agree or disagree with most strongly?

3. As you read, keep a written record of your summary of and comments on or responses to each paragraph. How do the ideas in this article speak to you personally?

4. Meet with one or more of your classmates during class or outside of class and discuss the different reactions and responses that you and your classmates have to the article. How are your interpretations similar to or different from those of your classmates?

Readings

Nobel Prizes are named after Alfred Bernhard Nobel (1833–1896), a Swedish chemist who invented dynamite. He was concerned about the potential uses of his invention to cause destruction and wanted to do something with his fortune to help humanity. Six international prizes are awarded annually by the Nobel Foundation for outstanding achievements in the fields of physics, chemistry, physiology or medicine, literature, economics, and for the promotion of world peace. Elie Wiesel, the author of the following article, received the Nobel Peace Prize in 1986.

When Passion Is Dangerous

BY ELIE WIESEL

A Nobel Peace Prize-winner explores the meaning of fanaticism

1 Fanaticism is all around us, and only we ourselves can stem it. That is because the hatred that underlies this ancient scourge is of human origin, and only human beings can trace its contours, measure its depth and realize its dangers before disarming it.

2 It flourishes today in lands near and far, and its victims are counted by the tens of thousands. Riots in Armenia and Azerbaijan, bloodshed in Yugoslavia, political convulsions in India, depredations against the Kurds in Iraq—all of these must be seen in the horrible context of a rising fanaticism.

3 Paradoxically, the current decade—the last of this century and this millenium—started rather well. A contagious current of liberty ran across much of the world, bringing *glasnost* and *perestroika* in the Soviet Union, the victory of Vaclav Havel in Czechoslovakia, the courageous student demonstration in China, the fall of the Berlin Wall, the growing strength of intellectual voices in Poland, Hungary, Bulgaria and Yugoslavia, the fall of dictatorships in Latin America.

4 Then came the disenchantment and the reversion to old patterns, reflected in the bloody repression in Beijing (which was accepted too fast by the so-called civilized world); the disturbing turnabouts in Soviet politics; the pardons of war criminals in Lithuania; the resurgence of anti-Semitism in Poland, Romania and Hungary; and the stirrings of racism in Germany, in France, in England and even in Scandinavia. What has become of the rising hope shared by so many? Was it, too, the victim of fanaticism on an international scale?

5 Forgive me if I expand a bit on the phenomenon of anti-Semitism—the oldest collective prejudice in history, one I've known since childood. Anti-Semitic fanaticism has passed through various phases over the centuries. The religious anti-Judaism of the Middle Ages has given way to a political anti-Semitism aimed at the State of Israel—although those who mount the attack may claim to be "merely" anti-Zionist. This political anti-Semitism is followed in its turn by an historical anti-Semitism that seems to me the most vicious and injurious of all. For historical anti-Semitism assaults the memory Jews hold of their own past suffering, as in the Holocaust. Its practitioners almost seem to become envious of those sufferings, first crying out, "The Jews are not the only ones who have suffered"; then, "Others have suffered more than the Jews"; and finally, "Others have been made to suffer by the Jews." Thus we are advised to speak more softly, to de-Judaize Jewish experience. If these new anti-Semites succeed in imposing their will, a Jew will no longer be able to speak of the Jewish tragedy.

6 Let us return to the problem of fanaticism in general by considering the question of whether fanaticism is nothing but a conviction pushed to excess—whether there exists a precise point at which the one is allowed to overflow into the other.

7 I would say that an idea becomes fanatical the moment it minimizes or excludes all the

ideas that confront or oppose it. In religion, it is dogmatism; in politics, totalitarianism. The fanatic deforms and pollutes reality. He never sees things and people as they are; his hatred makes him fabricate idols and images so ugly that he can become indignant about them. In his eyes he, and only he, has the right to put his ideas into action, which he will do at the first opportunity.

8   One can encounter fanaticism in the framework of all monotheistic religions—Christian, Jewish, Moslem—and extremism in any form revolts me. I turn away from persons who declare that they know better than anyone else the only true road to God. If they try to force me to follow their road, I fight them. Whatever the fanatic's religion, I wish to be his adversary, his opponent.

9   Does that mean I want to debate with him? My experience is that the fanatic hides from true debate. The concept of dialogue is alien to him. He is afraid of pluralism and diversity; he abhors learning. He knows how to speak in monologues only, so debate is superfluous to him.

10   Yes, the fanatic is passionate. But his passions can be dangerous. In religion, love is neither the problem nor the solution. The problem is exaggerated love, fanatical love, which turns religion into a personal battlefield that is dangerous to others and demeaning to the very faith it professes to cherish.

11   If religious fanaticism hides the face of God, so does political fanaticism destroy human liberty. In fact, there are some who, seeking to combat religious fanaticism, battle it with another kind of fanaticism that is equally evil. We cannot yield to fanaticism of any type. Fanaticism is a basic element of every dictatorship. In science, it serves death; in literature, it twists truth; in history, it tells lies; in art, it creates ugliness.

12   The fanatic never rests and never quits; the more he conquers, the more he seeks new conquests. For him to feel free, he must put everyone else into prison—if not physically, at least mentally. In doing so, he never realizes that he himself is in jail, as a guard if not as a prisoner. A fanatic has answers, not questions; certainties, not hesitations. In dictatorial regimes, doubts were considered crimes against the state. The philosopher Friedrich Nietzsche expressed it this way: *Madness is the result not of uncertainty but certainty.* Substitute the word fanaticism for madness, and the equation holds.

13   Now, on the threshold of the 21st century, it is our responsibility to combat the spreading cancer of fanaticism, which blocks the future of our children and ourselves. It must be constantly fought, because it leads to dehumanizing, degrading and contagious hatred. Nothing good, nothing worthy, nothing creative can be born of hatred. Hatred begets hatred. That is why we must keep it from our doors, send it away, repel it, disarm it—vanquish it before we even see the shadow of its shadow.

14   How can we do this? By celebrating, cherishing, defending the liberty of others—of *all* others. At stake is our cultural, ethical and moral future.

15   Let me conclude with a Midrashic story (of Rabbi Shimon bar Yohai), retold by the great Hasidic storyteller Rabbi Nahman of Bratslav:

16   A man is on a boat. He is not alone but acts as if he were. One night, he begins to cut a hole under his seat. His neighbors shriek: "Have you gone mad? Do you want to sink us all?" Calmly he answers them: "I don't understand what you want. What I'm doing is none of your business. I paid my way. I'm only cutting under my own seat."

17   What the fanatic will not accept, what you and I cannot forget, is that all of us are in the same boat.

Thinking Critically About the Reading

1. Where is the article's thesis statement? If the author does not provide a thesis statement, develop one that fits the article.

2. Wiesel states that the decade of the 1990s "started rather well." List three or four examples that he gives.

3. What are the translated meanings of *glasnost* and *perestroika* (paragraph 3)?

4. According to Wiesel, when does an "idea" become fanatical?

5. What does Wiesel mean when he says that "In science, it [fanaticism] serves death"?

6. What did the philosopher Friedrich Nietzsche say about madness? What is your understanding of this quotation?

7. In your own words explain the meaning of the story about the man on the boat.

8. Using a dictionary when necessary, define the following words in their appropriate context: fanaticism (paragraph 1); stem (1); scourge (1); depredations (2); paradoxically (3); disenchantment (4); resurgence (4); anti-Semitism (5); Zionist (5); Holocaust (5); dogmatism (7); totalitarianism (7); abhors (9); monologues (9); superfluous (9); demeaning (10); regimes (12); Midrashic (15); Hasidic (15).

What do the five Olympic rings represent? Do you believe that the Olympics help to promote the concept of world peace? Identify the flags of at least five countries.

A key term in Wiesel's essay is "fanaticism." Using this reading and a good dictionary, write an expanded definition of "fanaticism." Be sure to discuss the different kinds of fanaticism mentioned by Wiesel. As part of your definition, give two examples of fanaticism from Wiesel's essay and two examples not from the essay.

Explorations

1. Wiesel's 1992 article predates the events of September 11, 2001, by nine years. The dangers of fanaticism he describes were very real in 1992, but most of us were not aware of them. One could speculate that Wiesel could see into the future with his warning about fanaticism. Discuss with two or three of your classmates whether the warnings of "global warming" or "climate change" given by some scientists and environmentalists have any merit.

2. Engineer and architect Buckminster Fuller (1895–1983) spoke of "spaceship earth" and urged all nations to develop a global perspective about food, energy, and shelter. Learn about Fuller's life and inventions by doing research at the library and on the Internet. Give a report to the class about your findings.

Before You Read

1. Before reading the following article, take a moment to read just the opening and closing paragraphs. Put into your own words, either by telling a classmate or by writing in your notebook, what you believe to be the main point or thesis of the article.

2. Look at the bulleted, underlined subsections of the article. What do these subsections tell you about the article's major topics?

While You Read

1. As you read, underline or highlight key sentences. Remember, key sentences are often at the beginnings and ends of paragraphs.

2. What questions occur to you while you read this essay? Write these questions down. What do you agree or disagree with most strongly?

3. As you read, keep a written record of your summary of and comments on or responses to each body paragraph. How do the ideas in this essay speak to you personally?

4. Meet with one or more of your classmates during class or outside of class and discuss the different reactions and responses that you and your classmates have to the article. How are your interpretations similar to or different from those of your classmates?

The next essay, "We Are All Related" by Robert Moss, was first published in October 1992 to commemorate the 500th anniversary of Christopher Columbus's encounter with the indigenous people of the Americas in 1492. Columbus and his fellow sailors explored the world on a grand scale. Fortunately, we can explore the world much more safely and comfortably by traveling and even by taking advantage of the many opportunities in our own communities, opportunities such as reading, the Internet, television, taking college courses, meeting and getting to know people of different cultures.

The arrival of Columbus in this hemisphere led to the near-obliteration of the people already living here, but some of their most profound beliefs are still relevant today. In the following article Robert Moss analyzes some important aspects of Native American culture that hold relevance for today's world.

"We Are All Related"

BY ROBERT MOSS

1 No one is certain how many people were living on this continent when Columbus landed on an island he confused with the East Indies on Oct. 12, 1492. But everyone now agrees that Columbus did not "discover" America. It was here all along. The first inhabitants, ancestors of the American Indians, probably arrived from Asia at least 12,000 years ago, when the last Ice Age created a land bridge between Alaska and Siberia.

2 While Columbus often is venerated in our history books, he is no hero to most tribal peoples. For them, his voyages resulted in a sometimes unintended, but nonetheless real, catastrophe.

3 Before Columbus' time, Native Americans had domesticated a large number of wild plants, including maize, beans and squash; developed irrigation and terracing techniques; and invented accurate calendars. Some American Indians had developed thriving civilizations, while others survived in harsh environments as hunter-gatherers. Some Indian nations made war with each other, and warfare could be brutal. But others coexisted in peace.

4 Since Columbus' celebrated landing, native populations have been ravaged by disease, alcohol, heightened warfare, calculated acts of genocide, forced relocation and the destruction of their traditional ways of life. The survival of the American Indian over the past five centuries is remarkable in itself.

5 Native Americans continue to face tremendous challenges today. Their rate of alcoholism is approximately twice that of whites. Their unemployment rate is 45 percent on the reservations,

and an estimated 31 percent live below the poverty level. One study found that, among teenagers, twice as many Native Americans as whites attempt suicide.

6   American Indians continue to struggle to find a way to honor their traditional ways while living in a white man's nation. I think of a remarkable carving by Ben Thomas, a Mohawk sculptor, that shows an American Indian tearing his own body apart: Half of him, clad in a tuxedo, is grasping after a dollar while the other half is trying to cling to the old ways.

7   After years of urging Native Americans to take up our ways, however, we may have at last realized that it's time to take up theirs. This is not merely a venture into the exotic. As the year 2000 approaches, we are threatened by an environmental catastrophe and afflicted by a spiritual malaise. By providing a different way of looking at the world and what it means to be human, American Indian culture could be our salvation.

8   Many Indian nations have prophecies about the end of the world that resonate chillingly today. Tom Porter, a Bear Clan chief and spiritual leader of the Mohawks, related one: "First the elms will die. Then the maples. Then the fish will go belly-up in poison waters. The strawberries will no longer bear fruit, and then our world will be close to dying."

9   A Hopi leader, Thomas Banyacya, has warned: "We have a prophecy that a Gourd of Ashes will be thrown back and forth by the whites until there is a fire in the sky that no one can put out."

10   But while American Indian traditions offer many such warnings, they also offer us guidance on ways to restore our balance with the earth that sustains us. Native American cultures are rich and diverse—the Bureau of Indian Affairs recognizes more than 500 tribal groups—but they share an underlying view of the world and our relation to it. After talking with elders, clan mothers and spiritual leaders, I have discovered some values and beliefs they share that I believe could help our society.

Everything is spiritual. There is no exact 11 translation for the word "religion" in Indian languages, because in their traditions there is no clear divide between the sacred and the secular. Religious values are enacted in everyday life.

The late Jaime de Angulo, an anthropologist 12 who lived with the Pit River Indians of Northern California, observed: "The life of these Indians is nothing but a continuous religious experience. To them, the essence of religion is the 'spirit of wonder,' the recognition of power as a mysterious concentrated form of nonmaterial energy, of something loose in the world and contained in a more or less condensed degree by every object."

Spirituality can even be found in politics. "In 13 our ways, spiritual consciousness is the highest form of politics," says Leon Shenandoah, the chairman of the league of the Haudenosaunee, or Iroquois, whose Indian title is Tadodaho.

Hazel Dean-John, a Seneca clan mother, ex- 14 plains that the name for an Iroquois chief, Royaner, literally means "man of good mind." He is expected to have "a skin seven times thick" in the face of criticism, to control his own negative thoughts and feelings and to calculate the effects of his policies "down to the seventh generation."

"When a chief is raised up," Hazel Dean- 15 John adds, "he is told, 'Now you are poorer than any of us. Because you have lost yourself, you have become the nation.'" Among the Iroquois, a matriarchal people, it is the women who select the chiefs and have the power to impeach them if they fail in their obligations.

We are all related. The recognition that every- 16 thing is alive and everything is connected is at the heart of Native American spirituality.

Black Elk, the great spiritual leader of the La- 17 kota, has said: "Peace comes within the souls of men when they realize their relationship, their oneness, with the universe and all its powers, and realize that the center is really everywhere. It is within each of us."

18 "We have to respect all life, not just our own," Oren Lyons, an Onondaga chief, has said. The earth does not belong to us; we belong to the earth, and we have a sacred duty to protect it and to return thanks for the gifts of life.

19 *We must share the gifts of life.* The ritual year of American Indians, where the old ways are still alive, is a cycle of thanksgiving. This involves more than words. It means sharing with those in need. It means honoring life. It means working for peace and mutual understanding.

20 On the seventh day of the midwinter rites at the Cayuga longhouse near Brantford, Ontario, a speaker chants a prayer of thanksgiving to the Creator. He gives thanks for all that sustains us, for trees and birds, for wind and water. Nothing is taken for granted. Then, one by one, the Cayuga men start performing the *adowa* ceremony, singing their personal songs to the Creator out of their own truth.

21 Peace, in the American Indian conception, is not merely the absence of conflict. It is a positive force represented by the Iroquois as a great white pine, joining earth and sky, reaching to the four quarters to offer shelter.

22 *We must seek personal truth.* We all must engage in a personal quest for meaning, going beyond the demands of the ego to get in touch with the soul.

23 "When you respect yourself and treat yourself as sacred, you will respect all things and know all things are sacred," says Johnny Moses, a Nootka-Salish healer in the Pacific Northwest.

24 The first step is getting unclogged. Frank Fools Crow, a Lakota spiritual leader who died two years ago, compared the cumulative effect of negative emotions, addictions and bad habits to the buildup of rust and junk in an old pipe. "We must become hollow bones for the spirit to work through," he said. This may require solitude and sacrifice.

25 In the pursuit of self-knowledge, American Indian societies attribute extraordinary importance to dreams and visions. "The dream world," says a Native American healer in Santa Fe, "is the real world." The Iroquois believe dreams reveal "the secret wishes of the soul," on whose satisfaction the well-being—even the life—of the dreamer depends. Skeptics might be reminded that Carl Gustav Jung, the giant of modern psychology, was similarly guided throughout his career by personal adventures into "nonordinary reality" and that St. Paul was inspired by a vision to carry the Gospel to Europe.

26 The traditional wisdom of Native American cultures is that each of us has an obligation to seek our personal truth in the depths of our own souls. "The only thing of value in a man is the soul," an Inuit shaman, Inkinilik, told the Arctic explorer Knud Rasmussen early in this century. "It is the soul that makes us human."

27 To learn these lessons is to revive our sense of shared humanity with peoples of all races, cultures and conditions, to honor our obligations to the earth that sustains us and to remember that positive change begins with individuals. "If you want change to happen," said Freida Jean Jacques, an Onondaga clan mother, "begin by changing yourself."

28 Native Americans continue their struggle to change *and* to remember the old ways. As we celebrate Columbus Day and look toward the end of this century, we may do well to think of this Mohawk prophecy, as told by Tom Porter: "In the beginning, our Creator gave all the races of mankind the same songs and the same drums to keep in touch with Him, to keep faith. But people kept forgetting. In the fullness of time, the spiritual traditions of all the peoples—they are the same—will be united again in a great gathering of their secret leaders. And they will gain power to remake the world."

Thinking Critically About the Reading

1. Where is the article's thesis statement? If the author does not provide a thesis statement, develop one that fits the article.

2. What organizational device does Moss use to help readers follow the structure of the article?

3. How do some Native Americans relate spirituality to politics?

4. Among American Indians, what does the "cycle of thanksgiving" include?

5. What, according to some Native Americans, is "peace"?

6. What comparison do you find in paragraph 24? How does the comparison support the key belief indicated by the author in the first sentence of the pararagraph?

7. What importance do dreams have for many American Indians? What two examples does Moss cite of non-Indians who also believe that dreams are important?

8. What are the four major lessons that we can learn from Native Americans?

9. Using a dictionary when necessary, define the following words in their appropriate context: ravaged (4); calculated (4); genocide (4); malaise (7); culture (7); sustains (10); diverse (10); clan (10); secular (11); enacted (11); late (12); anthropologist (12); essence (12); condensed (12); matriarchal (15); impeach (15); obligations (15); ritual (19); mutual (19); conception (21); engage (22); quest (22); ego (22); cumulative (24); addictions (24); solitude (24); attribute (25); skeptics (25); psychology (25); shaman (26); prophecy (28).

JOURNAL WRITING

Choose two or three ideas from Moss's essay that particularly speak to you. Develop these ideas in relation to your life experiences.

Explorations

1. Traditionally, what are some of the achievements for which Christopher Columbus has been praised? What are some of the criticisms that have been leveled against Christopher Columbus recently?

2. How have Native Americans been depicted in books, movies, or television shows? What changes have these depictions undergone over the years? You may need to do some research to answer these questions.

Getting Started: Venturing Beyond Your Comfort Zone

As you may have already discovered, taking different college courses requires you to read and write outside of your "comfort zone." That is, you are asked to understand, analyze, and evaluate ideas that are unfamiliar to you and that you may not know very much about. This intellectual stretching may feel somewhat uncomfortable at first. However, just as you develop your strength and endurance by doing physical exercise, you develop your intellectual strength and endurance by engaging these new ideas through reading, writing, listening, and speaking about them.

As you delve into unfamiliar ideas, your frame of mind is important. Instead of thinking, "Darn, I have to read and study something that I may never need in my career," why not think, "Wow, I get to learn something new that may help me better understand myself, those around me, and the world!"

A few specific strategies may help ease the transition into studying and learning about new ideas.

First, try to relate new learning to what you already know. Build on the foundation you already have. Make connections between what you know and what you are studying.

Second, ask, "How does this new material speak to me personally?" Find ways to relate your own experiences to your topic of study.

Third, use reliable sources of information to supplement your study of new material. Reliable sources include your textbook, your instructor, your college librarians, and upperclass majors in the field that you are studying. Use the Internet cautiously; as you know, anyone can post just about anything on the Internet. You probably already know about the unreliability of the popular Wikipedia site, especially for doing research in college courses. In another chapter of this book we discuss ways to choose Internet sites carefully.

Finally, ask a lot of questions. Earlier in this book you learned about systematically exploring a topic by asking a series of questions, examining the topic from different perspectives.

Essay Assignments

Writing About the World

1. Probably the most horrific example of fanaticism that any of us can remember is the tragedy of September 11, 2001. Write an essay describing your reaction on that day. Where were you? How did you find out? What were your thoughts about the terrorists who planned and carried out the attacks?

2. Write about the impact of communication technology on our perception of the world. Has the world grown smaller? How does the extensive and continuous news coverage of world events change the way we feel about our role in the world?

3. Look through several issues of *Time* or *Newsweek* magazine, or locate a reputable online news source. Find an article about some aspect of political or religious fanaticism, or about a person or people who qualify as fanatics, using Wiesel's definition. Photocopy the article. Read the article at least twice, using active reading strategies. Write a 300- to 400-word summary of the article in your own words. Then show how this person or these people qualify as fanatics according to Wiesel's definition. Suggest some specific responses to counteract the fanaticism.

4. Find a person who is very different from you—culturally, ethnically, socially. Students from other countries are probably enrolled at your college. Try to find one of these international students. Develop a list of questions and interview this person, finding out as much as you can about this person's country and culture.

5. Look at the four major values/beliefs that Robert Moss discusses in his article:

   - Everything is spiritual.
   - We are all related.
   - We must share the gifts of life.
   - We must seek personal truth.

   In an essay with at least four body paragraphs, discuss the ways in which you have incorporated each of these values/beliefs into your life, OR ways in which you *could* incorporate these values/beliefs into your life.

6. You have probably heard, seen, or read about global warming or climate change. In order to learn more about some of the major issues surrounding this complex subject, do some reading and research, trying to sort out some of the major issues and arguments that have been used to support various points of view on this controversial subject. Write an essay in which you (1) summarize some of the most compelling arguments of those who believe that humans have caused global warming and that the world's nations must take immediate, decisive action to lessen or reverse the warming trend; and (2) summarize some of the most compelling arguments of those who believe that humans are not the main cause of global warming and that immediate, decisive action is not necessary.

Student Essay

This student essay was written in response to Essay Assignment 4.

Some Aspects of Indian Culture

Sue Williams
English 1301-012
Dr. Sabrio
October 25, 2007

1   One extra-curricular advantage of attending college is that students get to meet and learn from other students from all over the world. I was lucky enough to learn more about my English teacher, Tinu Sarma, who is a graduate teaching assistant finishing a master's degree in linguistics. She is from the state of Assam in northeastern India, and she agreed to let me interview her about India. During our conversation she spoke about what life is like for college students in India, customs pertaining to food, and practices concerning family, dating and marriage.

2   When asked about college life in India, Ms. Sarma mentioned that there are many differences compared with U.S. college life, but she focused on two. First, because the country's population is so large and because a college education at state and national universities is virtually free, the competition for admission to these universities is fierce. It would not be unusual for there to be one hundred applicants for each spot. Preparing for and taking national admissions tests is very tension-filled. Students who are lucky enough to be admitted to these universities are challenged with being in very large classes that are mostly given in a lecture format. Students tend not to interact with their professors. The second major difference is that most courses are two semesters long, and usually there is only one exam: the final exam at the end of the second semester. This high-stakes testing also adds to the tension and anxiety for students, especially as final exam time approaches.

3   As we might imagine for a country so populous and so diverse, there is no single food tradition in India. However, many Indians are vegetarians, not only because Hinduism, the major religion of India, does not sanction the eating of beef, but also because beef and other meats can be expensive for a large portion of the population. In Assam, where Ms. Sarma is from, people eat a lot of freshwater fish because of the large river flowing through this state. Food plays a large role in the lives of Indians. They show affection for others by offering them food. Ms. Sarma said that if one visits an Indian

home, one will almost always be fed. Guests are very important and are held in high regard. Ms. Sarma's mother used to say, "You never know if you are meeting God in disguise, so be nice to your guests." Guests are treated with great respect and honor, as shown through the offering of food. "If an Indian offers food to you," Ms. Sarma advises, "take it, because this is one of the ways Indians show that you are important to them." Ms. Sarma added that U.S. fast-food restaurants have made their way into India's urban areas. But at burger restaurants, diners are more likely to get a "maharaja burger," made of chicken, rather than a beef burger.

4   Ms. Sarma also spoke about the importance of family in India. Especially in smaller towns and rural areas, all adults feel responsible for all the children. So even when children are away from home playing with their friends, adults are always looking after the children and will not hesitate to correct them if they need correcting. Ms. Sarma said, "In India, family honor is extremely important. You are taught that from the very beginning, and God help you if you do anything that breaks family honor." Because there is this heightened sense of community, people rarely feel lonely and isolated. This is why Ms. Sarma says, "It breaks my heart to see people in homes for the aged here in the U.S. After all that they have done in their lives, this is where they end up. But I do understand that there is no other way for many families."

5   Because of the emphasis put on family honor in India, dating and marriage practices differ from those in the U.S. Many Indian teens and college students go out in groups, and usually the parents know everyone in the group. Even today in India many marriages are still arranged by the parents, who look for a suitable match for their son or daughter. In the past, the young woman had no say in the arrangement, but today that practice is changing. The couple is allowed to visit and go out together, and the parents do want their sons and daughters to be comfortable with the match. Marriage customs are influenced by the level of tradition practiced by the individual family involved. Still, however, Ms. Sarma added, "Parents are okay with their children having fun in groups, but are very wary of their children getting too serious too early."

6   I feel that I learned a lot about Indian culture from our interview, but Ms. Sarma cautioned me that India, with a population of over one billion people (more than three times the population of the U.S.), is extremely diverse in its people and culture. Life in the largest cities of India, such as Calcutta or Mumbai (Bombay), is similar to life in the largest U.S. cities, but very different from life in smaller towns and rural areas. Ms. Sarma had two final thoughts. First, if she had to recommend one film for Americans to watch to learn more about Indian culture, it would be *Monsoon Wedding*. Next, she stated that she feels very happy and fortunate to have the opportunity to study and live in the U.S.

Insightful Writing

Up to this point in *Insightful Writing* we have been reading, writing, listening, and speaking about ever-widening dimensions of our experiences. We began with learning and the self, moved to the family, then relationships beyond the family, then looked at language, then the nation, and finally the world. As an analogy, think of what happens when you throw a pebble into a small pond. When the pebble hits the surface of the water, concentric circles of ripples flow out from the point at which the pebble hit the water. Think of those concentric circles as ever-widening dimensions of our interactions. Notice too that when the ripples reach the edge of the pond, they rebound and flow back at various angles, intersecting with the ripples that were caused when the pebble hit the water. These intersecting patterns of ripples suggest the transactional, interactive nature of each aspect of our experience with the world around us.

We hope that, after you have become more aware of the multiple, ever-widening aspects of your experiences, you will notice connections, flashes of understanding, and moments of perception that lead to a better sense of who you are and your place in the world. These connections, understandings, and perceptions are your **insights**. You have probably already written about some of your insights, and you will certainly write about more as you continue growing into the best version of yourself.

We now move to Part III of *Insightful Writing*, which builds on what you have learned in Parts I and II and focuses on some practical aspects of writing: understanding, analyzing, and evaluating arguments; writing with sources; and writing in careers and professions.

PART III

Writing for a Purpose

Chapter 9: *Specialized Writing Tasks*

Chapter 10: *Argument and Persuasion: Influencing an Audience*

Chapter 11: *Research and Writing with Sources*

9 Specialized Writing Tasks

Examinations are formidable even to the best prepared, for the greatest fool may ask more than the wisest person can answer.

Charles Colton

During your college years and in your chosen career, there will be times when you have to write under the pressure and constraints of time. Whether you are taking an essay exam, writing an in-class essay, or taking a standardized test for graduate school admission, you will be required to produce an acceptable essay within a limited amount of time. To do this, you'll need to work as efficiently as possible.

You might object to such timed writings (or "fright writes" as they are sometimes called), pointing out, "My boss in the real world will never sit me down and order me to produce a completed written document in one hour." Perhaps not, but you will learn very quickly that college students and people in most careers and professions work against deadlines every day. Some of these deadlines can be quite demanding. In addition, people in virtually every profession sooner or later find themselves having to think and act quickly, without time to reflect and mull over alternatives.

What we are suggesting is that although writing under time pressure is not always the most effective way to write (especially if you are trying to write a complex paper the night before it is due!), it does give you practice in concentrating and focusing your energies on a limited task and in thinking and making decisions under pressure. Both of these abilities will serve you well in college and in your profession.

Think back to your own experiences with timed or in-class writing activities. How did you feel about these experiences? How did you handle them? What degrees of success or lack of success did you have? What was your most successful timed writing activity? What was your least successful? What would you do differently? What advice would you give to a friend who is facing a timed writing activity?

Essay Exams

You are most likely to encounter essay exams in your social science and humanities courses, such as history, political science, psychology, sociology, and English. We will divide our discussion into two parts: preparing for the essay exam and taking the essay exam.

Preparing for the Essay Exam

The following strategies are offered not as a substitute for study but as a means of organizing your study more effectively for better results.

You will usually have three sources of information from which to study for your essay exam: lecture notes, textbooks, and outside sources.

Lecture Notes Your lecture notes should summarize what goes on in class. You probably won't have time to write down everything your instructor says, so try to record the important points.

To help you remember the material that is presented in class, be sure to review your notes often. Ideally, you should read your notes after each class to make sure you understand what you wrote and to fill in any details that you did not have time to write during class.

PRACTICAL TIPS Taking Lecture Notes

Look for the following clues to identify the important points in a lecture:

1. The instructor may announce at the beginning of class what the main points will be.

2. The instructor may announce during the lecture which points are most important.

3. The instructor may summarize the more important points at the end of the lecture, or distribute a handout.

4. The main points of the lecture may be those that the instructor spends the most time talking about, or that are written on the board.

As you read over your lecture notes outside of class, look for connections between and among points in the notes. Take advantage of out-of-class study groups, online electronic bulletin boards, and chat rooms. Many times certain fuzzy points will be cleared up as you discuss them with classmates and get different perspectives. A word of caution is in order here: you may be tempted to save time by using "canned" (or paid-for) notes or note-taking services, but this shortcut is likely to backfire. A major benefit of taking notes yourself is that the act of physically writing the notes is a very powerful form of studying, engaging several of your senses: you hear the instructor speak, you see the instructor as he or she speaks and uses various visual aids, and you use your senses of touch and sight as you take notes. Most of these multisensory learning benefits are lost if you just get someone else's already-written notes.

If you really want to become familiar with your notes, you may want to rewrite your notes after each class, while making them more complete and detailed. This procedure takes time, but you will remember your notes better if you copy and expand them.

As you read over your notes, try to recognize the major points—the most important ideas. These may be the ones that recur most often.

Use an active method of studying. Ask yourself questions as you read your notes. Write these questions in the margin of your notebook or on a separate sheet of paper. You may even be able to anticipate one or more questions that will be asked on the essay exam.

Textbooks   Look for main points. We have mentioned repeatedly in *Insightful Writing* where to look for points of emphasis. These points usually occur at the beginnings and endings of the essay or article, of subsections, and of individual paragraphs. Textbooks contain similar points of emphasis. Look for these points in the preface, the introduction and conclusion of the book, and the beginnings and endings of each section or chapter. Some textbooks contain chapter summaries or outlines to help you get the overall picture before plunging into the chapters.

How does the textbook relate to the class lectures? Some instructors highlight and emphasize in their lectures certain points in the textbook. Other instructors provide in their lectures additional material not found in the textbook.

As in studying your lecture notes, study your textbook actively. The third best way to study your textbook is simply to read it. The second best way to study your textbook is to read, highlight, underline, and write down questions and comments about your reading. The very best way to study your textbook is to do all of the above and to talk about the main points with your classmates or your instructor.

Outside Sources   Some instructors may require you to read additional material that is not covered in the lectures and not found in the textbook. These outside sources may include parts of books, articles, or multimedia material; and they may be available at your campus library, course website, or learning lab. Instructors are usually impressed if you can relate this additional material to the lecture notes and the textbook.

After you have reviewed your three main sources of information for the essay exam, what else can you do? The first possibility is so obvious that many students overlook it or perhaps are too embarrassed to do it. Ask your instructor what will be on the test! Even if your instructor gives no specific information, you are no worse off than before you asked. Some instructors are willing to give specific information. Do they emphasize their lecture notes or the textbook on the essay exam? Will the question be broad, requiring that you pull together several main points, or will it be more narrow, asking about only one main point? Some instructors even allow students to look at test questions from previous terms.

What main points keep popping up in all three sources of information—notes, text, and outside sources? These main points may be the ones your instructor will ask about. Write down these points and talk about them with classmates. Remember, the more actively you study, and the more senses you involve in your study, the more successful you will be. Instead of lying on your bed and passively reading your study material, try organizing a study group at the library, your residence hall, or the student center. Try to anticipate several questions your instructor may ask, and then practice writing short essays in response to those questions.

Writing the Essay Exam

You have read, you have studied actively, you have prepared. The day has arrived. You go to class, get the exam, and panic. NO!

Here are some ideas for making the most of the time you have. We will discuss four strategies for writing an essay exam: budget your time; read, think, note; write your answer; and edit/proofread.

Budget Your Time   Before you begin writing, be sure to find out exactly how much time is allotted for each question. If you have to answer two questions in 50 minutes, then you should budget 25 minutes for each question. If you have four short answers to do, then budget 12 minutes for each question. One reason it is so important to budget your time is that most instructors would probably agree that it is better for students to answer all of the required questions—even if the answers are incomplete—than to give one or two full answers and leave some questions completely unanswered.

Read, Think, Note Read the question very carefully. As we tell our students, "When all else fails, read the directions." As you read the question, you will begin thinking of possible approaches to answering the question and of information to include in your answer. It's a good idea to jot down your thoughts on scratch paper. Get these notes down as fast as they occur to you. You will be surprised at how many notes you can write in a short time. Even five minutes' worth of planning is time well spent.

What exactly does the question ask you to do? Does it ask you to list, to discuss, to analyze, to compare/contrast, to discuss the causes or effects, to evaluate? You may even want to circle the key word or words in the question so that you won't lose your focus as you write your answer.

PRACTICAL TIPS | Key Terms in Exam Questions

As you read the exam question, underline, highlight, or circle key terms in the question. Then respond exactly as the question asks. Some key terms and their meanings follow:

▶ *Define:* to give the meaning or meanings of.

▶ *List:* to write down in some appropriate order.

▶ *Explain:* to make clear through appropriate details and examples.

▶ *Compare/Contrast:* to discuss similarities (comparison) and differences (contrast).

▶ *Analyze:* to separate a large or complex topic into its component parts and to explain each part in detail.

▶ *Discuss:* to consider or examine in detail. Because of time constraints, a discussion in an essay exam often focuses on just two or three topics.

▶ *Give causes:* to discuss the element or elements that produce a certain effect or result.

▶ *Give effects:* to discuss the results or consequences of a particular action or actions.

▶ *Argue:* to take a position or stand on an issue and support that position with reasons, evidence, and appropriate details.

▶ *Evaluate:* to judge or appraise something or someone. It is usually a good idea to give the standards or criteria that you are using to make the evaluation.

Write Your Answer   After you have read the question carefully, thought of ideas and approaches, and jotted notes, then you are ready to write your answer. If you are writing by hand, write as legibly as possible and with deliberate speed (not too fast, but not too slow). Don't be overly concerned with grammar, usage, punctuation, and spelling. Skipping lines as you write will leave you some room for making minor additions, neater cross-outs, and other minor changes. If you are writing on a computer, be sure to double space and save your answer frequently as you draft. Take advantage of a spell checker only when you have finished writing the entire answer.

Be sure to include specific details and examples, not just generalizations. Suppose, for example, you are writing an answer for an American history exam on the Civil War. An example of a generalization would be "The Union army had several advantages at the Battle of Gettysburg." A more specific, detailed statement would be, "The Union army had at least three advantages at the Battle of Gettysburg. They were led by officers determined not to be beaten again by Robert E. Lee. They were fighting in Pennsylvania, their 'home turf,' and they held the high ground." The second statement not only demonstrates your in-depth understanding of the material, but also sets up an easy-to-follow structure for the rest of your essay exam: each of these three advantages could serve as the topic sentence of a paragraph.

Remember, too, that if your essay response is longer than just one paragraph, you may want to include a very brief opening paragraph and a very brief closing paragraph. Your opening paragraph should introduce the main point or points you will cover in your body paragraphs.

In an essay or short-answer exam that includes multiple questions, we suggest that you begin answering the question that you know the most about. Beginning with your strongest answer will build your momentum and confidence and will eliminate panic-stricken, wasted time at the beginning of the exam.

Edit and Proofread   Leave enough time at the end of the essay exam to read over your answers one time carefully. You probably won't have time to make any major changes, but you will be able to make some minor modifications to your answers, and you should also be able to catch some oversights in grammar, usage, punctuation, and spelling.

One final word about taking an essay exam: Although you may be tired and want to leave the exam the moment you finish, get into the habit of using all of the time allotted to you. Instructors tend to take a dim view of essay exams that are turned in early and that contain under-developed answers or many careless oversights.

Sample Student Answers

We will illustrate here two essay answers to the same question in an American history course. These answers relate to an example used above. The question on the essay exam was "What advantages did the Union forces have at the Battle of Gettysburg?" The first answer lacks organization and contains an undifferentiated list of examples. The answer is not bad, but it pretty much gives back, in jumbled form, the material from the book and the lecture. Here is the first answer:

> The Union army had several advantages at the Battle of Gettysburg. The Union generals knew that public opinion was going against continuing the war because of recent Union defeats, so the generals knew they needed a victory. Union troops were better rested and did not have to march as far as the Confederate army. They fought a defensive fight, which is less difficult than an offensive campaign. Their flanks were strong and held together even under strong Confederate attacks. Their cannon fire was accurate and deadly. They had the advantage of going into the battle well supplied and well fed. When the major Confederate attack came, the Union troops stood their ground and poured volley after volley of accurate musket fire into the Confederate ranks.

Here is the second answer. Notice its organization and focus:

> The Union army had at least three advantages at the Battle of Gettysburg. They were led by officers determined not to be beaten again by Robert E. Lee. They were fighting in Pennsylvania, their home turf; and they held the high ground.
>
> The Union high command was desperate for a victory against the seemingly invincible Robert E. Lee. In the two previous major engagements in the east, Lee's army defeated Union General Burnside at Fredericksburg, Virginia, in December 1862, and crushed Union General Hooker at Chancellorsville, Virginia, in April–May 1863. Now, in the summer of 1863, the new Union commander General Meade and his now battle-hardened senior officers were determined to defeat Lee next time.

The second advantage enjoyed by the Union army is that it met Lee's army in southern Pennsylvania, its home turf. The Union supply lines back to Washington, D.C., were relatively short, and the people living in southern Pennsylvania welcomed and helped the Union forces with supplies and intelligence. The Union general staff also knew that if Lee won a victory on Union soil, public opinion might sway against continuing the war, and the U.S. might be forced to sign a peace treaty with the Confederacy. This would leave open the real possibility of a permanently divided country.

Perhaps the most important advantage of the Union troops at Gettysburg is that they held the high ground. Holding a strong defensive position, as the Union troops did, tends to be less difficult than attacking such a position, especially when the attacking force is outnumbered, as was the case here. The Union infantry forces were now battle tested, and their artillery officers used the high ground to their advantage. Although the Union armies sustained heavy losses during the course of the battle, their ranks held.

The Union forces had other advantages at Gettysburg, but these three especially helped turn the tide in favor of the Union at this crucial battle.

In-Class Essays

Although you are likely to meet essay exams in a wide range of social science and humanities courses, the in-class essay is most likely to be assigned in your composition class. Whether you have 50, or 75, or 100 minutes to write your in-class essay, you will benefit by using the four-step process discussed in the introduction and first two chapters of *Insightful Writing*. As you recall, the four steps are these:

1. Generating or preparing
2. Drafting or shaping
3. Revising
4. Editing and proofreading

Although these steps work best when spread out over time, you should be able to condense or "telescope" these steps into a shorter time frame.

Keep in mind that you will not have the luxury of time to reconsider major aspects of your essay, so it is important to plan carefully before you begin to write your essay. We suggest that you take the first five or ten minutes to generate and organize your ideas. Do this prewriting on scratch paper, or in a separate file for an online writing class. You probably will not have time to cover more than four topics in your in-class essay, so try to organize your ideas into two, or three, or four main topics. These main topics will become your body paragraphs.

Once you have generated and organized (or grouped) your ideas into two, three, or four separate topics, then you are ready to begin writing your essay. You will probably not have time to write both a rough draft and a final draft, so if you are writing by hand, be sure to write carefully and legibly. Most instructors will allow you to skip lines when you write, so that if you do have to make some revisions, you can use the blank lines that you skipped. Write revisions above the words that you crossed out.

As we said in Chapter 1, don't get bogged down trying to write the perfect opening sentence and paragraph. If you feel the least bit stuck, leave some blank space at the beginning of your essay and begin writing your first body paragraph. You may even feel more comfortable writing all of the body paragraphs first and then going back to write your opening and closing paragraphs. Obviously, if you are writing your exam on a computer, you will have the ability to easily move sentences and paragraphs from one part of the essay to another.

You may have a little time on in-class essays to do some limited revisions. You probably will not have time to do major organizational and content changes. You will, however, be able to revise for sentence quality and word choice (diction). Wait until you have finished your entire essay before going back to revise. (Be sure to answer all the required questions.) Look for oversights such as too many short sentences in a row, or a sentence that is so long that it is difficult to follow. Look for sentences that are unclear or awkward. If you are writing by hand and have to revise a sentence, just cross it out neatly and write the revised sentence on the blank line above it.

PRACTICAL TIPS | **Remember the DUCTT!**

Remember the **DUCTT** acronym for writing effective body paragraphs: **Development, Unity, Coherence, Transitions,** and **Topic Sentence.**

After you have spent some time revising, be sure to leave time to edit and proofread. By this time, you will probably be tired of looking at your essay, but take the time to read over your essay carefully. You will not be able to proofread your essay out loud, but you can read slowly, pointing to each word as you read it, mouthing the word silently with your lips.

Once again, we encourage you to use all the time allotted to you. We know that using the entire test period takes stamina and a strong will, but the potential benefits are worth the extra minutes you take with your essay.

Standardized Essay Exams

You may face another type of essay exam in order to advance to sophomore or junior status or to be accepted into one of the academic colleges at your university or a graduate program elsewhere.

All of the information we presented above for in-class essay exams and in-class essays will help you perform better on standardized essay exams. In addition, more and more states are moving toward competency-based instruction and insuring minimal levels of writing skills among students, and as a result you may be asked to pass a writing exam in order to graduate.

PRACTICAL TIPS   Evaluation Criteria for Standardized Essay Exams

Many standardized writing exams are graded or evaluated based on how well the essay meets established criteria or standards. Although the criteria for each examination vary with the exam's purpose, the following are basic guidelines by which you can expect all standardized writing to be judged:

▶ *Appropriateness:* the extent to which you address the topic and use language and style appropriate to the given audience, purpose, and occasion.

▶ *Unity and focus:* the clarity with which you state and maintain your main idea or point of view.

▶ *Development:* the amount, depth, and specificity of your supporting details.

▶ *Organization:* the clarity of your writing and the logical sequence of your ideas.

▶ *Sentence structure:* the effectiveness of your sentence structure and the extent to which your writing is free of errors in sentence structure.

▶ *Usage:* the extent to which your writing is free of errors in usage and shows care and precision in word choice.

▶ *Mechanical conventions:* your ability to spell common words and to use the conventions of capitalization and punctuation.

Some standardized writing exams might include general instructions similar to the following: "Be sure to write about the assigned topic and use multiple paragraphs. Please write legibly. You may not use any reference materials during the test. Remember to save some time to review what you have written and make any changes you think will improve your writing sample. The final version of your essay should conform to the conventions of edited American English."

Here are a few additional tips to help you prepare for a standardized writing exam: Most companies that administer standardized writing exams provide practice prompts for students. Take a practice exam; the experience is well worth the effort. Know ahead of time exactly what you can and cannot bring into the exam room with you: dictionary, food, water? Your campus testing center is a good source of information about standardized exams: how much they cost, where they are administered, and how to prepare for them.

Explorations

1. Using your campus testing center or counseling office, or test preparation books or websites, locate and list different kinds of advice and strategies for taking a standardized essay exam. Which of these strategies seem useful to you, either for a standardized essay exam or for your in-class essay writing in college?

2. Select several writing prompts from the sources listed in exploration 1 above and, individually or in groups, highlight key terms in the prompts that suggest what a student would need to know and what kind of essay a student should write in response to each prompt.

3. Pick a practice prompt at random from a study guide for a standardized essay exam, and practice doing a timed writing under test conditions. Ask your advisor, one of your instructors, or someone at your campus testing center to go over your essay with you. This activity will help you become familiar with the process of taking a standardized essay exam.

Insightful Writing

Instructors do not expect students to be brilliant every time they write an essay under time pressure. We have noticed, however, that a timed essay situation sometimes helps students to concentrate and focus their energies, resulting in an essay that is better than one or more of their out-of-class essays. These same energies of concentration and focus can help students get insights while doing timed writing activities.

Writing under time constraints also gives students experience in handling pressure and insight into how they respond to stress in the relatively safe environment of the classroom. Learning to think and perform under pressure will be useful in personal, family, and professional situations.

Think of different types of everyday situations that require quick thinking. On a personal level, for example, you may need to communicate clearly to a friend or acquaintance about something that might harm your relationship. In your community you may have to think quickly in responding to a teacher of one of your children, or perhaps to a city or county official about services that are not up to par. Maybe you would like to dash off a letter to the editor of the local newspaper about an issue on which you have strong feelings. In the workplace we can almost guarantee that you will sooner or later be put under pressure to get some writing done in an uncomfortably short period of time. This writing may be a memo, a report, a letter, a recommendation, or a proposal. Whenever you need to communicate quickly and effectively, you will be glad you have had experience writing under the pressure of time constraints.

10 Argument and Persuasion: Influencing an Audience

I argue very well. Ask any of my remaining friends. I can win an argument on any topic, against any opponent. People know this, and steer clear of me at parties. Often, as a sign of their great respect, they don't even invite me.

Dave Barry (born 1947), American writer and humorist

We have all either witnessed or been involved in an argument, a disagreement that often involves raised voices, uncomfortable confrontations, and, after the argument is over, hurt feelings and a sense that little or nothing was accomplished.

We may also know someone who, as in the quotation above, hates to lose any argument and who will do or say almost anything to "win" an argument.

However, when we write, read about, discuss, and analyze arguments in most academic and non-academic settings, we usually are not working with the kinds of arguments or arguers mentioned above. In professional, workplace, and academic situations, we argue not so much to "win" as to persuade, to call for action, to teach, and to learn.

In academic settings we learn to craft effective, well-organized arguments to take and defend a position on a controversial subject, and we read other writers' arguments to analyze their logic and determine whether we agree.

In non-academic settings we are bombarded with dozens of arguments every day as we read newspapers, magazines, or websites, listen to the radio, watch television, or even drive across town. Advertisements and commercials are very brief arguments that attempt to persuade us to buy a product or service (or perhaps not to buy a product, as in an anti-smoking campaign), or to vote for or against a candidate or a proposition.

Learning more about arguments and developing your ability to analyze arguments will bring many practical advantages. You will be able to get your point across more effectively and persuasively. You will be able to make more informed decisions about what to buy and whom to vote for. You will be able to make better decisions for yourself and your family, and you will be less likely to be taken advantage of by unscrupulous people who want something from you, such as your money or your vote.

JOURNAL WRITING

Think of several issues that you know something about, have some interest in, and on which you would be willing to develop an argument/persuasion essay. For starters, think locally. Perhaps your college or university has one or more policies or requirements that you do not agree with. Perhaps your town or city has one or more ordinances that you would like to see changed. Maybe there is something at your child's school that you would like to change. Perhaps the place where you work has a policy that you would like to see modified.

Develop a list of potential argument essay topics. The more you list, the more likely you will find one that you may be able to develop into an effective essay. Share your list with one or more classmates.

Readings

Here are two brief essays that take opposing sides on the issue of whether some kind of national service should be required of all able Americans. Both essays are adapted from the book *United We Serve: National Service and the Future of Citizenship* (2003). The first essay, by Robert E. Litan, director of the Economic Studies Program of the Brookings Institution, argues in favor of national service. (Both essays have been condensed to save space.)

The Obligations of September 11, 2001

BY ROBERT E. LITAN

1 Though one good reason for adopting universal service now is to respond to the military and homeland threat, universal service makes sense in other ways in this time of national peril.

2 First, universal service could provide some much-needed "social glue" in an embattled American society that is growing increasingly diverse—by race, national origin, and religious preference—and where many young Americans from well-to-do families grow up and go to school in hermetically sealed social environments. Twenty years ago, when America was much less diverse than it is now and is going to be, the editorial page of the *Wall Street Journal*

(of all places) opined that mandatory service would constitute a "means for acculturation, acquainting young people with their fellow Americans of all different races, creeds, and economic backgrounds."

3   Those words are as compelling today as when they were written. A service program in which young people from different backgrounds work and live together would do far more than college ever could to immerse young Americans in the diversity of our country. It would also help sensitize more fortunate young men and women, at an impressionable point in their lives, to the concerns and experiences of others from different backgrounds and give them an enduring appreciation of what life is like "on the other side of the tracks."

4   Second, universal service could promote civic engagement, which, as Harvard social scientist Robert Putnam has persuasively argued in *Bowling Alone,* has been declining—or at least was before September 11. Some who perform service for the required period may believe their civic responsibilities will thereby be discharged, but many others are likely to develop an appreciation for helping others that could change the way they lead the rest of their lives.

Third, young people serving in a civilian 5 capacity in particular would help satisfy unmet social needs beyond those associated with homeland security: improving the reading skills of tens of millions of Americans who cannot now read English at a high school level, cleaning up blighted neighborhoods, and helping provide social, medical, and other services to the elderly and to low-income individuals and families. Allowing individuals to delay their service until after college would enable them to bring skills to their service that could prove even more useful to society and thus may be a desirable option. But doing so would also reduce the benefits of added social cohesion from universal service because it would tend to create two tiers of service, one for those who don't go to college and another for those who do.

Finally, universal service would establish 6 firmly the notion that rights for ourselves come with responsibilities to others. Of course, the Constitution guarantees all citizens certain rights—free speech, due process of law, freedom from discrimination, voting—without asking anything of them in return. But why shouldn't citizens be required to give something to their country in exchange for the full range of rights to which citizenship entitles them?

The second essay, by Bruce Chapman, president and CEO of the Discovery Institute, argues against required national service.

A Bad Idea Whose Time Has Passed

BY BRUCE CHAPMAN

The Case Against Universal Service

1   Universal service never was a good idea, and it grows worse with time. It fails militarily, morally, financially, and politically.

For almost a century, universal service 2 has brought forth new advocates, each desiring to enlist all youth in something. Only the justifications keep changing. Today's justification is "homeland security." But is it realistic to suggest that youth who help guard a "public or private facility" (let alone those who stuff envelopes at some charity's office) are "shouldering the burden of war" in the same way as a soldier in Afghanistan?

3   I don't want to attach to Robert Litan all the customary arguments that universal service advocates have been promoting for years, especially because he states that a "reasoned debate about universal service before September 11 would have been unthinkable" (at least to him). Except in times of mass conflict, such as the Civil War and the two world wars, there has never been much of a reason for universal service. Still, the varied arguments for it need to be addressed.

No Military Case

4   Universal service is not needed on military grounds. We eliminated the draft three decades ago in part because the armed services found that they needed relatively fewer recruits to serve longer than conscription provided. As the numbers that were needed shrank, the unfairness of the draft became ever more apparent—and offensive. Youth, ever ingenious, found ways to get deferments, decamp to Canada, make themselves a nuisance to everyone in authority—and make those who did serve feel like chumps. Many of the young people who objected to military service availed themselves of alternative service, but no one seriously believed that most conscientious objectors were shouldering the burden of war in a way comparable to those fighting in the field. . . .

No Moral Justification

5   Trying to justify universal service on moral grounds is also a mistake, and a serious one. Morally, service isn't service to the extent it is compelled. Involuntary voluntarism is like hot snow. And allowing the pay to approach (let alone surpass) that available to ordinary workers of the same age performing the same tasks as the stipended and officially applauded "volunteers" stigmatizes the private sector. (The military recruit of today is sometimes called a volunteer only because he is not conscripted. His service is more commendable morally than that of some other paid employee because he is prepared to risk his life.)

6   Universal service advocates such as Litan are on especially shaky ground when charging that citizens should be "required to give something to their country in exchange for the full range of rights to which citizenship entitles them." This cuts against the grain of U.S. history and traditions. Citizens here are expected to be law-abiding, and they are called to jury duty—and to the military if absolutely necessary. They are encouraged (not forced) to vote and to render voluntary service—which Americans famously do. But to require such service before the rights of citizenship are extended is simply contrary to the purposes for which the country was founded and has endured. The Founders had a keen awareness of the ways that the state could tyrannize the people, and taking the people's liberty away to serve some specious government purpose unattached to national survival is a project that would horrify them. . . .

7   The way to get a nation of volunteers is to showcase voluntary service, praise it, reward it, and revere it. The way to sabotage voluntary service is to coerce it, bureaucratize it, nationalize it, cloak it in political correctness, and pay for it to the point where the "volunteer" makes out better than the poor soul of the same age who works for a living. Voluntary service blesses the one who serves as well as those to whom he renders service. Universal service would be civic virtue perverted into a civic vice.

1. What is the thesis of Litan's essay in favor of required national service?

2. What is the thesis of Chapman's essay opposing required national service?

3. List all the arguments in favor of national service in the first essay. What additional arguments in favor can you add to the list?

4. List all the arguments opposed to national service in the second essay. What additional arguments opposed to national service can you add to the list?

5. What is "civic engagement," mentioned in the first essay? Why does the author believe it is important? Give some specific examples of civic engagement.

6. More and more high schools and even some college courses are requiring service work or civic engagement as part of the educational experience. What experiences have you had with doing service work or civic engagement related to school or on your own?

Some Basics of Argument and Persuasion

In an argument/persuasion essay a writer takes a position or makes a claim on an issue about which there is some disagreement. The claim can also be called an argumentative thesis. The writer must support that claim with evidence and/or reasons why the claim is valid.

Some essay topics do not lend themselves to argument or persuasion. For example, an argument essay cannot be written about a matter of fact. "The capital of California is Sacramento" would not be a good claim for an argument essay because there is no disagreement about this statement. Nor would a matter of purely personal preference that has little or no effect on others be a good topic to argue about in an essay: "My favorite season of the year is spring." In making this statement, you are probably not trying to convince others to adopt spring as their favorite season. An essay based on your favorite season might make a good expository essay in which you explain why you like spring, give some insight into your personality, and perhaps include some appealing descriptions of past springs that you have experienced.

An argument essay often focuses on an issue about which people hold differing, often conflicting points of view. Also, an argument essay often focuses on an issue, such as a law or policy, that may regulate people's actions. A claim or argumentative thesis often (but not always) includes the word "should" or "ought."

Thinking Critically About Claims and Evidence

Look at the following claims or argumentative thesis statements. We have provided some evidence in support of and in opposition to the first claim. Working in pairs or small groups, consider the other claims below and provide evidence on both sides of each issue (pro and con):

1. First-year college students should be required to live in the residence halls. Evidence in support of the above claim might be that students who live on campus are more likely to use the campus's resources to help students succeed. A second bit of evidence might be that students who live on campus may identify and bond with roommates and hall mates and thus establish a support system. Evidence opposed to the above claim might be that many first-year college students are "non-traditional" students and already have families and homes. Other support for this position is that some students live with their parents in the town where the college is located and should not be forced to pay extra money to live on campus when they can live at home for free.

2. The college should provide more parking closer to classroom buildings than is now available.

3. College students who do not attend the college's athletic activities should not be required to pay the athletic activity fee each semester.

4. Drivers should not be allowed to use hand-held communication devices (such as cell phones) while driving.

5. Uniforms or coordinated dress should be required in public school classrooms.

6. College students should be allowed to design their own degree plans and should not be required to take any courses unrelated to their field of study.

Four Common Strategies to Strengthen Arguments

Whether you are writing your own argument essay or analyzing someone else's argument essay, it is important to know some of the common strategies used to get one's point across to the reader effectively. These strategies have withstood the test of time, having been used effectively in argumentative speaking and writing for more than two thousand years. Speakers and writers have used four basic strategies or "appeals" to get audiences and readers to agree with them. Depending on the situation and audience, speakers and writers usually emphasize one or more of the following strategies.

Rational or Logical Appeal   The first strategy and the one that is emphasized when students are learning how to argue effectively is the appeal to reason or logic, sometimes known as the rational or logical appeal. The Greek word associated with the logical appeal is "logos," which literally means "word," but here refers to the logical principles used in argument. When we argue, we hope that our readers are logical, rational beings like us. We hope that if we are reasonable, our readers will hear us out and give our argument serious consideration. The logical appeal is almost always the best strategy to use for a wide range of audiences.

Suppose, for example, you are arguing for an expanded, modernized animal shelter for your hometown. Logical appeals or arguments might be that the town has a small budget surplus, that the state mandates a minimal level of animal care for municipal animal shelters, and that the current shelter was built forty years ago and does not meet current fire and electrical codes.

Emotional Appeal   The second strategy is the appeal to our audience's emotions and feelings, sometimes known as the emotional appeal. The Greek word associated with the emotional appeal is "pathos," meaning "suffering." When we use the emotional appeal, we hope to evoke in our audience a feeling of compassion, of pity for our situation. If our audience feels sorry for us or for the subject of our argument, they might be more likely to agree with our position and perhaps do what we ask. In the kinds of arguments written and analyzed in academic settings, the emotional appeal is usually secondary to the logical appeal in carrying the weight of the argument. The emotional appeal, however, can be used in appropriate situations, such as when the speaker or writer has few or weak rational arguments. One area in which emotional appeals are used frequently is advertising.

Continuing with the animal shelter argument above, you might add an emotional appeal: You could describe the overcrowded, filthy, smelly conditions that currently exist in the pens. Or better yet, your emotional appeal would include taking the town council members on a tour of the shelter so they can see and smell for themselves the animals and their living conditions. Appeals to emotion often include the addition of visual dimensions to an argument. If you cannot take the town council members on a tour of the shelter, photos of the shelter's filthy, crowded conditions would strengthen your position.

Ethical Appeal   The third strategy is the ethical appeal. This is your attempt to establish yourself as a trustworthy person, someone in whom your readers can have confidence. The Greek word associated with the ethical appeal is *ethos,* meaning "custom," "habit," or "character." It usually takes time to build up one's ethical appeal, so this strategy may be difficult to use extensively during a fifteen-week academic term. Students can, however, build up their ethical appeal by doing good academic work: coming to class prepared, getting work done on time, being trustworthy, and showing commitment to doing the best work possible.

Continuing with the animal shelter argument, the extent of the ethical appeal may depend on who is making the argument to the town council. If the arguer is a lifelong town resident who has developed a reputation over the years for honesty, reliability, and fairness, then this person's arguments will probably be heard with a great deal of attention and perhaps with an inclination to accept the arguments. If you do not have this kind of established reputation, other ways that you can establish a strong sense of ethos include presenting yourself professionally, presenting facts and situations accurately, practicing strong interpersonal skills, and maintaining an even temperament.

Stylistic Appeal   Suppose you look at two argument essays on the same subject. Both argue for the same position, and both use similar argument strategies. The first essay is well organized and clearly written. The second essay's organization, however, is hard to follow, some of the language is inappropriate for the situation, and the essay contains proofreading and editing errors. You would probably be more inclined to be swayed by the first essay.

A well-organized, effectively written argument essay that considers the needs of its audience will almost always influence readers more positively than a poorly organized, sloppily written essay. The stylistic appeal is using the essay's "style," the way it is written, to further your purpose of influencing your readers. Earlier chapters of this text discuss many ways of improving your essay's style.

The stylistic appeal is not usually included among the preceding three traditional appeals, but it can be a very powerful strategy to induce your readers to accept your arguments.

Continuing with the example of the animal shelter, a presentation to the town council that is clear, well organized, and easy to follow is more likely to influence the council than a presentation that strays off subject, repeats itself, and is difficult to follow.

Looking at Different Perspectives on an Issue

No matter which side of an argument you choose to support, it is always a good idea to write down as many different perspectives on the argument as you can think of. We do this because most argument essays consist not only of presenting one's own side of the argument, but also responsibly considering and refuting opposing viewpoints. A useful way to develop this strategy, which is called *rebuttal,* is to use a "T-chart" in the pre-writing or idea-generating step of the writing process. At the top of the "T" is your claim or argumentative thesis. On one side of the T-chart will be a list of all the arguments supporting your claim, and on the other side of the T-chart will be a list of all the arguments opposing your claim. A T-chart for our sample issue might look something like this:

Claim or Argumentative Thesis: Our town should build a new animal shelter

Pro (For)	Con (Against)
1. Town has a budget surplus	1. There are more pressing needs.
2. Shelter does not meet current fire and electrical codes.	2. Building could be updated.
3. Number of animals has far outstripped shelter capacity.	3. Surplus animals could be euthanized.
4. Shelter is dirty and may potentially spread disease.	4. Ad campaign could be started for increasing the number of animal adoptions.
5. Shelter does not meet minimal state guidelines for animal shelters.	

Organizing an Argument Essay

Speakers and writers have used many different ways to organize argument essays, but we will suggest a basic organizational strategy to get you started. As you develop more experience and more confidence, you may want to modify this basic structure. A T-chart like the one used above will help you organize your essay more effectively. As usual, begin your opening paragraph with one or two sentences in which you orient readers to your subject. Then focus down on your narrowed subject and include toward the end of the paragraph your argumentative thesis statement or claim. This is your position on whatever issue you are arguing for or against. Often the claim of an argument essay contains the word "should" or "ought." For example, "The town council *should* build a new animal shelter for the town."

In order for your audience to be sufficiently oriented to your subject, you may need to give some background information so that readers are in a better position to evaluate your arguments. Whether or not you need a paragraph with background information will depend on your subject and audience. But if you do need such a paragraph, a good place for it is immediately following the opening paragraph.

After the background paragraph, you begin presenting your own evidence or reasons for taking the stand you take. One reason and accompanying support per paragraph usually works well. For example, the first reason for arguing for a new animal shelter is that the town has a small budget surplus this year. So a draft of this body paragraph might look something like this:

> One of the main reasons why we should build a new animal shelter is that the town has a budget surplus. All of our commitments to our citizens have been met in terms of city services. We now have the luxury of addressing the town's needs lower down on the priority list. The reason for the budget surplus is that the town's population has grown, and this growth has led to an increase in the number of stray and abandoned animals. It's better to address the issue now while we have a small surplus, rather than wait until we have a crisis.

In the next body paragraph you give your second reason and accompanying support for your claim:

> The current animal shelter was built forty years ago and does not meet the current fire and electrical codes. All city buildings are required to have fire-resistant construction materials, sprinkler systems, and smoke detectors. In addition, all electrical lines are required to be hidden or enclosed in weather-resistant material, and to be heavy enough to carry higher electrical loads. When the current shelter was constructed, no such fire and electrical codes existed. The current shelter, therefore, is a potential danger for both the humans who work there and the animals that live there.

If you have a third reason in support of your position, you would develop it in the next paragraph.

After you have presented all the reasons and accompanying evidence supporting your claim, you now should be ready to consider and rebut any arguments in opposition to yours. Suppose other townspeople have other plans for the town's budget surplus. Why should the surplus (or part of it) be spent on this particular project? Could a renovation of the shelter accomplish nearly the same results for less money? Suppose the animal population of the shelter could be reduced by increasing adoptions, euthanizing animals, or a combination of both. You might be able to answer all of the opposing arguments in one well-developed paragraph. If, however, there are several opposing arguments, or if your response to one of the opposing arguments will require more space than the others, then you may have to use two or more body paragraphs to respond to the opposing arguments.

Finally, end your essay with a closing paragraph in which you reword your claim or argumentative thesis. After the reworded claim, add a couple of sentences relating your subject to a more general issue.

PRACTICAL TIPS   Basic Structure of an Argument Essay

A stripped-down, basic structure of an argument essay might look something like this:

ɿ Introduction with claim/argumentative thesis statement

ɿ Background information if necessary

ɿ Reason/evidence supporting your thesis

ɿ Second reason/evidence supporting your thesis

ɿ Third reason/evidence supporting your thesis

ɿ Response to one or more opposing arguments

ɿ Response to one or more opposing arguments

ɿ Closing paragraph, beginning with reworded claim/argumentative thesis statement

---

Putting It All Together

Sample Student Essay

Let's take the claim that the town should build a new animal shelter and put together a draft based on the materials above. Here is what it would look like:

It's Time for a New Animal Shelter

When our town's first animal shelter was constructed in 1967, the population of our town was only 15,000, and the number of stray and unwanted animals was very low. Today, forty years later, the situation has changed drastically. The town's population is now 25,000, and there has been an explosion in the number of stray and unwanted animals, along with a significant increase in the number of wild animals roaming the town as it has expanded into formerly wooded areas. The time has come for the town council to address this growing problem by approving the funding to construct a new animal shelter.

One of the main reasons why we should build a new animal shelter is that the town has a budget surplus. All of our commitments to our citizens have been met in terms of city services. We now have the luxury of addressing the town's needs lower down on the priority list. The reason for the budget surplus is that the town's population has grown. Unfortunately, this growth has led to an increase of the number of stray and abandoned animals. It's better to address the issue now while we have a small surplus, rather than wait until we have a crisis.

The current animal shelter was built forty years ago and does not meet the current fire and electrical codes. All city buildings are required to have fire-resistant construction materials, sprinkler systems, and smoke detectors. In addition, all electrical lines are required to be hidden or enclosed in weather-resistant material and to be heavy enough to carry higher electrical loads. When the current shelter was constructed, no such fire and electrical codes existed. The current shelter, therefore, is a potential danger for both the humans who work there and the animals that live there.

Because of the town's growth, the number of stray and unwanted animals that wind up in the shelter has exploded to the point of being unsafe and unsanitary. Every cage is occupied by more animals than it was designed for, leading to fights and injuries among the animals. The large number of animals has also overwhelmed the efforts to keep the shelter sanitary. There are not enough personnel to keep up with cleaning the cages and disposing of the growing amounts of waste. Fortunately, widespread disease has not yet broken out at the shelter, but our consulting veterinarian says it may be only a matter of time before there is a major die-off caused by disease.

Yet another reason why we need a new shelter is that the number of people visiting the shelter (mainly to drop off unwanted animals) or calling the shelter to report stray animals has increased steadily along with the town's population. As the following graph shows, the number of visits and/or

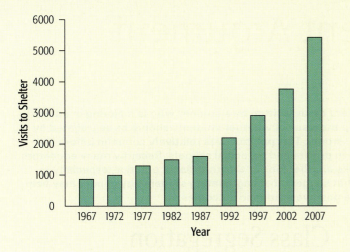

Visits to Shelter

Year

calls to the shelter has risen from an average of fewer than three per day in 1967 to an average of over 14 per day in 2007, the last year for which statistics are available. The vertical axis represents the number of visits and/or calls to the shelter. The horizontal axis represents the years in which the data were collected.

Finally, over the past forty years the state has developed guidelines for the safe, sanitary operation of animal shelters, and our shelter has fallen below the minimal standards. So we are required by state law to address the shelter's shortcomings.

We understand that there is some opposition to our proposal that a new shelter be built. Some have suggested that the town has more pressing human needs. While this may be true, it is also true that poverty in our town is on the decrease, thanks especially to the federal grant we received several years ago. Others have said that the shelter could be upgraded to meet the minimal state requirements. But an upgrade would be only a short-term solution to a problem that is getting bigger every day. The local SPCA has recommended that the town start an "adopt-a-pound-puppy-or-kitty" campaign. Unfortunately, only a relatively small number of animals have been adopted from the shelter. There is also the last resort: the relatively inexpensive option of euthanizing surplus animals. Sad to say, but this option is already being used on sick, injured, or feral animals.

We therefore propose that a portion of the town's surplus funds be used to construct a new, expanded shelter that meets all local and state codes. A relatively minor investment now may prevent a major problem in the near future. A new facility, combined perhaps with a community outreach/education officer, just might have the doubly positive effect of getting more animals adopted and fewer animals abandoned.

Student Argument Essay

Here is an argument essay written by a student who is majoring in education. She takes up the issue of whether students should be segregated by gender in the classroom. This practice was relatively common before the 1970s, especially in private and parochial schools. Recently many educators have begun to take another look at this traditional practice, especially in light of studies that suggest that segregating students by gender may help bring about some positive academic outcomes.

Class Segregation

Jessica Ryan
Prof. Sabrio
Feb. 9, 2006

Argumentative thesis statement

1   In the past few years, males have been falling behind academically compared to females. Many possible factors may have contributed to this academic decline, and this essay will address a possible remedy for the problem. Because male and female adolescents benefit from different learning techniques, students should be segregated in core classes in sixth through eighth grades.

First argument (topic sentence) in support of thesis

Support of first argument

2   Historically, if educators focus on one gender, the other suffers. Thirty years ago, "girls . . . were lagging behind" academically and feminists fought to "provide equal opportunities for girls in the classroom" (Newsweek 47). Educators revised curricula in order to provide an optimal learning situation for the females. For example, "teachers increasingly put an emphasis on . . . sitting quietly and speaking in turn" (Newsweek 48). Once girls began to excel, feminists continued to promote higher academic opportunities for females (Newsweek 47). However, in the meantime, the academic welfare of boys has been overlooked. An obvious solution to this problem is to identify the best learning situation for both genders and apply the two curricula separately in segregated classrooms.

Second argument (topic sentence) in support of thesis

Support of second argument

3   Teaching males and females in the same classroom does not make sense from a biological standpoint. Scientific studies have shown that the male and female brains show the most difference in development during the adolescent years. The part of the brain that controls organizational skills, among other skills, develops in females approximately eighteen months before it develops in males (Newsweek 50). This means that females have a biological advantage over males for a year and a half. Also, while the genders show

little difference in mental processing speed at age five and eighteen, females outperform their male counterparts during adolescence (Newsweek 50). If the male and female brains do not operate similarly in this age group, why are they being taught with similar methods? Additionally, students reach puberty at this age, and accommodating both sexes in the same classroom may prove to be a distraction. Many males are raised to be independent and competitive. They may be unwilling to ask for help lest they be seen as weak by females in the classroom. Instead, many males may refrain from asking questions and simply continue on in confusion of the subject matter.

Acknowledgment of one opposing argument

Response to opposing argument

4   Some critics may argue that gender segregation in middle school may not be socially beneficial to the students, and I would agree. That is why the genders should not be segregated by schools, but only in the core classes. If segregated by schools, the genders may not learn the crucial social skills needed for communicating with the opposite sex in the real world. However, if the genders are kept in the same school but simply segregated in core classes such as reading, math, English, and science, males and females still have the opportunity to interact. These core classes are important since they provide a base of fundamental knowledge on which to build.

Restatement of argumentative thesis

5   For some reason or perhaps many different reasons, boys are obviously falling behind, and by having the United States public schools segregate core classes in sixth through eighth grades, many possible causes of this problem may be remedied. In the real world, although this would be an ideal teaching situation, it probably will not be implemented for many years, if ever.

Some Common Fallacies

A logical mistake or error in an argument is called a fallacy. A fallacy weakens your argument and leaves your argument open to rebuttal. Those who study logic have named well over one hundred fallacies. For our purposes, we will list and explain some of the more common fallacies found in the essays of beginning college writers. Recognizing these fallacies will help you avoid them in your own essays and will help you detect them in essays, texts, ads, and commercials.

Hasty Generalization   This fallacy makes the mistake of generalizing on the basis of just a few experiences or inadequate evidence. A person might say, "I don't go to that restaurant anymore because it's always crowded." How many times did the person go? When did the person go? Were reservations made?

Stereotyping   This is similar to the hasty generalization fallacy. Stereotyping is drawing a conclusion about an entire group of people based on just a few experiences, or based on what you may have heard others say.

Stereotyping applies labels to entire groups without considering individual differences or characteristics of members of the group. Examples of stereotypes might be "People from the northeastern part of the U.S. are rude and unfriendly" or "Students from that college are spoiled, rich kids."

False Cause   This fallacy claims that if event A happened before event B, then event A caused event B. This fallacy sometimes goes by the Latin name *post hoc ergo propter hoc,* which means "after this, therefore because of this." An example of this fallacy might be "Ever since the new mayor took office, the crime rate has dropped. The mayor must be tough on crime." A falling crime rate is usually too complex a phenomenon to be attributed to any one cause. Perhaps the police happened to break the town's largest burglary ring two days before the mayor was elected.

Oversimplification   This is the fallacy of looking at a complex problem and pronouncing a quick fix. An example might be "The way to end the teen pregnancy problem in this country is to teach abstinence." This approach may help in some circumstances, but the problem of teen pregnancy in our country is very large, very complex, and requires a multifaceted approach to help remedy it. Minor problems usually do not grow into major problems unless they are very complex and involve many variables that are difficult to deal with.

Either-Or Fallacy   This fallacy oversimplifies a situation into only one of two courses of action. This fallacy is often seen in political campaigns and advertising: "We either support the Patriot Act, or the terrorists will win" or "If the government does not fix the social security situation right now, all those retiring after 2035 will not see any social security checks." In both of these situations, there are many possible positions between the two extremes mentioned.

Faulty or False Analogy   An analogy is a comparison, usually between two unlike things, to help an audience better understand one of them. A faulty or false analogy is the fallacy of comparing two things, situations, or experiences that have some minor similarities but are essentially different. An example might be "The federal and local governments responded to the September 11 attacks in New York City quickly. Why couldn't the government respond to the Hurricane Katrina disaster quickly?"

Ad Hominem   This is Latin for "against the man" (or against the person). The ad hominem fallacy consists of criticizing a person directly rather than arguing against the issues: "This candidate favors tax cuts because he is very wealthy and wants a tax break for himself" or "The governor is proposing mandatory flu shots for everyone over the age of

50 because she has stock in the drug company that manufactures the flu vaccine."

Red Herring   A red herring is a smoked fish that can get very smelly. Dragging a red herring across the track that dogs are following will cause the dogs to follow the strong scent of the red herring and leave the track. The red herring fallacy involves introducing an unrelated or false issue into an argument or debate in order to lead attention away from the issue being argued. An example might be "I can't support her for county treasurer because her father was convicted of embezzling funds when he worked for the bank."

Bandwagon   This fallacy, often used by advertisers, urges people to make a hasty decision without much forethought, or "jump on the bandwagon," before they get left behind. Examples include "Don't wait another minute to buy this product! We have only a few more left, and they are going fast!" or "Everyone is going to the beach for spring break this year! You'd better reserve your room right now, before all the hotel rooms are sold out!"

Begging the Question   This fallacy is sometimes called "circular reasoning." It assumes that a proposition is true even if it has not been proven yet. The conclusion, or a variation of it, is used as a premise:

"Students at that college are very smart."

"How do you know?"

"Because only intelligent students go there."

Appeal to False Authority   According to this fallacy, a person who is an authority in one field attempts to use his or her authority to influence people in another field unrelated to his or her expertise. You may have seen magazine ads featuring young, attractive celebrities with "milk mustaches" advertising the benefits of drinking milk. While it is true that certain kinds of milk may be healthful for most people, the majority of celebrities have no special expertise in the field of health and nutrition.

Non Sequitur   This is a Latin term that means "it does not follow." A non sequitur fallacy is committed when one attempts to relate two ideas that have no logical connection. An example might be "Representative Smith is not qualified to make any decisions affecting the U.S. armed forces because she has never served in the armed forces." This statement assumes that one has to have direct experience with a situation in order to be able to make responsible decisions about that situation. While experience may certainly help, people make responsible decisions all the time without direct experience. For example, physicians can diagnose and treat diseases without experiencing those diseases. First-time parents have little or no experience in being parents, but most do a good job of raising their children.

Thinking Critically About Fallacies

Analyze the following statements and, working with one or two classmates, see if you can agree on the fallacy being committed in each. Some statements include more than one fallacy.

1. I heard a movie star say in an interview that mothers who experience postpartum depression should not take medication for their depression. I'm going to tell my friend to stop taking her anti-depression medication.

2. We visited Los Angeles last summer, and everybody there is laid back, self-absorbed, and looking for an easy way to make money.

3. The way to reverse global warming is to develop hydrogen-powered vehicles and build more nuclear power plants.

4. Do we really want to elect a president who attended an Islamic school when he was younger?

5. If we continue to let Iran develop its nuclear capability, we will have another Nazi Germany on our hands. The allies did not stop Hitler when he was gaining power, and look what he did.

6. The speed limit on South Staples Street should be lowered from 50 miles per hour to 40. Why? Because 50 mph is too fast.

7. That's the first and last time I'm flying with that airline. The flight was overbooked, it was late, and my luggage was lost.

8. I'm looking at the Shopping Network right now, and they have only 1000 Super Chef's Knives to sell, and the count on the screen says they have already sold 689 in the first ten minutes of advertising. I'd better order one right now before they run out.

9. The situation in Afghanistan is simple to deal with. We should pull out all NATO and U.S. troops right now. If that's unacceptable, we should send in 100,000 more troops immediately and crush the Taliban once and for all.

10. I don't think she would make a good principal of our high school. Neither of her parents finished high school, and her sister has a baby and is unmarried.

11. Six months after he was elected President, the country's unemployment rate went up and the stock market fell. I told you his economic policies were not good for the country.

12. I think she will be a good company president. She is attractive and dresses well.

1. Look at the title of this short story. How can the concepts of "love" and "fallacy" be said to belong to two very different ways of making sense of human experience?

2. This short story was first published in 1951. How might the narrator's attitude toward Polly reflect the culture of that time?

While You Read

1. List and explain the fallacies that the narrator Dobie Gillis teaches to Polly.

2. List and explain the fallacies that Polly points out as Dobie Gillis attempts to persuade her to return his affection for her.

Reading

This is an old but very funny short story, first published in 1951, about a law school student, Dobie Gillis, trying to teach Polly Espy, the person he wants to be his girlfriend, about logic. He "succeeds" with unintended consequences.

Love Is a Fallacy

BY MAX SCHULMAN

1 Cool was I and logical. Keen, calculating, perspicacious, acute and astute—I was all of these. My brain was as powerful as a dynamo, as precise as a chemist's scales, as penetrating as a scalpel. And—think of it!—I was only eighteen.

2 It is not often that one so young has such a giant intellect. Take, for example, Petey Bellows, my roommate at the university. Same age, same background, but dumb as an ox. A nice enough fellow, you understand, but nothing upstairs. Emotional type. Unstable. Impressionable.

Worst of all, a faddist. Fads, I submit, are the very negation of reason. To be swept up in every new craze that comes along, to surrender yourself to idiocy just because everybody else is doing it—this, to me, is the acme of mindlessness. Not, however, to Petey.

3 One afternoon I found Petey lying on his bed with an expression of such distress on his face that I immediately diagnosed appendicitis. "Don't move," I said. "Don't take a laxative. I'll get a doctor."

4   "Raccoon," he mumbled thickly.

5   "Raccoon?" I said, pausing in my flight.

6   "I want a raccoon coat," he wailed.

7   I perceived that his trouble was not physical, but mental. "Why do you want a raccoon coat?"

8   "I should have known it," he cried, pounding his temples.

9   "I should have known they'd come back when the Charleston came back. Like a fool I spent all my money for textbooks, and now I can't get a raccoon coat."

10   "Can you mean," I said incredulously, "that people are actually wearing raccoon coats again?"

11   "All the Big Men on Campus are wearing them. Where've you been?"

12   "In the library," I said, naming a place not frequented by Big Men on Campus.

13   He leaped from the bed and paced the room. "I've got to have a raccoon coat," he said passionately. "I've got to!"

14   "Petey, why? Look at it rationally. Raccoon coats are unsanitary. They shed. They smell bad. They weigh too much. They're unsightly. They—"

15   "You don't understand," he interrupted impatiently. "It's the thing to do. Don't you want to be in the swim?"

16   "No," I said truthfully.

17   "Well, I do," he declared. "I'd give anything for a raccoon coat. Anything!"

18   My brain, that precision instrument, slipped into high gear. "Anything?" I asked, looking at him narrowly.

19   "Anything," he affirmed in ringing tones.

20   I stroked my chin thoughtfully. It so happened that I knew where to get my hands on a raccoon coat. My father had had one in his undergraduate days; it lay now in a trunk in the attic back home. It also happened that Petey had something I wanted. He didn't *have* it exactly, but at least he had first rights on it. I refer to his girl, Polly Espy.

21   I had long coveted Polly Espy. Let me emphasize that my desire for this young woman was not emotional in nature. She was, to be sure, a girl who excited the emotions, but I was not one to let my heart rule my head. I wanted Polly for a shrewdly calculated, entirely cerebral reason.

22   I was a freshman in law school. In a few years I would be out in practice. I was well aware of the importance of the right kind of wife in furthering a lawyer's career. The successful lawyers I had observed were, almost without exception, married to beautiful, gracious, intelligent women. With one omission, Polly fitted these specifications perfectly.

23   Beautiful she was. She was not yet of pin-up proportions, but I felt sure that time would supply the lack. She already had the makings.

24   Gracious she was. By gracious I mean full of graces. She had an erectness of carriage, an ease of bearing, a poise that clearly indicated the best of breeding. At table her manners were exquisite. I had seen her at the Kozy Kampus Korner eating the specialty of the house—a sandwich that contained scraps of pot roast, gravy, chopped nuts, and a dipper of sauerkraut—without even getting her fingers moist.

25   Intelligent she was not. In fact, she veered in the opposite direction. But I believed that under my guidance she would smarten up. At any rate, it was worth a try. It is, after all, easier to make a beautiful dumb girl smart than to make an ugly smart girl beautiful.

26   "Petey," I said, "are you in love with Polly Espy?"

27   "I think she's a keen kid," he replied, "but I don't know if you'd call it love. Why?"

28   "Do you," I asked, "have any kind of formal arrangement with her? I mean are you going steady or anything like that?"

29   "No. We see each other quite a bit, but we both have other dates. Why?"

30   "Is there," I asked, "any other man for whom she has a particular fondness?"

31   "Not that I know of. Why?"

32   I nodded with satisfaction. "In other words, if you were out of the picture, the field would be open. Is that right?"

33   "I guess so. What are you getting at?"

34   "Nothing, nothing," I said innocently, and took my suitcase out of the closet.

35   "Where you going?" asked Petey.

36   "Home for the week end." I threw a few things into the bag.

37   "Listen," he said, clutching my arm eagerly, "while you're home, you couldn't get some money from your old man, could you, and lend it to me so I can buy a raccoon coat?"

38   "I may do better than that," I said with a mysterious wink and closed my bag and left.

39   "Look," I said to Petey when I got back Monday morning. I threw open the suitcase and revealed the huge, hairy, gamy object that my father had worn in his Stutz Bearcat in 1925.

40   "Holy Toledo!" said Petey reverently. He plunged his hands into the raccoon coat and then his face. "Holy Toledo!" he repeated fifteen or twenty times.

41   "Would you like it?" I asked.

42   "Oh yes!" he cried, clutching the greasy pelt to him. Then a canny look came into his eyes. "What do you want for it?"

43   "Your girl," I said, mincing no words.

44   "Polly?" he said in a horrified whisper. "You want Polly?"

45   "That's right."

46   He flung the coat from him. "Never," he said stoutly.

47   I shrugged. "Okay. If you don't want to be in the swim, I guess it's your business."

48   I sat down in a chair and pretended to read a book, but out of the corner of my eye I kept watching Petey. He was a torn man. First he looked at the coat with the expression of a waif at a bakery window. Then he turned away and set his jaw resolutely. Then he looked back at the coat, with even more longing in his face. Then he turned away, but with not so much resolution this time. Back and forth his head swiveled, desire waxing,

resolution waning. Finally he didn't turn away at all; he just stood and stared with mad lust at the coat.

49   "It isn't as though I was in love with Polly," he said thickly. "Or going steady or anything like that."

50   "That's right," I murmured.

51   "What's Polly to me, or me to Polly?"

52   "Not a thing," said I.

53   "It's just been a casual kick—just a few laughs, that's all."

54   "Try on the coat," said I.

55   He complied. The coat bunched high over his ears and dropped all the way down to his shoe tops. He looked like a mound of dead raccoons. "Fits fine," he said happily.

56   I rose from my chair. "Is it a deal?" I asked, extending my hand.

57   He swallowed. "It's a deal," he said and shook my hand.

58   I had my first date with Polly the following evening. This was in the nature of a survey; I wanted to find out just how much work I had to do to get her mind up to the standard I required. I took her first to dinner. "Gee, that was a delish dinner," she said as we left the restaurant. Then I took her to a movie. "Gee, that was a marvy movie," she said as we left the theater. And then I took her home. "Gee, I had a sensaysh time," she said as she bade me good night.

59   I went back to my room with a heavy heart. I had gravely underestimated the size of my task. This girl's lack of information was terrifying. Nor would it be enough merely to supply her with information. First she had to be taught to think. This loomed as a project of no small dimensions, and at first I was tempted to give her back to Petey. But then I got to thinking about her abundant physical charms and about the way she entered a room and the way she handled a knife and fork, and I decided to make an effort.

60   I went about it, as in all things, systematically. I gave her a course in logic. It happened that I, as a law student, was taking a course in

logic myself, so I had all the facts at my finger tips. "Polly," I said to her when I picked her up on our next date, "tonight we are going over to the Knoll and talk."

61   "Oo, terrif," she replied. One thing I will say for this girl: you would go far to find another so agreeable.

62   We went to the Knoll, the campus trysting place, and we sat down under an old oak, and she looked at me expectantly.

63   "What are we going to talk about?" she asked.

64   "Logic."

65   She thought this over for a minute and decided she liked it. "Magnif," she said.

66   "Logic," I said, clearing my throat, "is the science of thinking. Before we can think correctly, we must first learn to recognize the common fallacies of logic. These we will take up tonight."

67   "Wow-dow!" she cried, clapping her hands delightedly.

68   I winced, but went bravely on. "First let us examine the fallacy called Dicto Simpliciter."

69   "By all means," she urged, batting her lashes eagerly.

70   "Dicto Simpliciter means an argument based on an unqualified generalization. For example: Exercise is good. Therefore everybody should exercise."

71   "I agree," said Polly earnestly. "I mean exercise is wonderful. I mean it builds the body and everything."

72   "Polly," I said gently, "the argument is a fallacy. Exercise is good is an unqualified generalization. For instance, if you have heart disease, exercise is bad, not good. Many people are ordered by their doctors not to exercise. You must *qualify* the generalization. You must say exercise is *usually* good, or exercise is good *for most people*. Otherwise you have committed a Dicto Simpliciter. Do you see?"

73   "No," she confessed. "But this is marvy. Do more! Do more!"

74   "It will be better if you stop tugging at my sleeve," I told her, and when she desisted, I continued. "Next we take up a fallacy called Hasty Generalization. Listen carefully: You can't speak French. I can't speak French. Petey Bellows can't speak French. I must therefore conclude that nobody at the University of Minnesota can speak French."

75   "Really?" said Polly, amazed. *"Nobody?"*

76   I hid my exasperation. "Polly, it's a fallacy. The generalization is reached too hastily. There are too few instances to support such a conclusion."

77   "Know any more fallacies?" she asked breathlessly. "This is more fun than dancing even."

78   I fought off a wave of despair. I was getting nowhere with this girl, absolutely nowhere. Still, I am nothing if not persistent. I continued. "Next comes Post Hoc. Listen to this: Let's not take Bill on our picnic. Every time we take him out with us, it rains."

79   "I know somebody just like that," she exclaimed. "A girl back home—Eula Becker, her name is. It never fails. Every single time we take her on a picnic—"

80   "Polly," I said sharply, "it's a fallacy. Eula Becker doesn't cause the rain. She has no connection with the rain. You are guilty of Post Hoc if you blame Eula Becker."

81   "I'll never do it again," she promised contritely. "Are you mad at me?"

82   I sighed. "No, Polly, I'm not mad."

83   "Then tell me some more fallacies."

84   "All right. Let's try Contradictory Premises."

85   "Yes, let's," she chirped, blinking her eyes happily.

86   I frowned, but plunged ahead. "Here's an example of Contradictory Premises: If God can do anything, can He make a stone so heavy that He won't be able to lift it?"

87   "Of course," she replied promptly.

88   "But if He can do anything, He can lift the stone," I pointed out.

89   "Yeah," she said thoughtfully. "Well, then I guess He can't make the stone."

90 "But He can do anything," I reminded her.

91 She scratched her pretty, empty head. "I'm all confused," she admitted.

92 "Of course you are. Because when the premises of an argument contradict each other, there can be no argument. If there is an irresistible force, there can be no immovable object. If there is an immovable object, there can be no irresistible force. Get it?"

93 "Tell me some more of this keen stuff," she said eagerly.

94 I consulted my watch. "I think we'd better call it a night. I'll take you home now, and you go over all the things you've learned. We'll have another session tomorrow night."

95 I deposited her at the girls' dormitory, where she assured me that she had had a perfectly terrif evening, and I went glumly home to my room. Petey lay snoring in his bed, the raccoon coat huddled like a great hairy beast at his feet. For a moment I considered waking him and telling him that he could have his girl back. It seemed clear that my project was doomed to failure. The girl simply had a logic-proof head.

96 But then I reconsidered. I had wasted one evening; I might as well waste another. Who knew? Maybe somewhere in the extinct crater of her mind a few embers still smoldered. Maybe somehow I could fan them into flame. Admittedly it was not a prospect fraught with hope, but I decided to give it one more try.

97 Seated under the oak the next evening I said, "Our first fallacy tonight is called Ad Misericordiam."

98 She quivered with delight.

99 "Listen closely," I said. "A man applies for a job. When the boss asks him what his qualifications are, he replies that he has a wife and six children at home, the wife is a helpless cripple, the children have nothing to eat, no clothes to wear, no shoes on their feet, there are no beds in the house, no coal in the cellar, and winter is coming."

100 A tear rolled down each of Polly's pink cheeks. "Oh, this is awful, awful," she sobbed.

101 "Yes, it's awful," I agreed, "but it's no argument. The man never answered the boss's question about his qualifications. Instead he appealed to the boss's sympathy. He committed the fallacy of Ad Misericordiam. Do you understand?"

102 "Have you got a handkerchief?" she blubbered.

103 I handed her a handkerchief and tried to keep from screaming while she wiped her eyes. "Next," I said in a carefully controlled tone, "we will discuss False Analogy. Here is an example: Students should be allowed to look at their textbooks during examinations. After all, surgeons have X rays to guide them during an operation, lawyers have briefs to guide them during a trial, carpenters have blueprints to guide them when they are building a house. Why, then, shouldn't students be allowed to look at their textbooks during an examination?"

104 "There now," she said enthusiastically, "is the most marvy idea I've heard in years."

105 "Polly," I said testily, "the argument is all wrong. Doctors, lawyers, and carpenters aren't taking a test to see how much they have learned, but students are. The situations are altogether different, and you can't make an analogy between them."

106 "I still think it's a good idea," said Polly.

107 "Nuts," I muttered. Doggedly I pressed on. "Next we'll try Hypothesis Contrary to Fact."

108 "Sounds yummy," was Polly's reaction.

109 "Listen: If Madame Curie had hot happened to leave a photographic plate in a drawer with a chunk of pitchblende, the world today would not know about radium."

110 "True, true," said Polly, nodding her head. "Did you see the movie? Oh, it just knocked me out. That Walter Pidgeon is so dreamy. I mean he fractures me."

111 "If you can forget Mr. Pidgeon for a moment," I said coldly, "I would like to point out

that the statement is a fallacy. Maybe Madame Curie would have discovered radium at some later date. Maybe somebody else would have discovered it. Maybe any number of things would have happened. You can't start with a hypothesis that is not true and then draw any supportable conclusions from it."

112   "They ought to put Walter Pidgeon in more pictures," said Polly. "I hardly ever see him any more."

113   One more chance, I decided. But just one more. There is a limit to what flesh and blood can bear. "The next fallacy is called Poisoning the Well."

114   "How cute!" she gurgled.

115   "Two men are having a debate. The first one gets up and says, 'My opponent is a notorious liar. You can't believe a word that he is going to say.' . . . Now, Polly, think. Think hard. What's wrong?"

116   I watched her closely as she knit her creamy brow in concentration. Suddenly a glimmer of intelligence—the first I had seen—came into her eyes. "It's not fair," she said with indignation. "It's not a bit fair. What chance has the second man got if the first man calls him a liar before he even begins talking?"

117   "Right!" I cried exultantly. "One hundred per cent right. It's not fair. The first man has *poisoned the well* before anybody could drink from it. He has hamstrung his opponent before he could even start. . . . Polly, I'm proud of you."

118   "Pshaw," she murmured, blushing with pleasure.

119   "You see, my dear, these things aren't so hard. All you have to do is concentrate. Think—examine—evaluate. Come now, let's review everything we have learned."

120   "Fire away," she said with an airy wave of her hand.

121   Heartened by the knowledge that Polly was not altogether a cretin, I began a long, patient review of all I had told her. Over and over and over again I cited instances, pointed out flaws, kept hammering away without letup. It was like digging a tunnel. At first everything was work, sweat, and darkness. I had no idea when I would reach the light, or even if I would. But I persisted. I pounded and clawed and scraped, and finally I was rewarded. I saw a chink of light. And then the chink got bigger and the sun came pouring in and all was bright.

122   Five grueling nights this took, but it was worth it. I had made a logician out of Polly; I had taught her to think. My job was done. She was worthy of me at last. She was a fit wife for me, a proper hostess for my many mansions, a suitable mother for my well-heeled children.

123   It must not be thought that I was without love for this girl. Quite the contrary. Just as Pygmalion loved the perfect woman he had fashioned, so I loved mine. I decided to acquaint her with my feelings at our very next meeting. The time had come to change our relationship from academic to romantic.

124   "Polly," I said when next we sat beneath our oak, "tonight we will not discuss fallacies."

125   "Aw, gee," she said, disappointed.

126   "My dear," I said, favoring her with a smile, "we have now spent five evenings together. We have gotten along splendidly. It is clear that we are well matched."

127   "Hasty Generalization," said Polly brightly.

128   "I beg your pardon," said I.

129   "Hasty Generalization," she repeated. "How can you say that we are well matched on the basis of only five dates?"

130   I chuckled with amusement. The dear child had learned her lessons well. "My dear," I said, patting her hand in a tolerant manner, "five dates is plenty. After all, you don't have to eat a whole cake to know that it's good."

131   "False Analogy," said Polly promptly. "I'm not a cake. I'm a girl."

132   I chuckled with somewhat less amusement. The dear child had learned her lessons perhaps too well. I decided to change tactics. Obviously the best approach was a simple, strong, direct

declaration of love. I paused for a moment while my massive brain chose the proper words. Then I began:

133   "Polly, I love you. You are the whole world to me, and the moon and the stars and the constellations of outer space. Please, my darling, say that you will go steady with me, for if you will not, life will be meaningless. I will languish. I will refuse my meals. I will wander the face of the earth, a shambling, hollow-eyed hulk."

134   There, I thought, folding my arms, that ought to do it.

135   "Ad Misericordiam," said Polly.

136   I ground my teeth. I was not Pygmalion; I was Frankenstein, and my monster had me by the throat. Frantically I fought back the tide of panic surging through me. At all costs I had to keep cool.

137   "Well, Polly," I said, forcing a smile, "you certainly have learned your fallacies."

138   "You're darn right," she said with a vigorous nod.

139   "And who taught them to you, Polly?"

140   "You did."

141   "That's right. So you do owe me something, don't you, my dear? If I hadn't come along you never would have learned about fallacies."

142   "Hypothesis Contrary to Fact," she said instantly.

143   I dashed perspiration from my brow. "Polly," I croaked, "you mustn't take all these things so literally. I mean this is just classroom stuff. You know that the things you learn in school don't have anything to do with life."

144   "Dicto Simpliciter," she said, wagging her finger at me playfully.

145   That did it. I leaped to my feet, bellowing like a bull. "Will you or will you not go steady with me?"

146   "I will not," she replied.

147   "Why not?" I demanded.

148   "Because this afternoon I promised Petey Bellows that I would go steady with him."

149   I reeled back, overcome with the infamy of it. After he promised, after he made a deal, after he shook my hand! "The rat!" I shrieked, kicking up great chunks of turf. "You can't go with him, Polly. He's a liar. He's a cheat. He's a rat."

150   "Poisoning the Well," said Polly, "and stop shouting. I think shouting must be a fallacy too."

151   With an immense effort of will, I modulated my voice. "All right," I said. "You're a logician. Let's look at this thing logically. How could you choose Petey Bellows over me? Look at me—a brilliant student, a tremendous intellectual, a man with an assured future. Look at Petey—a knothead, a jitterbug, a guy who'll never know where his next meal is coming from. Can you give me one logical reason why you should go steady with Petey Bellows?"

152   "I certainly can," declared Polly. "He's got a raccoon coat."

Thinking Critically About the Reading

1. Using the Internet or some other resource, find a brief summary of the mythological story of Pygmalion. How is this short story related to the Pygmalion myth?

2. What might Polly's choice of Petey Bellows to be her boyfriend, instead of the narrator Dobie Gillis, say about the relation of logic and love?

A good source of fallacies is letters to the editor of a newspaper or magazine. For several days in a row, read at least ten different letters to the editor, either in print or posted on a newspaper's or magazine's website. Also, look for unedited comments that people can post to a newspaper or online magazine discussion board. These postings are also good sources of fallacies. Find letters that show different fallacies from the list of fallacies you learned about above. Bring to class the letters, or printouts if you found the letters online, and be prepared to point out and explain the different fallacies you spotted.

Rogerian Argument

Carl Rogers (1902–1987) was a clinical psychologist who spent years helping people communicate more effectively. During his many years of counseling and therapy sessions, he became convinced of the importance of communicating in a non-threatening way, especially in emotionally charged situations in which people hold conflicting positions.

In the 1970s Rogers's ideas were adapted for use in argument/persuasive essays and speeches. In a "Rogerian" argument essay, the writer makes an effort to find common ground with the opponent. The writer also restates the opponent's position to show that the writer understands the opposing position. In addition, the writer emphasizes shared values, shared goals, and points of common agreement with the opponent.

The overall organization of a Rogerian argument looks different from that of a more conventional argument outlined previously. A typical Rogerian argument looks like this:

- Introduction. The writer looks for common ground with opponent, what they both can agree on. The writer may not even state a thesis here.

- Writer states opponent's position as fairly and accurately as possibly, showing that the opponent's position is understood.

- Writer concedes or acknowledges that opponent's position is valid in certain situations or contexts.

- Writer presents his or her own perspective and arguments, showing the situations or contexts in which his or her own position is valid.

- Writer closes with a carefully worded thesis statement, emphasizing the points of agreement with the opponent. The closing paragraph focuses on common ground and shared beliefs.

Sample Rogerian Essay

As a way to compare a traditional argument essay's structure with that of a Rogerian essay, we will take the animal shelter essay above and recast it into a Rogerian form.

How Can We Best Help the Animals?

This town has always been proud of the way it comes together to help those less fortunate than we are. Business and church groups often respond to those in need even before various levels of government respond. A situation in our town requires our attention before the conditions worsen. We are referring to the town's animal shelter with its overcrowded, unsanitary conditions and its violation of town and state codes. Although there may be some disagreement about the most prudent course of action to improve the animal shelter, the great majority of citizens agree that something must be done to help some of the most defenseless creatures among us.

We understand that a wide range of options, some less costly than others, are available to alleviate the current conditions at the shelter. Perhaps the least expensive option is to euthanize even more animals than are now euthanized. Most townspeople are probably not aware that a number of sick, injured, and feral animals are now euthanized weekly; the practice of putting animals down could be extended to the healthy ones, but we are not sure if this practice would have widespread support. Another suggestion is to upgrade the current shelter so that it meets all town and state building codes in the areas of electricity, fire detection, sanitation, number of animals per pen, and supervision. This renovation option is definitely worth investigating and may provide a short-term solution.

A more general difference of opinion exists on what to do with the town's small budget surplus. Some would argue that it is always more appropriate to spend money on people rather than on animals. While we tend to agree with this sentiment, we do not see the situation as an "either people or animals" choice. We believe that there is enough in the budget surplus to continue funding all the current assistance programs, while at the same time earmarking a relatively small sum for the shelter. In addition, we suggest that a modern, efficiently run shelter will benefit the townspeople as well as the animals: Fewer stray and feral animals will roam the streets, lessening the exposure of our children and pets to bites and disease.

We believe that a city-wide campaign of business and church group support, along with judicious use of some of the budget surplus, will result in something that we all desire: a safer town for our people and better shelter conditions for the animals. The town already owns the land where the current shelter is located, so there would be no land costs. Some of the budget surplus could be used for designing a new shelter and building the parts that require special expertise. Most of the other construction work could be done by selected town employees with construction experience and volunteers from various business and church groups. This involvement of the townspeople would highlight the importance of pet care, getting pets spayed and neutered, and taking steps around our property to discourage wild animals from coming into town from the surrounding rural areas. We will arrange with the local SPCA to provide volunteer community outreach/education officers to teach pet owners to be more responsible. The SPCA will also spearhead an "adopt-a-pound-puppy-or-kitty" campaign to help keep the number of shelter animals to a minimum.

In the end we will have a situation that everyone can be proud of—a new shelter built at minimal cost to the taxpayers, an involved citizenry, more responsible pet owners, a safer town, and happier animals. We believe everyone will agree that these results are better than what we have now. Won't you join us?

Evaluation: A Common Form of Argument

In our everyday lives we constantly have to make choices between or among alternatives. What school should I go to? What school should I send my children to? What vehicle should I buy? Where can I be the most useful volunteer? How should we raise money for the neighborhood block association? Which health plan is best for me and my family?

In academic situations professors may ask students to evaluate written works, political or economic theories, ways of doing something or solving a problem. Evaluation often involves comparing and contrasting two items or plans or approaches and deciding which is better.

No matter what we are evaluating, we have to be clear from the start about the standards or criteria (plural of "criterion") we use to make the evaluation. A criterion is a standard by which one makes a judgment. We often use more than one standard on which to make a judgment. For example, when evaluating what kind of vehicle to buy, we may decide the three most important standards or criteria by which to judge a vehicle are frequency of repair, gas mileage, and safety. With those criteria established, we now have common standards by which to judge every vehicle we look at. Another example would be establishing criteria by which to decide where to attend college. You might decide that the three most important standards are cost, closeness to where you live, and whether the college offers the program of study you are interested in.

Notice that the standards or criteria for making a judgment about a situation may not be the same for everyone. The examples above, buying a vehicle and choosing a college, illustrate the point. If someone is in the landscaping business, perhaps the criteria for buying a vehicle may include cargo space to carry lawn care equipment, and an engine strong enough to tow a trailer loaded with a backhoe. These criteria lead to the conclusion that a certain kind of truck is necessary. In choosing a college, suppose the student decides that she would like to experience living on the campus of a college with a strong liberal arts curriculum. Then that student may have to travel farther away from home and pay more for her education.

Other situations that call for establishing criteria for evaluation might include some like the following: For a class in the humanities, you may be asked to evaluate a play at your college theater or an art exhibit at your college gallery. A class in marketing might ask you to evaluate different advertising campaigns for their ability to reach a target market. And a group project in a civil engineering class might require you to collaboratively discover the safest and most cost-effective strategy for building a bridge. An effective approach to each assignment begins with a careful assessment of the criteria you will use, based on the purpose of the evaluation you are asked to make.

Exploration

Two very common kinds of evaluation essays are film reviews and restaurant reviews. Go to a newspaper or magazine—in print or online—and copy or print out one of each kind of review. Many newspapers run these kinds of reviews in the Friday issue to give readers some entertainment ideas during the weekend. Read each review carefully and find the criteria or standards the writer uses to evaluate the film or restaurant. Sometimes the criteria are stated explicitly; sometimes they are not. Bring the reviews to class and discuss with one or two classmates each other's findings.

Student Evaluation Essay

Here is an essay written in response to prompt #4 in the Essay Assignments on page 212. Notice how the writer includes her criteria in the topic sentences of her body paragraphs.

Lost Maples State Natural Area

Elizabeth J. Cook
English 1301
Prof. Sabrio
October 6, 2006

Thesis statement

1   Families are often looking for inexpensive, healthful ways of spending vacation time together. If your family likes being outdoors, getting some exercise, and staying away from large crowds, then you would probably love hiking the scenic trails of Lost Maples State Natural Area in the Hill Country of Texas.

Topic sentence (first standard or criterion of evaluation)

Development of topic sentence

2   The accessibility and admission price of a vacation spot are important considerations for families wanting to have a good time without going into debt. Located in the middle of the Texas Hill Country near Vanderpool, Lost Maples is easily accessible for a day trip by the thousands of people living in or near Austin, San Antonio, Corpus Christi, or anywhere in central Texas. Those living in the Dallas and Houston areas could easily plan a two-day vacation to Lost Maples. In addition, the admission fee ranges from three to six dollars per person, depending on one's age and when during the year one visits. So instead of fretting about how they are going to pay for their vacation, families can relax and enjoy themselves.

Topic sentence (next two standards or criteria of evaluation)
Development of topic sentence

3   Two of the major attractions of Lost Maples are its beauty and remoteness. The park gets its name from isolated stands of bigtooth maple trees that thrive in the area's unique microclimate. During autumn (November is often the best time) these trees are transformed into gorgeous sentinels with leaves of red, orange, yellow, and many combinations of these colors. Even if autumn is not a convenient time to visit, the park always offers breathtaking vistas of river valleys, wooded hills, limestone canyons, clear streams, and grassy plateaus. All of this beauty is tucked into an isolated, sparsely populated area of the Texas Hill Country. No major highways cut through here, and the nearest town, Vanderpool, boasts a population of 20. Twelve miles south of the park is Utopia—no kidding! Those who visit the park during a weekday may not see or hear another person on a trail. The only sounds will be the wind rustling through the wooded slopes and bird chatter in the distance.

Topic sentence (next standard or criterion of evaluation)
Development of topic sentence

4   For families that like hiking, Lost Maples offers eleven miles of well-marked trails, divided into four trails of varying distances and degrees of difficulty. The Maple Trail, the least strenuous and shortest at eight-tenths of a mile, takes hikers to the stands of bigtooth maples. The most challenging and longest trail (nearly five miles long) is the West Trail, which wends its way through aptly named Mystic Canyon, a narrow, rugged path cut deep into the limestone. Artifacts found here and in other places in the park suggest that Native Americans lived in these areas for many hundreds of years. Although the elevations in the park (from 1800 to 2250 feet) are nothing compared to the elevations of mountain ranges in the western U.S., certain sections of some trails are daunting because of the steep slopes combined with loose, fist-sized rubble stones that sometimes shift under a hiker's weight. For these trail sections, light to medium weight hiking boots with ankle support are recommended.

Transition and topic sentence (next standard or criterion of evaluation)
Development of topic sentence

5   Hiking is only one of many activities offered at Lost Maples. For those who want a less strenuous experience, picnicking and RV camping are available just inside the park's entrance. For the more adventurous vacationers, backcountry tent camping and fishing are available with permits. Those who enjoy seeing animals in their natural habitat may get a glimpse of white-tailed deer, fox, armadillo, raccoon, bobcat, squirrel, javelina, and many species of birds, including hawks and turkey vultures. The friendly, knowledgeable park rangers at the station near the park's entrance provide information, answers, and maps to visitors.

Restatement of thesis

6   Lost Maples State Natural Area is a true bargain. There are not too many places left that can offer accessibility, value, beauty, no crowds, good hiking, and many other activities. Families could spend a lot more money for a much less satisfying experience. If you cannot visit Lost Maples, I suggest you check out nearby parks in your state.

Getting Started: Constructing Effective Arguments

In popular culture the art of arguing effectively has often degenerated into combative, contentious shouting matches in which the volume of one's voice and the cheering of the audience determine the "winner." Anyone who has watched *The Jerry Springer Show* can attest to this degeneration of the art of argument. In addition, the polarizing tendencies of political debates in the U.S. have further eroded notions of what constitutes an effective argument.

In situations that require you to argue for or against a particular position, we recommend that you go against this popular trend. More often than not, the best results are achieved by a careful, rational, calm approach to argumentation. The Rogerian tactic of finding common ground and emphasizing what opponents can agree on often leads to the best likelihood of success in an argument. It is very easy to lose one's cool when arguing and to be tempted to belittle one's opponents. We admit that it temporarily feels good to fire off a good insult or make an opponent look bad in public. Unfortunately, the short-term satisfaction you may get rarely outweighs the long-term good will and respect you would have gained by focusing on the issues, arguing rationally, and refraining from personal attacks.

Your instructor may ask you to look for—in print, online, or even in television or film—and bring to class examples of the two approaches to argument that we have discussed in the preceding two paragraphs.

Essay Assignments

Writing Evaluations

Look at the following topics. Choose three or four criteria or standards that you might use to evaluate each item. Remember, these criteria may differ from student to student. Your instructor may ask you expand one of these topics (or another suitable topic) into a journal entry or complete essay.

1. Evaluate a play or an art exhibit in your community.

2. Evaluate a nearby restaurant.

3. Evaluate an item that you recently purchased or will soon purchase.

4. Evaluate a nearby state or national park as a possible vacation spot.

5. Evaluate a television show or film that you enjoy.

6. Evaluate a course that you recently took in high school or college.

7. Evaluate some aspect of your college, such as the bookstore or the financial aid office.

8. Evaluate an athletic team that you follow.

9. Evaluate a hobby or pastime that you participate in, in terms of whether others might want to take it up as their hobby or pastime.

Evaluation of Visual Media

An area that brings together several elements of argument and evaluation, and an area that we are all very familiar with, is magazine advertising. Every magazine advertisement is a mini-argument which most often attempts to convince the reader to buy something. Advertisements use the major appeals we discussed earlier: logical, emotional, ethical, and stylistic. Advertisers are sometimes guilty of using fallacies in their ads.

JOURNAL WRITING

Look at the following ads and point out the various appeals and fallacies used, denotations and connotations of words, pictures and other visuals, the overall structure of each ad, and anything else that strikes you as important.

Essay Assignments

Evaluating Advertisements

This assignment brings together several aspects of the study of argument and evaluation. Find two magazine ads for similar products, such as two cell phone ads, two shampoo ads, two makeup ads, two ads for vehicles that are of the same general class and price, or two ads for similar medications. Your purpose is to decide which ad is more effective in selling its product to the consumer. Devote at least one body paragraph to each of the following topics:

1. *Audience.* What audience or group of readers is each ad directed to? The product being sold will help you determine the audience. What magazine(s) do the ads come from? The magazines will also help you determine the readers the ads are directed to.

2. *Words.* How effective are the words used in each ad? What are the denotations and connotations of the key words?

3. *Pictures.* How effective are the pictures in each ad? What is particularly striking about the pictures?

4. *Appeals.* What appeals are used? Logical, emotional, ethical, stylistic? What fallacies, if any, are used in the ad?

The criteria or standards you are using to evaluate the ads are the ways the advertisers use all aspects of the ads to make them cause the viewer to buy the product advertised. You must take a stand and state clearly which ad is more effective in selling its product. Use the point-by-point or part-to-part method of organization that was discussed in Chapter 5.

Student Essay
Comparing Two Ads

Secret vs. Soft & Dri

HOLLY REMMERS

Dr. Sabrio
English 1301-013
27 January 2005

Thesis statement

1   Today's world is surrounded by advertisements. Every company and industry out there wants consumers to buy the new product that they have. Many items are similar, causing some consumers difficulty in choosing. I have found numerous products out there and have had some difficulty in choosing which product is better for me. One such case of this involves women's deodorant. I found these two ads in *Seventeen* magazine, which appeals to teenage girls and young women. After I reviewed the advertisements for Secret Tropical Radiance and Soft & Dri deodorants, I found that the ad for Secret deodorant is more appealing and effective.

Topic sentence
Development of topic sentence

2   First of all, I will discuss one of the most important aspects of any advertisement, the photography. The ad for Secret Platinum Tropical Radiance has a beautiful, brightly colored background. It looks similar to what you would see at dusk on a Hawaiian island, a sight of pure magnificence. Hues of bright orange, yellow, and red blend together to illuminate the model and her gown. There is a woman in the center of the advertisement wearing a beautiful, brightly colored dress. Pink flamingos, palm trees, a monkey, flowers, and luscious tropical foliage surround her. Sparkling gems cascade around her presence. The Soft & Dri advertisement is more subdued. Everything is in a dull black and white scheme. The model is wearing a hot pink dress. A visualization of the product and the model are the only two things in color. A construction site is in the background of the top half of the page. The bottom half of the page is solid black with the exception of the product photo and a few words. She is holding a large wrench with a solid, stern look on her face. The way she holds her body makes her seem tough and strong. I would rather look at the Secret Platinum Tropical Radiance advertisement simply because the model looks like she is enjoying herself. Her big smile is much more pleasant than a harsh look.

Transition
Topic sentence
Development of topic sentence

3   Visualizations are not the only key aspect of a good, effective advertisement. Words also play a major role. First of all, there are not very many

words in either of the advertisements. The slogan "When you're strong, you Sparkle" is headlining the advertisement for Secret Platinum Tropical Radiance. The fact that there are not very many words makes this advertisement more effective because it is simple and gets to the point right away. In the Soft & Dri advertisement the slogan "Strong & Beautiful" runs across the middle of the page. "Strong" plays up the model's harsh look and the fact that she's holding a wrench in front of a construction site with heavy machinery, which is typically a brawny male's territory. There is a sentence at the bottom of the page giving some highlights about the deodorant. It is a little lengthy and just describes what the deodorant is supposed to do for the consumers' skin. I feel that a lengthy explanation is unnecessary and most people probably will not read the sentence. It is in a place that most people may not look at right away. Many consumers want a short, simple catchphrase that is easily remembered. The model is called the "Transmission Tamer," as it says in the short description in the top left corner of the advertisement. This was redundant because the description is only claiming that she is wearing the deodorant. Common sense would say that since she is promoting the product, she would be wearing it.

Transition and topic sentence
Development of topic sentence

4   Finally I will describe some of the tactics used to get the consumers' attention. As I mentioned before, visual stimulation is a key element in advertising. There is much more imagery for the eye in the Secret Platinum Tropical Radiance advertisement than there is in the Soft & Dri advertisement. In the Secret Tropical Radiance ad the model has her hands lifted above her head, as if they were trying to reach the banner with the slogan, "Tropical Radiance." Our eyes will naturally follow her arms above her head so that we will focus in on the banner. The two flamingos have their beaks pointing down towards the lower banner and the picture of the product. There is also a monkey looking up at the deodorant and the lower banner. The pictures of the fruit also drew my attention down to the picture of the deodorant and the banner with the other scents in the collection. As I wrote earlier, there is not that much visual stimulation in the advertisement for Soft & Dri deodorant. The model's gaze seems to drift down towards the slogan in the middle of the page. The photograph of the product is slightly larger than the product in the Secret deodorant ad. Also, the picture is a focus since the product is pink and the background is solid black. It seems to pop off the page toward the consumer.

Topic sentence
Development of topic sentence

5   Both advertisements are appealing to young women and teenagers. All women want to feel strong and beautiful. These deodorant products are saying that they are strong enough to protect a strong and beautiful woman. Actually it seems as if the Secret Tropical Radiance advertisement plays up the beautiful aspect more than the strength aspect which is clearly evident in the Soft & Dri advertisement. The woman in the Soft & Dri Advertisement exudes strength while maintaining her beauty, whereas the model in the Secret Tropical Radiance advertisement exudes beauty. Young women

are especially keen on wanting to feel strong and beautiful, which is what both products claim to provide.

Restatement of thesis 6   After looking at the strengths and weaknesses of both ads, I have found that the advertisement for Secret Platinum Tropical Radiance is more effective and appealing than the Soft & Dri advertisement. Visualizations, slogans, and tactics are used more effectively to gain the young female readers' attention, which essentially leads to a more appealing advertisement.

Insightful Writing

Studying arguments and evaluations is not just a dry academic exercise. People make arguments, either orally or in writing, all the time in their everyday activities and in their professions. People must evaluate arguments every day when making decisions at work, as consumers, as voters, and as family members. People must evaluate products, courses of action, and even other people. The more you know about arguments and evaluations, the more likely you will be able to make informed decisions that affect you and your loved ones.

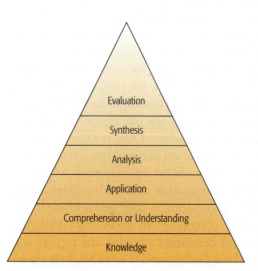

Evaluating arguments, or any form of evaluation for that matter, is not always easy. In one of the most famous and most frequently cited classifications in U.S. educational history, Benjamin Bloom (1913–1999), who was an influential education professor at the University of Chicago, ranks "evaluation" as the most complex and abstract form of intellectual behavior in learning. Bloom's well-known hierarchy or "taxonomy" ranks the various forms of intellectual behavior as shown in the accompanying diagram, from lowest level to highest level:

Bloom and his colleagues found that the order in which most people learn is somewhat similar. Learning at the two lower levels of knowledge and comprehension builds a foundation on which the so-called "higher-order thinking/learning skills" are developed. You'll notice that the writing assignments in this book are usually sequenced from lower level to higher level learning/thinking activity, with analysis, synthesis, and argument/evaluation coming mostly in later chapters.

11

Research and Writing with Sources

A world of facts lies outside and beyond the world of words.

Thomas Huxley

Get the facts, or the facts will get you. And when you get 'em, get 'em right, or they will get you wrong.

Thomas Fuller

Several assignments in earlier chapters required you to research various topics. Sometimes the process is relatively painless. Writing about your own family traditions (Chapter 4) will not require hours in the library searching through files or conducting searches on the Internet. Instead, information is probably readily available from your own memories and some conversations with relatives. However, if you choose to compare three different religions (Chapter 7) in an essay, it becomes necessary to do a little research. Similarly, an essay on fanaticism (Chapter 8) requires you to look through several issues of *Time* or *Newsweek* magazine and pick an article about a person or people who might fit the definition of a "fanatic" as defined by Elie Wiesel. The information in this chapter shows you how to research a topic and use the sources (books, articles, websites, interviews, etc.) to support your essay's thesis.

One major challenge of writing a research paper is deciding how much and what kind of information to include. So much information is available, both printed and electronic, that it would be impossible to read everything about a topic you choose to research. The time alone required to do so would be prohibitive. This chapter gives a concise overview of how to access the information you need, evaluate the information for accuracy, and use the information to accomplish a specific purpose such as completing a project or solving a problem.

Another important topic covered in this chapter is the subject of plagiarism. You will learn how to avoid plagiarism and give the proper credit to the sources you use when writing a research paper.

Were you required to write a research paper in high school? What was your topic? Were you able to complete the paper and turn it in to the teacher on time? List three things that you learned from the experience. If you had a chance to go back in time, would you choose to write about the same topic? Why or why not?

We live in a time period where the concept of "literacy" has expanded beyond just the ability to read and write. If you know how to use the basic software programs available on a computer, you are considered "computer literate." Most of us have heard this terminology before, but you may not be familiar with the term "information literacy." The Association of College and Research Libraries has developed standards for becoming an "information literate student." Keep these standards in mind as we explore ways to research and write with sources.

Finally, be sure to supplement the general guidelines and advice for conducting research and writing from sources covered in this chapter with the detailed instructions that you can access in a writing handbook or similar reference texts readily available at your college library or a bookstore. Your campus writing center, a reference librarian, and your writing teacher can assist you in finding and evaluating different kinds of information.

PRACTICAL TIPS   The Information Literate Student

▶ Standard One: The information literate student determines the nature and extent of the information needed.

▶ Standard Two: The information literate student accesses needed information effectively and efficiently.

▶ Standard Three: The information literate student evaluates information and its sources critically and incorporates selected information into his or her knowledge base and value system.

▶ Standard Four: The information literate student, individually or as a member of a group, uses information effectively to accomplish a specific purpose.

▶ Standard Five: The information literate student understands many of the economic, legal, and social issues surrounding the use of information and accesses and uses information ethically and legally.

Planning Your Research

Whenever you embark upon a research project, remember the Five P's rule: *Prior Planning Prevents Poor Performance*. Prior planning can also eliminate the stress caused by running out of time on an assignment. Despite what some of your friends may say, writers generally do their best work when they have had enough sleep. Fatigue does not sharpen the mind.

Use the following checklist to make sure you are able to finish your assignment on time. Before you begin to fill in the checklist you should read your assignment carefully. Make sure that you understand what

---

PRACTICAL TIPS | **Build a Research Paper Timeline**

Stage 1: Preparing or Generating

Read the assignment carefully to understand the requirements.

Choose your topic or narrow the topic given by the instructor.

Conduct searches on library databases and the Internet to make sure you have enough sources.

Develop a research question or thesis statement.

Read and evaluate the sources you plan to use.

Set a target date for completion of Stage 1: _____

Stage 2: Organizing/Drafting/Shaping

Make copies of online articles and photocopies or notes of library materials.

Develop an outline of the paper and organize your sources.

Collect more sources if necessary as you complete the outline.

Choose quotations and write summaries or paraphrases of sources you might want to use.

Write the first draft.

Set a target date for completion of Stage 2: _____

Stage 3: Revising

Get feedback from your instructor and classmates.

Conduct more research, if necessary, to address comments or concerns from your instructor or classmates.

Evaluate the first draft.

Revise the draft (global, body paragraphs, and sentence level).

Set a target date for completion of Stage 3: _____

Stage 4: Editing/Proofreading

Format paper to conform to MLA guidelines.

Prepare the Works Cited page.

Edit and proofread paper.

Prepare final draft.

Set a target date for completion of Stage 4: _____

your instructor is asking you to do. How many words will the final paper contain? How many sources (books, reference books, magazines, newspapers, journals, articles from the Internet) need to be used?

Selecting a Topic, Research Question, and Thesis

Research paper topics come in various flavors and shades. The topic could be historical, literary, political, scientific, or even some aspect of you as an individual. You can search for a topic as you go about your daily activities of watching TV, browsing the Internet, reading magazines, and talking with friends. Keep in mind that you will be writing your paper for a specific audience and that the topic should be appropriate for your readers. This will help you begin the process of narrowing your topic and developing your research question and framing a thesis statement that will serve as the framework for your paper.

Topics

Choose a topic that you are interested in knowing more about. Since you will be spending a considerable amount of time researching and writing about your topic, it will make the experience more enjoyable if you are genuinely interested in the subject matter.

Even if the general topic for a research paper is assigned by your instructor, you can focus on the aspect of the topic that interests you the most as you narrow the broad topic into a suitable topic for a research paper. The process is similar to developing an essay thesis. You "narrow down" your topic by limiting its scope. The process involves going from the *general* to the *specific*. Below are examples:

Broad topic:	Mental illnesses
Narrowed-down topic:	Depression
More narrow:	Different types of treatment for depression
Broad topic:	Violence in schools
Narrowed-down topic:	Bullying
More narrow:	Bullying behavior by boys in elementary schools
Broad topic:	Drug abuse
Narrowed-down topic:	Drug abuse by athletes
More narrow:	Anabolic steroid use by bodybuilders

Once you have decided on a suitable topic, generate a list of possible sources to begin researching. It is important to make sure that your topic will have enough credible (scholarly and trustworthy) sources to allow you to complete your assignment. Conduct a preliminary search to determine how much and what type of information is available. As you read the titles and summaries of the articles, begin formulating some possible research questions for your paper.

Research Questions

What makes a good research question? Your question should focus on a specific aspect of your topic and should contain the key terms that you can use for a successful search for sources. Here are some sample research questions based on the narrowed-down topics just listed:

1. What different types of treatment for depression are available to people living in rural America?

2. Do patients receive different types of treatment for depression based on their age, gender, and socioeconomic status?

3. Does bullying behavior by boys in elementary school predict future behavior problems in school and life?

4. Does bullying behavior by boys in elementary school cause lifetime problems for their victims?

5. What are the long-term effects of anabolic steroid use by body-builders on their careers and health?

6. Is anabolic steroid use by bodybuilders continuing to grow, and what steps are athletic and law enforcement officials taking to curb the growth?

You might need to revise your research question if you discover that there are not enough sources available. Another reason for changing your research question is realizing that too much information is available and covering the topic would involve discussing too many issues and would take too much time. The research question should transition into and be logically connected to your thesis statement.

Thesis Statement

Your thesis statement focuses your paper on specific aspects of the topic and provides a way to answer your research question through examples, evidence, evaluation, arguments, and other forms of support. Please note that the thesis statement is not merely a statement of fact; it is a statement that can be developed and supported throughout the paper. You will take a position on a topic and hold or defend that position by providing relevant information, examples, and logical arguments that support your position. Below are two sample thesis statements related to the research questions shown earlier:

1. Age, gender, and socioeconomic status are important factors that affect what type of treatment for depression a person receives.

2. The long-term negative effects of bullying behavior by boys include a greater risk of developing depression in adulthood for the victims and an increased probability of criminal activity in later life by those who act as bullies.

Finding and Evaluating Sources

The best places to begin your research are the campus library and the Internet. Your campus library is a great place to start working on your assignment. The staff of the library, especially the reference librarians, can be one of your greatest resources for completing your assignment. Ask your library staff about opportunities such as free workshops to explain the services and resources available to students. You will learn what types of reference books are available and learn how to look for specific books related to your topic. Many libraries also have searchable databases that list articles from thousands of magazines and scholarly journals. If you do not have Internet access in your home or dormitory room, almost every library offers access to computers connected to the Internet. In addition, many colleges have computer labs with Internet access available for student use.

What kind of information would you find if you conducted a Google search for the specific topic of "anabolic steroid use by bodybuilders"? When these words were typed into the Google search engine (on June 13, 2007), more than 500,000 articles were found. Based on the search results you can determine that there are many sources for your paper. While this is still a large amount of information to consider, the number of "hits" is considerably smaller than a Google search for the words "anabolic steroids," which returned over 1.2 million articles. However, the mere *quantity* of articles that you find should not be your only concern. You also need to determine whether the *quality* of the articles you are going to use is appropriate for your assignment. The same search conducted on Google Scholar will yield approximately 3700 articles. The Google Scholar search results also show how many times each article was cited by other scholars conducting research. You could read through several hundred articles and see if the authors are reputable, or you could use a database that already makes an attempt to eliminate unreliable and disreputable sources.

Evaluating the Credibility of Online Sources

The next step is to determine whether there are enough credible (authoritative and believable) sources for your topic. Two major advantages of using your college library's databases for conducting research are (1) the number of articles will be much smaller, and (2) the quality of the information you find will be reliable. Many sites on the Internet contain credible and useful information, but not every source on the Internet can be used in a research paper. Websites may be sponsored by an unscrupulous person or organization that uses misleading or false information to promote a specific viewpoint on an issue. Also, remember that some websites are commercial enterprises designed for promoting a product, political opinion, or industry rather than providing scholarly information for research purposes.

Finding Online Sources

Check with your library reference desk or library website for a list of reputable websites. Many magazines, newspapers, and radio and television news broadcasts have online versions, and there are reliable online libraries such as the Internet Public Library, the Library of Congress, and Presidential libraries.

Evaluating a Website

If you find a promising online source for your research paper, you will need to rely on your own critical thinking skills to evaluate its reliability and timeliness. Below are several questions that will help you determine the usefulness of an online source for your research purposes.

What Type of Website or Webpage Is It?   Look at the web address of the page. The address is sometimes referred to as the URL, which stands for Uniform Resource Locator. The URL is a unique address for a web document. Part of the URL contains the domain name of the website. Examining the domain name can tell you what type of organization published the page. A ".com" ending on the domain name lets you know that the site is a commercial site owned by a business or individual. An ".org" ending usually tells you that a nonprofit organization published the website (e.g., www.ipl.org). Universities and colleges usually have an ".edu" ending, while government agencies have an ".org" or ".gov" ending. As the Internet grows, additional URL endings will be created. It is up to you to discover the owner and purpose of the website.

How Did It Become a Website?   Who is the person or group responsible for creating the webpage? Who is listed as the author of the page? How often has the information on the page been updated? Look for links on the page that can direct you to information about the author and publishers. These links are often labeled "About Us," "Background," "Mission Statement," or something similar.

How Useful Is the Website for Your Specific Assignment? Compare the information presented on the webpage with the domain name. Scholarly publications contain links or footnotes that credit the sources of information (facts, data, etc.) presented. Does the author have credentials that qualify him or her to speak as an expert on the topic? Are there links on the website to other resources related to the topic? Do the links actually work? Are the links well organized, and do they offer a balanced perspective on the topic? Does the author list credible sources as part of the information presented rather than simply presenting personal opinions? Does the webpage contain numerous grammatical and spelling errors?

Should You Use the Webpage as a Source? Consider all of the above factors to determine whether the source is trustworthy and credible. As mentioned earlier, the staff at the library is always willing to help if you are uncertain. Instructors are also a good resource. Ask yourself if the information from this site is as good as or better than what you could find through typical library resources (online databases, Facts on File, reference books, scholarly journals, etc.). If you are unable to locate the name of an author, the author's credentials, or publisher and purpose of a webpage, you probably should not use the information from the site in your research.

Evaluating the Credibility of Print Sources

Articles and books should be evaluated for the quality as well as the timeliness of the information they contain. Recognizing and evaluating scholarly and trustworthy print sources is an important part of the research process. Often you can get help with this task by asking a librarian or instructor about the article or book you are considering as a potential research source for your project. Periodicals consist of scholarly journals (e.g., *Sociological Methods & Research, American Educational Research Journal, Culture & Psychology*), popular magazines (e.g., *Scientific American, Psychology Today, Time, Newsweek*), and newspapers (e.g., *The New York Times, Wall Street Journal, USA Today*). These publications are called periodicals because they are published on a set schedule over a period of time (i.e., daily, weekly, monthly, quarterly, yearly).

A scholarly article in a journal contains the author's name and usually describes his or her background and credentials. The work of other scholars who have written about the topic will be mentioned in the form of in-text citations or footnotes and a bibliographical list of sources used by the author. Articles in scholarly journals go through a peer review process before they are accepted for publication. This means that other experts in the academic world will have read the article and decided whether it is worthy of publication. You can scan an article and read the "Abstract," "Conclusions," or "Recommendations for further research" sections to see if it contains useful information for your research project.

Magazines such as *Scientific American* or the *Smithsonian* contain in-depth articles designed for readers who have a specific interest in science or history. The articles usually contain references at the end and offer a serious treatment of a topic. Articles in magazines such as *Time* and *Newsweek* are written for a general audience and address current events and popular culture. These articles provide substantive news and information, but they are usually shorter and contain fewer references than magazines targeted to specific interests. Less suitable for academic research are articles in magazines such as *National Enquirer* or *Star Magazine* that are designed to entertain readers by treating topics in a sensational manner. These publications, which often do not name the authors of articles, contain the latest gossip about celebrities and sometimes questionable news stories about monsters and aliens.

Like magazines, newspapers come in various shades of reputation and trustworthiness. Major national publications pride themselves on journalistic integrity, but even some of the largest and best-known newspapers have been known to print biased and poorly researched stories. It is important to check the sources for the information you plan to use in a research paper.

When you plan to use a book as a source, research the author thoroughly. Look at the brief description of the author on the book's jacket or in the last pages. Is the author a recognized expert or authority on the topic? Check the Internet to see what other books have been written by the same author. Check the date of publication to confirm that the source's information is timely (although, of course, there are certain classics of scholarship that will always be considered worthy of your attention). The table of contents will give you a general idea of what is covered in the book; looking up key words about your topic and research question in the index will help determine the extent of that coverage. Skim the preface and the first and last paragraphs of each chapter. Sometimes there is only one chapter in a book related to your topic, and skimming through the book will help you save time by limiting how much you read.

Interviews

Conducting research does not always involve reading a book, article, or webpage. Sometimes it is necessary to interview someone to find specific information. You may also gain access to the records of someone who has conducted interviews of people on the topic you are researching. An interview with a person can be used as a source for writing a research paper.

It is important to make sure that the person interviewed has the necessary authority and expertise to provide reliable information. For instance, if you were working on a paper that compared various religions, you might want to interview a local rabbi, priest, or minister to get information that supports or refutes information you have found in books or articles. You should plan carefully to document your interview by following the same procedure or "protocol" with each person you interview. Develop a list of questions to ask each person you interview, and take notes that faithfully reflect what happened in each interview. It is a good idea to have your instructor look at your list of questions before you begin. Using a list of questions that do not create an unfair or biased interview is an important ethical consideration, and it is also simply good manners not waste a person's time by going to an interview unprepared.

If your research has led you to a source consisting of interviews or personal observations, make sure that the subjects being interviewed possess the credentials or background to make them authoritative sources. Field notes, logs, and journals are possible sources of information to use

PRACTICAL TIPS   Effective Interviews

Before the interview
- ▶ Plan well in advance.
- ▶ Contact potential interviewee and give the big picture.
- ▶ Set up interview.
- ▶ Develop open-ended questions.

During the interview
- ▶ Use your written questions.
- ▶ Let interviewee do most of the talking.
- ▶ Be open to unanticipated directions of interview.
- ▶ Ask permission to record interview.
- ▶ Ask for clarification if necessary.
- ▶ Thank interviewee.

After the interview
- ▶ Develop notes immediately.
- ▶ Use the interview information appropriately.

in your research, but you should evaluate their trustworthiness the same way you would do with books and articles.

You can also interview someone via e-mail. Establish contact first with a courteous (and brief) e-mail introducing yourself and describing your project. If the person agrees to assist you, ask them to respond to a list of well-phrased and key questions. One advantage of an e-mail interview is that both you and the interviewee have time to compose thoughtful and detailed questions and answers. In addition, the person's words will be much easier to quote. Check your handbook or ask your instructor about the appropriate citation styles for e-mails, and be sure to thank your interviewee with an e-mail or even a handwritten note.

Developing a Working Bibliography

A bibliography is a list of the books, articles, and online sources an author consulted or referred to as he or she produced a book or article. A "working bibliography" for your research paper may be a group of note cards or computer files that contain the information mentioned in the "Practical Tips" box.

> ### PRACTICAL TIPS | Information to Record in a Working Bibliography
>
> ▶ Author or editor name(s): Starting with the last name, write the name of each author. If the work does not have an author or editor listed, record the name of the corporation, organization, or governmental agency. Often no author or editor will be listed for entries in a reference book such as a dictionary or encyclopedia.
>
> ▶ Title and subtitle
>
> ▶ Publisher
>
> ▶ Edition
>
> ▶ Volume number
>
> ▶ Date of publication
>
> ▶ Internet address (URL)
>
> ▶ Document name
>
> ▶ Date of access
>
> ▶ Name of online database
>
> ▶ Brief notes with the page numbers and key words of quotations from the sources you are considering.

Organize your research information alphabetically by the last name of the author or authors. You can add a new source or decide not to use a particular source as you work on your paper. Keeping a careful record of the sources will help you compose an accurate Works Cited page and avoid plagiarism. The working bibliography can be used to help write an annotated bibliography. The annotated bibliography contains the same basic information as your working bibliography, but it also has a summary of the article as well as comments about how you plan to use the information in your paper. This is also a good place to write your evaluation of the credibility and trustworthiness of the source and author.

Avoiding Plagiarism

The first step in avoiding plagiarism is to understand what your instructor means when he or she tells you not to commit plagiarism. If you use the ideas or writings of someone else without acknowledging the sources of these ideas or writings, then you are committing plagiarism. In effect, you are taking credit for something that you did not create or think of yourself. This is considered a serious offense in college and could result in an F on an assignment or even more severe consequences. Ultimately, you are cheating yourself out of an opportunity to learn from doing the work on your own.

You are probably aware that it is unacceptable to copy test answers from a classmate or to turn in an essay written by someone else. In the same way, it is unacceptable to copy part of an article or book and pretend that you wrote it yourself. However, it is perfectly acceptable to use information that you have discovered through your research in the library or on the Internet in a research paper. When you use the exact words from a source, you will need to enclose the passage in quotation marks (" ") and make sure the words are attributed to the author and source. If you are summarizing or paraphrasing rather than directly quoting someone's words, you will not use quotation marks, but you must mention the author and source. You can avoid plagiarism by following the accepted rules for documenting your sources. The first step in the process of avoiding plagiarism is to develop good note-taking skills.

How to Take Notes from Sources and Document Them

As you begin to organize and shape your research paper, take notes by summarizing, paraphrasing, and quoting to identify possible examples and information that will support your thesis. Developing good note-taking skills will help you throughout your academic career. Listening to lectures, watching video clips, reading lengthy assignments, and conducting observations all require you to identify the main ideas and relevant information that might appear on a test. Skillful note-taking will lead to successful completion of college courses.

Summarizing the Main Ideas

A summary presents the main ideas of a source in a concise manner. The source could be an entire article or a book or just a passage from an article or book. In each case you should begin by mentioning the author or source and use your own wording to describe the most important information in the same sequence it appears in the original text. Sometimes you may want to use the exact wording for a particular phrase or sentence in your summary. Just make sure that these phrases or sentences are enclosed in quotation marks. Do not get carried away by quoting long passages. By its very nature a summary is much shorter than the original. Do not include your thoughts or insights about the writing in the summary. Your purpose is to provide the reader with pertinent information from the source in a brief form. Use the complete writing process (preparing/generating, organizing/drafting, revising, editing/proofreading) as you construct a summary. Here are some steps to follow when you summarize an article. The same steps can be adapted for summarizing a book, speech, or even a movie.

Use the reporter's formula (who, what, when, where, why, and how) as you read the original-source text and make notes or underline/highlight key concepts and important words. Pay particular attention to the title, subtitle, and subheadings. These will give you many of the main ideas and show the overall organization of the text. Next, reread the first paragraph and last paragraph of the text. These are key paragraphs in most articles, and carefully reading them will often reveal the author's major points. Identify the topic sentence in each of the body paragraphs of the article. Frequently, but not always, these are the first sentence in a paragraph. Organize your notes as an outline. Develop your first draft by writing (in your own words) one or two sentences for each major point in the article. As you revise your summary, exclude supporting examples and illustrations of the major points. Remember that this is a summary and you are not trying to write the entire article. At the end of your summary be sure to cite the page numbers of the source. This lets the reader know where the summary ends and where your own interpretations and thoughts about the topic begin.

To illustrate the process of writing a summary, we have provided an original-source text followed by examples of unacceptable and acceptable summaries. Explanatory notes can be found in the margins.

Reading

Original-Source Text

"How Do Our Kids Get So Caught Up in Consumerism?"

BY BRIAN SWIMME, PH. D. (from paragraph 5)

The advertisers of course are not some bad persons with evil designs. They are just doing their job. On the other hand, we can also say that their primary concern is not explicitly the well-being of our children. Why should it be? Their objective is to create ads that are successful for their company, and this means to get the television viewer interested in their product. But already we can see that this is a less than desirable situation. After all, we parents demand that our children's teachers, to take just one example, should have our children's best interests foremost in mind. Such teachers will shape our children when they are young and vulnerable, so of course we want this shaping to be done only by people who care. So to hand over so much of our children's lives to people who obviously do not have our children's well-being foremost in mind is at the very least questionable. But at a deeper level, what we need to confront is the power of the advertiser to promulgate a world-view, a mini-cosmology, that is based upon dissatisfaction and craving.

Author not mentioned.

The words "they are just doing their job," "well-being," and "shape our children" are not in quotation marks.

Personal opinions and evaluation of the writing should not be included in a summary.

Example of Unacceptable Summary

Advertisers are not evil people. They are just doing their job, but they are not concerned about the well-being of our children. The primary goals of the advertiser are to create interest in a product and produce sales for their company. Parents would not allow their children to be taught by teachers that were indifferent to their children's well-being, but advertisers are allowed to shape our children's world-view and to encourage them to crave new products. I think we give too much power to advertisers to influence our children.

[187 words in original text; 86 words in summary.]

Example of Acceptable Summary

Title and author are mentioned.

Judicious use of a quote is acceptable.

In the paragraph from *How Do Our Kids Get So Caught Up in Consumerism?* by Brian Swimme, the author questions the wisdom of letting advertisers shape our children's "world-view." Unlike teachers who we assume care about the healthy development of children, advertisers just want to sell their product and do not necessarily care about how it will affect children. We should examine the impact of advertisers on children's attitudes toward what is important in life.

[187 words in original text; 77 words in summary.]

Paraphrase

Paraphrasing a passage from an original source allows you to provide more details to your reader than would be found in a summary. A paraphrase is often almost as long as the original text. You are not trying to condense the information you are sharing. Instead, you are using your own words to express the information and arguments of the author. A well-written paraphrase shows that you fully understand the author's perspective of the ideas he or she has presented. This is one reason why many writing instructors encourage students to use paraphrasing as a tool for taking notes. Take care not to use the same wording or copy the sentence structure too closely. You might inadvertently commit plagiarism if you do not take the time to compare your paraphrase with the original text.

Example of Unacceptable Paraphrase

Sentence structure and wording "bad people" is too much like the original.

Brian Swimme does not believe that advertisers are bad people with evil plans. They are employees. As employees their primary concern is not the well-being of children who are exposed to their ads. They want the television viewer to become interested in the product or service they are selling and they want their company to reap the profits of a successful ad campaign. We see a big problem with this situation. For example, parents demand that teachers actually care about children's well-being. Parents realize that teachers shape the ideas and beliefs children have about the world. They are only willing to let teachers play this role if the motives of the teachers are in line with the best interests of the children they serve. It is questionable to give advertisers the power to shape our children's world-view by making them unsatisfied with their life so that they crave new products.

Throughout this paraphrase there are numerous examples of picking up exact wording without using quotation marks and of copying the sentence structure of the original text.

[187 words in original text; 148 words in paraphrase.]

Example of Acceptable Paraphrase

Brian Swimme points out advertisers are not sinister people planning to harm our children. Their job is to create ads that stimulate interest in products or services and produce sales for the company they represent.

On the other hand, Swimme believes we should not assume that advertisers are concerned about how the ads they create might have adverse effects on children. Parents would not want their children to be taught by teachers who did not have a sincere desire to do what is best for children. Children are very impressionable and Swimme asserts that it is unwise to let advertisers exert so much influence on them when the motivation is just to create new customers, not actually improve lives. We need to examine the profound impact advertisers have on these future consumers. It does not seem reasonable to let the lifelong habits and values of children be to buy the newest, most appealing, or popular products (paragraph 5).

[187 words in original text; 156 words in paraphrase.]

Quotation

Chances are pretty good that you have photocopied many of your sources or saved parts of articles on computer files. Sometimes a particular passage will draw your attention by the author's clever use of the English language. Also, as you read about a technical or complex subject, a key idea will be defined or illustrated with vivid language. Highlight these passages for possible use in your research paper. Remember that one of the techniques for grabbing your readers' interest is to begin or end an essay with a relevant quotation. As you process all of the source material you have gathered in your research, keep looking for possible quotes that would support your thesis or help support a key point.

Use direct quotations when you want readers to hear directly from an authoritative source or when paraphrasing would not convey the precise point that you want to make. This can be tricky because it is easy to decide that you really cannot say what you want to say without quoting extensively from a source text. Ask yourself why you need to quote a passage instead of paraphrasing. Perhaps you need to attempt to paraphrase first and then make a decision. Pay careful attention to the quote when you take notes to prevent making mistakes. As you blend a quote into your narrative you must use the same words and punctuation found in the original text. Quotations longer than four lines from an article or book are indented rather than enclosed in quotation marks. Begin the quotation on a new line and document the source by citing the page number in parentheses at the end of the passage after the period. A final word of advice about quotations is to use them sparingly. Your instructor wants to read what you think about a topic and not just the opinions of others.

Example of Unacceptable Quotation

Brian Swimme argues that advertisers do not always have children's "best interests" foremost in mind. He also states, "But at a deeper level, what we need to confront is the power of the advertiser to promulgate a world-view, a mini-cosmology, that is based upon dissatisfaction and craving."

Example of Acceptable Quotation

Brian Swimme argues that advertisers are not like teachers, and therefore parents should not expect advertisers to "have our children's best interests foremost in mind" (page number).

Example of Acceptable Quotation

Swimme asserts the fundamental problem is "the power of the advertiser to promulgate a world-view, a mini-cosmology, that is based upon dissatisfaction and craving" (page number).

Example of Acceptable Long Quotation

Brian Swimme describes the motivations of people who influence the minds and hearts of children. Teachers are required, as part of their job description, to foster the healthy development of children. Parents realize that the significant time spent in school has a great impact on their children's values and beliefs. Children also spend a large amount of time watching television and are bombarded with numerous commercials. Swimme comments:

> The advertisers of course are not some bad persons with evil designs. They are just doing their job. On the other hand, we can also say that their primary concern is not explicitly the well-being of our children. Why should it be? Their objective is to create ads that are successful for their company, and this means to get the television viewer interested in their product. But already we can see that this is a less than desirable situation. (page number)

Other Strategies for Avoiding Plagiarism

Whenever you use another writer's words or ideas as part of your paper, make sure you give credit to the original author and text. Plagiarism can occur through carelessness or on purpose. In each case it is still a violation of academic integrity. Even if you plagiarize unintentionally, there are severe consequences. Reporters, researchers, computer programmers, and even weathermen have been fired for committing plagiarism.

PRACTICAL TIPS | Key Strategies for Avoiding Plagiarism

1. Plan your time wisely to avoid the temptation of committing plagiarism because your paper is due tomorrow and you just got started.

2. Keep careful records of the author, title, and publisher of your source materials.

3. Develop a method for taking notes that ensures proper documentation. Always include the author's name in your notes and indicate whether it is a summary, paraphrase, or quote.

4. Do not use a passage from a source when you have lost the name of the author and title.

5. Remember that summaries and paraphrases have to give proper credit to the author of the ideas as well as the words.

6. If someone offers to sell you an essay, just say no. Purchasing someone else's work will not help you to develop the skills necessary to successfully complete assignments.

7. Double check each quote against the original text for spelling and punctuation, and provide proper documentation. Make sure that key words or phrases used in the original text are enclosed in quotation marks.

Essay Assignment

Research Essay: The Day I Was Born

In this essay you will do research on what the world was like on the day you were born. Since you will not be able to discuss everything that was happening on the day of your birth, you will have to choose the four or five main topics that interest you the most or those that have had the most influence on you.

Here are some topics to consider: What was a significant international event, or national event, or state event, or local event on the day of your birth? What wars (if any) were being fought? What political issues were important? What was going on in the area of popular culture, such as sports, music, fashion, television, movies? What consumer products were popular?

If you could go back to your birth date and be the same age then as you are now, what kinds of activities would you like to do? What would you like to see, wear, experience?

How or in what ways do you believe you are a "product" of the time of your birth? That is, how have you been affected by the time and place of your birth?

What generalizations can you make about the kind of place the United States (or the country of your birth) was on the day you were born? What were some of the concerns, hopes, preoccupations, contradictions, oppositions of the time?

The purpose of your essay is to communicate to your audience a sense of what the world and culture were like at the time you were born. You also want to give a personal perspective on the time of your birth, not the impersonal perspective of many history books. Another purpose of this essay is to help you understand yourself better.

You must use at least six different sources for this essay. You must use two different newspapers, one of which must be *The New York Times.* You must use two different weekly magazines, such as *Time, Newsweek,* or a specialized magazine on some topic of your interest (such as *Sports Illustrated*). You must use at least one almanac or yearbook, and at least one person (such as a family member or relative) who can tell you something about the time of your birth. The librarian will help you locate some of the resources. Remember to keep careful notes of authors, titles, dates, page numbers, and other bibliographic information for your Works Cited page. It is strongly recommend that you photocopy all the materials that you use.

The length of the essay will be 700 to 900 words. Keep a copy of the essay for yourself and put it away so that your descendants can look at it.

Student Essay

The following paper was written in response to the essay assignment on "The Day I Was Born."

Title is centered.

On This Day in 1986

Amy Wolter

Instructor's name   Dr. Sabrio

College course   English 1302

Date   7 March 2005

Thesis is stated.

Preview of paper's organization and subtopics

1   As the eighties phrase goes, "Take a chill pill" and prepare to be transported back in time to the year 1986. It may sound "cheesy," another eighties word, but the year 1986 is particularly significant to me because it is the year in which I was born. By extensively researching on what the world was like around June 19, 1986, I have discovered that quite a bit has changed in the world since then. Issues focusing on South African apartheid, abortion rights, and the status of NASA were prominent around that time. Also, one

can discover what shaped a time period by evaluating the pop culture trends found in music, movies, television and fashion.

Development of sub-topic "apartheid"

2   A storm of controversy was brewing in South Africa surrounding the time in which I was born. The controversy dealt with the apartheid system that was once prominent in South Africa. Apartheid can be defined as "the former policy of the South African government designed to maintain the separation of Blacks and other non-Whites from the dominant Whites" (Gwertzman A10). The article is from the June 20, 1986 edition of *The New York Times*, "U.S. to Cite Vote to Press Pretoria." The desire of the Reagan administration was to persuade Pretoria, the capital of South Africa, to end its corrupt apartheid system. Unless the South Africa government took significant steps to end this system, they would face new sanctions. The United States encouraged the establishment of a representative form of government by their continued involvement in reform. The article ends by stating that "American business in South Africa is helping to break apartheid. They've led the way in promoting an end to segregation in the workplace" (A10). Accordingly, in another article I came across in *The New York Times* entitled "African Leader Seeks Sanctions," Abdou Diouf, leader of the Organization of African Unity pleads for multinational companies to suspend their investments in South Africa in order to put an end to the corrupt system of apartheid that was being practiced. President Diouf argued that the rights of black workers in South Africa were being unduly violated because of the system of racial segregation known as apartheid (A10). Another article titled "Embargo on Trade" describes how the Senate approved imposing a trade embargo on South Africa. The 280 American companies would have to halt trade there within a time span of 180 days if the measure was approved by President Reagan (Lewis A1).

Citation for quotation of work by one author

Citation for quotation of work by one author
Transition to next subtopic

3   In addition to the controversy brewing in South Africa, the issue of abortion was a hot topic in the United States. The article entitled "Abortion Storm" in the June 23, 1986 issue of *Newsweek* discussed this conflict. Abortion is not only an issue between organizations such as the National Right to Life Committee and the National Organization for Women. It is also another issue that has been used to divide the views of some Republicans and Democrats. The National Right to Life committee as well as other pro-life organizations expressed their desire to elect a Republican presidential hopeful while the abortion advocates were confident that the Democrat presidential hopefuls shared their views on abortion. The article says, "The most divisive issue in American politics is rolling again. The U.S. Supreme Court struck down state restrictions on a woman's right to choose an abortion" (McDaniel et al. 26). Justice Harry A. Blackmun spoke about how the court was affirming its decision from the previous Roe v. Wade trial that "created a constitutional right to have an abortion" (qtd. in McDaniel et al.). But, the article brought to light the fact that court decisions concerning Roe v. Wade trial might soon be changing because four out of the five justices

Citation for quotation of work with four or more authors

who brought about that ruling were over 77 years old. The article ends with the phrase, "The politics of abortion is not for the uncommitted or the faint of heart" (McDaniel et al. 26).

4   Another issue of great importance around the time of my birth was the reforms that the Space agency had to face after the explosion of the space shuttle *Challenger* on January 28, 1986. The *U.S. News* published an article in the June 16, 1986 edition called "Military Agenda for NASA." After the shuttle disaster, the goals for the space agency were uncertain as well as the monetary support. The article said, "As the nation struggles to resume space operations after the program's worst setbacks in history, the inspiration of manned exploration and the thrill of scientific discovery seem forgotten" (Powell, Thornton, and Sheler 14).

Citation for quotation of work with three authors

5   Tragically, as reported in *The New York Times* on June 18, 1986, an "Air Crash Kills 25 at Grand Canyon." The accident was the result of a collision between a twin-engine plane and a helicopter. The airplane was carrying 18 passengers and the helicopter was carrying five. Both were carrying vacationers and sightseers over the south rim of the canyon. The authorities stated that the accident left no survivors. The only evidence left of the crash was blackened plane fuselage. The accident brought the ongoing debate on whether flights over the Grand Canyon should be restricted back to the discussion table (Cummings A10).

Citation for summary of work by one author
Transition to next subtopic

6   On a lighter note, trends in popular culture have certainly changed since the time around my birth. According to my mother's documentations in my baby book, one of the most popular songs playing on the radio was "Dancing on the Ceiling" by Lionel Ritchie. My mom also recorded some of the most popular fads in fashion in my book. They were spiky hair cuts, high-top tennis shoes, big shirts, and wild socks. It is funny when I reflect on the days in high school when I used to wear wild socks. One of the best-loved shows on television at that time was *The Cosby Show*. I even remember watching that show when I was growing up. In fact, I still watch reruns of it from time to time. According to the June 20, 1986 edition of the *Corpus Christi Caller Times*, one of the movies showing in theaters was *Karate Kid II*. Another film showing was *Ferris Bueller's Day Off*, which was the story of a rebellious teenage boy in high school ("New Movies" A12). Some of the popular cartoons according to the "T.V. Guide" in the *Corpus Christi Caller Times* were *Sesame Street*, *Mister Rogers*, *The Jetsons*, and *The Flintstones*, just to name a few. I learned a lot growing up from watching wholesome shows such as *Sesame Street* and the lovable *Mister Rogers*.

Transition to next subtopic

7   Who could forget the fashion in the 80s? According to the June 18, 1986 edition of the *Corpus Christi Caller Times*, one of the most popular forms of workout wear was the leotard. The article stated that leotards come in many styles such a "leotards made of lace, leotards with wrap fronts, leotards with boat necks, and leotards with zippered fronts just to name a few" (Sherwood). Another trend was red hair, as discussed in a section of the June 22,

1986 edition of the *San Antonio Star*. The author said, "Millions of women are having more fun as redheads." "Whether natural or bottled, red is classy or sassy (Stefanie Powers, Molly Ringwald), even punky or funky (Cyndi Lauper, Annie Lennox or Sissy Spacek)" (Dorsey 23–25).

Concluding paragraph 8   From what I read, world events during the time around my birth centered mostly on the South African apartheid issue. As I reflect back, I can think of ways in which I am a product of the time of my birth. For example, I am not really computer savvy. I like to use the excuse that I am this way because computers were not as prominent and as advanced in 1986 as they are currently. On the other hand, I feel that the television shows I grew up watching in the 80s were a lot more wholesome than the array of reality shows that infest the television stations today. It is appropriate to end the paper with this quote, "What lies behind us and what lies before us are small matters compared to what lies within us" by Ralph Waldo Emerson. In actuality, we cannot dwell on the past. The events that were taking place around the time I was born have not determined who I am today. Even though quite a bit has changed in the world since June 19, 1986, I have developed the strength inside of me to embrace the time I live in now and make the most of it.

Works Cited page with centered title and sources listed alphabetically

Works Cited

"African Leader Seeks Sanctions." *The New York Times*. 19 Jun. 1986: A10.

Cummings, Judith. "Air Crash Kills 25 at Grand Canyon: Plane and Helicopter Collide While on Tourist Flight." *The New York Times*. 19 Jun. 1986: A10.

Dorsey, Lynne. "Red Heads." *The San Antonio Star*. 22 Jun. 1986: 23–25.

Gwertzman, Bernard. "U.S. to Cite Vote to Press Pretoria: Reagan Aides Say Sanctions Will Be Used in Seeking Shifts on Racial Policy." *The New York Times*. 20 Jun. 1986: A10.

Lewis, Neil. "Embargo on Trade: Measure Sent to Senate-Reagan Aide Again Voices Opposition." *The New York Times*. 19 Jun. 1986: A1.

McDaniel, Ann, and Borger, Gloria and Fineman, Howard and Williams, Elisa. "Abortion Storm: A Court Decision Heats up a Highly Divisive Political Issue." *Newsweek*. 1986:26.

"New Movies." *Corpus Christi Caller Times*. 20 Jun. 1986: A12.

Powell, Stewart, Thornton, Jeannye, and Sheler, Jeffrey. "Military Agenda for NASA." *U.S. News*. 16 Jun. 1986: 14–15.

Sherwood, Mary. "Leotard." *Corpus Christi Caller Times*. 18 June 1986.

"T.V. Guide." *Corpus Christi Caller Times*. 18 Jun. 1986.

Wolter, Carrie. Personal Interview. 19 Mar. 2005.

Insightful Writing

When you immerse yourself in the research process, you may uncover surprising facts about a topic. Sometimes it is the combination or two or more apparently unrelated events or sources of information that leads to true insight about a situation. Research is as much about exploration as about "writing." Look for connections among the various sources you use in the writing process. What is the major difference in two opposing viewpoints on a controversial topic? Is there common ground upon which a compromise could be built? Did historical events shape the personalities of famous individuals? How does the topic you are researching affect you personally? How does the topic you are researching affect your friends, relatives, and strangers? Answers to these types of questions can lead to insights about your academic and professional interests. You have been introduced to the process of research and writing with sources. Develop and use your skills to help yourself and others. When it comes time to purchase a major item like a car, research to find the best deal for you or a family member. When it comes time to look for a job, research the job market for a great career. A world of information is at your disposal. Use it.

PART IV

A Portfolio of Readings

Chapter 12: *Cultural Identities*

Chapter 13: *Work*

Chapter 14: *Consumerism*

Chapter 15: *The Environment*

12 Cultural Identities

No culture can live, if it attempts to be exclusive.

Mahatma Gandhi

The test of courage comes when we are in the minority. The test of tolerance comes when we are in the majority.

Ralph W. Sockman

Culture is the totality of patterns of behavior, or way of life, that each person learns in order to live in a society. Culture is a complex web of doing and thinking that influences every aspect of our lives. Important aspects of culture include the ways our families are organized, the food we eat, the language we speak, the education we receive, the entertainment we participate in; and the customs, beliefs, and traditions we follow.

We all identify with and belong to certain cultures and overlapping subcultures. Cultures and subcultures are influenced by race, ethnicity, gender, age, nationality, socioeconomic level, class, religion, profession, education level, and other factors. The readings in this section reflect the centrality of culture in shaping people's identities during the course of their lives.

Examining one's own culture may be difficult because we are all so unconsciously embedded within our cultures that we have a hard time stepping back and attempting to analyze the various cultural influences working in us and through us.

Learning to Let Go: Tradition Binds College Hopefuls to Families

BY VANESSA COLON

1 Seventeen-year-old Tiffany Renteria plans to leave Reedley [California] for college on the East Coast in 2005. Her parents will go with her.

2 "Some people find it funny that they want to follow me. Some students have said, 'Don't you want your own independence?'" Tiffany says. "I would want them to go with me. That way, I don't have to support myself. I can just focus on my education." Frank and Josephine Renteria say they want to go to great lengths to protect their daughter and maintain traditional Latino beliefs. They say single daughters should get an education—but live with or near their parents until they are older or married.

3 In the Latino culture, a young woman who lives on her own before marriage may be criticized, shunned or disowned.

4 It's a view that's more prevalent in first and second-generation Latino families, particularly those in which the parents have little or no education. A few Latina women who have left home to pursue higher education say their parents worry about them becoming sexually liberal.

5 The culture is blamed for limiting the number of Latinas who pursue postsecondary education, which spurs some local leaders to seek ways to change beliefs.

6 Tiffany, who is finishing her junior year at Reedley High School has a 3.9 grade-point average. She is a member of the Ivy League Leadership Project, a program that encourages students to seek enrollment in Ivy League universities.

7 Tiffany will choose between Brown University in Providence, R.I., and Columbia University in New York. She hopes to study business.

8 Her parents say they are willing to relocate. Frank Renteria is a handyman and carpenter, and Josephine Renteria is a nurse. They were born in the United States and are of Mexican descent.

9 "I tell her, you are not going to get rid of me," Frank Renteria says with a laugh. "It's really not safe. There's people out there that will take advantage of a girl like my daughter. We are willing to sacrifice for her.

10 "We just don't trust people out there. That's why a lot of parents don't want their daughters to go."

11 Many Latinas are opting for middle ground —mainly, community colleges.

12 Statewide, Latinas make up about 15% of the student body at commsunity colleges, 13% in the California State University system and 7% at University of California campuses, according to a 2003 report by Hispanas Organized for Political Equality.

13 "The majority go to community colleges because it's closer to home and it's affordable," says Elmy Bermejo, board president of HOPE.

14 Fresno State's Latina enrollment is strong. The school says that 650 Latinas are expected to receive bachelor's and graduate degrees for the 2003–04 school year—nearly 17% of the 3,908 total.

15 At Fresno City College, the percentage of Latinas earning associate degrees was 21%, the school says.

16 But there's more work to be done, says Martina Granados, director of the Upward Bound program at California State University, Fresno. The program prepares high school students for college by placing them on campus for five weeks in the summer to take college preparation classes in the morning and live in dormitories.

17 "We are not breaking the cycle at home or at school," Granados says. "[Some] parents are still traditional. They want them to go to school, but Latinas still have pressure from the family. If they are moving out of the house and they are not married, they [parents] see it as something negative."

18 Many of the Latinas interviewed for this story say they chose to attend a community college, Fresno State, Fresno Pacific University or other colleges nearby so they could continue helping their families—often doing traditional chores such as cleaning, cooking and doing laundry.

19 A 2000 report by the American Association of University Women Educational Foundation found that those extra tasks sometimes interfere with postsecondary education.

20 Household responsibilities are a strain for 22-year-old Maria Ramirez, who lives with her parents and attends West Hills College's Firebaugh campus.

21 She says she works 16 to 19 hours a week at the college, cooks and takes care of her mother, who has diabetes and is schizophrenic. She gets up at about 6 a.m. to cook breakfast for her stepfather. In the evening, she makes dinner.

22 Seventeen-year-old Sanger High School student Carmen Hernandez and her sisters faced similar challenges of juggling housework and school duties.

23 This fall, Carmen plans to attend Cornell University in New York. Carmen was part of the Upward Bound program but says her parents, Antonio and Maria Hernandez, didn't approve of her college plans until her Spanish teacher and her husband intervened.

24 Her parents still have mixed feelings about her going to a university on the East Coast.

25 "I can't tell her, 'You can't go, you have to stay,'" Antonio Hernandez says in Spanish. "I want something better for her."

26 He works in the fields and packages peaches and cherries for about $6 an hour.

27 Carmen says: "My mom is like, 'Why so far? I won't be able to see you and take care of you.'"

28 Adalid Alejandre says tradition dictated what he expected of his daughter—until he saw how dedicated she was to her studies.

29 His daughter, 21-year-old Glafira Alejandre, came from Mexico to Del Rey when she was 17. She has a 4.1 grade-point average at Sanger High School, where she learned to speak English. She hopes to attend Fresno State and then continue her education at Stanford or another out-of-area university.

30 "My mom always supported me, but my father didn't. He now understands," she says in Spanish. "My dad didn't like me applying far away."

31 Adalid Alejandre says he grew up seeing women stay at home until they got married. Once they married, they had children and remained at home.

32 Eliseo Gamino, an associate dean at West Hills' Firebaugh campus, says that girls in traditional Latino households carry the reputation of the whole family. He recalls a father who stopped talking to his daughter when she left home to go to college.

33 "It brought me to tears. . . . He then showed up for the graduation," Gamino says.

34 The lack of awareness of what higher education can do for Latinas plays a huge role in whether parents will encourage their daughters to go to college, Gamino says.

35 To help overcome these obstacles, some educators have turned to promoting plays, summer programs and conferences for Latinos:

36 • Gamino and Ruben Fuentes helped start Teatro Tortilla, a group that performs plays to educate parents and students at West Hills about issues including obstacles Latinas face in pursuing higher education.

37 • Fresno State's Upward Bound continues to guide high school students on ways to prepare for their careers and introduces parents to the idea of college.

38 • The Hispanic Female Conference exposes Latinas to college. The conference involves Clovis West High School and Kastner Middle School.

39 • Parlier Junior High School's Ivy League Leadership Project encourages students to pursue higher education and consider attending an Ivy League university.

Educators and organizers say the programs have offered a glimmer of hope to students. Margarita Luna Robles, who is a founder of the Hispanic Female Conference, says: "Now, the sentiment has changed. The girls have taken ownership of the conference. For many who never thought about college, they now think of it." 40

Questions

1. What is the article's thesis? If the author does not provide one, develop a thesis that fits the article.

2. A statement in paragraph 2 suggests that supporting oneself while at college and focusing on one's education are not possible. Suggest some ways in which these two activities can be done successfully at the same time.

3. In paragraphs 2 and 3 there are references to "traditional Latino beliefs" and "Latino culture." To what extent are these things unified and monolithic, or varied and diverse? Can a culture be both? How? Give examples from your own culture and experiences.

4. According to the article, what aspects of Hispanic culture tend to limit the number of Hispanic women who go to college? What other aspects of one's culture might hinder a person's going to college? What aspects of one's culture might promote one's attendance at college?

5. Paragraph 16 mentions the Upward Bound program. What do you know about this program from personal experience? If you have not participated in the program, find out about the program and describe it in 100 to 200 words.

6. Make a T-chart (see page 189) showing the advantages and disadvantages of living at home while attending college.

7. Make a T-chart (see page 189) showing the advantages and disadvantages of living on or near campus while attending college.

8. Using a dictionary when necessary, define the following words in their appropriate context:
   traditional (2); culture (3); prevalent (4); liberal (4); Ivy League (6); opting (11); intervened (23); dictated (28); reputation (32); promoting (35).

For Further Discussion and Writing

1. How would you feel if your parents said they were moving to the place where you were attending college in order to help you? What advantages and disadvantages would you see in this arrangement?

2. What elements or people in your immediate family and culture have helped you or hindered you (or both) in your pursuit of postsecondary education?

3. What programs, if any, did or does your high school or nearby college have for encouraging students to continue their education beyond high school?

4. Think of the three people who offered you the most encouragement to continue your education beyond high school. Were they teachers, counselors, family members, friends, or mentors in the working world? In what specific ways did each person encourage you to continue your education? Your instructor may ask you to develop your answer to this question into a journal entry or essay.

When did your ancestors first become United States citizens? How might becoming a citizen change the attitude of an immigrant? Where is this ceremony taking place?

Lessons from Executive Order 9066

BY ROY H. SAIGO

1 Sixty-five years ago today [Feb. 19, 2007], on Feb. 19, 1942, President Franklin D. Roosevelt signed an order to allow the incarceration of 120,000 people of Japanese descent—more than two-thirds of them American citizens—for the duration of World War II.

2 I was not yet 2 years old when his Executive Order 9066 sent my parents, my older brother and sister and me into the Arizona desert to be held in a federal "Relocation Center," which was a euphemism for a prison encampment.

3 We could bring only what we could carry, leaving behind a household, memorabilia and personal possessions that would never be returned.

4 During our three years there, we lived in a 20-by-25 foot section of a tarpapered wooden barracks, sharing public cooking and latrine facilities. We were inside barbed-wire fences with armed guards in towers.

Wrongs to remember

5 While my own memories of life in Arizona are faint, I remember the impact the internment had on my family, and I recall the prejudice, suspicion and hatred we experienced after re-joining American society. The lessons from the experience remain vivid.

6 • **Lesson 1:** the power of education. My parents were resolved to instill in their children a respect for education as the great equalizer, the source of a better life, something "they can't take away from you."

7 Today I am president of Minnesota's second-largest public university. I am a product of the great American tradition of opportunity through public education, and have been privileged to perpetuate this opportunity to many thousands of students over nearly 40 years in higher education.

8 • **Lesson 2:** the need to fight prejudice and discrimination. The damage my family experienced gave me a determination to fight prejudice in any form, to stand up to bullies who treat others unfairly and to help prevent a recurrence of such persecution.

9 • **Lesson 3:** the power of firsthand international and multicultural learning experiences. More than ever, it is necessary for schools, colleges and universities to help students gain a world perspective. This is a pragmatic approach in light of our increasing global interdependence. And it is even more important for developing the critical and empathetic understanding that helps us all to avoid stereotyping people and to see opportunities for relationships instead of allowing fear to separate us.

10 The incarceration of Japanese and Japanese-Americans during World War II is not the worst example of horrific human actions toward other humans. It is but one item on a shamefully long list of deliberate actions to degrade, subjugate and even eradicate subsets of people because they are different in some way. Unfortunately, the list will continue to grow unless humankind finds better ways to cultivate understanding and acceptance among people.

11 No Japanese-American was found guilty of subversive behavior during or after WWII, and families in the camps saluted the American flag each morning. They sent their sons to fight alongside other American soldiers. Our fellow Americans succumbed to a common weakness of human nature—distrusting those who do not resemble us.

Ethnic scapegoating

12 Now, in our post-9/11 world, that weakness has again showed its face. This time it is directed toward the men, women and children who are, or appear to be, of Middle Eastern ancestry.

13 Ours is an increasingly diverse country. If we succumb, again, to the temptation of ethnic scapegoating, to choose entire categories of people we trust and don't trust, we will be jeopardizing our future as a democracy, repudiating the fairness we celebrate, sacrificing our many freedoms and shirking our proud, historic role as a compassionate beacon of liberty for the world.

14 Sixty-five years later, we must heed the lessons of this un-American chapter in our history.

Questions

1. What is the article's thesis? If the author does not provide one, develop a thesis that fits the article.

2. What three lessons does the author emphasize?

3. Saigo's lesson 3 is related to international and multicultural learning experiences. Reflect on your education (high school, college, and non-school-related experiences) and give some examples of how you have gained multicultural understanding and wider perspectives on world issues.

4. Using a dictionary when necessary, define the following words in their appropriate context:
   incarceration (1); duration (1); euphemism (2); memorabilia (3); latrine (4); faint (5); internment (5); prejudice (5); suspicion (5); vivid (5); instill (6); perpetuate (7); discrimination (8); recurrence (8); persecution (8); pragmatic (9); interdependence (9); empathetic (9); stereotyping (9); horrific (10); degrade (10); subjugate (10); eradicate (10); cultivate (10); subversive (11); succumbed (11); post (12); ethnic (13); scapegoating (13); jeopardizing (13); repudiating (13); shirking (13); compassionate (13); beacon (13).

For Further Discussion and Writing

1. Find out if any of your family members or friends of your family were affected by Executive Order 9066. If so, prepare a brief report on their experiences. If not, go online or to some other source to read a brief first-person account by someone who was affected. Prepare a brief report and be ready to share it with your classmates and instructor.

2. In what possible ways would Americans react if the U.S. government rounded up thousands of first- and second-generation people of Middle Eastern descent and put them into "Relocation Centers"?

3. What similarities and differences do you see between Executive Order 9066 and the U.S. government's practice of establishing reservations for Native Americans?

4. In paragraph 13 Saigo mentions and defines "ethnic scapegoating." Do some research on recent ethnic scapegoating somewhere in the world. Possible places and peoples to research include the Darfur region of Sudan, the Kurds of northern Iraq; the various peoples of the former country of Yugoslavia (Serbs, Kosovars, Albanians); and the Hutu and Tutsi tribes of Rwanda and Burundi in East Africa. What connections do you find with terms such as "ethnic cleansing" and "genocide"?

5. To what extent might ethnic scapegoating be said to exist in the United States today? Give examples.

6. How are cultural and ethnic identities established in the first place? At what point does a cultural or ethnic identity become a stereotype? What are some positive aspects of one's cultural or ethnic identity? What are some potentially negative aspects of cultural and ethnic identities?

It Could Happen Here

LAILA AL-MARAYATI

1 Not long ago I rented the movie *The Count of Monte Cristo* to watch with my two sons, who I thought would enjoy the exciting, action-packed tale. My 11-year-old surprised me, though, by becoming very agitated as the protagonist, Edmond Dantes, was banished to the Chateau d'If, a grisly prison on a desolate island where torture was the order of the day.

2 "Are people tortured in prison today?" he asked.

3 "Well, yes," I admitted.

4 "What about here, here in America?"

5 "No, of course not," I reassured him. "It's something that only happens in other countries."

6 "Can they take you out of prison here and send you somewhere else to get tortured?" he asked.

7 I am usually honest with my children. But not this time. I had recently read that U.S. officials had admitted to sending detainees abroad to countries with regimes that have no qualms about using torture to get people to cooperate. This was not information my son needed to hear.

8 "Absolutely not!" I assured him. "Why are you so worried about this?"

9 "Well, what if they make a mistake and you get taken to jail even though you didn't do anything wrong? I mean, what if they sent you

to jail just for being Muslim? Everyone thinks Muslims are terrorists and bad people."

10 His fear of arbitrary arrest and torture disturbed me, especially since this is the reality for some Muslims here and many more abroad who have been incarcerated as suspects in the "war on terrorism."

11 Our family has roots in Palestine and Iraq, so naturally we are preoccupied with events overseas, but we limit the exposure of our children to media coverage of the Middle East. We don't discuss the threats to their civil liberties at the dinner table.

12 Though our children are proud of their ethnic heritage, they identify themselves as Americans. At their Islamic school, parents and teachers reinforce the notion of an integrated Muslim American identity. Muslim values, they learn, can contribute to the betterment of their country. Some of the kids have ties "back home," visiting frequently, perhaps creating a dual allegiance. Not so in our family. We don't spend our summer vacations in Baghdad or the Gaza Strip.

13 I don't have the heart to tell my boys that, if pending legislation passes, our security as Muslims living in America—even as citizens by birth, will be at risk, or that my son's question might foretell his own future.

14 Earlier this year, the Justice Department prepared a draft proposal to revise the USA Patriot Act, a post-Sept. 11 law that greatly expanded the ability of law enforcers to track suspected terrorists. If the Domestic Security Enhancement Act of 2003 outlined in the memo (known widely as Patriot II) is ultimately passed by Congress, the government would, in the name of fighting terrorism, be granted sweeping new surveillance powers, more leeway to detain citi-

zens indefinitely without charge and the ability to present secret evidence against those accused of supporting terrorism. The death penalty would be expanded to include certain terror-related crimes. The government would also have the authority to strip Americans of their citizenship for providing support to an organization deemed a "terrorist group," a term that is broadly and vaguely defined.

15 I want to tell my children that as law-abiding American citizens, they have nothing to worry about. But I know that simply obeying the law won't keep them from being profiled at the airport, monitored while attending the mosque or wiretapped if they participate in Muslim-oriented activities on campus when they go to college. The truth is, they will be suspects, simply because of their identity as young adult Americans who also happen to be male, Muslim and of Arab descent.

16 We can hope that our elected officials won't agree to the further erosion of civil liberties and will refuse to pass Patriot II. But if they lack the resolve to question something that wouldn't make us more secure but would render America unrecognizable to our founding fathers, then we're all in trouble.

17 *The Count of Monte Cristo* raised frightening issues for my sons. But it also made an important point. When Dantes was at the height of despair during his imprisonment, he rejected God for having abandoned him. Later, when the words etched on his cell wall, "God will give me justice," were proved true, he vowed never to lose faith again. His troubles may have caused my son to agonize about the injustices that could befall him one day, but perhaps he also learned from the film that God's justice prevails despite man's injustice to man.

Questions

1. What happens in the movie, *The Count of Monte Cristo,* that causes Al-Marayati's son to become worried?

2. How did the author avoid giving her son information about the possible torture of detainees sent to other countries?

3. Why is the author concerned about the USA Patriot Act and the Domestic Security Enhancement Act of 2003?

4. Why does the author send her children to an Islamic school?

5. Using a dictionary when necessary, define the following words in their appropriate context:
   protagonist (1); arbitrary (10); profiled (15); mosque (15)

For Further Discussion and Writing

1. Do you agree or disagree with the author that the civil liberties of Muslims and Americans in general are in jeopardy?

2. Do you know of other religions that have private schools for members of their faith? Do you know someone who attended such a school? How would attending such a school affect a person's identity as an American? Prepare a brief report on the history of faith-based schools in your city or region. How is "home schooling" related to historical reasons for establishing private faith-based schools?

3. Compare and contrast the USA Patriot Act with Executive Order 9066 mentioned in the previous essay.

4. Watch the movie mentioned in the essay with a group of friends. What other themes are presented in the movie that seem important to you? Does your cultural heritage affect how you view the movie? Report your findings and write a "movie review" for the class. Be sure to include information about the author of the book upon which the movie is based.

The Great Divide

BY MICHAEL QUINTANILLA

1 Virginia Gomez wanted to share a story.

2 The 13-year-old eighth-grader and her friends—all American-born Latinas—were walking past three Mexican immigrant sixth-graders after school recently. One of the younger children was sipping from a soda can. Suddenly,

one of Virginia's friends bopped the bottom of the can.

3 "Wham! The soda spilled all over the little girl," Virginia recalled. As she and her friends walked away, the immigrant student muttered a Spanish obscenity.

4 "What? You want to start something?" Virginia's friend asked the now-frightened girl. "Tell me to my face . . . Wetback!"

5 "We're all proud of being Mexican," said Virginia—who was born in Los Angeles to immigrant parents—as she talked about the on-campus incident the day after it occurred at Nimitz Middle School in Huntington Park.

6 "But the thing is we see ourselves as different even though we have the same culture," she said. "We're American and they're not."

7 Virginia's story embodies all the elements of a conflict that plagues many Latino students today: the alienation and prejudice that divide American-born Latino kids and their immigrant classmates. The students often segregate themselves during lunchtime, on the basketball court, at school dances, and while hanging out on campus before and after school.

8 A language barrier coupled with an unfamiliar teen culture—the culture of the popular American Latino kids who wear baggy clothes with Doc Martens or Nikes and listen to deep-house and hip-hop—adds to the problem of assimilation for immigrant students.

9 In most cases, students agree, it's the American-born Latinos who ridicule the immigrants.

10 They make fun of the immigrant boys who dress in white buttoned shirts instead of T-shirts and high-water cotton trousers instead of oversized jeans. They ridicule the immigrant girls in their ruffled starched blouses and pleated skirts and braids tied with bows. They make fun of the immigrant children's shyness, respectfulness and dedication to academics.

11 The U.S.-born Latinos call the Mexican kids "*quebradita* people" because of their banda music and *quebradita* dances. They make fun of the immigrants' "nerdy" Mickey Mouse–adorned backpacks and have even coined a term for them: "Wetpacks."

12 They call the immigrant students other names—"beaner," "Wehac" (a derogatory term for a Mexican immigrant of Indian descent) and tell them to "go back where you come from." Immigrant students at Nimitz reported that when they run around the track in gym class, American-born teens shout "Corrale! Corrale! La Migra! La Migra!" ("Run! Immigration!").

13 Brad Pilon, a bilingual school psychologist with the Los Angeles Unified School District, works with about 70 schools—most with a majority Latino enrollment—in the mid-city area, including Belmont High School's Newcomer Center, which helps hundreds of recent non-English-speaking immigrants adjust in school.

14 "These kids feel the segregation, they live it," Pilon said. "They get beat up, get lunches stolen, are laughed at in their faces" by U.S.-born Latinos, he said. Often the immigrant student is too scared to report the harassment. Also, Pilon said, students soon learn that if they were to report such incidents, "nothing would be done" because overloaded teachers and administrators often aren't aware the problem exists.

15 "The immigrant kids, especially the newest arrivals, are naive, open and most of all vulnerable when they come to school," Pilon said. "When they first come here, like anybody who moves anywhere, they are faced with the problem of fitting in."

16 For most, fitting in is their dream even though they often view American kids as lazy, unmotivated and disrespectful to their parents and teachers.

17 Ramon A. Gutierrez, director of the Center for the Study of Race and Ethnicity at the University of California, San Diego, said this Latino rift is not something new. He cited a 10-year-old study conducted in the San Jose area, where a researcher found four Latino groups

that segregated themselves from each other in one school—"the recent lower-income Mexican immigrant; the middle-class Mexican immigrant; the acculturated Chicano kids and the cholo kids: lower-income Mexican Americans."

18 "There have always been tensions and stresses between individuals of a remote immigrant past and recent immigrants," he said. "What it boils down to is discrimination based not only on immigrant status," Gutierrez said, but also on language and social class.

19 "If you went to Beverly Hills High, you'd find lower-class white kids segregated from the wealthier kids. It's segregation based on social standing," he said.

20 Rene Estrella, a leadership class adviser and biology teacher at Belmont High School, where 90% of the 4,500 enrollment is Latino, said immigrant Latino students "take the brunt of discrimination" from American-born students because "the people who are privileged to be born here think that they are superior to the person who was not.

21 "I think most kids who come to Belmont don't have too much to feel good about, growing up in the area. They don't get out of this area very much and anything they can hold onto to get a better identity, even if it means making others feel lower, makes them feel important."

22 Estrella said storytelling sessions in his classes helped bring students together last semester, and he probably will continue them. For several minutes at the start of each class, students shared their lives with other classmates. Immigrant students spoke about their homelands, family members killed in their war-torn countries and their adjustment to life in the United States.

23 "Hearing each other's stories united the students. It made the American-born kids understand the struggle so many of the newcomers have experienced and the struggle they still face, especially when they are segregated," Estrella said.

24 "We are oppressing each other and that bothers me," said Lupe Simpson, principal of Nimitz, the second-largest middle school in the country. The school has an enrollment of 3,200 students—97% Latino, one-fifth of that number recent immigrants.

25 Simpson said she is deeply concerned about the "anti-Mexican" feelings of some of her students as well as the isolation and disaffection immigrant children deal with daily. "But I don't see this as a defeat," she said. "It's a challenge."

26 She hopes students will embrace her plan for a buddy program that would pair native and immigrant Latinos so they could help and learn from each other. Another idea she is exploring is to have award assemblies for the whole student body, instead of the English as a Second Language students having their assemblies separately, as they do now. And she wants to speak to teachers and administrators about integrating students in classrooms, during sporting events and at school dances.

27 "We have to do something so the kids can see that that kind of thinking prevails in their lives and where does it end? We have to start ending it with ourselves. We have to show our kids that we are more alike than we are different," she said after listening to some of the students express their feelings in recent interviews at the school.

28 Gabriela Rico, 13, a Nimitz eighth-grader from Mexico, said she is mocked in gym class because she doesn't always understand the games.

29 "The Chicanos don't speak to us at all. They don't try to teach us. That's what we want most of all—to learn the games, to learn English, to be like them," she said, as other immigrant children nodded.

30 "I know they make fun of me," Gabriela said, her eyes on a book on her lap. "I tell my mother and she tells me not to be like them and show off, not to place value on materialistic things

like clothes or shoes or to care too much about appearances."

31 Julio Bejarano, an 11-year-old sixth-grader also from Mexico, said he gets along fine with kids in his neighborhood, many of them American-born. But at school, it's a different world. He said he is not accepted "as a friend by the Latino Americanos," never invited to join in a game of basketball or to sit with them at lunchtime "because they think we are inferior to them because we were not born here." His eyes water. The room is silent for a few seconds.

32 Language is the biggest obstacle, he said, even though it should be the key to bridging the communications gap because an over-whelming majority of the American Latinos are bilingual.

33 "We talk to them in Spanish because we don't know English and even though they know how to speak Spanish, they talk to us in English. Why don't they want to communicate with us?" Julio said.

34 Nancy Garcia, also 11, said she has an American Latina "good friend," but still there's no escaping the prejudice. "My friend tells me that she is superior to me," Nancy said, even though Nancy's grades are better.

35 "I don't know why she says that," Nancy paused. "I think she might be envious of us because we are so proud of our culture."

36 Still, she said she yearns to one day be accepted by her American-born Latino class-mates because "I love the get-togethers they have at school, the way they dress, the way they dance, their music."

37 Image, said American-born classmate Lisa Moreno, 13, plays a big role in the self-imposed segregation at her school. "You have to know how to dress so you can be in the 'in-crowd.' Immigrant girls wear Payless shoes."

38 Peer pressure keeps them from befriend-ing the immigrants, students said. "If I were to hang around with them, then I wouldn't be in the in-crowd anymore," explained Lisa.

39 Said Virginia Gomez: "Straight out, we haven't welcomed the Mexicans with open arms. We're like, 'You want to be with us? I don't think so.'"

40 "It shouldn't be this way—two groups," said Virginia, who is student body president at Nimitz. "But what can you do to stop it? Some people are not going to change no matter what you do."

41 Rudy Lopez, a Los Angeles–born 13-year-old Latino at Nimitz, agreed that both groups should be united, especially "when they haven't done anything to us to treat them bad."

42 That's a sentiment shared by several students at Belmont.

43 Sandra Flores, 16, a 10th-grader born in Los Angeles, said, "I have newcomer friends and it's very hard for them. I think they are afraid to talk to U.S. Latinos because they are expecting us to put them aside, you know, ignore them. That's why they come to their own little groups."

44 "It's sad to see us segregated like that, espe-cially when the immigrant students have such a big enthusiasm for learning, for having better futures. They are really smarter than us," she said.

45 Ernesto, a 16-year-old Guatemalan (who preferred not to use his surname), said he chooses to remain a loner because he doesn't want to be rejected as he was last year in junior high school.

46 "We get rejected because of the way we dress, talk, the way we are," he said. So he and his immigrant friends hang out together, en-courage each other, lift each other's spirits. As a group, they are secure and safe. It's what gets them through the day.

47 Still, it's unfathomable sometimes to Ernesto and other immigrant young people that they have left one war to face another.

48 "We come from war-torn countries," he said. "Our families have struggled to come here for a better future and then we still have to struggle with people who are from our own race."

Questions

1. What are the two population groups separated by "The Great Divide"?

2. List three or four factors that contribute to the "divide."

3. What classroom activity is mentioned in paragraph 22 that seems to help unite the students? Why do you think this activity might help?

4. How does peer pressure keep some American-born Latinos from making friends with the immigrant students?

5. Which of the two groups demonstrate the most discrimination toward the other group? Why do you think this is true?

6. List three of the examples given by the author of how the American-born Latinos exhibit discrimination toward immigrant classmates.

7. Using a dictionary when necessary, define the following words in their appropriate context:
   bopped (2); wetback (4); plagues (7); segregate (7); Doc Martens (8); assimilation (8); high-water (10); naïve (15); acculturated (17); disaffection (25); sentiment (42); unfathomable (47)

For Further Discussion and Writing

1. Who do you believe is the intended audience for Quintanilla's article? Support your choice with examples of word choice from the article.

2. Have you ever noticed incidents of prejudice between members of the same ethnic group? Who? What? When? Where? How? Write a paragraph describing the incident. Write a short dialogue that dramatizes the incident. How does the opening of the article by Quintanilla set the stage for later discussion?

3. Conduct a research activity to discover the population demographics of your city, region, or state. Prepare a short report that examines the trends in ethnicity and socioeconomic status. What changes will take place in the next twenty years? A good source for this type of information is the U.S. Census Bureau.

4. This chapter presented readings about Hispanics, Muslims of Arab descent, and Japanese Americans. What other ethnic groups or members of a religion are you interested in knowing more about? Form a group with three or four classmates and prepare a presentation for the class about a different ethnic group or religion. Provide information on traditions and cultural heritage for the class in a PowerPoint presentation or poster project.

13 Work

Pleasure in the job puts perfection in the work.

Aristotle (384 BC–322 BC)

The more I want to get something done, the less I call it work.

Richard Bach

Hundreds of thousands of Americans spend thirty, forty, fifty years or more working at various jobs during their lives. One of the first questions we often ask when meeting someone is "What do you do?" Right or wrong, fair or unfair, people are often associated with the work they do. Some professions and careers carry favorable associations; while others carry less favorable associations.

One tension within post-secondary education and among those in the workforce is the ongoing debate about the "best" preparation for professions and careers. Should a person seek a broad, liberal education that teaches one how to think, analyze, and continue learning? Or should one develop a more focused approach to learning, concentrating on a specific discipline in a particular profession? Of course, this "either-or" situation quickly breaks down, because in actuality many people do a little of both in their education.

The following articles focus on the world of work that most college students are presumably preparing themselves for.

Ten Majors That Didn't Exist 10 Years Ago

BY BRIDGET KULLA

1 Want to try something new? Really new? That list of majors in the course catalog isn't static. As technology advances and business evolves, fields of study that weren't imagined or that may have been limited to a few specialized classes emerge as full-blown majors. Check out these 10 fields of study that hardly existed a decade ago.

1. New Media

2 Online media is one of the fastest growing areas of journalism. New media majors combine traditional journalism studies with courses on the design and management of digital media.

3 Some programs, like the new media program at the Academy of Art University in San Francisco, concentrate on computer skills and design of online media. Other programs, like the one at Indiana University/Purdue University, Indianapolis, integrate communications and digital skills.

2. Biotechnology

4 Biotechnology combines biology and technology to solve agricultural, food science and medical issues. It is an interdisciplinary field and is often combined with a business degree, like the joint degree program at Johns Hopkins University. Most biotechnology degrees are at the master's level, yet bachelor's degrees in biotechnology, like the one at Delaware State University, are starting to emerge as this field becomes more in demand.

5 Related fields include bioinformatics and biomedical engineering.

3. Organic Agriculture

6 The first organic agriculture program in the U.S. began at Washington State University (WSU) in 2006. Demand for those knowledgeable in organic agriculture is growing. "Large corporations increasingly are interested in meeting the nation's growing appetite for organic foods [and] are seeking employees who understand organic agriculture systems," says Dr. Cathy Perillo, coordinator of WSU's organic agriculture program, in a press release.

7 This major is not widespread, but other institutions are looking into adding an organic agriculture degree program, including University of California, Davis. The University of Florida also launched an organic agriculture major in 2006.

4. Homeland Security

8 New degree programs in homeland security have been established since the 9/11 terrorist attacks. Homeland security majors study everything from psychology to disaster relief and federal law to handling hazardous materials. The U.S. Department of Homeland Security offers scholarships and fellowships for homeland security majors and runs an intensive 18-month degree program at the Center for Homeland Defense and Security.

9 Homeland security education is expanding rapidly at community colleges. Close to 85 percent of students trained in homeland security-related fields graduate from community colleges, according to the American Association of Community Colleges.

5. E-Business/E-Marketing

10 This field focuses on buying, selling and marketing items on the Internet and may also include communicating with customers, employees and business partners. Demand for employees in this field is expected to grow faster than average, according to U.S. Bureau of Labor Statistics.

11 Degree programs in e-marketing are usually in universities' business schools and are more common at the graduate level. Some schools, like the University of Akron, offer bachelor's programs in e-marketing, while others, like Missouri State University, offer a minor for business students.

6. Computer Game Design

12 Students playing video games in their dorm rooms can now avoid a lecture from their parents by majoring in computer game design. Computer game design programs were nearly nonexistent a decade ago. Today more than 150 colleges offer programs and courses in game design.

13 Some programs, like the computer games development program at DePaul University, focus on the programming of games while others, like the game art and design program at the Art Institute of Phoenix, concentrate on the visual design. Michigan State University is launching a Serious Game Design master's degree program in the fall of 2007 for students with "a desire to create and study games which change the world." The International Game Developers Association offers resources, including a scholarship, for students interested in game design.

7. Forensic Accounting

14 The controversy surrounding recent corporate scandals has drawn attention to the expanding field of forensic accounting. While it has existed for many years, forensic accounting is now the fastest-growing field of accounting. Forensic accountants are like money detectives—they investigate suspected financial mishandling and assist in legal matters. Forensic accountants must have a broad understanding of business practices beyond standard accounting skills.

15 Bachelor's degrees in forensic accounting, like the program offered at Franklin University, are required for most careers in this field.

Students can also earn a master's degree and post-graduate certificate through a program like the one at West Virginia University.

8. Human Computer Interaction

16 Human computer interaction (HCI) majors focus on designing ways to improve human experiences and work practices with technology. HCI investigates the impact of technology on individuals and organizations. While courses in this field have been offered since the 1960s, degree programs in HCI have been growing. Human computer interaction majors are usually located in schools of computer science, but studies are multidisciplinary.

17 Most HCI programs are at the graduate level, like the program at Iowa State University, but some, like the HCI program at the New Jersey Institute of Technology, have a bachelor's degree program.

9. Society and the Environment

18 Society and environment majors study the interactions between society and the environment. Degree programs in this field go by slightly different names, like Indiana University's joint environmental science and public affairs degree and Columbia University's climate and society program. Students in these majors apply social science theories to environmental issues. Most programs are at the master's degree level, but programs like the one at UC-Berkeley offer undergraduate degrees as well.

10. Nanotechnology

19 Developments in technology have made it possible to control matter at smaller and smaller levels. The field of nanotechnology works with systems at the molecular level and can be applied across many different disciplines, including physics, engineering and chemistry. Interest in nanotechnology is growing and is being encouraged by the National Nanotechnology Initiative, organized in 1998.

20   Most nanotechnology programs are at the graduate level, but several programs provide a background in nanotechnology studies, like bachelor's program in nanosystems engineering at Louisiana Tech University.

Questions

1. Of the ten new majors, how many involve computers? What conclusions can you draw from this observation?

2. In the "computer game design" section, there is a reference to creating and studying "games which change the world." What computer game(s) might be said to change the world?

3. Using a dictionary when necessary, define the following words in their appropriate context:
   static (1); technology (1); evolves (1); digital (2); bioinformatics (5); psychology (8); forensic (14); environment (18); climate (18); nano (19) as a prefix.

For Further Discussion and Writing

1. Find someone who works or teaches in one of these new fields and interview him or her. (For information on how to prepare for and conduct a useful interview, see Chapter 11.) Your purpose is to learn more about a particular field of study. If you cannot find anyone to interview, use the Internet to gather more information on one of the above majors that you would like to know more about. Be prepared to share your findings with your classmates and instructor.

2. Think of one or two new majors that are not on the list but should be or might be. That is, take a look at the world around you and think of a college major that is not yet available (or at least not widely available) but that might be useful in the next ten years.

3. According to the U.S. Department of Labor Statistics, the top fifteen groups of workers with the largest projected increases in the U.S., through the year 2010, are the following:

   1. Food-preparation and -serving workers, including fast food
   2. Customer-service representatives
   3. Registered nurses

4. Retail salespeople
5. Computer support specialists
6. Cashiers (except gaming)
7. Office clerks, general
8. Security guards
9. Computer-software engineers, applications
10. Waiters and waitresses
11. General and operations managers
12. Truck drivers, heavy and tractor trailer
13. Nursing aides, orderlies, and attendants
14. Janitors and cleaners
15. Postsecondary teachers

As you have noticed, at least nine of these fifteen groups of workers do not need a college degree for the work they do. Keeping this information in mind, how would you justify obtaining a college degree, especially with all the hard, time-consuming studying and reading, and the potential for going into debt and in many cases putting off earning a full-time salary for two or more years?

Have you ever taken public transportation, like the subway in the photograph, to work or college on a daily basis? Notice the poster in the photograph that says "Life Begins at 80." What do you think it might be advertising?

Find Work That You Love

BY BARBARA MOSES

1 . . . "Do what you love." "Follow your bliss." We have all heard this type of apparently impractical advice for job seekers. But this advice is actually very practical. All things being equal, the chances are that you will do better and be happier doing work that you love than work to which you are indifferent—or actively dislike.

2 But finding work that you love is not as blissfully easy as the peppy self-help books might suggest. You may have to make considerable sacrifices and difficult trade-offs, but becoming an activist in your career means you will be in a position to make choices. If you never even look for the work you love, your life will be poorer for it.

3 Knowing what you love starts with **knowing what is important to you**. Knowing your personal priorities and values is crucial in ensuring your career satisfaction . . .

Be Who You Are

4 Marian, a successful senior manager, recently quit her job. Warm and expressive with her friends and family, she found herself becoming increasingly "cold and hard" to survive in an unrelentingly tough corporate environment. "It was getting to the point where I no longer recognized myself. I had to get out of there or go crazy," she said.

5 Don't try to be something you're not. Be who you are—your authentic self. Find an organizational culture that reflects your personal needs and values, an environment that allows you to be you. You'll be happier. And in the long run, you'll probably be more successful.

6 One study looked at the characteristics of 55 successful women executives who held powerful positions in major American corporations. One of the most striking things they had in common was their honesty and directness. They didn't pretend to be something they weren't. They expressed their own individuality. They weren't defensive or "political." And their careers flourished.

7 Being who you are may mean **refusing to "worship the new market god."** Five years ago, you would routinely hear parents make comments about their children such as, "I don't really care what they decide to do as long as they're happy." I don't hear anyone make this comment today. It's almost as if the stakes have become so high that people feel that happiness as an end in itself is an indulgence one can ill afford. Never before has people's measure of worth and "fitness" been so intimately tied to their economic viability.

8 People turn themselves inside out to fit into positions that are a fundamentally awful match with their skills, interests, and values because they are so terrified of being without a job. They make career choices on the basis of how it will look on their résumé. They work excessive hours at the expense of their health, their children, and their personal relationships.

9 At some point, we have to step back and refuse to worship blindly at the altar of the market god—to do what we want to do rather than contorting ourselves into whatever shape the market currently happens to demand.

10 Instead, we must learn to **play to our strengths**. Each of us brings to the table a unique set of skills and attributes that describe who we are and how we can add value. When we stray too far from these core strengths, we invite trouble.

11 Increasingly, I see people worrying because their organization has decided that in order

for them to be successful they have to possess certain attributes and competencies. For example, they need to "be creative," to "have good leadership skills," or to "be able to withstand enormous pressure." In evaluating themselves against these competencies, people often identify one or two areas where they are not as strong, and ask: "How can I become more creative? How can I be a better leader? How can I become more effective under pressure? What does it mean if I have a liability or weakness in a particular area?"

12 Self-help books and motivational courses would have us believe that we can be whatever we want to be, if we only try hard enough. I think this is psychologically naïve. We are all different, and each of us has our own unique portfolio of strengths and aptitudes.

The 12 New Rules for Career Success

13 It is not enough to know what the new emerging careers are for building a successful future for yourself. The job market isn't that stable anyway. The workplace has changed, and the rules of career success have changed along with it.

1. Ensure Your Marketability

14 Ben, 45, was a middle manager in a company that eradicated its entire middle-management ranks. It took him 18 months to find another job—and two years to recover emotionally. Now, Ben says, "Every six months I take out my résumé, and if I can't think of one thing I've accomplished that I can add, I know that I've been slacking off."

15 It may no longer be realistic to believe that job security exists anywhere anymore. But you can have security in the marketability of your skills. To make yourself marketable:

- Think of everyone you work for as a client rather than a boss.
- Know your product: yourself and the skills you have to offer, your assets, strengths,

potential liabilities, and how you can add value to an employer or client.

- Know your market: both current and prospective clients.

2. Think Globally

16 Philip, a Toronto architect, struggled for a few years in what he described as a dying profession. "They're no longer building office towers," he complained. "They were all done in the 1980s." But he secured a new livelihood by going online and networking to find new clients as far away as Saudi Arabia. Philip still lives in Toronto but travels back and forth to the Middle East.

17 Today's technology allows you to work anywhere, anytime. And in a global economy, you may have to. In the borderless work world, where the entire world is a potential market, the ability to speak other languages and be comfortable with other cultures will be crucial. Globalization means an expansion of work opportunities, making you less reliant on the local economy. And living and working internationally helps you gain richer concepts not only in the mechanics of business, but also in the principles of life and work. As organizations increasingly move into new international markets, they will be looking for individuals who can adapt readily to other cultures.

3. Communicate Powerfully, Persuasively, and Unconventionally

18 Adrienne is an international art dealer who is now selling much of her art on the Internet rather than through face-to-face communication; she has had to learn a completely new set of communication skills. In the past, she would build relationships and establish credibility with people over time through "schmoozing," charm, and professional expertise. To do the same thing online, she says, "I had to learn to use the written word the way I speak. I had to learn how to become an evocative writer—to

charm, to talk about the feeling of a picture in a few powerful and suggestive words."

19 People with finely honed communication skills have always been valued, but advances in telecommunications, geographically dispersed project work, and everyone's information overload mean that efficient and effective communication is needed more than ever. You must be able to:

- Quickly capture your listener's attention and get your message across.
- Use words to paint a picture, tell a story, make information vivid.
- Write clearly, persuasively, and with impact.
- Zero in on key concepts and translate them appropriately for your listener's requirements.

4. Keep on Learning

20 With constantly changing work and skill requirements, "lifelong learning" will be more than just a catchphrase. It will be a necessity. Rules of lifelong learning include:

- Stay current in your own field, and continue to develop skills and knowledge outside it.
- Take courses, read books and journals, develop and practice new skills.
- Look at periods of full-time education between periods of work not as "time off," but as smart career moves preparing you for the future.

21 When considering learning, don't confine yourself to traditional institutions or modes of learning. Perhaps the most important learning "event" of recent years has been the number of people who have become computer literate—something achieved almost exclusively outside the traditional classroom.

22 As more and more educational institutes are going online, offering diverse learning experiences over the Internet (including graduate degrees), it will be much easier to meet the need for lifelong learning.

5. Understand Business Trends

23 I am always amazed at how many people have only the narrowest knowledge of specific trends in their profession and even less knowledge of broader business trends—whether economic, demographic, or cultural. I routinely ask people, "What international trends will affect your business?" and "Globally, what is your major source of competition?" Even among senior managers, only a handful of people say they are as well informed as they should be.

24 Test yourself: Do you regularly read the business section of your newspaper? Can you identify three trends that will have significant impact on your industry in the next five years? Do you know what new technologies might shape your industry in the next five years? Do you know what the potential threats are to your industry or profession?

25 In a very complex and rapidly changing work world, it is crucial to be aware of key trends in business, society, and politics. Not having the time to keep up simply doesn't cut it as an excuse. Read the business press or keep current through electronic media and keep track of the fast-changing economic and social landscape. Understand the competitive environment. Get information from a variety of sources and maintain an independent and critical perspective.

6. Prepare for Areas of Competence, Not Jobs

26 Recently someone suggested computer animation as a possible future career for Barry, a teenager with storytelling, graphics, and media abilities. Barry replied, "The work I choose now might not even exist by the time I'm old enough to do it. Or if it does exist, the technology may have changed to require completely different skills."

27 Intuitively, Barry understood a key maxim of the new economy: Don't prepare for jobs, prepare for areas of competence. Like many of yesterday's jobs that have now vanished, the "hot jobs" of today may not exist tomorrow.

28 It is important, then, to think of roles, not jobs. You may have a single job title but many, many roles: leader, change agent, coach, problem solver, troubleshooter, team builder, consensus builder, mentor, facilitator, and so on. Think also of marketable skills that are independent of your technical abilities, such as resilient, resourceful, opportunity seeking, time urgent, market driven, high-impact risk taker, and insatiable learner. These are the self-management attributes and skills that employers are looking for and that will determine your future success in the new economy.

7. Look to the Future

29 You can't rely on the accuracy of long-term occupational projections, nor should you try to make career choices based on what kind of work you think will be "hot," rather than what you are best suited to do. But it is still helpful to monitor demographic, economic, and cultural trends.

30 Based on current trends, here are some of the fields that should be fairly buoyant:

- **Medicine.** Many of the new openings will be at the lower end of the scale (e.g., home care workers and nursing assistants), but there will also be openings for occupational and physical therapists, pharmacists, and radiologists, as well as specialties that will help keep an aging population active and youthful looking: plastic surgery, for instance.

- **Education.** School boards are cutting back on jobs for teachers, but educators and entrepreneurs alike will be able to profit from the growth of private tutoring services and centers.

- **Edutainment.** The growth of electronic media and the emphasis on lifelong learning add up to tremendous opportunities for people who can combine the excitement of computer graphics and animation with educational content—everyone from the entrepreneurs who package and market the products to computer programmers, graphic artists, animators, and educators.

31 Other "hot" areas include recreation, the environment, biotechnology, pharmaceuticals, communications, computers, and personal services of all kinds.

8. Build Financial Independence

32 When your finances are in good shape, you can make career decisions based on what is really important to you. A financial planner can help you take steps toward financial independence. Most recommend that you save about 10% of your pretax income and keep six months' salary in the bank.

33 Rethink your relationship to money: Does all the stuff you buy contribute to your happiness? If not, could you give up buying it? You might take a lesson from the "voluntary simplicity" movement, in which people have actively decided to pursue a life outside the continual push to "buy, spend, consume." What do you really need?

9. Think Lattice, Not Ladders

34 Corporate downsizing and flattened hierarchies have carved out half the rungs in the traditional career ladder. Now, the career ladder is more like a lattice: You may have to move sideways before you can move up.

35 In a lattice, everything is connected. Each step will take you somewhere, though sometimes in unpredictable directions. You must measure progress in new ways. Each new work assignment should contribute to your portfolio of skills, in increasing both your breadth and depth, while you stay motivated and challenged.

36 Be creative in seeking out new opportunities. When 42-year-old Ira was told that he would never make partner at his accounting firm, he looked for opportunities not only to keep himself challenged, but also to maintain his visibility and value to the firm. Every two years or so, Ira takes on a high-profile assignment, thus making himself an indispensable contributor to the firm.

37   If you're feeling stuck in your current role, consider the possibilities for job enrichment: a lateral move into a new work assignment that offers opportunities for learning and development, opportunities to mentor younger staff, participation in task forces, and interesting educational programs.

38   Track your career progress by your work, not your level. Judge your progress by the depth of content of your work, its importance to the organization and to customers, and whether you are still learning and having fun.

10. Be a Generalist with a Specialty or a Specialist Who's a Generalist

39   Will you be better off in the future as a specialist or as a generalist? The answer is, Both. You need to have strong enough specialist skills to get you in the door—something that makes you unique and puts you in a position to add value to a client. But that is no longer enough.

40   You also need to be able to use those specialist skills in high-pressure environments and in teams of people from different disciplines. You also need to be able to organize your work, manage your time, keep a budget, and sell a project. So the question is not so much one of either/or, but one of degree. Should you be *more* of a specialist or *more* of a generalist?

41   If you prefer to specialize, conduct a searching self-assessment to make sure you have what it takes to rise to the top of your profession. Take an equally careful look at market conditions to make sure that you are investing your career assets in an in-demand specialty. Stay on top of the newest trends and information in your profession. And don't give up on your general skills.

11. Be a Ruthless Time Manager

42   We are working in a world where fast enough never is and where speed is prized above all else. With so many demands on us, it's crucial to be ruthless in managing time.

43   Evaluate every time commitment. Are you doing something because it needs to be done or because it's there? What are you not doing that may be more important? Become vigilant in saying "no" to excessive work demands. Know your limitations. Work strategically rather than just staying busy. If you are working excessively long hours over an extended period of time, you may lose productivity.

44   Set priorities, including personal priorities. Use the weekend to refresh yourself—turn off the cell phone. Go someplace where you can't be reached.

12. Be Kind to Yourself

45   Instead of beating yourself up over things that didn't work out, remind yourself of your successes. Celebrate them!

46   Set realistic expectations of what's doable. Learn to live with the best you can do at this point, to live with less-than-perfect. Congratulate yourself on your successes. When you've done a good job, pat yourself on the back. Regularly keep track of your successes, no matter how apparently small, and take credit where it's due. Above all, be kind to yourself.

Questions

1. Why does the author believe it is practical to choose a career that involves doing work that you truly enjoy?

2. What does the author mean when she advises readers to refuse to "worship the new market god?" How is this advice related to the concept of knowing what is important to you?

3. In the author's twelve rules for career success, the first rule is "Ensure Your Marketability" and the fourth rule is "Keep on Learning." Explain the concept of "lifelong learning." How is this concept related to ensuring your marketability?

4. What is the "voluntary simplicity" movement mentioned in Rule 8? Do you agree or disagree with the advice given?

5. Using a dictionary when necessary, define the following words in their appropriate context:
unrelentingly (4); organizational culture (5); indulgence (7); viability (7); résumé (8); portfolio (12); eradicated (14); liabilities (15); honed (19); catchphrase (20); consensus builder (28); resilient (28); insatiable (28); hierarchies (34); lattice (35).

For Further Discussion and Writing

1. What would be your choice of the top three "rules" described in the reading? Explain your choices.

2. Visit the career center at your college and ask to take an "interest inventory" to help you decide upon a career. Share your experience with a friend. Were you surprised at the suggestions for possible careers? Did you consider the experience worthwhile?

3. How does the advice contained in Rule 7 (Look to the Future) compare to the information in the previous article by Bridget Kulla, "Ten Majors That Didn't Exist 10 Years Ago"? Write an essay in which you compare and contrast the value of the two readings to your personal search for a career.

4. What would be your "dream job" ten years in the future? In a short essay, describe a typical day in your life ten years from today. Include a description of your job as well as recreational activities.

Working Just to Live Is Perverted into Living Just to Work

BY ANA VECIANA-SUAREZ

1 He's hardly ever home. The children are asleep when he leaves for the office, asleep when he returns. He misses most of their activities. On Sundays, if there's no paperwork to finish, no meetings, no community demands, he's too tired to be much fun.

2 His son learned to fish without him. His daughter became a young woman before he

realized it. He turned gray, it seemed, overnight. He gave up tennis and soccer and took up spreadsheets. They sold their pop-up camper because it gathered dirt and leaves in the driveway.

3   I was told this by someone who knows: his wife.

4   "He has no life," she says matter-of-factly.

5   I imagine she meant something more, too: We have no life together, as a family.

6   I hear and witness these transformations more than I care to, enough that it has become a regular refrain of mine: We work so hard, so long, that there is often nothing left for us and our families by the end of the day, and certainly not by the end of the week.

7   We think of this as a new phenomenon, a product of downsizing and corporate mergers. Hardly. A friend sent me the words to "My Little One," an 1890s Yiddish song that resounds with concerns of today:

> I have a son, a little son,
> A boy completely fine.
> When I see him it seems to me
> That all the world is mine.
> But seldom, seldom do I see
> My child awake and bright;
> I only see him when he sleeps;
> I'm only home at night.
> It's early when I leave for work;
> When I return it's late.
> Unknown to me is my own flesh,
> Unknown is my child's face . . .

8   A century later, we are stuck in an endless, destructive cycle, simultaneously addicted to and repulsed by our work, at once proud of our long hours and frightened by what they mean. Even as we are compulsive in chasing the next career rung, many of us profess to be burned out.

9   Are we confused, or delusional?

10   I'm not sure. I used to believe that my generation was disillusioned with the demands and the emotional price tag of their fathers' careers and would change things. But as we approach middle age, when the psychological commitments of child-rearing and family care-taking intensify, work for many has become an end in itself and a means to get away from our homes and ourselves.

11   Sure, some work long and hard of necessity. Most of those I know, though, work more to make more money to buy more and bigger things. We want, we want, we want. So we work, we work, we work.

12   The job comes to do more than define us. It owns us. We live to work, and as a result, the job comes with us whoever we are—by fax at home, by beeper at the ballet recital, by cellular phone in the car. We have become so efficient—we expect ourselves to be so efficient—that work is no longer something we do solely in an office. Those boundaries have been erased.

13   So we answer client mail between innings at our son's games. We jot notes for tomorrow's job presentation while our toddler plays in her sandbox. We organize our briefcase in the pediatrician's waiting room.

14   I love my job. I love putting together the words, the turn of phrase, that will make a reader savor the sound of language. I wonder, though, after drifting back from columnland into my children's conversations, if I'm turning over too much of me. Or maybe the question really is: Am I giving up too much of them for my own pleasure and ambition?

15   Part of the problem stems, I believe, from the way we describe the integration of our work and family lives, with words that imply we can do both well if only we organize, prioritize, set our minds to it. Juggle this. Balance that.

16   Conspicuously absent in discussions is the admission that much of life turns out to be a series of either-or choices, not merely a matter of better management or improved organization.

17   We don't talk so readily of giving up, putting aside—and maybe that's exactly what we need to do.

18   Some competing demands can't be reconciled. Sometimes, we need to surrender some of our ambition. That's life, or at the least the life we all claim we want to live. Because if we're not careful, our sons will learn to fish alone and our daughters will grow up before we know it.

Questions

1. In one or two sentences, write the main idea of the article.

2. When the wife of the overworked man described at the beginning of the article says that "He has no life," what does the author believe she really means?

3. How long does the author say there has been a problem balancing work and family life?

4. What examples does the author give to illustrate her point that the boundaries between office and home have been erased and "The job comes to do more than define us. It owns us"?

5. Why does the author believe that it may not be possible to always balance the demands of work and family life? What is her solution?

6. Using a dictionary when necessary, define the following words in their appropriate context:
   spreadsheets (2); refrain (6); phenomenon (7); resounds (7); simultaneously (8); columnland (14); prioritize (15).

For Further Discussion and Writing

1. Do you think that more men than women become "owned by their job," or do you believe that similar percentages of career-oriented men and women become compulsive workaholics (someone addicted to work)? Do you personally know of someone who seems to have sacrificed his or her family life and/or personal life in order to succeed in a career?

2. Make two lists. In the first, list jobs or careers that you believe would interfere with a quality personal life. In the second, list jobs or careers that you believe lend themselves to having more of a balance between work and personal time. Compare your list with those of two classmates. Are they similar?

3. Listen to or read the lyrics of the song, "The Cat's in the Cradle" by Jim Croce. Compare the sentiments expressed in the song to the 1890s

Yiddish song, "My Little One." Do you know of any other songs or works of art that express similar ideas?

4. The author mentions transformations of people who are "working just to live" into people who are "living just to work." Do other countries have similar problems, or is this transformation more common in the United States? Conduct research at the library and on the Internet to discover the average number of hours in a work week in five other countries. Be sure to check France and Japan. Report your findings to the class either orally or as a PowerPoint presentation.

It's Time to Make Up Your Mind

BY WINSTON FLETCHER

1 . . . Every day we all make hundreds of decisions with hardly a thought. We decide what to have for breakfast, what to wear, which bits of the newspaper to read and which to ignore. Yet most of us feel guiltily indecisive at work, much of the time. In our hearts, we alone know what terrible procrastinators we are.

2 Can you improve yourself? You bet. First and foremost, in any situation, you must determine your objectives. The ends will almost always justify the means—but you must be absolutely clear about the ends you're aiming for. Are you willing to let your personal life suffer, or do you want to keep work and home life in balance? Are you keen to be popular or don't you give a stuff? Are you willing to be ruthless in pursuit of your ambitions or do you find ruthless behavior unethical? The more guidelines you can lay down for yourself, the faster you will decide which activities will help you achieve your goals and which won't. If you constantly hum and haw about where you are going, you'll never decide how to get there.

3 On any project, one of the immediate analyses you need to make is: does it need to be perfect or does it need to be fast? As in cooking, excellence often takes time—time that may not be available. . . . There is never any excuse for shoddiness, but there is often a trade-off between speed and perfection. Find out what's needed before you start or you'll end up falling out of the frying pan and into the fire. . . .

4 Next, evaluate the downside. What is the worst that can happen if things go pear-shaped? When you're making a decision, carefully analyze the consequences of everything coming utterly unstuck. The downside will rarely be quite as disastrous as it first appears.

5 Then, don't delay—but don't rush. If you have a little time in hand, take it: you'll find the decision keeps resurfacing in your mind, helping you to reexamine all the angles. Many of the most senior and successful business managers I have met view themselves as rather cautious decision-makers. They're not, of course. Their skill is to act as quickly as the circumstances dictate, while taking as much time as the circumstances allow. "More haste less speed" is as true in business as in life generally.

6 A couple more tips. If you are hesitating, ask yourself how somebody you admire would tackle the problem: the head of the company, perhaps, or a previous boss you really rated. Put

them in your shoes and see what they would do. It will force you to look at the problem from a different standpoint. Similarly, don't be too proud to ask for advice. Phrase your enquiry properly and it won't make you look stupid; it will make you look smart. Whereas you will indubitably look a right idiot if you make the wrong decision when your colleagues knew the right one all along. The propensity of managers to re-invent wheels is prodigious. Don't do it.

Probably the best single decision-making aid ever devised was invented by the great American wit, thinker, and businessman Benjamin Franklin over 200 years ago. Franklin had made enough by the age of 42 to retire, which was probably even more difficult then than now. And he did it with the help of his "pros and cons" lists. He analyzed every decision into its pros and cons and wrote down the two lists, facing each other, on a single sheet of paper. (Today you can do it on a computer, but it's one of the few pieces of analysis I still find faster by old-fashioned pencil and paper.) The pros and cons must each be boiled down to a few words—the act of compression makes you think hard about them. And it's essential they are written down (or typed). If you try to carry them in your head, you'll get yourself into an unholy, confused, and thoroughly indecisive mess. But if you make out Ben Franklin's pros and cons lists properly, they will always help you to speedy, but considered, decisions.

Dig Deep into Your Pocket

Another system I've used and like I stole from Bob Jacoby. Bob Jacoby was the dynamic supremo of the Ted Bates advertising agency for many years, and is credited with having made more money out of advertising than any other individual in history—over $100 million. (He then retired, too.) Jacoby jotted down decisions that were nagging at his mind on small pieces of paper. He put the pieces in his jacket pocket, together with other bits of paper with other difficult decisions. Whenever he had a spare moment, he would pull one of the pieces of paper from his pocket at random, and concentrate on it for a few minutes. It might not work for everyone, but it worked for him, and it has worked for me, though I still prefer Franklin's pros and cons list.

There I go again: indecisive even about the best way to become more decisive. That must be why I'm never going to be head honcho at Chrysler. But maybe you could. Stop procrastinating and get on with it.

Questions

1. What does the author say you should do first to improve your ability to make difficult business decisions?

2. What are some other techniques to help you make decisions?

3. What decision does the author say you must make about any project?

4. Using a dictionary when necessary, define the following words in their appropriate context:
   procrastinators (1); analyses (3); shoddiness (3); pear-shaped (4); utterly (4); circumstances dictate (5); rated (6); indubitably (6); propensity (6); prodigious (6); compression (7); supremo (8).

For Further Discussion and Writing

1. Do you agree with the author that many of us are procrastinators? Brainstorm with the class for ways to overcome the habit of putting off doing class assignments such as research papers and essays.

2. Have you ever found yourself in a position where you had to make a difficult decision? Did you use any techniques like the ones mentioned in the reading to help you come to a final decision? Give examples you are comfortable sharing with your classmates.

3. Do you think any of the advice given in this reading selection could help explain how people find themselves "owned by the job," as described in the previous reading selection, "Working Just to Live Is Perverted into Living Just to Work" by Ana Veciana–Suarez? How are the two authors' approaches to making a difficult decision similar? How are they different?

4. Think of as many examples as you can where it would be reasonable to make a "trade-off between speed and perfection" when you are doing a project, task, or job. What kind of project or job would not allow you to make such a trade-off?

5. Following the technique attributed to Benjamin Franklin, develop lists with the pros and cons of two or more possible career choices. Use information from the other reading selections in this chapter and your own research on the Internet to discover your ideal career.

14 Consumerism

You can tell the ideals of a nation by its advertisements.

Norman Douglas, South Wind, *1917*

I think that parents only get so offended by television because they rely on it as a babysitter and the sole educator of their kids.

Trey Parker and Matt Stone, South Park, *"Death," 1997*

The United States' economic engine is fueled by millions of consumers buying goods and services every day, year after year. The multi-billion-dollar advertising industry sees to it that we are bombarded daily with hundreds of advertisements and logos (in print, online, on radio and television, and on billboards) exhorting us to spend and buy. Americans face a dizzying number of choices about how to spend their dollars. Is it any wonder that we are the most consumer-driven society in history?

With regard to accumulating consumer goods, how much is enough? How much is too much? How do we know? Why do Americans, as a society, carry more debt today than ever before? What is the "right" standard of living for us? How do we handle the tug-of-war between our desire to consume and our desire to be responsible stewards of our environment?

The following articles address these questions and more.

Living 'Poor' and Loving It

BY DONNA FREEDMAN

1 I don't consider myself deprived, although I can see why some people might think so. I don't own a laptop computer, television, DVD player, stereo, iPod, video-game system, Black-Berry or many of the other things marketed as necessities.

2 But I have food, shelter, family, friends, a radio, a bus pass, a library card and the chance to attend a respected university. How could I consider myself "poor" when so many people have nothing to eat, nowhere to sleep and no chance to improve their situations?

3 Yet there is another reason I hesitate to call myself poor—the cultural baggage associated with the word: Poor people are lazy, stupid, immoral, shameless and incapable of making smart decisions. Poor people are losers; our country loves winners. We want poor people to trade their rags for riches. We want them to embody the American dream.

4 Most of all, we want to believe that poor people are shiftless and depraved and always to blame for their poverty. Otherwise, we'd have to face the possibility that someday we, too, could wind up on the business end of the bread line.

Blaming the Victims?

5 I'm not naive enough to think that some people don't make bad choices. But I'm not mean-spirited enough to believe that poor people are poor only because they're pathologically incapable of wealth. Lots of them are where they are because of sickness, unemployment, a lack of education, a dearth of opportunities. More than a few of my relatives are among them. I joked to a cousin that our family has been practicing "how to be poor" all our lives. She agreed. "Poor just is," she said, "and you don't question, 'How?' You just do it."

6 I grew up fairly broke and stayed that way until my early 20s. Marriage and a career kept me comfortably middle class for more than two decades. Now I'm a divorced student and broke again.

7 Scratch that. I'm not broke. I'm poor. I'm redefining the word so that it will lose its power to harm. Being poor is what my dad would call a "useful life skill." (He used this phrase when he wanted us to carry cinder blocks or weed the tomato patch.) And I happen to believe it's a life skill that plenty of Americans could use, saddled as they are with credit card debt, college loan debt and mortgage debt. Being "poor" for a while—that is, making a conscious choice to manage money differently—would be good for them.

8 Here, then, are the rules for How to Be Poor:

Rule 1: Have very little money.

Rule 2: Live on it.

Rule 3: Rule 2 will change your life, if you let it.

9 Being poor means taking a hard look at your needs and getting ruthless about separating them from the wants. (I *need* food. I *want* steak.)

10 It means not behaving as though you still have money because you don't have money—you have credit cards. Using them to live beyond your means is financial suicide.

11 Whether you're in debt because of bad luck or bad choices doesn't matter. What matters is taking charge of your situation. As the old saying goes, when you find yourself in a hole, stop digging. In other words, stop spending. Dinners out, vacations, electronic toys, shopping trips, cable TV, tickets to sporting events—you simply can't have these things right now.

12   But here's the good part: Once you can afford them again, you may not care if you get them. That's where Rule 3 comes in.

An Attitude of Gratitude

13   My most important money-management tool hasn't been figuring out how to get more but rather discovering how little I really need and how much I already have. Sure, I look for practical ways to save. The local electric company has a reduced rate for lower-income users. I cook simple meals that cost practically nothing. I shop for loss leaders and use coupons and rebates. About once a month, I go to a food bank. Yard sales, thrift shops and dollar stores supply most other requirements.

14   But how I save money isn't the point. What's important is knowing that I have everything I need and some of what I want. Although I have never been more broke, more tired or more uncertain about the future, I've also never been happier. I'm no Zen master, but I can say that having less makes you that much more grateful for what's in front of you. I've also learned that paring down possessions means a lot more room in your life as well as in your house.

15   I might not have selected this scenario for my life. But now that I have it, I'm going to see what I can learn from it. My hope is that it will make me wiser about what I eventually seek.

Here's what I've already learned: Being poor 16 doesn't mean not wanting things; it means wanting the right things for the right reasons. When these clothes wear out, I'll get new ones. In time, I'll want a new computer for my freelance writing work. Several family members are struggling financially, so I'd like to help them. Certainly, I'd love to travel. Someday I'll treat myself one of those small-but-mighty bookshelf sound systems so that music will fill my apartment with momentous impact. And I want to donate to a couple of education foundations so that others can have the same opportunities I'm getting.

Those are all nice goals, but I can still be 17 happy if I don't get all (or any) of them. Should I earn a good salary one day, I'll decide which are most important and make them happen. But it won't matter if I don't get a high-paying job because I know how to be poor: You live as well as you can on what you earn and look for ways to improve your life.

True prosperity is more than just a healthy 18 bottom line. Being rich wouldn't necessarily make me happy or generous. Those two states of mind have nothing to do with your bank balance. There's a world of difference between poverty and poverty of spirit.

Not that being poor makes me noble. It 19 doesn't. It just makes me careful. And grateful.

Questions

1. What is the article's thesis? If the author does not provide a thesis, develop one that fits the article.

2. In paragraph 3 the author mentions "the American dream." What is your understanding of the American dream?

3. In paragraph 4 the author states that many people want to believe that poor people are "always to blame for their poverty." What specific

situations does the author mention that might contribute to people's poverty, and for which they may not be wholly responsible? What situations can you add that the author does not mention?

4. In paragraph 7 the author's father calls being poor "a useful life skill." In what ways might this be true?

5. What are the author's three rules for "how to be poor"?

6. In paragraph 9 the author distinguishes between "needs" and "wants." How do (or how should) you and your family distinguish between needs and wants?

7. What "practical ways to save" does the author mention? What practical ways to save can you add to the list?

8. In paragraph 18 the author makes some interesting philosophical distinctions among key concepts discussed in the article: "prosperity," "rich," "state of mind," "poverty," "poverty of spirit." Discuss and elaborate on some meanings of these concepts and how they relate to the subject of this article.

9. Using a dictionary when necessary, define the following words in their appropriate context:
   deprived (1); embody (3); shiftless (4); depraved (4); bread line (4); pathologically (5); dearth (5); mortgage (7); ruthless (9); means (10); loss leaders (13); Zen (14); paring (14); scenario (15); momentous (16); bottom line (18); noble (19).

For Further Discussion and Writing

1. What is your definition of "poor"? In what ways can a person be poor? What is your definition of "rich"? In what ways can a person be rich?

2. Think of the two or three poorest people you know personally. In what ways are they poor? How would you describe their attitudes about life? Now think of the two or three richest people you know personally. In what ways are they rich? How would you describe their attitudes about life?

3. In what ways does the American consumer culture and advertising influence people's ideas about being poor and being rich?

4. How is "poverty" defined by the federal government? Do some research on poverty levels in your community. What percentage of your community's population live below the poverty line? What generalizations, if any, can you make about the kinds of people in your community who are more likely to be poor?

5. Spiritual wealth has often been associated with material poverty. For example, members of many religious communities around the world take a vow of poverty. Also, the great spiritual and political leader of

India, Mohandas Gandhi (1869–1948), lived an extremely simple life free of most material possessions. What are some reasons why spiritual wealth has been associated with material poverty?

6. Watch the American film classic *It's a Wonderful Life* (1946), directed by Frank Capra. What points about poverty and wealth can you derive from this film? What other films, books, plays, and TV shows can you think of that explore the relationship between wealth and poverty?

How Do Our Kids Get So Caught Up In Consumerism?

BY BRIAN SWIMME

In the Merck Family Fund's Yearning for Balance national survey, 86 percent of people agreed or strongly agreed that "today's youth are too focused on buying and consuming things." This is a touchstone issue for children and the future. The following book excerpt deals with how children today discover what it means to be human.

1 Where are we initiated into the universe? To answer we need to reflect on what our children experience over and over again, at night, in a setting similar to those children in the past who gathered in the caves and listened to the chant of the elders. If we think in terms of pure quantities of time the answer is immediate: the cave has been replaced with the television room and the chant with the advertisement. One could say that the chant has been replaced with the television *show*, but at the core of each show, driving the action, and determining whether or not the show will survive the season, is the advertisement. That is the essential message that will be there night after night and season after season. Television's *Bonanzas*, *Cheers*, and *Cosby* shows all come and go; the advertisement endures through every change.

2 What is the effect on our children? Before a child enters first grade science class, and before entering in any real way into our religious ceremonies, a child will have soaked in thirty thousand advertisements. The time our teenagers spend absorbing ads is more than their total stay in high school. None of us feels very good about this, but for the most part we just ignore it. It's background. It's just there, part of what's going on. We learned to accept it so long ago we hardly ever think about it anymore.

3 But imagine how different we would feel if we heard about a country that programmed its citizenry in its religious dogmas in such a manner. In fact, it was just such accounts concerning the leaders of the former Soviet Union that outraged us for decades, the thought that they would take young children and subject them to brainwashing in Soviet lies, removing their natural feelings for their parents or for God or for the truth of history, and replacing these with the assumptions necessary for their dictatorship to continue its oppressive domination.

4 Immersed in the religion of consumerism, we are unable to take such comparisons seriously. We tell ourselves soothing clichés, such as

the obvious fact that television ads are not put on by any political dictatorship. We tell ourselves that ads are simply the efforts of our corporations to get us interested in their various products. But as with any reality that we rarely pay any serious attention to, there may be a lot more going on there than we are aware of. Just the sheer amount of time we spend in the world of the ad suggests we might well devote a moment to examining that world more carefully.

5   The advertisers of course are not some bad persons with evil designs. They are just doing their job. On the other hand, we can also say that their primary concern is not explicitly the well-being of our children. Why should it be? Their objective is to create ads that are successful for their company, and this means to get the television viewer interested in their product. But already we can see that this is a less than desirable situation. After all, we parents demand that our children's teachers, to take just one example, should have our children's best interests foremost in mind. Such teachers will shape our children when they are young and vulnerable, so of course we want this shaping to be done only by people who care. So to hand over so much of our children's young lives to people who obviously do not have our children's well-being foremost in mind is at the very least questionable.

6   But at a deeper level, what we need to confront is the power of the advertiser to promulgate a world-view, a mini-cosmology, that is based upon dissatisfaction and craving.

7   One of the clichés for how to construct an ad captures the point succinctly: "An ad's job is to make them unhappy with what they have."

8   We rarely think of ads as being shaped by explicit world-views, and that precisely is why they are so effective. The last thing we want to think about as we're lying on the couch relaxing is the philosophy behind the ad. So as we soak it all up, it sinks down deep in our psyche. And if this takes place in the adult soul, imagine how much more damage is done in the psyches of our children, which have none of our protective cynicisms but which draw in the ad's imagery and message as if they were coming from a trusted parent or teacher.

9   Advertisers in the corporate world are of course offered lucrative recompense, and, with that financial draw, our corporations attract humans from the highest strata of IQs. And our best artistic talent. And any sports hero or movie star they want to buy. Combining so much brain power and social status with sophisticated electronic graphics and the most penetrating psychological techniques, these teams of highly intelligent adults descend upon all of us, even upon children not yet in school, with the simple desire to create in us a dissatisfaction for our lives and a craving for yet another consumer product. It's hard to imagine any child having the capacities necessary to survive such a lopsided contest, especially when it's carried out ten thousand times a year, with no cultural condom capable of blocking out the consumerism virus. Could even one child in the whole world endure that onslaught and come out intact? Extremely doubtful. Put it all together and you can see why it's no great mystery that consumerism has become the dominant world faith of every continent of the planet today.

10   The point I wish to make is not just that our children are such easy prey. It's not just that the rushing river of advertisements determines the sorts of shoes our children desire, the sorts of clothes and toys and games and sugar cereals that they must have. It's not just the unhappiness they are left with whenever they cannot have such commodities, an unhappiness that in many cases leads to aggressive violence of the worst kinds in order to obtain by force what their parents will not or cannot give them. All of this is of great concern, but the point I wish to focus on here has to do with the question of how we are initiated into a world.

11   Advertisements are where our children receive their cosmology, their basic grasp of the

world's meaning, which amounts to their primary religious faith, though unrecognized as such. I use the word "faith" here to mean cosmology on the personal level. Faith is that which a person holds to be the hard-boiled truth about reality. The advertisement is our culture's primary vehicle for providing our children with their personal cosmologies. As this awful fact sinks into awareness, the first healthy response is one of denial. It is just too horrible to think that we live in a culture that has replaced authentic spiritual development with the advertisement's crass materialism. And yet when one compares the pitiful efforts we employ for moral development with the colossal and frenzied energies we pour into advertising, it is like comparing a high school football game with World War II. Nothing that happens in one hour on the weekend makes the slightest dent in the strategic bombing taking place day and night fifty-two weeks of the year.

12   Perhaps the more recalcitrant children will require upward of a hundred thousand ads before they cave in and accept consumerism's basic world-view. But eventually we all get the message. It's a simple cosmology, told with great effect and delivered a billion times each day not only to Americans of course but to nearly everyone in the planetary reach of the ad: *humans exist to work at jobs, to earn money, to get stuff.* The image of the ideal human is also deeply set in our minds by the unending preachments of the ad. The ideal is not Jesus or Socrates. Forget all about Rachel Carson or Confucius or Martin Luther King, Jr., and all their suffering and love and wisdom. In the propaganda of the ad the ideal people, the fully human humans, are relaxed and carefree—drinking Pepsis around a pool—unencumbered by powerful ideas concerning the nature of goodness, undisturbed by visions of suffering that could be alleviated if humans were committed to justice. None of that ever appears. In the religion of the ad the task of civilizations is much simpler. The ultimate

meaning for human existence is getting all this stuff. That's paradise. And the meaning of the Earth? Premanufactured consumer stuff.

13   I have mentioned only television here, but of course that is simply one part of the program. To wade into a fuller awareness we need bring to mind our roadside billboards, the backs of cereal boxes, the fifty thousand magazines crammed with glossy pitches, the lunch boxes wrapped with toy advertisements, the trillion radio commercials, the come-ons piped into video programs, the seductions pouring into the telephone receiver when we're put on hold, the corporate logos stitched into our clothes and paraded everywhere and so on and so on. Literally everywhere on Earth, the advertising continues its goal of becoming omnipresent, even entering into space on the surfaces of our capsules.

14   None of what I have said here concerning ads and their effects on children will be news to those educators who for decades have been lamenting this oppressive situation in America. But I bring up the issue for two reasons.

15   The fact that consumerism has become the dominant world faith is largely invisible to us, so it is helpful to understand clearly that to hand our children over to the consumer culture is to place them in the care of the planet's most sophisticated preachers. If those bizarre cults we read about in the papers used even one-tenth of 1 percent of the dazzling deceit of our advertisers, they would be hounded by the federal justice department and thrown into jail straight away. But in American and European and Japanese society, and increasingly everywhere else, we are so blinded by the all-encompassing propaganda we never think to confront the advertisers and demand they cease. On the contrary, as if cult members ourselves, we pay them lucrative salaries and hand over our children in the bargain.

16   The second reason for bringing up the advertisement's hold on us has to do with my

fundamental aim in presenting the new cosmology. If we come to an awareness of the way in which the materialism of the advertisement is our culture's primary way for shaping our children, and if we find this unacceptable, we are left with the task of inventing new ways of introducing our children and our teenagers and our young adults and our middle-aged adults and our older adults to the universe. These notes on the new cosmology are grounded in our contemporary understanding of the universe and nourished by our more ancient spiritual convictions concerning its meaning. These notes then are a first step out of the religion of consumerism and into a way of life based upon the conviction that we live within a sacred universe.

Have you ever spent more money than you meant to when you went shopping? Why did you do it?

Questions

1. What has replaced the "cave" and "chant of the elders" described in paragraph 1?

2. According to the author, how many advertisements will a typical child see before he or she enters first grade?

3. Does the author believe that advertisers are evil? Does he believe that advertisers care about the welfare of children? How does the author support his viewpoint on the motives of advertisers in paragraph 5?

4. What is the author's greatest concern about the role advertisements play in children's lives? Do you agree or disagree with his argument?

5. Who are Rachel Carson, Confucius, and Martin Luther King Jr.?

6. Using a dictionary when necessary, define the following words in their appropriate context:
dogmas (3); clichés (4); promulgate (6); succinctly (7); psyche (8); protective cynicisms (8); lucrative (9); recompense (9); cosmology (11); crass (11); recalcitrant (12); alleviated (12); pitches (13); omnipresent (13).

For Further Discussion and Writing

1. Research the author's background to determine what his motives are for writing the article. Do you believe he is sincere in his beliefs about the dangers of advertisements? Why or why not?

2. Write a summary of the article following the guidelines in Chapter 11. Notice that one paragraph from this reading was used to provide examples for writing a summary, paraphrase, and quote.

3. Do you believe that you have been personally influenced by advertisements? Do you believe it has affected what you believe, how you dress, or what restaurants you choose to patronize? Give specific examples.

4. In paragraph 13 the author mentions several different media for advertisements to reach us. Have you noticed an increase in the number of advertisements that come to you by e-mail? Is this a problem for you personally? Would you be willing to pay a penny for every e-mail you send if it meant that unwanted advertisements would virtually disappear? Why or why not?

5. Evaluate the argument presented in this reading by referring to Chapter 12. Write your evaluation in the form of a short essay that considers the logical and emotional appeals used by the author.

In Defense of Consumerism

BY LLEWELLYN H. ROCKWELL, JR.

1 I'm beginning to think that the epithet "consumerism" is just another word for freedom in the marketplace.

2 It's true that the market is delivering goods, services, and technological advances by leaps, day after day. People claim that they are so inundated with techno advances that they don't want anymore. Say no to the latest gizmo!

3 But we really don't mean it. No one wants to be denied web access, and we want it faster and better with more variety. We want to download songs, movies, and treatises on every subject.

No amount of information is too much when it is something specific we seek.

4   And that's not all.

We want better heating and cooling in our homes and businesses. We want more varieties of food, wine, cleaning products, toothpaste, and razors. We want access to a full range of styles in our home furnishing. If something is broken, we want the materials made available to repair it. We want fresh flowers, fresh fish, fresh bread, and new cars with more features. We want overnight delivery, good tech support, and the newest fashions from all over the world.

5   The libraries are going online, as is the world's art. Commerce has made the shift. New worlds are opening to us by the day. We find that phone calls are free. We can link with anyone in the world through instant messaging, and email has become the medium that makes all communication possible. We are abandoning our tube-televisions and landline telephones—staples of 20th-century life—for far superior modes of information technology.

6   We want speed. We want wireless. We want access. And improvements. Clean and filtered water must flow from our refrigerators. We want energy drinks, sports drinks, bubbly drinks, juicy drinks and underground spring water from Fiji. We want homes. We want safety and security. We want service. We want choice.

7   We are getting all these things. And how? Through that incredible production and distribution machine called the market economy, which is really nothing but billions of people cooperating and innovating to make better lives for themselves. There's no dog-eat-dog. Competition is really nothing but entrepreneurs and capitalists falling over themselves in a quest to win the hearts and minds of the consuming public.

8   Sure, it's easy to look at all this and shout: ghastly consumerism! But if by "consume" we meant to purchase products and services with our own money in order to improve the human condition, who can't help but plead guilty?

9   The whole history of ideas about society has been spent trying to come up with some system that serves the common man rather than just the elites, the rulers, and the powerful. When the market economy, and its capitalistic structure, came into being, that institution was finally discovered. With the advent of economic science, we came to understand how this could be. We began to see how it is that billions of unplanned economic choices could conspire to create a beautiful global system of production and distribution that served everyone. And how do the intellectuals respond to this? By denouncing it as providing too much to too many.

10   But are people buying superfluous things that they can do without? Certainly. But who is to say for sure what is a need as versus a mere want? A dictator who knows all? How can we know that his desires will accord with my needs and yours? In any case, in a market economy, wants and needs are linked, so that one person's necessities are met precisely because other people's wants are met.

11   Here is an example.

If my grandchild is desperately sick, I want to get her to a doctor. The urgent care clinic is open late, as is the drug store next door, and thank goodness. I'm in and out, and I have the medicine and materials necessary to restore her to health. No one would say that this is a superficial demand.

12   But it can only stay open late because its offices are nestled in a strip mall where the rents are low and the access is high. The real estate is shared by candy stores, sports shops selling scuba gear, a billiard hall, and a store that specializes in party favors—all stores selling "superficial" things. All pay rent. The developer who made the mall wouldn't have built the place were it not for these less urgent needs.

13   The same is true for the furniture and equipment and labor used in the urgent-care clinic.

They are less expensive and more accessible than they otherwise would be due to the persistence of non-essential consumer demands. The computers they use are up-to-date and fast precisely because technicians and entrepreneurs have innovated to meet the demands of gamers, gamblers, and people who use the web to do things they shouldn't.

14   The same point can be made about "luxury goods" and bleeding-edge technologies. The rich acquire them and use them until the bugs are gone, the imitators are aroused, capitalists seek out cheaper suppliers, and eventually prices tumble and the same technology hits the mass market. Moreover, it is the rich who donate to charity, the arts, and to religion. They provide the capital necessary for investment. If you think through any service or good that is widely considered to be a need, you will find that it employs products, technologies, and services that were first created to meet superficial demands.

15   Maybe you think quality of life is no big deal. Does it really matter whether people have access to vast grocery stores, drug stores, subdivisions, and technology? Part of the answer has to do with natural rights: people should be free to choose and buy as they see fit. But another argument is buried in data we don't often think about.

16   Consider life expectancy in the age of consumerism. Women in 1900 typically died at 48 years old, and men at 46. Today? Women live to 80, and men to 77. This is due to better diet, less dangerous jobs, improved sanitation and hygiene, improved access to health care, and the entire range of factors that contribute to what we call our standard of living. Just since 1950, the infant mortality rate has fallen by 77 percent. Population is rising exponentially as a result.

17   It's easy to look at these figures that suggest that we could have achieved the same thing with a central plan for health, while avoiding all this disgusting consumerism that goes along with it. But such a central plan was tried in socialist countries, and their results showed precisely the opposite in mortality statistics. While the Soviets decried our persistent poverty amidst rampant consumerism, our poverty was being beaten back and our longevity was increasing, in large part because of the consumerism for which we were being reviled.

18   Nowadays we are being told that consumption is aesthetically displeasing, and that we should strive to get back to nature, stop driving here and there, make a compost pile, raise our own vegetables, unplug our computers, and eat nuts off trees. This longing for the primitive is nothing but an attempt to cast a pleasing gloss on the inevitable effects of socialist policies. They are telling us to love poverty and hate plenty.

19   But the beauty of the market economy is that it gives everyone a choice. For those people who prefer outhouses to indoor plumbing, pulling their teeth to dentistry, and eating nuts from trees rather than buying a can of Planters at Wal-Mart, they too have the right to choose that way of life. But don't let them say that they are against "consumerism." To live at all requires that we buy and sell. To be against commerce is to attack life itself.

Questions

1. This article presents a different opinion about the value of consumerism. What is the main idea of this essay? Do you agree with the author's assertion that "consumerism" can be defined as "freedom in the marketplace"?

2. What example does the author provide to support his argument that stores selling consumer goods help make vital services more available?

3. What are the author's views on the value of luxury goods, video games, and online gambling?

4. What other evidence does the author present to persuade the reader that consumerism has benefited society in the United States?

5. Using a dictionary when necessary, define the following words in their appropriate context:
epithet (1); inundated (2); entrepreneurs (7); elites (8); superfluous (10); exponentially (16); amidst (17); rampant (17); aesthetically displeasing (18); compost pile (18).

For Further Discussion and Writing

1. Write a summary of this essay and compare it with the essay by Brian Swimme. Both authors use the argument that the health and well-being of people will be increased if you follow their advice. However Swimme says this will happen if we limit consumerism. On the other hand, Rockwell says consumerism has improved people's health and standard of living. Which author do you think has the more convincing argument?

2. How effective are the author's examples about the benefits of consumerism? Would you be happy in a society that did not have television, telephones, and the Internet?

3. Do you agree with the author's opinions regarding everyone's "right to choose" what we buy? How do you decide what you really need as opposed to what you want?

4. Imagine that the two authors (Rockwell and Swimme) are having a conversation about consumerism. Write a short dialogue that portrays their imagined conversation and perform it as a skit for the class.

As Consumerism Spreads, Earth Suffers, Study Says

BY HILLARY MAYELL

1 Americans and Western Europeans have had a lock on unsustainable over-consumption for decades. But now developing countries are catching up rapidly, to the detriment of the environment, health, and happiness, according to the Worldwatch Institute in its annual report, *State of the World 2004.*

2 Perfectly timed after the excesses of the holiday season, the report put out by the Washington, D.C.-based research organization focuses this year on consumerism run amuck.

3 Approximately 1.7 billion people worldwide now belong to the "consumer class"—the group of people characterized by diets of highly processed food, desire for bigger houses, more and bigger cars, higher levels of debt, and lifestyles devoted to the accumulation of non-essential goods.

4 Today nearly half of global consumers reside in developing countries, including 240 million in China and 120 million in India—markets with the most potential for expansion.

5 "Rising consumption has helped meet basic needs and create jobs," Christopher Flavin, president of Worldwatch Institute said in a statement to the press. "But as we enter a new century, this unprecedented consumer appetite is undermining the natural systems we all depend on, and making it even harder for the world's poor to meet their basic needs."

6 The report addresses the devastating toll on the Earth's water supplies, natural resources, and ecosystems exacted by a plethora of disposable cameras, plastic garbage bags, and other cheaply made goods with built-in product obsolescence, and cheaply made manufactured goods that lead to a "throw-away" mentality.

7 "Most of the environmental issues we see today can be linked to consumption," said Gary Gardner, director of research for Worldwatch. "As just one small example, there was a story in the newspaper just the other day saying that 37 percent of species could become extinct due to climate change, which is very directly related to consumption."

From luxuries to necessities

8 Globalization is a driving factor in making goods and services previously out of reach in developing countries much more available. Items that at one point in time were considered luxuries—televisions, cell phones, computers, air conditioning—are now viewed as necessities.

9 China provides a snapshot of changing realities. For years, the streets of China's major cities were characterized by a virtual sea of people on bicycles, and 25 years ago there were barely any private cars in China. By 2000, 5 million cars moved people and goods; the number is expected to reach 24 million by the end of next year.

10 In the United States, there are more cars on the road than licensed drivers. Increased reliance on automobiles means more pollution, more traffic, more use of fossil fuels. Cars and other forms of transportation account for nearly 30 percent of world energy use and 95 percent of global oil consumption.

11 Changing diet, with a growing emphasis on meat, illustrates the environmental and societal toll exacted by unbridled consumption.

12 To provide enough beef, chicken, and pork to meet the demand, the livestock industry has moved to factory farming. Producing eight ounces of beef requires 6,600 gallons (25,000 liters) of water; 95 percent of world soybean crops are consumed by farm animals, and 16 percent of the world's methane, a destructive greenhouse gas, is produced by belching, flatulent livestock. The enormous quantities of manure produced at factory farms becomes toxic waste rather than fertilizer, and runoff threatens nearby streams, bays, and estuaries.

13 Chickens at a typical farm are kept in cages with about nine square inches (about 60 square centimeters) of space per bird. To force them to lay more eggs, they are often starved. Chickens slaughtered for meat are first fattened up with hormones, sometimes to the point where their legs can no longer support their weight.

14 Crowded conditions can lead to the rapid spread of disease among the animals. To prevent

this, antibiotics are included in their feed. The World Health Organization reports that the widespread use of these drugs in the livestock industry is helping breed antibiotic-resistant microbes, complicating the treatment of disease in both animals and people.

15 Inroads are being made. In 2002, McDonald's announced it would stop buying eggs from suppliers who keep chickens confined in battery cages and that are forced to lay additional eggs through starvation. By 2004, the fast-food chain will require chicken suppliers to stop giving birds antibiotics to promote growth. Wendy's, Burger King, and Kentucky Fried Chicken have all hired animal welfare specialists to devise new animal care standards.

16 The World Bank has also rethought its policy of funding livestock factory farming. In 2001, a World Bank report concluded "there is a significant danger that the poor are being crowded out, the environment eroded, and global food safety and security threatened."

Not much happier

17 The increase in prosperity is not making humans happier or healthier, according to several studies. Findings from a survey of life satisfaction in more than 65 countries indicate that income and happiness tend to track well until about $13,000 of annual income per person (in 1995 dollars). After that, additional income appears to produce only modest increments in self-reported happiness.

18 Increased consumerism evidently comes at a steep price.

People are incurring debt and working longer hours to pay for the high-consumption lifestyle, consequently spending less time with family, friends, and community organizations.

19 "Excess consumption can be counterproductive," said Gardner. "The irony is that lower levels of consumption can actually cure some of these problems."

20 Diets of highly processed food and the sedentary lifestyle that goes with heavy reliance on automobiles have led to a worldwide epidemic of obesity. In the United States, an estimated 65 percent of adults are overweight or obese, and the country has the highest rate of obesity among teenagers in the world. Soaring rates of heart disease and diabetes, surging health care costs, and a lower quality of day-to-day life are the result.

21 Some aspects of rampant consumerism have resulted in startling anomalies. Worldwatch reports that worldwide annual expenditures for cosmetics total U.S. $18 billion; the estimate for annual expenditures required to eliminate hunger and malnutrition is $19 billion. Expenditures on pet food in the United States and Europe total $17 billion a year; the estimated cost of immunizing every child, providing clean drinking water for all, and achieving universal literacy is $16.3 billion.

22 There is, of course, no easy solution to the problem. The authors call for green taxes (to reflect the true environmental costs of a product), take-back programs that require manufacturers to recycle packaging or goods, and consumer education and awareness programs.

23 But first and foremost we need to reorient our way of thinking, says Gardner.

"The goal is to focus not so much on sacrifice, but on how to provide a higher quality of life using the lowest amount of raw materials," he said. "We need to change the way we produce goods and the way we consume them."

Questions

1. What is the World Watch Institute? What is the purpose of the organization? Who owns the organization?

2. According to the article, how many global consumers reside in developing countries?

3. According to the article, what items that were once considered luxuries are now considered necessities?

4. What argument does the author present to convince the reader that increased prosperity does not lead to increased happiness? Do you agree or disagree?

5. Using a dictionary when necessary, define the following words in their appropriate context:
unsustainable (1); detriment (1); plethora (6); product obsolescence (6); globalization (8); flatulent (12); estuaries (12); antibiotic-resistant microbes (14); battery cages (15); the World Bank (16); increments (17); obesity (20); anomalies (21); green taxes (22)

For Further Discussion and Writing

1. Using the author's definition of the "consumer class" (paragraph 3), prepare a questionnaire to be taken by members of the class. Report the results of the questionnaire to the class.

2. The article mentions several fast food restaurants that are making changes in the way they purchase eggs and chickens. What types of eggs and chickens are available for you to purchase at the grocery store? Prepare a report to illustrate the different choices that individuals have when they purchase eggs and chickens. Conduct research on the "battery cage" chickens mentioned in the article. What is the difference between "cage" and "free range" chickens and the eggs they lay? Some brands advertise that their eggs have superior nutrition for the consumer. How can you verify the claims?

3. The first sentence of paragraph 17, "The increase in prosperity is not making humans happier or healthier, according to several studies," seems to disagree with the rest of the paragraph. The rest of the paragraph actually says that prosperity does make people happier, but that after reaching around $13,000 annual income (in 1995 dollars) the gains are quite small. Perhaps there is more evidence in the original report, but does the author present it in the article? Do you believe the report is biased? Why or why not?

4. Write a research paper on the topic of "green taxes" to evaluate the potential of such policies to reduce the effects of pollution.

15 The Environment

I would feel more optimistic about a bright future for man if he spent less time proving that he can outwit Nature and more time tasting her sweetness and respecting her seniority.

E. B. White (1899–1985)

Adapt or perish, now as ever, is nature's inexorable imperative.

H. G. Wells (1866–1946)

Few issues have attracted more worldwide interest in the twenty-first century than the environment. What began as a kind of fringe issue in the 1960s has now blossomed into a mainstream concern. The environmental issue that has been the focus of so much attention recently is climate change. Few people deny that the earth's climate is changing and that the earth's average temperatures are slowly rising. But there is a great deal of debate over what should be done about the situation and the urgency with which action should be taken.

The following readings address some of the issues associated with the environment and climate change. The first two readings take the form of a debate about climate change.

Climate change is a bigger issue than ever, with Al Gore testifying before Congress that we face a civilization-threatening crisis. Here, two physics-trained, math-savvy, educated-layman observers, without political or institutional axes to grind, take a look at some of the pros and cons of climate change concern.

Debate, What Debate?

BY MITCHELL E. GOLDEN

1 Hmm, I'm asked to write a piece for Health-FactsAndFears about climate change. I suppose I could marshal the evidence that global warming is real, that it's caused by human emissions of greenhouse gases, and that it will raise the temperature of the earth somewhere between 1.5 and 4 degrees Celsius during this century. Maybe I could throw in a photo of a melting glacier or two.

2 Nope, not going to do that—there are already lots of resources out there from which an interested layman can learn about the science of climate change.

3 I mean, if you can learn about climate from the National Center for Atmospheric Research, wouldn't you prefer to do that than read me?

4 But since we are all here, let me tell you why the greenhouse effect makes sense.

5 First of all, it's derived from basic physical principles. The earth is hot because it's warmed by the sun, and at night it cools down by radiating to space. Greenhouse gasses lower the ability of the earth to re-emit, and there's no reason to expect that the earth won't heat up. Simple, right? If the earth isn't going to warm up, you'll need a mechanism to explain why not. Unfortunately for us, no one has thought of any.

6 You see, I am the sort of guy who finds that a very persuasive argument. I have a Ph.D. in theoretical physics. I like it on those occasions when you can actually analyze a problem from first principles, make predictions, and see them come true.

7 Now, yes, the Earth is a very complicated system. But so are lots of other systems we know a lot about. Like, say, the bond market—lots of my friends who have the same sorts of Ph.D.s I do are off working on that (and they make much more money than I do, unfortunately). The bond market has millions of human actors—which are much more complicated to model than infrared radiation. But by building proper models you get to make lots of predictions that work.

8 Now look, I'm not a climate expert. I read about it a lot. But I have a day job, just like everyone else. Since I'm not *really* an expert, I can't say that I've read the code of the Goddard Institute for Space Studies climate model or that I have looked into the details of cloud formation. Like everyone else, I have to depend at least partially on the people who really are experts—they're the ones who have hashed all of this out in the peer-reviewed literature.

9 Here's a partial list of organizations that have made official statements supporting the conclusion that climate change is real and that it's largely caused by human-generated greenhouse gases:

- American Association for the Advancement of Science
- American Geophysical Union
- American Meteorological Society

- The Academies of Science of Brazil, Canada, China, France, German, India, Italy, Japan, Russia, UK and US (joint statement)
- The Academies of Science of Australia, Belgium, Brazil, Canada, Caribbean states, China, France, Germany, India, Indonesia, Ireland, Italy, Malaysia, New Zealand, Sweden, and UK (joint statement)

10   Not to mention a parade of reports written by impartial scientists in the National Academy of Sciences going all the way back to 1979—long before this was a political issue. And there's the well-known Intergovernmental Panel on Climate Change Report.

11   But I know scientists—I used to hang with scientists. They'll bicker over everything. Surely those scientific professional organizations must be driven by controversy, splitting into factions over this very important contemporary issue. But no, I haven't heard about any mass resignations. That's because, among scientists, this isn't actually controversial.

12   Again, I'm not an expert in climate science. But then, neither is the guy writing the article on the other side of this HealthFactsAndFears debate. And frankly, neither are most of the people writing about it—no, not Al Gore either. I hear lots of silly stuff said about climate. But because I have a technical background, I can at least go look up the primary sources and see what they actually say. And when I do, the stuff I hear from the climate "skeptics" in particular seem to crumble to dust under closer examination.

13   For instance, Richard Lindzen (a scientist who seems to be quoted in virtually every news report) says that there's been "almost no" temperature rise since 1986. Here: go look at the graph of global temperatures. Doesn't his statement just seem tendentious and silly?

14   Similarly, I'll often hear someone telling a general audience to go read the technical literature, knowing full well that they won't. Like the time John Stossel went on MSNBC's *Scarborough Country* and implored the audience to read for themselves the June 22, 2006 National Academy report, rather than relying on "the liberal media," because the academy "said they can't rule out that [global warming is caused by] all natural influences." I'm enough of a dweeb to do just that. So I know that, in fact, the report in question wasn't really about what might have caused global warming, and to the extent it briefly touched on the subject its conclusion was the opposite of what Stossel implied: there are "multiple lines of evidence supporting the conclusion that climate warming is occurring in response to human activities."

15   Here's the thing: many people think that believing in the reality of global warming is an ideological question. It isn't. I'm a dyed-in-the-wool capitalist. I've founded companies, sold them, and made money doing it. I am not a political idealist and don't care whether all the scientific conclusions described above are termed a "crisis" or not—I just want the scientists listened to and policy made in response to what is actually known.

16   Even the President of Shell Oil says it's "a waste of time to debate" because climate science is settled. It's time to move on. Let's debate something interesting—like what to do about it.

Questions

1. What is the author's thesis? If the author does not provide a thesis, develop one that fits the article.

2. According to Golden, what is the "greenhouse effect"?

3. One way in which Golden supports his position that global warming is real is to refer to scientific organizations that have stated that global warming is real. What organizations does he mention?

4. List the main arguments that Golden uses to support his position "that global warming is real, that it is caused by human emissions of greenhouse gasses, and that it will raise the temperature of the earth" (paragraph 1).

5. Using a dictionary when necessary, define the following words in their appropriate context:
   marshal (1); emissions (1); layman (2); emit (5); hashed out (8); peer-reviewed (8); impartial (10); riven (11); factions (11); skeptics (12); tendentious (13); dweeb (14); ideological (15); dyed-in-the-wool (15).

List the details in the photograph and consider them as possible symbols. How would you interpret the rainbow, the high-voltage power lines, and the sheep? Is this a peaceful coexistence or an ironic juxtaposition of symbols?

Rumors of Our Climatic Demise Have Been Greatly Exaggerated

BY CHUCK BLAKE

1 Amid much media flurry, the International Panel on Climate Change (IPCC) delivered its fourth summary for policy makers (SPM), the Academy of Motion Pictures Arts and Sciences gave an Oscar to a *An Inconvenient Truth*, and Gore testified before Congress that the very survival of our civilization is at stake. The media is replete with global climate change horror stories. We are told that the scientific debate is over, that killer storms, heat waves, droughts, and epidemic diseases lie in wait. We are told that the oceans will swallow our cities and tend to hear about climatological records broken when they are broken in the direction of concern. Gore, to mix animal metaphors, portrays polar bears as canaries in a coal mine, stalked by apocalyptic horsemen—signs of what is to come for humans.

2 Yet the World and American Meteorological Associations refuse to support specific claims on future weather impact, such as storm intensity. Their reluctance owes to the lack of evidence for storm-intensification trends over the twentieth century, though it saw a 1 C rise in temperature, over one third of the projected rise for the twenty-first century. At best, only the North Atlantic seems to show any such relationship, and it is weak in magnitude. Other regions show opposite effects. Unless one delves into technical literature, one never hears that the theory suggests only 3% more force in the tiny fraction of storms that reach their maximum intensity, or that initial studies' implications often resulted from gerrymandering the boundaries of storm categories. (See Curry, Webster, and Holland, *Mixing Politics and Science in Testing the Hypothesis That Greenhouse Warming Is Causing a* *Global Increase in Hurricane Intensity,* American Meteorological Society, August 2006.)

Beasts and beastly storms?

3 Meanwhile, polar bear demographers count many healthy polar bears thriving in warmer climes, their population doubling in the past twenty years. We are barraged by iconic pictures of bears "stranded" on ice in summertime—yet often within safe swimming distance of shore and able to hop off as they like.

4 Claims about "records" being set often abuse the underlying statistics. On the one hand it may be warmer than it has been in recent years, but on the other it was also warmer a long while ago with no supposed human influence and no ensuing catastrophe. Records of local phenomena can be very misleading. (See Redner and Petersen, "Role of Global Warming on the Statistics of Record-breaking Temperatures," *Physical Review*, v74, 061–114.)

5 Paul Reiter, a top French insect and infectious disease contributor, felt the IPCC message about warming-boosted mosquito populations and other disease threats was so skewed from the facts that he had to resign from the IPCC in protest—and threaten legal action to get his name removed. He tells us that mosquitoes are not necessarily more likely to thrive in warmer times: Siberia has had malaria-carrying mosquitoes forever; mosquito-dominated regions are closer to, not farther from, equatorial regions than a hundred years ago; and none of the new diseases Gore talks about can be attributed to warming.

6 Even using data from the current IPCC report, we see the projections of sea level rise by

2100 are about the same as the non-catastrophic rise from 1850 to present. The same report also can substantiate no net acceleration of net ice loss from a hundred years ago to the present.

What we don't know—and why science works

7 To a quantitative eye, the IPCC's summary for policy makers includes a chart indicating that our ignorance about the influence of man is almost as great as our knowledge. The role of carbon dioxide (CO_2), generally assumed to be the cause of our impending overheating, is overplayed because it is better understood. The role of aerosols such as dust is underplayed because it is poorly understood—though it is about as large as that of CO_2 and in the opposite direction. Historically, atmospheric CO_2 tends to rise centuries *after* temperatures rise, and there have been epochs with an order of magnitude more CO_2 *during ice ages*. In general, in the climate change debate as shaped by IPCC, qualitative accounts ("bad things will happen") are poorly supported by the underlying quantitative tables.

8 Science is better than myth-telling because science's future predictions acquire credibility in proportion to the fulfillment of past predictions. Quantitative science on complex, poorly understood systems requires special cautions. We surely require pharmacologists to use proper double-blind clinical trials rather than just trusting anecdotal evaluations or theoretical blood chemistry beliefs. We don't believe stock market forecasters who lose money. In climate science, a handful of weak, qualitative predictions are often presented as the fruits of a mature, reliable science, while a half dozen unresolved deep issues and poor quantitative confirmation are ignored.

9 See, for example, the main IPCC Working Group I chapters when they are released or the 2006 paper by Hansen, Sato, et al., for the National Academy of Sciences. Though alarmist in tone, Hansen admits that the agreement of his 1988 climate prediction models with later data was "accidental," that seventeen years is too brief a time to quantitatively validate the model, and that it is likely to prove wrong anyway. Climate scientists are fond of saying projecting climate is different from weather—climate is like predicting average rainfall, not rain tomorrow. How then should we take climatologists' self-acknowledged failure to accurately predict even regional climate or anything close to average precipitation? Or their failure to foresee the *cooling* of the oceans during 2003–2005, the largest oceanic cooling event in decades? (See Lyman, Willis, and Johnson, "Recent Cooling of the Upper Ocean," *Geophysical Research Letters*, September 2006.)

10 Hawking-class physicist Freeman Dyson is a long-time critic of presumed model-reliability, saying they use fudge factors for important processes.

Fear not

11 Even if models were reliable, there is no clear cause for fright. Consensus for *slightly elevated temperatures and vague causation* is misrepresented as consensus for *alarm*. More and more climate scientists are feeling the need to back away from the unrealistic histrionics of politicians and the media. As Mike Hulme, director of Britain's Tyndall Center for Climate Change Research said: "It seems that it is we, the professional climate scientists, who are now the (catastrophe) skeptics."

12 There is some hope, though, that the public is developing a thick skin with regard to exaggerated claims. After a little persuasion by Michael Crichton, Richard Lindzen, and Philip Stott at a recent debate hosted by Intelligence Squared in Manhattan, skepticism about an impending crisis won majority support from an audience that had initially self-identified as being mostly believers in a man-made climate crisis. That audience's change in opinion could be the real harbinger of things to come.

Questions

1. What is the author's thesis? If the author does not provide one, develop a thesis that fits the article.

2. Explain the last sentence in paragraph 1—the reference to polar bears and canaries in a coal mine.

3. What are Blake's main arguments supporting his position?

4. There are at least three instances in these two articles of each author (Golden or Blake) citing the same source, or using a different side of the same argument, to support his position. Find these three instances. What does this tell us about using sources to support one's position?

5. Using a dictionary when necessary, define the following words in their appropriate context.
   climatic (title); demise (title); flurry (1); replete (1); epidemic (1); metaphors (1); apocalyptic (1); delves (2); gerrymandering (2); demographers (3); barraged (3); iconic (3); ensuing (4); skewed (5); substantiate (6); net (6); quantitative (7); epochs (7); qualitative (7); pharmacologists (8); double-blind (8); anecdotal (8); validate (9); Hawking (10); fudge factor (10); consensus (11); histrionics (11); harbinger (12).

For Further Discussion and Writing

1. Which writer, Golden or Blake, does a more effective job of supporting his position persuasively? Why?

2. Find an article that does an effective job of explaining the climate change or global warming debate in terms that non-specialists can understand. Bring the article to class and be prepared to give a brief report to your classmates and instructor.

A New Student Generation Accepts the Global Warming Challenge

BY KYEANN SAYER

1 Though many Americans are beginning to accept that every time we switch on a light or start the ignition we contribute to global warming, it's hard to know exactly what to do about it. News of rising ocean levels and displaced Alaskan villagers make most of us want to tune out on the couch with a DVD and a tub of ice cream.

2 Imagine what the climate-change era is like for college students. In addition to juggling classes and post-graduation uncertainty, they're forced to define their futures alongside regular news of looming planetary disaster and the pressure to radically shift the ways we consume energy.

3 Luckily, students like Claire Roby and Carlos Rymer are applying pragmatic approaches to their deep concern, challenging traditional assumptions about environmental activists, and giving us all reasons to get off the couch.

"These are not liberal, hippie environmental issues"

4 "Students are seeing that climate change is the issue of our generation, and we have to enact broad change to protect our future," says Claire Roby, a sophomore at American University and president of the environmental organization Eco-Sense. "We can't wait to find out what the exact answer is," Roby says. "We have to act now or else it's going to be too late."

5 When she was a freshman in the spring of 2006, Roby led a referendum on clean energy (alternative energy that significantly reduces emission of air pollution and greenhouse gases). The measure—calling for the university to buy at least 50 percent wind power by 2012 through a $10 annual increase in student fees—passed by 71 percent, and attracted the highest voter turnout to date in a campus election.

6 Ten other core Eco-Sense members worked on a spirited campaign that included an open-air battle between a wind turbine and a smokestack, and get-out-the-vote pinwheels. The effort received recognition from the National Wildlife Federation. "We had the support of the former treasurer of the college Republicans," Roby says. "These are not liberal, hippie environmental issues. We're seeing broad support."

7 Cornell University sophomore Carlos Rymer notes a similar trend. "At Cornell, we've really noticed a big change," he says. "Last year when we started campaigning, most people were really apathetic. This year, after 'An Inconvenient Truth' (the Al Gore documentary about global warming) came out, we would say 'global warming' and students would stop and sign the petition. Students are getting aware of the problem and want to do something about it."

8 After campaigning for a year and gathering over 5,000 student, faculty and departmental signatures, student group KyotoNOW! convinced Cornell to commit its Ithaca, New York campus to carbon neutrality. This means that after taking action to significantly reduce CO_2 emissions through clean energy use and other means, efforts will be made to counter-balance what global warming impact remains. Thus, overall, the college will have "net zero impact" on climate. In February, President David J. Skorton joined more than 80 of his contemporaries in signing the American University and College Presidents Climate Commitment.

9   Rymer and four other KyotoNOW! students each worked about 10 hours per week for months—tabling, meeting with the administration and coordinating with 100 additional members.

10   Both Rymer and Roby worked with the Campus Climate Challenge, a project of the Energy Action coalition. The network of over 30 youth organizations in the United States and Canada provides support to local groups who want to encourage carbon neutrality on their campuses.

"This was not like preventing development to save an owl species"

11   What makes a student rise to this level of environmental commitment?

12   "Neither of my parents are outspoken environmentalists," Roby says. "As a family we would go fishing and camping. My grandfather was a farmer, and my family still has a small piece of land that my great-great grandfather staked in the land run that set up Oklahoma as a state. A strong connection to the land and the environment in our lives is where I developed my personal environmental ethic."

13   This sensibility led Roby to study environmental policy, but she never imagined taking up student organizing when she left Tulsa. "I had worked on a couple of electoral campaigns as a phone banker and was interested in environmental policy, but had no idea of the world of activism, probably because I'm from a conservative area of the country," Roby says. "I was called to activism because it allows me to effect policy change while I'm still in school."

14   Why choose global warming as an area of focus? "It was seeing general scientific reports about climate changes," says Roby. "This was not just a traditional environmental issue like preventing development to save an owl species. This is going to have vast effects on human life, affecting the daily lives of everyone in the world."

15   Rymer grew up a world away from Tulsa, dividing his childhood time between Union City, New Jersey and the Dominican Republic. While an American Chemical Society internship made him interested in environmental issues as a high school junior, it was the record temperatures of 2005 that truly activated the then-incoming Cornell freshman.

16   "New Jersey and lower New York state suffered a drought and 100-degree temperatures. I realized the seriousness—how a few degrees' increase had a big effect on water supply for one year. I read more and got the sense that it was an issue affecting the entire world and would worsen. It made me feel that young people needed to start working for right technologies, appropriate land use and everyday behaviors that would rise to combat the problem."

17   In addition to his work at Cornell, the 19-year-old Rymer has founded an organization in the Dominican Republic called Romana Sostenible (Sustainable Romana). The group advocates a wind energy proposal that would escalate to 20 percent by 2012 and 50 percent by 2020 and be financed by tourism taxes, similar to a carbon neutrality scheme that Costa Rica has recently taken on.

"My family wasn't aware of environmental problems"

18   We can't all be global warming superstars. How do regular people react when their children or friends suddenly become activists?

19   Rymer says, "My family wasn't aware of any environmental problems. They've all been open to listening and doing things that I recommend. My mother, grandmother and aunt now purchase clean energy from Clean Energy Choice programs."

20   Many local utilities now have plans that allow consumers to buy energy from sources like solar or wind.

21   Roby also receives encouragement from her family. While laughing at the irony, she says, "My mother is an accountant for an electric

company, and my father invests in real estate development." These seemingly un-environmental occupations do not cause a rift, however. "My family is definitely supportive and proud of my efforts," Roby says. "My friends are also supportive."

22   "I helped one friend move into his new apartment at the beginning of this school year," Roby continues. "When we went to Target for supplies, I didn't have to pester him. He picked up the compact fluorescent."

23   Compact fluorescent light bulbs use two-thirds less energy than incandescent bulbs, and generate about 70 percent less heat. According to the Environmental Protection Agency, each bulb can prevent the release of 450 pounds of power-plant emissions over its lifetime.

"We can all be part of the solution"

24   This year [2007], Roby and American University's Eco-Sense are lobbying the administration for a transportation overhaul. Suggestions include building a green fleet of biodiesel shuttles and fuel-efficient cars, and integrating commuting suggestions like providing more bike racks, incentives for hybrids and car pooling, and adding bike routes on campus maps.

25   Rymer is now turning his attention to the New Jersey Climate March. From April 13 to 16 [2007], citizens will walk from Rutgers to New Brunswick to Princeton to the College of New Jersey, before finishing in Trenton with a rally to support politicians sponsoring the New Jersey Global Warming Response Act. The bill would mandate reductions of greenhouse emissions in the state by 20 percent by the year 2020 and 80 percent by 2050.

26   "We want to help pass the act and show Congress in particular that we ought to be passing these kinds of laws," Rymer contends. "We want comprehensive legislation that is going to be affecting people in all sectors."

27   Romey reflects, "Each individual has a role. When we turn on that light, we're not separate individuals—we're all a part of this issue, and I think we can all be part of the solution."

Questions

1. What is the article's thesis? If the author does not provide one, develop a thesis that fits the article.

2. Who is Claire Roby, and what did she do in response to concerns about global warming?

3. Who is Carlos Rymer, and what did he do in response to concerns about global warming?

4. Explain "carbon neutrality" in such a way that non-specialists can understand the explanation.

5. What suggestions did Roby and her group propose to help the environment at American University?

6. Using a dictionary when necessary, define the following words in their appropriate context:
looming (2); pragmatic (3); referendum (5); emission (5); greenhouse gases (5); hippie (6); apathetic (7); CO_2 (8); net (8); tabling (9); outspoken (12); ethic (12); sensibility (13); escalate (17); utilities (20); irony (21); rift (21); lobbying (24); comprehensive (26).

1. Using the Internet or other sources, find out more about one of the following organizations mentioned in the preceding article: Eco-Sense; KyotoNOW; Campus Climate Challenge; Energy Action; Clean Energy Choice.

2. View "An Inconvenient Truth," the award-winning documentary about climate change by former Vice-President Al Gore. Write a brief summary of and reaction to the documentary. Be prepared to report to your classmates and instructor.

3. Learn about what initiatives and actions, if any, are being implemented on your campus in response to concerns about climate change. Be prepared to make a report to your classmates and instructor.

4. In paragraph 23 the author mentions using compact fluorescent light bulbs as a small, practical response to climate change. What other actions or steps can ordinary people take in their everyday lives to help protect the environment?

5. Look around your campus and propose some practical ways that your campus community can be more environmentally responsible.

A Fable for Tomorrow

BY RACHEL CARSON

1 There was once a town in the heart of America where all life seemed to live in harmony with its surroundings. The town lay in the midst of a checkerboard of prosperous farms, with fields of grain and hillsides of orchards where, in spring, white clouds of bloom drifted above the green fields. In autumn, oak and maple and birch set up a blaze of color that flamed and flickered across a backdrop of pines. Then foxes barked in the hills and deer silently crossed the fields, half hidden in the mists of the fall mornings.

2 Along the roads laurel, viburnum and alder, great ferns and wildflowers delighted the traveler's eye through much of the year. Even in winter the roadsides were places of beauty, where countless birds came to feed on the berries and on the seed heads of the dried weeds rising above the snow. The countryside was, in fact, famous for the abundance and variety of its bird life, and when the flood of migrants was pouring through in spring and fall people traveled from great distances to observe them. Others came to fish the streams, which flowed clear and cold out of the hills and contained shady pools where trout lay. So it had been from the days many years ago when the first settlers raised their houses, sank their wells, and built their barns.

3 Then a strange blight crept over the area and everything began to change. Some evil spell had

settled on the community: mysterious maladies swept the flocks of chickens; the cattle and sheep sickened and died. Everywhere was a shadow of death. The farmers spoke of much illness among their families. In the town the doctors had become more and more puzzled by new kinds of sickness appearing among their patients. There had been several sudden and unexplained deaths, not only among adults but even among children, who would be stricken suddenly while at play and die within a few hours.

4   There was a strange stillness. The birds, for example—where had they gone? Many people spoke of them, puzzled and disturbed. The feeding stations in the backyards were deserted. The few birds seen anywhere were moribund; they trembled violently and could not fly. It was a spring without voices. On the mornings that had once throbbed with the dawn chorus of robins, catbirds, doves, jays, wrens and scores of other bird voices there was now no sound; only silence lay over the fields and woods and marsh.

5   On the farms the hens brooded, but no chicks hatched. The farmers complained that they were unable to raise any pigs—the litters were small and the young survived only a few days. The apple trees were coming into bloom but no bees droned among the blossoms, so there was no pollination and there would be no fruit.

6   The roadsides, once so attractive, were now lined with browned and withered vegetation as though swept by fire. These, too, were silent, deserted by all living things. Even the streams were now lifeless. Anglers no longer visited them, for all the fish had died.

7   In the gutters under the eaves and between the shingles of the roofs, a white granular powder still showed a few patches: some weeks before it had fallen like snow upon the roofs and the lawns, the fields and the streams.

8   No witchcraft, no enemy action had silenced the rebirth of new life in this stricken world. The people had done it themselves.

9   This town does not actually exist, but it might easily have a thousand counterparts in America or elsewhere in the world. I know of no community that has experienced all the misfortunes I describe. Yet every one of these disasters has actually happened somewhere, and many real communities have already suffered a substantial number of them. A grim specter has crept upon us almost unnoticed, and this imagined tragedy may easily become a stark reality we all shall know.

Questions

1. How does the author describe the town's condition in times past? Does her choice of words help create a picture of the town?

2. What happens in the small town that causes concern?

3. How does the information shared in the last paragraph create an impressive conclusion and grab the attention of the reader?

4. Using a dictionary when necessary, define the following words in their appropriate context:
   fable (title); checkerboard (1); viburnum (2); blight (3); maladies (3); brooded (5); droned (5); withered (6); specter (9).

For Further Discussion and Writing

1. "A Fable for Tomorrow" is taken from Rachel Carson's influential book *Silent Spring*, first published in 1962. Go online and find a summary or review of this book. Be prepared to make a brief report in class.

2. What types of problems with pollution are you aware of today? What would the author say about global warming?

3. What can people do to help prevent pollution from ruining their towns? Write a newspaper article in which you express your concerns about the effects of pollution in your local area. Submit the article for publication in the school or local newspaper.

4. The government knew about the environmental effects of pesticides as early as 1962 when the book *Silent Spring* first appeared. What progress has been made combating the spread of pollution? What new government agencies have been created to make sure industry and individuals do not harm the environment? Has the creation of Earth Day helped raise awareness?

5. Do some people and organizations go too far in fighting pollution? Give a report on ecoterrorists. What are some of the tactics used by organizations like Greenpeace? Are these tactics justified?

6. Use of the pesticide DDT is now outlawed in most countries, but from 1945 until the mid-1960s it was considered by many farmers and scientists to be a safe chemical. It was very effective in killing unwanted insects but had serious side effects on ecological systems. For example, dead insects containing DDT were eaten by birds. The DDT stayed in the birds' bodies and led to birds laying eggs with shells that were too thin to allow for survival. Can you think of other examples of chemicals that were once considered safe but are now known to be harmful to the environment? What are some ways that problems similar to those associated with DDT can be avoided in the future?

Glossary

[Note: These terms are defined in the context of a writing course as they apply to the field of rhetoric.]

ad hominem Latin for "against the man" (or against the person). The ad hominem fallacy consists of criticizing a person directly rather than arguing against the issues that he or she raises.

analogy Comparison between two objects or concepts, usually using a more familiar object or concept to explain a less familiar object or concept.

analysis The act of taking something complex and breaking it down into its component parts in order to understand the whole object better. Similar to division/partition.

appeal to false authority A fallacy in which one uses a person who is an authority in one field to attempt to influence people in a field unrelated to the authority's area of expertise.

argument Taking a stand for or against a proposition and supporting one's position with reasons.

audience The readers of an essay. A key, early consideration in the writing process is the audience for whom the essay is written.

bandwagon This fallacy, often used by advertisers, urges people to make a hasty decision without much forethought, or "jump on the bandwagon," before they get left behind.

begging the question This fallacy is sometimes called "circular reasoning." It assumes that a proposition is true even if it has not been proven yet. The conclusion, or a variation of it, is used as a premise.

brainstorming One method for generating ideas early in the writing process. The writer gets together with one or more helpers, and they begin talking freely about the essay's subject. Notes are kept and used as possible material/ideas for the essay.

cause Something that occurs so as to produce a specific result; the reason or motive for some action. Essays often discuss the causes of a particular event.

claim In an argument, a claim is an assertion that must be supported or proven with reasons.

classification The act of taking many items or people and sorting them into groups based on some similarity or principle of classification.

clustering/mapping One method for generating ideas early in the writing process. Especially useful for visual learners. Key ideas are written inside ovals or rectangles and connected by lines to sub-ideas, which are also inside ovals or rectangles. (See diagram on page 28.) Also called bubble mapping or webbing.

coherence Logical connection in which the topic of one sentence flows into the next. Paragraphs should have coherence.

comma splice Two complete sentences that are joined together by just a comma. Two complete sentences should be joined by a period, a semicolon, or a comma followed by a coordinating conjunction.

comparison/contrast Discussing similarities (comparison) and differences (contrast). Comparison/contrast is a common method of organizing an essay.

composing process Another term for writing process. *See* writing process.

cooperative learning The use of highly structured (by the instructor), student-led learning teams in the classroom. Cooperative learning works best in small teams (two or three students per team).

coordinating conjunction Word used to join other words, phrases, or sentences. A coordinating conjunction joins grammatical elements of equal rank. The seven coordinating conjunctions form the acronym "FANBOYS": for, and, nor, but, or, yet, so.

definition The act of making definite, distinct, or clear; a statement of the meaning or significance of a word or concept. A definition can range from a few words to a few sentences to an entire essay.

description An account or representation that uses words to appeal to one or more of the reader's five senses: sight, hearing, smell, taste, touch. One common method of developing paragraphs and essays.

development Using specific details to expand or elaborate ideas. Also called *elaboration*.

division/partition Taking one object and dividing or partitioning it into its component parts in order to understand the whole object better. This is a common method of organizing essays.

edited American English *See* Standard Written English.

editing Activity done to a draft of an essay near the end of writing process, involving especially the improvement of sentence quality and word choice.

effect Result; consequence. Essays often discuss the effects of a particular event.

either-or fallacy A fallacy in which one oversimplifies a situation to make it seem as though it involves only two potential courses of action.

emotional appeal In an argument essay, this is the appeal to the reader's feelings or emotions.

essay A multi-paragraph piece of written discourse focusing on a particular, limited subject. In an essay a writer often gives his or her own perspective on a subject. An essay may be based on the writer's experience, personal opinion, research, or a combination of these sources.

ethical appeal In an argument essay, this is the writer's attempt to convince readers that the writer is honest and trustworthy.

evidence In an argument essay, evidence is what the writer uses to support his or her position or to convince readers to agree with the writer's position.

example A particular instance used to show the character of the whole, or to illustrate whatever is being discussed. Using examples is a common method for developing paragraphs and essays.

exemplification Explaining by giving examples, details, and illustrations. The kind of writing done in many college classes is exemplification.

exposition The act of explaining or setting forth details. Related to this word is *expository*, which means "serving to explain." The kind of writing that is done in many college writing classes is expository writing.

fallacy Some kind of error in reasoning or logic that makes one's arguments invalid and open to rebuttal.

false cause A fallacy in which one claims that if event A happened before event B, then event A caused event B. This fallacy sometimes goes by the Latin name *post hoc ergo propter hoc*, "after this, therefore because of this."

faulty or false analogy A fallacy in which one compares two things, situations, or experiences that have some minor similarities but that are essentially different.

focused freewriting One method for generating ideas early in the writing process. The student focuses on the subject of the essay and writes freely and quickly any ideas that come to mind on that subject.

global revision Revision of large aspects of a draft, such as order of paragraphs, paragraph development, inclusion of all relevant topics, and cutting topics that do not clearly support the essay's thesis.

hasty generalization A fallacy that makes the mistake of generalizing on the basis of just a few experiences or inadequate evidence.

illustration The act of clarifying or explaining.

insight The ability to perceive the true nature of a situation or to understand the hidden nature of something. There are systematic ways to develop one's ability to gain insights into situations.

journal In writing classes, a journal is usually an informal piece of writing in which a student develops one or more ideas/topics. Journals often are used as prewriting for essays.

logical/rational appeal In an argument essay, this is the appeal to the reader's sense of reason.

narration Telling a story or relating a series of events. Narration is one common method of developing an essay.

non sequitur Latin for "it does not follow." A non sequitur fallacy is committed when one attempts to relate two ideas that have no logical connection.

oversimplification A fallacy in which one looks at a complex problem and pronounces a quick fix.

paragraph Usually a group of sentences that develop one topic. The paragraph is the building block of an essay or article. The three main types of paragraphs are the introductory or opening paragraph, the body paragraph, and the concluding or closing paragraph.

peer response Activity during the revision step of the writing process in which one or more classmates respond to a classmate's draft in order to help the classmate improve the draft. Peer response is usually guided by some sort of checklist that students use to respond to a classmate's draft.

persuasion The act of convincing or inducing someone to do something or not do something, or to change his or her thoughts or position on a particular subject.

plan of development A statement often appearing near the beginning of an essay listing the major topics to be discussed in the essay. The plan of development often follows the thesis statement and is sometimes incorporated into the thesis statement.

prewriting An early step in the writing process. Prewriting involves preparing or generating ideas and all the thought processes that go along with beginning a writing project.

process A series of steps, usually taken in a particular order. A process essay tells how to do or make something, or how something is done or made, or how something happens.

prompt (noun) The essay or journal assignment that guides the writer's response. For example, your instructor might say, "Be sure to read the prompt carefully so that your written response is appropriate."

proofreading Activity done to a draft of an essay at the end of the writing process, involving the improvement of elements such as grammar, usage, punctuation, spelling, and format.

purpose The reason why one writes an essay; aim or goal. One main purpose for writing is to communicate ideas clearly to an audience.

red herring A red herring is a smoked fish that can get very smelly. Dragging a red herring across the track that dogs are following will cause the dogs to follow the strong scent of the red herring and not the true track. The red herring fallacy involves introducing an unrelated or false issue into an argument or debate in order to lead attention away from the issue being argued.

reporter's questions/reporter's formula Questions that reporters or journalists often ask when gathering material to write a news article. These questions, which begin with the words who, what, when, where, why, how, work especially well when writing about an event. Finding answers to these questions can help writers generate material for an essay or a paragraph.

revision/revising Looking again at a draft of an essay in order to improve it; a key step in the writing process.

rhetoric The art of using language effectively. In an English or writing course, the focus is on writing effectively. In a speech course, the focus is on speaking effectively.

Rogerian argument Non-threatening, non-confrontational approach to writing argument essays that emphasizes establishing common ground between writer and reader. Developed by clinical psychologist Carl Rogers.

run-on/fused sentence Two complete sentences that have no punctuation between them.

sentence fragment A group of words that is punctuated like a sentence but for some grammatical reason does not qualify as a sentence.

Standard Written English Widely accepted form of written English, used especially in academic, business, and professional settings.

stereotyping A fallacy in which one draws a conclusion about an entire group of people based on just a few experiences, or based on what others may have said. This is similar to the hasty generalization fallacy

stylistic appeal In an argument essay, this is the appeal to the reader's desire to read something that is clearly organized and effectively written.

thesis statement The main idea or key point of an essay or article. The thesis statement is often found near the beginning of an essay or article.

topic sentence The sentence that gives the main idea or key point of a body paragraph. The topic sentence often appears at the beginning or near the beginning of a body paragraph.

transitions Words, phrases, or sentences that help join or link the various parts of an essay. Transitions are found within paragraphs and often between paragraphs.

unity The quality of being related or connected. Body paragraphs usually focus on one topic, with each sentence developing that topic.

writing process Steps that writers follow to complete a writing project. The steps include preparing or generating ideas, organizing or arranging the ideas into a draft, revising the draft, and proofreading and editing the draft.

Credits

Index

AAVE (African-American Vernacular English), 123
Academic essay format, 37
Acronyms
    ART, for examples, 91, 105
    DUCTT, for body paragraph traits, 31–32, 52, 105, 177
    FANBOYS, for coordinating conjunctions, 65
    usefulness of, 31
Active reading
    effectiveness of, 25
    strategies for, 26
    studying for essay exams, 171–172
Ad hominem fallacy, 196–197
Advertisements. *See also* Consumerism (readings)
    as brief arguments, 181
    evaluation argument for, 213–217
    "Secret vs. Soft & Dri" (student essay), 216–218
African-American Vernacular English (AAVE), 123
"Alienated Asian, An" (Verderber), 60–61
Al-Marayati, Laila, 252
American Baby magazine, 80
American English (Wolfram and Schilling-Estes), 127
"America's Religious Mosaic" (Moyers), 108, 138–140
Analogy
    body paragraph strategy, 109–110
    faulty or false, 196
    focused freewriting using, 113
Analysis
    exam questions asking for, 173
    skills developed by writing, 19
    strategy for body paragraphs, 108
And (coordinating conjunction), 65
Animal shelter argument
    argument essay example, 191–193
    emotional appeal, 187
    ethical appeal, 188
    organization for an essay, 189–190
    rational or logical appeal, 187
    Rogerian argument example, 207–208
    stylistic appeal, 188

Appeal to false authority fallacy, 197
Appropriateness, in standardized exam evaluation, 178
Argument and persuasion
    in academic vs. non-academic settings, 181
    in advertisements, 181, 213–217
    background information paragraph, 189–190
    "Bad Idea Whose Time Has Passed, A" (reading), 183–184
    basic structure of essay, 191
    Bloom's hierarchy or taxonomy, 217–218
    "Class Segregation" (student essay), 194–195
    considering opposing viewpoints, 188–189
    emotional appeal, 187
    eroded notions of, 212
    in essay exams, 173
    ethical appeal, 187–188
    evaluation argument, 208–217
    example essay, 191–193
    exam questions asking for, 173
    fallacies, 195–198
    focus of argument essays, 185
    "Lost Maples State Natural Area" (student essay), 210–211
    "Love Is a Fallacy" (reading), 199–205
    "Obligations of September, 11, 2001, The" (reading), 182–183
    organizing an argument essay, 189–191
    practical advantages of learning, 181–182, 217
    rational or logical appeal, 187
    Rogerian argument, 206–208, 212
    "Secret vs. Soft & Dri" (student essay), 216–218
    strategies common to, 186–188
    stylistic appeal, 188
    T-chart for rebuttal, 188–189
    topics suitable for, 185
Aristotle, 259
ART acronym for examples, 91, 105
Arthur, Orry, 148

"As Consumerism Spreads, Earth Suffers, Study Says" (Mayell), 286–288
Audience or readers
    choosing ideas suitable for, 87
    considering before writing, 20, 87
    grabbing interest in opening paragraph, 32, 33
    importance of determining, 85
    paragraphs as aid to, 30
    questions for determining, 86
Authority, appeal to false, 197
Awkward sentence construction, 66

Bach, Richard, 259
"Bad Idea Whose Time Has Passed, A" (Chapman), 183–184
Baker, Sheridan, 34
Bandwagon fallacy, 197
Barber, Benjamin, 1
Baron, Dennis, 122, 123
Barry, Dave, 181
Beam, Cris, 80
Begging the question fallacy, 197
Bibliography
    working, 229–230
    Works Cited page, 242
Biotechnology majors (reading), 260
Blake, Chuck, 294
Block, writer's, 32
Block method (comparison/contrast), 107
Blog, for journal writing, 24
Bloom, Benjamin, 217–218
Bodily-kinesthetic intelligence (reading), 11–12
Body paragraphs, 30–32, 105–110
    analogy strategy for, 109–110
    for argument essays, 189–191
    ART acronym for examples, 91, 105
    background information for argument, 189–190
    cause/effect strategy for, 108
    classification strategy for, 109, 110
    comparison/contrast strategy for, 107–108

Body paragraphs (*continued*)
definition strategy for, 109
description in, 87, 106
developing, 31, 90–91, 105–110
division or partition strategy for, 108
DUCTT acronym for traits, 31–32, 52, 105, 177
in essay structure, 21
examples in, 52, 91, 105, 106
explanation in, 106
facts in, 109
narration strategy for, 105
process organization for, 106–107
questions answered by, 85
statistics in, 109
topic sentence of, 32
underlying structure of, 52–53
writing before introduction and conclusion, 21, 30, 32
Books as sources, 227
Brainstorming, 27–28
Brill, Pamela, 44
Burchfield, Mitchel, 10
But (coordinating conjunction), 65

Canales, David, 88
Careers. *See* Work
Carson, Rachel, 300
Castro, Janice, 118
Cause/effect
exam questions asking for, 173
focused freewriting using, 113
strategy for body paragraphs, 108
Chaika, Elaine, 127
"Changing American Family, The" (Beam), 80–83
Chapman, Bruce, 183
Checklists
peer response for essay drafts, 56
timeline for research papers, 221
Chicago Tribune, 147
Christian, Kenneth W., 44
Chronological narrative, 8
Circular reasoning, 197
Clarity
developing fluency first, 66, 67
dividing or shortening long sentences, 67–68
editing for, 65–68
methods of achieving, 66
in speech vs. writing, 63, 65–66
Classification strategy
for body paragraphs, 109, 110
focused freewriting using, 113

Classmates. *See also* Peer response
cooperative learning with, 54–55
discussing lecture notes with, 171
feedback for revision from, 54
studying sentence fragments by, 64
"Class Segregation" (Ryan), 194–195
Climate change (readings)
"Debate, What Debate?" 291–292
"New Student Generation Accepts the Global Warming Challenge, A," 297–299
"Rumors of Our Climatic Demise Have Been Greatly Exaggerated," 294–295
Closing paragraph, 34–35
for argument essays, 191
in essay exam answers, 174
in essay structure, 21
inverted funnel structure of, 34
not introducing new topics, 34
rewording thesis statement in, 34, 35, 191
in Rogerian argument, 206
summarizing main topics, 34
writing after drafting body, 21, 30, 32
Clustering for generating ideas, 28
Coherence
defined, 31
in DUCTT acronym, 32, 52, 105, 177
College Hill Independent, 132
Colon, Vanessa, 246
Colton, Charles, 169
Combining sentences for variety, 66–67
.com ending of URL, 225
Comfort zone, venturing beyond yours, 161
Comma splices, 64–65
Communication
as key to healthy relationships, 95
writing as important skill for, 19
Comparison/contrast
exam questions asking for, 173
focused freewriting using, 113
strategy for body paragraphs, 107–108
Composing process, 20. *See also* Writing process
Computer game design majors (reading), 261
Concluding paragraph. *See* Closing paragraph
Conjunctions, coordinating, 65
Consumerism (readings)
"As Consumerism Spreads, Earth Suffers, Study Says," 286–288

"How Do Our Kids Get So Caught Up In Consumerism?" 279–282
"In Defense of Consumerism," 283–285
"Living 'Poor' and Loving It," 276–277
Cook, Elizabeth, 106, 210
Cooking stage of writing, 26
Cooperative learning. *See also* Classmates; Peer response
peer response checklist, 56
practicing, 54–55
tips for peer response, 57
Coordinating conjunctions, 65
Criteria, establishing for evaluation, 209
Critical thinking, skills developed by writing, 19
Cultural identities
"Alienated Asian, An" (student essay), 60–61
culture, defined, 245
"Great Divide, The" (reading), 254–257
"It Could Happen Here" (reading), 252–253
"Learning to Let Go: Tradition Binds College Hopefuls to Families" (reading), 246–248
"Lessons from Executive Order 9066" (reading), 250–251
"Some Aspects of Indian Culture" (student essay), 163–164
"Spanglish Spoken Here" (reading), 118–119
"We Are All Related" (reading), 157–159
Cynic's Calendar, The (Mumford), 95

Deadlines, essay exams as preparation for, 169
"Death" (*South Park* episode, by Parker and Stone), 275
"Debate, What Debate?" (Golden), 291–292
Decision-making (reading), 272–273
Definition
exam questions asking for, 173
focused freewriting using, 113
strategy for body paragraphs, 109
Description
defined, 87
for developing body paragraphs, 87, 106
focused freewriting using, 113

Development
   in body paragraphs, 31, 90–91,
      105–110
   in DUCTT acronym, 31, 52, 105, 177
   of fluency, 23–24, 66, 67
   in standardized exam evaluation,
      178
Diary keeping vs. journal writing, 24
Dimas, Brittney A., 133
Discuss, as key term in exams, 173
Dividing long sentences, 67–68
Division or partition strategy, 108
Domestic Security Enhancement Act
      of 2003 (reading), 252–253
Douglas, Norman, 275
Drafting, 21–22. *See also* Organization
Drum playing (student essay), 38–39
DUCTT acronym for body paragraph
      traits, 31–32, 52, 105, 177

Ebonics (reading), 123–124
E-business/e-marketing majors (read-
      ing), 260–261
Edison, Thomas, 112
"Edited American English," 114
Editing and proofreading
   for clarity and eliminating awk-
      wardness, 65–68
   combining sentences for variety,
      66–67
   for comma splices, 64–65
   dividing or shortening long
      sentences, 67–68
   essay exam answers, 174
   in-class essays, 178
   from last to first sentence, 69
   leaving time before, 69
   leaving to the end, 62, 67
   reading for, 69
   for run-on or fused sentences, 65
   for sentence fragments, 63–64, 65
   for sentence quality, 43, 63–65
   strategies for, 69
   timeline for research papers, 221
   writing process step, 22
Educational system, 136
Effort, importance of, 112–113
Either-or fallacy, 196
E-mail interviews, 130, 219
Emotional appeal, 187
Environment (readings)
   "Debate, What Debate?" 291–292
   "Fable for Tomorrow, A," 300–301
   "New Student Generation Accepts
      the Global Warming Chal-
      lenge, A," 297–299

"Rumors of Our Climatic Demise
      Have Been Greatly Exagger-
      ated," 294–295
society and the environment
      majors, 261
Essay exams
   asking what will be on the test, 172
   budgeting time for, 172–173
   editing and proofreading your
      answer, 174
   example answers, 175–176
   finding main points, 171, 172
   in-class essays, 176–178
   key terms in questions, 173
   lecture notes for, 170–171
   making notes and planning your
      essay, 173
   outside sources for, studying, 172
   preparing for, 170–172
   reading questions carefully, 173
   real-world deadlines and, 169
   standardized, 178–179
   textbooks for, studying, 171–172
   usefulness of, 169, 179–180
   using all the time allotted, 174
   writing the exam, 172–174
   writing under time pressure, 169
Ethical appeal, 187–188
Ethos, 187
Evaluate, as key term in exams, 173
Evaluation argument, 208–217
   in Bloom's hierarchy or taxonomy,
      217–218
   establishing criteria, 209
   "Lost Maples State Natural Area"
      (student essay), 210–211
   in reviews of films and restaurants,
      209–210
   "Secret vs. Soft & Dri" (student
      essay), 216–218
   usefulness of, 208–209
   for visual media, 213–217
Examples
   accurate details in, 91
   articles using as major method, 106
   choosing to suit audience, 87, 91
   for developing body paragraphs, 106
   effective, ART acronym for, 91, 105
   focused freewriting using, 113
   relating to thesis, 91
   specific, for effectiveness, 52
Exams. *See* Essay exams
Executive Order 9066 (reading),
      250–251
Explanation
   for developing body paragraphs,
      106

exam questions asking for, 173
focused freewriting using, 113

"Fable for Tomorrow, A" (Carson),
      300–301
"Fabric of a Nation, The" (Reyes),
      96–99, 110
Facts
   for developing body paragraphs,
      109
   focused freewriting using, 113
Fallacies in arguments
   ad hominem, 196–197
   appeal to false authority, 197
   bandwagon, 197
   begging the question, 197
   defined, 195
   either-or, 196
   false cause, 196
   faulty or false analogy, 196
   hasty generalization, 195
   "Love Is a Fallacy" (reading),
      199–205
   non sequitur, 197–198
   oversimplification, 196
   red herring, 197
   stereotyping, 195–196
False cause fallacy, 196
Family
   "Changing American Family, The"
      (reading), 80–83
   developing body paragraphs for
      essay, 90–91
   "Family Values" (student essay),
      88–90
   "Learning to Let Go: Tradition
      Binds College Hopefuls to
      Families" (reading), 246–248
   "My Family Traditions" (student
      essay), 92–93
   as oldest social institution, 73
   Peoplemaking excerpt (reading),
      75–77
   preparing and generating step for
      essay, 85–87
"Family Values" (Canales), 88–90
Fanaticism
   defining, 156
   "When Passion Is Dangerous"
      (reading), 153–154
FANBOYS acronym for coordinating
      conjunctions, 65
"Fashion" (Rosenkrantz), 98–99
"Fashion of the Times" (Varela),
      110–112
Faulty or false analogy, 196

Feedback
   peer response, 54, 56
   sources for revision, 53–57
   from your classmates, 54
   from your instructor, 53
   from yourself, 55–57
Film reviews, 209–210
"Find Work That You Love" (Moses), 264–268
Five P's rule for research, 221
Five Ws and one H, 106
Fletcher, Winston, 272
Flexibility in learning styles, 14
Fluency
   defined, 23
   developing before clarity, 66, 67
   in focused freewriting, 27
   journal writing for developing, 23–24
Focus, in standardized exam evaluation, 178
Focused freewriting, 26–27, 113
Fong-Torres, Ben, 47
Fonts for academic essays, 37
"Food" (Sandoval), 97–98
For (coordinating conjunction), 65
Forensic accounting majors (reading), 261
Formal vs. informal writing, 23, 114
Format for academic essays, 37
Fragments, sentence, 63–64, 65
Freedman, Donna, 276
Freewriting, focused, 26–27, 113
Fright writes. See Essay exams
Fuller, Buckminster, 156
Fuller, Thomas, 219
Funnel structure for opening and closing paragraphs, 34
Fused or run-on sentences, 65

Gandhi, Mahatma, 245
Gardner, Howard, 10, 11, 12–13, 108
Gender bias (reading), 124
Generalization, hasty, 195
Generating ideas. See Preparing and generating
"Getting Yourself Back on Track" (Hales), 44–46, 107
Give causes/effects, as key term in exams, 173
Global affairs. See World events
Globalization
   of daily life, 96
   reality of, 151
Global revision, 42, 43

Global warming (readings)
   "Debate, What Debate?" 291–292
   "New Student Generation Accepts the Global Warming Challenge, A," 297–299
   "Rumors of Our Climatic Demise Have Been Greatly Exaggerated," 294–295
Godden, Rumer, 41
Golden, Mitchell E., 291
Google, 224
Google Scholar, 224
Gottlieb, Linda, 1
.gov ending of URL, 225
"Great Divide, The" (Quintanilla), 254–257

Hales, Dianne, 44, 106
Hasty generalization fallacy, 195
HCI (Human computer interaction) majors (reading), 261
Herford, Oliver, 95
"He Wails for the World" (Fong-Torres), 47–49
Highlighter, using when reading, 26
History courses, 147
Hobbies (student essay), 38–39
Homeland security majors (reading), 260
House of Four Rooms (Godden), 41
"How Do Our Kids Get So Caught Up In Consumerism?" (Swimme)
   acceptable long quotation, 235
   acceptable paraphrase, 233–234
   acceptable short quotation, 235
   acceptable summary, 232–233
   original-source text excerpt, 232
   reading, 279–282
   unacceptable paraphrase, 233
   unacceptable quotation, 235
   unacceptable summary, 232
"How to" method of organization, 106–107
Human computer interaction (HCI) majors (reading), 261
Humphrey, Hubert H., 151
Huxley, Thomas, 219
Hyatt, Carole, 1

Ideas, generating. See Preparing and generating
Illiteracy, 116–117, 126–127
In-class essays, 176–178
Incubating stage of writing, 26

"In Defense of Consumerism" (Rockwell), 283–285
Indian culture (student essay), 163–164
Informal vs. formal writing, 23, 114
Information literacy, 220
Instructor, feedback from, 53
Intelligence Reframed: Multiple Intelligences for the Twenty-First Century (Gardner), 12–13
Intelligences, multiple, 10–13, 16
Internet sources. See Online sources for research
Interpersonal intelligence (reading), 12
Interviews
   conducting, 130–131, 227–228
   e-mail, 130, 219
   sources consisting of, 228–229
   tips for, 131, 228
Intrapersonal intelligence (reading), 12
Introductory paragraph. See Opening paragraph
"It Could Happen Here" (Al-Marayati), 252–253
"It's Time to Make Up Your Mind" (Fletcher), 272–273

Jackson, Jesse, 136, 137
Japanese-American incarceration during WWII (reading), 250–251
Jobs. See Work
John Marshall Fundamental Secondary School, 101–103
Journals, scholarly, 226–227
Journal writing
   blog for, 24
   diary keeping vs., 24
   fluency developed by, 23–24
   length of entries, 24
   suggestions for, 24–25
   writer's notebook, 135

Kulla, Bridget, 260

Language. See also Editing and proofreading; Speaking
   formal vs. informal, 23, 114
   interviews and conversations, 130–131
   "Language and Society" (reading), 123–127
   power of, 114–115

"Reading and Writing" (student essay), 133–134

"Shameful Secret of Illiteracy in America, The" (reading), 116–117

"Spanglish Spoken Here" (reading), 118–119

writing the way you speak, 23

"Language and Society" (Baron), 123–127

Language: The Social Mirror (Chaika), 127

Latino culture
"Great Divide, The" (reading), 254–257
"Learning to Let Go: Tradition Binds College Hopefuls to Families" (reading), 246–248
"Spanglish Spoken Here" (reading), 118–119

Learning
cooperative, 54–55
in groups vs. alone, 3–4, 9
learners vs. nonlearners, 1
as lifelong activity, 1, 20
"Not a Perfect Person" (student essay), 14–15
"splitters" vs. "lumpers," 4, 9
styles of, 2–9, 14, 16
writing as a means of, 16, 19
writing skills, capability of, 39

Learning styles
defined, 2
developed by writing, 16
flexibility and building on strengths in, 14
questionnaire, 6–8
reading, 2–4

"Learning Styles" (Sabrio), 2–4

"Learning to Let Go: Tradition Binds College Hopefuls to Families" (Colon), 246–248

Lecture notes, 170–171

"Lessons from Executive Order 9066" (Saigo), 250–251

Linguistic intelligence (reading), 10

List, as key term in exams, 173

Litan, Robert E., 182

Literacy
information literacy, 220
in "Language and Society" (reading), 126–127
"Reading and Writing" (student essay), 133–134
"Shameful Secret of Illiteracy in America, The" (reading), 116–117

"Living 'Poor' and Loving It" (Freedman), 276–277

Logical fallacies. *See* Fallacies in arguments

Logical-mathematical intelligence (reading), 10–11

Logical or rational appeal
animal shelter argument example, 187
fallacies, 195–198
overview, 187

Logos, 187

Long sentences, dividing or shortening, 67–68

Los Angeles Times, 147

"Lost Maples State Natural Area" (Cook), 106, 210–211

"Love Is a Fallacy" (Schulman), 199–205

"Lumpers" vs. "splitters," 4, 9

MacNeil, Robert, 110, 114, 115, 131

Magazines, 147, 225, 226–227

Mapping for generating ideas, 28

Margins for academic essays, 37

Maycll, Hillary, 286

Mechanical conventions in standardized exam evaluation, 178

Mexican immigrants (reading), 254–257

Mizner, Addison, 95

Mosaic
"America's Religious Mosaic" (reading), 138–140
defined, 138

Moses, Barbara, 264

Moss, Robert, 157

Moyers, Bill, 108, 137, 138

Mullen, Marissa, 92, 106

Multiple intelligences, 10–13, 16

"Multiple Intelligences" (Sabrio and Burchfield), 10–13, 108, 109

Multiple Intelligences: The Theory in Practice (Gardner), 10

Mumford, Ethel Watts, 95

Musical intelligence (reading), 11

"My Family Traditions" (Mullen), 92–93, 106

"My Hobby" (Varela), 38–39

Nanotechnology majors (reading), 261–262

Narration strategy
for body paragraphs, 105
for developing ideas, 9

dividing events into paragraphs, 9, 105
focused freewriting using, 113

Narrowing research topics, 222

Nation, the
"America's Religious Mosaic" (reading), 138–140
educating oneself about issues, 147
educational system and strength of, 136
"Tragedy of September 11, 2001" (student essay), 148–149
voicing insights about issues, 150
"We Choose Honor" (reading), 143–145

Native American culture (reading), 157–159

Naturalistic intelligence (reading), 12–13

Newman, Beatrice, 57

New media majors (reading), 260

Newspapers and newsmagazines, 147, 225, 227

"New Student Generation Accepts the Global Warming Challenge, A" (Sayer), 297–299

Newsweek, 147

New York Times, The, 147

Niebuhr, Reinhold, 73

Nobel, Alfred Bernard, 153

Nobel Peace Prize, 153

Nonlearners vs. learners, 1

Non sequitur fallacy, 197–198

Nor (coordinating conjunction), 65

"Not a Perfect Person" (Saavedra), 14–15

Notebook, writer's, 135

Note taking
from lectures, 170–171
paraphrasing, 233–234
quotations, 234–236
from sources, 230–236
summarizing main ideas, 231–233

"Obligations of September, 11, 2001, The" (Litan), 182–183

Online sources for research
evaluating credibility of, 225
evaluating Websites, 225–226
finding Websites, 224, 225
library databases, 224, 225
national information, 147
periodicals and broadcasts, 225
quantity vs. quality, 224
search engines, 224

"On This Day in 1986" (Wolter), 237–240
Opening paragraph, 32–34
  for argument essays, 189
  in essay exam answers, 174
  in essay structure, 21
  funnel structure of, 34
  grabbing the reader's interest, 32, 33
  perfect, avoiding waiting for, 25
  in Rogerian argument, 206
  thesis statement in, 29, 32–33
  writing after drafting body, 21, 30, 32
Or (coordinating conjunction), 65
Organic agriculture majors (reading), 260
Organization. *See also* Body paragraphs; Thesis statement
  for argument essays, 189–191
  closing paragraph, 21, 30, 32, 34–35, 174, 191, 206
  funnel structure for paragraphs, 34
  opening paragraph, 21, 25, 29, 30, 32–34, 174, 189, 206
  paragraphs as basic tools for, 29–30
  plan after thesis statement, 29
  of Rogerian argument, 206
  in standardized exam evaluation, 178
  structure of an essay, 21
  stylistic appeal of argument and, 188
  T-chart for rebuttal, 188–189
  three-part structure, 21
  timeline for research papers, 221
  topic sentence, 32
  underlying structure of body paragraphs, 52–53
  writing process step, 21–22
.org ending of URL, 225
Outside sources for essay exams, 172
Oversimplification fallacy, 196

Page numbering for academic essays, 37
PARADE magazine, 44, 47, 101, 142
Paragraphs
  background information for argument, 189–190
  body, 21, 30–32, 52–53
  closing, 21, 34–35
  defined, 29
  dividing narratives into, 9, 105
  opening, 21, 32–34
  overview, 28–29
  reader helped by, 30
  structure of an essay, 21

topic sentence of, 32
writer helped by, 30
Paraphrasing research findings
  acceptable example, 233–234
  avoiding plagiarism, 230, 233
  overview, 233
  quotations vs., 234
  unacceptable example, 233
Parker, Trey, 275
Partition or division strategy, 108
Part-to-part method (comparison/contrast), 107–108
Pathos, 187
Peer response. *See also* Classmates
  cooperative learning, 54–55
  defined, 54
  for feedback for revision, 54
  guide for essay drafts, 56
  self-evaluation for, 60
  tips for, 57
Pen or pencil, using when reading, 26
Peoplemaking excerpt (Satir), 75–77, 108
Periodicals
  magazines, 147, 225, 226–227
  newspapers, 147, 225, 227
  online, 225
  scholarly journals, 226–227
  types of, 226
Permission to Succeed (St. John), 45
Persistence, importance of, 112–113
Persuasion. *See* Argument and persuasion
Plagiarism, avoiding
  consequences of plagiarism, 230, 236
  key strategies for, 236
  in paraphrases, 230, 233–234
  quotations for, 230, 234–235
  in summaries, 230, 232–233
  understanding what it means, 230
Point-by-point method (comparison/contrast), 107–108
Political science courses, 147
Post hoc ergo propter hoc fallacy, 196
Poverty (reading), 276–277
Preparing and generating, 25–29
  for achievement essay, 51–52
  audience considerations, 20, 85, 86, 87
  brainstorming, 27–28
  clustering or mapping, 28
  cooking or incubating stage, 26
  defining your purpose, 20, 85
  for family essay, 85–87
  focused freewriting, 26–27, 113

for in-class essays, 176–177
pre-writing, 21, 51–52
questions for generating ideas, 85, 86
subconscious process of, 25–26
thesis statement, 29, 85, 86, 87
timeline for research papers, 221
waiting for perfect opening, avoiding, 25
writing process step, 20, 21
Preparing for essay exams
  asking what will be on the test, 172
  finding main points, 171, 172
  lecture notes, 170–171
  outside sources, 172
  studying actively, 171–172
  textbooks, 171–172
Preschool teachers (student essay), 35–36
Pre-writing, 21, 51–52. *See also* Preparing and generating
Print sources, evaluating credibility of, 226–227
Process organization
  for body paragraphs, 106–107
  focused freewriting using, 113
Proofreading. *See* Editing and proofreading
Public education system, 136
Punctuation
  of sentence fragments, 63
  in speech, 63
  in standardized exam evaluation, 178
Purpose of writing project. *See also* Thesis statement
  considering before writing, 20
  determining, 85

Questionnaire on learning styles, 6–8
Quintanilla, Michael, 254
Quotations
  acceptable example, 235
  avoiding misquotes, 235
  from interviews, 130–131
  overview, 234
  paraphrasing vs., 233
  unacceptable example, 235

Rational or logical appeal
  animal shelter argument example, 187
  fallacies, 195–198
  overview, 187
Readers. *See* Audience or readers

Reading
  active or effective, 25, 26
  civic responsibilities and, 136
  for editing and proofreading, 69
  purposes of, 25
  strategies for, 26
  writing competency linked to, 40
"Reading and Writing" (Dimas),
    133–134
Readings
  "America's Religious Mosaic"
    (Moyers), 138–140
  "As Consumerism Spreads, Earth
    Suffers, Study Says" (Mayell),
    286–288
  "Bad Idea Whose Time Has Passed,
    A" (Chapman), 183–184
  "Changing American Family, The"
    (Beam), 80–83
  "Debate, What Debate?" (Golden),
    291–292
  essay exam answers, 175–176
  "Fable for Tomorrow, A" (Carson),
    300–301
  "Fabric of a Nation, The" excerpts,
    96–99
  "Fashion" (Rosenkrantz), 98–99
  "Find Work That You Love"
    (Moses), 264–268
  "Food" (Sandoval), 97–98
  "Getting Yourself Back on Track"
    (Hales), 44–46
  "Great Divide, The" (Quintanilla),
    254–257
  "He Wails for the World" (Fong-
    Torres), 47–49
  "How Do Our Kids Get So Caught
    Up In Consumerism?"
    (Swimme), 279–282
  "In Defense of Consumerism"
    (Rockwell), 283–285
  "It Could Happen Here" (Al-
    Marayati), 252–253
  "It's Time to Make Up Your Mind"
    (Fletcher), 272–273
  "Language and Society" (Baron),
    123–127
  "Learning Styles" (Sabrio), 2–4
  "Learning to Let Go: Tradition
    Binds College Hopefuls to
    Families" (Colon), 246–248
  "Lessons from Executive Order
    9066" (Saigo), 250–251
  "Living 'Poor' and Loving It"
    (Freedman), 276–277
  "Love Is a Fallacy" (Schulman),
    199–205

"Multiple Intelligences" (Sabrio and
    Burchfield), 10–13
"New Student Generation Accepts
    the Global Warming Chal-
    lenge, A" (Sayer), 297–299
"Obligations of September, 11, 2001,
    The" (Litan), 182–183
Peoplemaking excerpt (Satir), 75–77
"Rumors of Our Climatic Demise
    Have Been Greatly Exagger-
    ated" (Blake), 294–295
"Shameful Secret of Illiteracy in
    America, The" (Wild), 116–117
"Spanglish Spoken Here" (Castro),
    118–119
"Ten Majors That Didn't Exist 10
    Years Ago" (Kulla), 260–262
"We Are All Related" (Moss),
    157–159
"We Choose Honor" (Wiesel),
    143–145
"We Just Forge Ahead and Believe"
    (Relin), 101–103
"When Passion Is Dangerous"
    (Wiesel), 153–154
"Working Just to Live Is Perverted
    into Living Just to Work"
    (Veciana-Suarez), 269–271
Rebuttal
  defined, 188
  T-chart for, 188–189
Red herring fallacy, 197
Relationships beyond the family
  common needs as foundation
    for, 95
  communication as key ingredient
    for, 95
  "Fabric of a Nation, The" excerpts,
    96–99
  "Fashion of the Times" (student
    essay), 110–112
  organizing ideas for the essay,
    105–110
  "We Just Forge Ahead and Believe"
    (reading), 101–103
Religion
  "America's Religious Mosaic" (read-
    ing), 138–140
  "When Passion Is Dangerous"
    (reading), 153–154
Relin, David Oliver, 101
Remmers, Holly, 216
Reporter's Formula or Questions, 106
Research. See also Sources
  as exploration, 242
  finding and evaluating sources,
    224–229

Five P's rule, 221
  information literacy, 220
  interviews for, 130–131, 227–229
  online sources, 224–226
  paraphrasing, 233–234
  plagiarism, avoiding, 230–236
  planning, 221–222
  preliminary search, 223
  print sources, 226–227
  quantity vs. quality, 224
  questions for, 223
  quotations from, 234–236
  summarizing main ideas, 231–232
  taking notes from sources, 230–231
  thesis statement, 223–224
  timeline for papers, 221
  topic selection, 222–223
  working bibliography, 229–230
  Works Cited page, 242
Restaurant reviews, 209–210
Revision. See also Editing and
    proofreading
  defined, 22, 42
  feedback sources for, 53–57
  global, 42, 43
  of in-class essays, 177
  leaving time before, 56
  need for, 42
  for sentence quality, 43, 63–65
  successful writing due to, 42
  timeline for research papers, 221
  writing process step, 22
Rockwell, Llewellyn H., Jr., 283
Rogerian argument
  effectiveness of, 212
  organization, 206
  origins of, 206
  sample essay, 207–208
Rogers, Carl, 206
Rosenkrantz, Linda, 98
Ruiz, Don Miguel, 116
"Rumors of Our Climatic Demise
    Have Been Greatly Exagger-
    ated" (Blake), 294–295
Run-on or fused sentences, 65
Ryan, Jessica, 194

Saavedra, Richie, 14
Sabrio, David, 2, 10
Saigo, Roy H., 250
St. John, Noah, 45
Sandoval, Ricardo, 97
Santana, Carlos (reading), 47–49
Sarma, Tinu, 163–164
Satir, Virginia, 75, 108, 110
Sayer, Kyeann, 297

Schilling-Estes, Natalie, 127
Scholarly journals, 226–227
Schulman, Max, 199
Scott, Melissa Anne, 35
Search engines, 224
Secret ad
    illustrated, 214
    "Secret vs. Soft & Dri" (student essay), 216–218
"Secret vs. Soft & Dri" (Remmers), 216–218
Segregation (student essay), 194–195
Self-discovery
    four rooms exercise, 41–42
    writing as a tool for, 41
Self-Responding Worksheet, 58–59
Self-revision
    strategies, 56–57
    worksheet for, 57, 58–59
Senses, appealing to the reader's, 87
Sentences
    average length of, 58, 66
    awkward construction of, 66
    combining for variety, 66–67
    comma splices, 64–65
    defined, 66
    fragments, 63–64, 65
    as guideposts of draft, 59
    long, dividing or shortening, 67–68
    problems not noticed in speech, 63
    proofreading from last to first, 69
    revision for quality, 43, 63–65
    run-on or fused, 65
    standardized exam evaluation of, 178
    topic sentence, 32, 52
    varying length of, 58, 66–69
September 11, 2001
    "Obligations of September, 11, 2001, The" (reading), 182–183
    "Tragedy of September 11, 2001" (student essay), 148–149
    "We Choose Honor" (reading), 143–145
"Shameful Secret of Illiteracy in America, The" (Wild), 116–117
Shaping, 21–22. *See also* Organization
Shortening long sentences, 67–68
So (coordinating conjunction), 65
Society
    "Language and Society" (reading), 123–127
    society and the environment majors (reading), 261
Sockman, Ralph W., 245
Soft & Dri ad
    illustrated, 215

"Secret vs. Soft & Dri" (student essay), 216–218
"Some Aspects of Indian Culture" (Williams), 163–164
Sources. *See also* Research
    avoiding plagiarism, 230–236
    evaluating credibility of, 225–227
    interviews, 130–131, 227–229
    library, 224, 225, 226
    online, 224–225
    paraphrasing, 233–234
    print, 226–227
    quantity vs. quality, 224
    quotations from, 234–236
    studying for essay exams, 172
    summarizing main ideas, 231–232
    taking notes from, 230–231
    working bibliography for, 229–230
    Works Cited page, 242
South Park (Parker and Stone), 275
South Wind (Douglas), 275
Spacing for academic essays, 37
"Spanglish Spoken Here" (Castro), 118–119
Spatial intelligence (reading), 11
Speaking
    in brainstorming sessions, 27–28
    civic responsibilities and, 136
    clarity in writing vs., 63, 65–66
    formal vs. informal, 23, 114
    sentence problems not noticed in, 63
    writing the way you speak, 23
"Splitters" vs. "lumpers," 4, 9
Sporn, Eliza, 132
Standardized essay exams, 178–179
Standards for information literacy, 220
"Standard Written English," 114
Statistics
    for developing body paragraphs, 109
    focused freewriting using, 113
Stereotyping fallacy, 195–196
Stone, Matt, 275
Structure. *See* Organization
Student essays
    "Alienated Asian, An" (Verderber), 60–61
    "Class Segregation" (Ryan), 194–195
    "Family Values" (Canales), 88–90
    "Fashion of the Times" (Varela), 110–112
    "Lost Maples State Natural Area" (Cook), 210–211
    "My Family Traditions" (Mullen), 92–93

    "My Hobby" (Varela), 38–39
    "Not a Perfect Person" (Saavedra), 14–15
    "On This Day in 1986" (Wolter), 237–240
    "Reading and Writing" (Dimas), 133–134
    "Secret vs. Soft & Dri" (Remmers), 216–218
    "Some Aspects of Indian Culture" (Williams), 163–164
    "Tips for a New Preschool Teacher" (Scott), 35–36
    "Tragedy of September 11, 2001" (Arthur), 148–149
Studying
    actively, 171–172
    finding main points, 171, 172
    lecture notes, 170–171
    outside sources, 172
    textbooks, 171–172
Styles
    of learning, 2–9, 14, 16
    of writing (formal vs. informal), 23, 114
Stylistic appeal, 188
Subject-by-subject method (comparison/contrast), 107
Summarizing research findings
    acceptable examples, 232–233
    avoiding plagiarism, 230–236
    main ideas, 231–233
    paraphrasing, 233–234
    unacceptable examples, 232, 233
Sunada, Roy, 101–103
Swimme, Brian, 232–235, 279

Taking notes
    from lectures, 170–171
    paraphrasing, 233–234
    quotations, 234–236
    from sources, 230–236
    summarizing main ideas, 231–233
T-chart for rebuttal, 188–189
Teaching preschoolers (student essay), 35–36
"Ten Majors That Didn't Exist 10 Years Ago" (Kulla), 260–262
Textbooks, studying, 171–172
Thesis statement
    for argument essays, 189, 191
    defined, 29
    formulating, 29, 52
    importance of, 29
    in opening paragraph, 32–33
    plan of organization after, 29

questions answered by, 85, 86
for research papers, 223–224
rewording in closing paragraph, 34, 35, 191
supporting, 87
using examples related to, 91
Thinking. *See also* Preparing and generating
civic responsibilities and, 136
skills developed by writing, 19
in writing process, 20, 21
Three-part structure of essays, 21
Timed writings. *See* Essay exams
Timeline for research papers, 221
Time magazine, 147
"Tips for a New Preschool Teacher" (Scott), 35–36
Title format for academic essays, 37
Topic selection for research paper, 222–223
Topic sentence
in body paragraph structure, 52
defined, 32
in DUCTT acronym, 32, 52, 105, 177
position in paragraph, 32
Torture (reading), 252–253
"Tragedy of September 11, 2001" (Arthur), 148–149
Transitions
in body paragraph structure, 52
defined, 32
in DUCTT acronym, 32, 52, 105, 177

Underachievement (reading), 44–46
United We Serve: National Service and the Future of Citizenship, 182
Unity
in body paragraphs, 31
in DUCTT acronym, 31, 52, 105, 177
in standardized exam evaluation, 178
Universal service
case against (reading), 183–184
case for (reading), 182–183
URL (Uniform Resource Locator), 225
Usage, in standardized exam evaluation, 178

U.S. Bureau of Labor Statistics survey, 20

Varela, Ricky, 38, 110
Veciana-Suarez, Ana, 269
Verderber, Michael, 60
Vietnamese culture (student essay), 60–61

Waco, Texas (reading), 139–140
"We Are All Related" (Moss), 157–159
Websites. *See also* Online sources for research
evaluating, 225–226
finding, 224, 225
"We Choose Honor" (Wiesel), 143–145
"We Just Forge Ahead and Believe" (Relin), 101–103
Wells, H. G., 290
"When Passion Is Dangerous" (Wiesel), 153–154
When Smart People Fail (Hyatt and Gottlieb), 1
White, E. B., 290
"Who, What, When, Where, Why, and How," 106
Whole-to-whole method (comparison/contrast), 107
Wiesel, Elie, 142, 143, 152, 153, 219
Wild, Penni, 116
Williams, Sue, 163
Winner's Way, The (Brill), 44
Wolfram, Walt, 127
Wolter, Amy, 237
Word processing, format for academic essays, 37
Wordstruck (MacNeil), 114
Work
debate about education, 259
"Find Work That You Love" (reading), 264–268
"It's Time to Make Up Your Mind" (reading), 272–273
need for writing in, 20
"Ten Majors That Didn't Exist 10 Years Ago" (reading), 260–262

"Working Just to Live Is Perverted into Living Just to Work" (reading), 269–271
Working bibliography, 229–230
"Working Just to Live Is Perverted into Living Just to Work" (Veciana-Suarez), 269–271
Works Cited page, 242
Worksheets for self-revision, 57, 58–59
World events
importance of being informed about, 151
ripple metaphor for, 165
"Some Aspects of Indian Culture" (student essay), 163–164
venturing beyond your comfort zone, 161
"We Are All Related" (reading), 157–159
"When Passion Is Dangerous" (reading), 153–154
Writer's block, 32
Writer's notebook, 135
Writing process, 20–22
audience considerations, 20
begun before actual writing, 20, 21
as composing process, 20
dividing time for, 69
editing and proofreading step, 22
for in-class essays, 176–177
as a learning tool, 16, 19
organizing/drafting/shaping step, 21–22
preparing and generating step, 21
purpose of project, 20
revising step, 22
self-evaluation for, 60
timeline for research papers, 221
varying nature of, 20, 22, 68, 70
Writing with sources. *See* Research; Sources

Yet (coordinating conjunction), 65
Your Own Worst Enemy: Breaking the Habit of Adult Underachievement (Christian), 44